MARK D. MINEVICH is a worn
executive management consurt.
Currently serving as an exeig
Global Ventures Inc, anig
partnership, Mr. Minevich in,
commercialization, outsourcing, and international strategy.

Mr. Minevich earlier served as a CTO and Senior Strategist of IBM Next Generation Group. Mark has formed a strategy for Incubator Innovation and Going Global programs at IBM Company. Mark has worked in senior leadership and strategic management positions at USWEB/CKS, Qwest, Comcast, and Geotek. As an entrepreneur, Mr. Minevich has founded Vitasave (Healthcare), ClubMom (Community), and Silicon Jersey (Executive Recruitment). He has advised US Government (Department of Commerce and Department of State) on innovation and bilateral relationship with emerging economies such as Russia, and has served as Advisor to high growth companies, innovation centers, emerging incubators and venture community.

Mr. Minevich is world recognized speaker at internationally renowned global events, technology conferences and symposiums, universities, venture capital roundtables and United States Government events. Mark is a member of CIO Collective, and US Russian Business Council. Mr. Minevich has been awarded a leadership recognition award at IBM, and best intranet portal award from Microsoft.

Mr. Minevich holds a B.S. in Computer Science, and an M.B.A. in Information Management.

The CTO Best Practices Handbook

The Indispensable Technology Management Resource

Mark D. Minevich

VISION BOOKS
(Incorporating Orient Paperbacks)
New Delhi • Mumbai • Hyderabad

www.visionbooksindia.com

> Vision Books are available for bulk purchases at special discounts. Corporates use them for a variety of purposes, including customer acquisition, customer retention, incentives and premiums, in-house staff and management education, and for promotions. If you are interested in purchasing bulk copies for your company or team on discount prices, please email: visionbk@vsnl.com

Authorized edition for sale in the
Indian Sub-continent and South-East Asia

ISBN 81-7094-651-4

© Aspatore, Inc., 2004

All rights reserved
Originally published as *The CTO Handbook*
www.aspatore.com

Published in 2005 by
Vision Books Pvt. Ltd.
(Incorporating Orient Paperbacks and CARING imprints)
24 Feroze Gandhi Road, Lajpat Nagar-3,
New Delhi-110024, India.
Phone: (+91-11) 2983 6470; 2983 6480
Fax: (+91-11) 2983 6490
E-mail: visionbk@vsnl.com

Printed at
Rashtra Rachna Printers
C-88, Ganesh Nagar, Delhi 110092, India.

Contents

Part I

Chapter 1:	**Introduction**	13
	• Summary of Roles and Responsibilities	13
	• Fundamentals of the CIO/CTO Role	14
	• Importance of the CTO/CIO Profession	16
	• Background of CTO/CIO Profession	18
Chapter 2:	**Change and Transformation**	20
	• Globalization Perspective	20
	US Government Perspective	20
	McKinsey Perspective	22
	Goldman Sachs Analysis Report	25
	Natural Maturation of Markets and Efficiency	26
	Competitiveness Issues	28
	• Current Economic Climate and Changes	31
	General IT Climate	31
	New Generation and Digital Revolution	33
	Women as CIO/CTOs	34
	Are CIOs in Decline?	35
	Changing Environment in Context	39
	• Outsourcing and Offshoring	41
	Changes Leading up to Mainstream Outsourcing-Offshoring Model	41
	Trends and Figures	43
	Challenges in Offshoring	45
	Offshoring Maturing	47
	Risk Management	49
	What Does It Mean for the US IT Market?	50
	What Does It Mean for CIO?	52
	New Paradigm	52
	• New Economy — Creating Value for Customers	53
	CTO/CIO — Change and Transformation	55
	Type of Companies — Focused on Customer Value	58

6 / The CTO Handbook

Chapter 3:	**CTO Priorities: Defined by Media, Analysts and Corporations**	**60**
	▪ *BusinessWeek's* Technology Overview	60
	▪ *CIO Magazine*	61
	▪ Gartner Group	61
	▪ Morgan Stanley	64
	▪ META	64
	▪ CSO Magazine Online	65
	▪ Top Industry Players	65
Chapter 4:	**Emerging Technology Direction and Vision**	**68**
	▪ Next Generation Consulting Harvard Report	68
	▪ Future Growth Opportunities and Technologies	69
	Enablers and Drivers and Globalization	69
	Predictions	70
	▪ Vance Chan Associates	71
	▪ George Washington University and Future of Technologies	71
	▪ *BusinessWeek* Predictions of New Technologies	74
	BusinessWeek — Innovation 2004	74
	▪ Batelle—The Top Strategic Technologies	77
Chapter 5:	**Strategic and Influential Relationships: Empowering a CTO —**	
	A Complex Ecosystem	**82**
	▪ Community	82
	▪ CEO-Executives	83
	▪ CIO	84
	▪ Chief Scientist	85
	▪ Marketing and Sales	86
	▪ Research	86
	▪ Values Based Organizations	87
Chapter 6:	**CTO Strategic Roles and Responsibilities**	**88**
	▪ Skills and Competencies of an Effective CTO: Technology Summary	88
	Technology	88
	Strategy	88
	Business Growth	88
	Interpersonal Skills	89
	Executive Relationships	89
	▪ CTO — Leadership and Coaching	89
	▪ Technology Decision Maker	91
	Act as the Technical Conscience	91
	Provide technology oversight for the enterprise	91
	▪ CTO and the Emerging and Competitive World	92
	Monitoring and Assessing New Technologies	92
	▪ CTO—Strategic Planning and Direction	94
	Development of a Technological Strategic Plan	94
	▪ CTO Innovation and Commercialization	97
	Chief Technology Transfer Office	97
	Strategic Innovation	97

Commercialization	99
• CTO and the Evangelist	101
• CTO and Globalization	102
• CTO — Merger & Acquisition	103
• CTO — Marketing and Media Role	104
• CTO — Government, Academia and Professional Organizations	104
• CTO and Company Culture	105
• CTO — Emerging Business Technology Role	106
• CTO — Change Agent Roles	108
• CTO — Chief Creative Officer: Latest Trend	111

Chapter 7: Conclusion   114

Part II: Best Practices

Chapter 8: **Opportunities for Large and Small Software Companies for Today and Tomorrow**
Michael George   119

Chapter 9: **Software Savvy: Taking and Keeping Your Place in the Software Market**
John Chen   128

Chapter 10: **Basics of the Business**
Gerald D. Cohen   137

Chapter 11: **Closing the Gap between What Technology Can Do and What People Want It to Do**
Dr. Carl S. Ledbetter   146

Chapter 12: **Creating and Enriching Business Value**
Richard Schroth   165

Chapter 13: **Bridging Business and Technology: Keeping Things as Simple as Possible**
Mike Ragunas   178

Chapter 14: **The Art of Being a CTO — Fostering Change**
Rick Bergquist   187

Chapter 15: **Keep Your Blade Sharp**
Jeff P. Van Dyke   200

Chapter 16: **Intelligent Enterprises Everywhere**
Arun Gollapudi   212

Chapter 17: The Changing Face of Technology
Tom Salonek   222

Chapter 18: Major Dilemmas Facing Privacy Practitioners
William B. Wilhelm, Jr.   242

Chapter 19: Managing Privacy
W. Riker Purcell   252

Chapter 20: The Myth of Privacy
William Sterling   262

Chapter 21: Starting From Scratch
Richard Brock   275

Chapter 22: Relationship Management
Richard Hochhauser   286

Chapter 23: Finding the Right Fit
Jeffrey Rodek   296

Chapter 24: How to Make Every Customer a Repeat Customer
Lloyd G. "Buzz" Waterhouse   305

Chapter 25: Best Practices for Offshore Software Development Outsourcing
Eugene Goland   317

Appendix 1: Tips and Guidelines   324
- Tips and Guidelines for Upcoming CTO/CTOs   324
    - *CIO Magazine's* 12 Step Program for Aspiring CIOs   324
    - Four Ways to Move up a Line   326
- Tips and Guidelines for Existing CIO/CTO's   327
    - CIO Challenges   327
    - 90-Day Plan   328
    - Round-the-year Resolutions for CTO/CIOs   329
    - Top Tips to Increase Influence   330

Appendix 2: Technology Brainstormers   332

References   335

Dedicated to

My dear wife, Susanna, and to my dear parents

and

*To the memory of my dear friend and mentor,
the late Sam Albert*

Part I

Chapter 1: Introduction

Chapter 2: Change and Transformation

Chapter 3: CTO Priorities — Defined by Media, Analysts and Corporations

Chapter 4: Emerging Technology Direction and Vision

Chapter 5: Strategic and Influential Relationships: Empowering a CTO — A Complex Ecosystem

Chapter 6: CTO Strategic Roles and Responsibilities

Chapter 7: Conclusion

Chapter 1

Introduction

For many years, CIOs and CTOs have been working hard to secure a place at the top management table. Now some business and industry gurus say IT is no longer strategic, it's just becoming a commodity and can't give a competitive advantage. Are they right?

The book will review all of the current events, and thought leadership to become a CTO or a CIO. This book also acts as a complete reference guide. It is important to note that the CTO and CIO terms will be used interchangeably throughout the book due to increasingly integrated focus. We will separate the role when required to make the necessary points.

Throughout the book, we will use CTO and CIO's terminology interchangeably, but it is important to summarize and define Key Technology Leaders from the initial start. In reality, facing new economic climate, one person will be assigned to handle technology leadership in a corporation.

Summary of Roles and Responsibilities

CTO

- **Technology Strategy.** The CTO's primary responsibility is contributing to the strategic direction of the company by identifying the role that specific technologies will play in its future growth. The CTO looks for contributions that technology can make to the competitive advantage of the company.
- **Internal Coordination.** Identification of the best technologies usually comes from a strong internal network of people who are in touch with the latest technologies and understand their potential.
- **External Partnerships.** Like all business professionals, the CTO will be part of a strong network that includes business partners, academics, government officials, and technology thought leaders.

CIO
- **Information Technology Application.** The CIO leads the application of information technology to internal processes and services. This person is responsible for improving the efficiency of internal systems like payroll, accounting, accounts receivable, labor recording, benefits management, human resources records, government reporting, and a number of others.
- **Reduce Internal Operating Costs.** The CIO's systems are focused on reducing the costs associated with the company operations listed above.
- **Improve Services to Employees and Partners.** CIOs and IT departments have provided fantastic improvements in employee services in the last two decades. They have also built systems that allow better information and financial exchange with business partners.

Chief Scientist
- **Technology Creation.** Chief Scientists lead teams that are focused on creating new technologies. Given strategic direction from management, these teams work to create products or services that make the company's strategy possible and that do so in a manner superior to their competitors.
- **Recognized Leader.** Chief Scientists should be recognized leaders in their technical field. They should be actively involved in professional associations and conferences with their peers in industry and academia.

Fundamentals of the CIO/CTO Role

As discussed in a summary, Chief Technology Officer is more and more integrated and evolving into the role of Chief Information Officer. Chief Information Officer is the senior executive responsible for all aspects of a company's information technology and one of the most complex of all corporate officer positions. This book reviews current responsibilities and expectations of the role, and showcases how CIOs apply the right skills to meet the challenge.[17]

We start with a definition and proceed to the main qualities demanded of the role, which is very complex. These include knowledge of and experience in a specific industry, relationship skills and international or global experience. Only CEOs require a similar cross-functional and broad-based background. The unique cornerstone of the CIO role — and its fundamental mission — is having expertise in aligning and leveraging technology for the advantage of the enterprise. A decade ago, CIOs emerged as vision builders, relationship builders, tacticians and deliverers. Today many requirements have been added such as mirroring the continuing transformation in both IT and the business at large: strategist, architect, reformer and alliance manager. I believe that there will be transformation of the role in the next five years.

The scope of this role is too broad for any one guide to cover definitively. We focus on the most common and troublesome challenges, such as keeping up with technology (and technologists) and communicating value. I slant some material toward the CTO and CIO with a transformational role that may be new to the role or the company. It is this book's intent to help him or her establish a firm grounding. CIOs and CTOs who are new to their positions can navigate the territory with guidance and mentoring. We will learn that it is important to establishing credibility at the start. Through my research and direct correspondence, CIOs advise their associates to build credibility fast by addressing relatively minor complaints about IT and paying special attention to the immediate frustrations and needs of their new manager.

Although information technology is better understood than ever by the business community and management, there are a lot of expectations for a CIO. Not only must the CIO have all the answers, but he must complete every project on time and under budget, even as users squeeze every moment of his staff's day with the same mundane tech support questions. The book will explain that it is possible to take control in a number of ways. First, CIOs must foster trust within the senior executive team. They must be mediators when conflicts arise, learn how to manage up, delegate, prioritize and encourage responsibility in others. CIOs and CTOs in this book discuss the most critical skills for their jobs today as the ability to communicate effectively, to understand business processes and operations, and to engage in strategic planning and thinking. It's great to know what skills to leverage, but it's even better to know how to bone up on those skills. We share advice on skill cultivation. CIOs who find themselves doing IT on behalf of the company should transition as fast as possible. Also known as the federated model, it holds business units responsible for the "what" of IT, while IT is responsible for the "how".

A good relationship with senior executives is a necessary for CIO success. Learning about your industry and about your company is a core requirement. Jim Sphorer, from IBM, and Sam Albert mention this in our discussions.[83] "Learn more about your competition, about the performance of your company. What's your revenue? What is your main product? What's profitable? What isn't? Start thinking as if you were CEO", the CIO recommends. "That way, when you're in the group, they'll start looking to you for technology solutions, but they'll also realize that you're a business person."

Some of the companies where we work are decentralized. It's even tougher to keep connected in a decentralized company .It is important to be able to compare and contrast global priorities, US corporate priorities and regional CIOs' priorities, moving priorities from one pile to another and then back again to help determine where to focus first. We can learn of priorities from leading media and analyst sources.

One of the hardest languages for the CIO to explain is their value. We define the value, and the best ways to communicate the value of information technology projects to company executives. Perhaps the most extreme dichotomy of the role is that not only must the CIO go toe-to-toe with its peers and shareholders to prove the value of proposed investment, he or she must also be able to inspire, motivate and manage technologists. This is an ultimate dilemma. Consider, for instance, that technical people are generally uncomfortable with uncertainty.

Yet, driving to a conclusion in an established time frame is important to success. Technologists are typically stuck in the world of solutions. Being a successful CIO requires a continuing search for knowledge. In a short period of time, CIOs could be absorbing new insight on the technologies and processes of e-commerce and CRM, and also building better skills for leadership and communication. CIOs must be open to all sources of learning. In this book, we provide associations and references of media, computer industry publications that are the best sources of learning. We review different roles of a CTO, an ecosystem of relationships, and the continuing struggle to define the role, and find and retain staff with the right skills. In all of the areas, it is important to focus on strategic thought process.

To help IT leaders regain a little of that time they lack, we have a reference section that offers check lists, tips and guides to help contend with executives, and win political battles. It is important to note that CIOs or CTOs new on the scene must be careful to avoid being swept into immediate projects without taking time to survey the environment and playing field.

We have consolidated a lot of research, correspondence and analysis. Some conversations were done directly and some through other media and 3rd party sources. Therefore, we have included the comprehensive research, as well as all of the necessary references that would be of interest including people, media sources, articles, and associations.

Importance of the CTO/CIO Profession

We must state the unique role and charter of the CTO (Chief Technology Officer) as well as the CIO (Chief Information Officer). The role is changing, and at the same time becoming very important in the scope, organization and direction of the organizations leveraging information and emerging technology for competitive advantage. Computerworld recently noted that "While used by nearly 10% of major companies, the title of chief technology officer has yet to develop into a clearly defined role, according to a New York executive management search firm. And if the CTO /CIO title ever does gain full acceptance, it will likely take at least 10 years — the same length of time it took for companies to embrace the CIO title."[59] I have to take an opposite view that without this major shift in thinking of a senior technology executive, an element of our economic market model would be seriously challenged. Strategic business decisions today have created the need for executives that are properly aligned to understand technology with profitable business opportunities, services, and processes. There is a growing need for a new type of a Technology Leader — The Leader that transforms the strategy of an organization. It may take the form of CTOs who are exclusively focusing on monitoring new technologies and assessing their potential to become new business opportunities, commercializing technologies and projects to increase value added to the organization, strategic and technical due diligence of mergers and acquisitions, evangelizing the company's future to the global community, and actively participating in government, academic, and industry econets to expand new channels and opportunities as well as to promote the company's vision. It could also be used as a vehicle to capture a significant knowledgebase of information. It demonstrates that the business visionary leaders clearly are on the same wavelength in terms of long-term technology direction and strategy. Most CTO executives agree that CTOs are long-term technology business visionaries focusing on a transformation of the company.

The path that we are describing is now moving the modern CTO into the least understood area of "distributed capitalism", an area of globalization with a focus on consumer and value based organizations that leverage emerging growth, strategy and transformation. We already see a tremendous change in the growth of innovation in organizations and corporations around the world, the competitive strategy of tomorrow that will combine the strategic thought leadership, emerging technology growth, and next generation strategy to deal with global issues. In fact, the strategy of organization will depend heavily on the role and responsibilities of the CTO. This convergence of knowledge and business is very important to the next movement of CTO. This book will clearly outline the set of new responsibilities for a CTO, and provide a sense of direction for CTOs focusing on Emerging Growth and Strategic Transformation. In this transitional period, many senior executives express confusion about what is and should be the exact role of the CTO with strategy, research, development, innovation and thought leadership. However, they do recognize that those areas need to intersect to combine a powerful leader. A majority of the people that we had discussions with mentioned that the role of the CTO is changing, and it will have even greater impact on the company, industry and our society. We will see how a CTO's role is going to be involved with emerging growth, strategy, globalization, commercialization, value added economy, strategic future, and competitive impact on the organization. Is this returning to a traditional CIO role? Those CTO/CIO roles that we are discussing will transform the existing companies and technologies, develop emerging business areas and technologies, and provide and improve on competitive advantage for the company. Of course, a lot of factors will depend on how actively the company is involved in the transformation and emerging growth areas. Hopefully, the role of CTO or CIO in emerging and transformational growth areas will significantly enhance business opportunities for the company and industry. Leveraging the new vision and role of a CTO with business corporate strategy will require the unique ability of a CTO to leverage internal, external, customer and management relationships to the full extent.[5]

This book will also provide guidelines on strategic thought technology leadership for the company which is set to focus on growth or transformation. In one aspect, the Emerging CTO may focus on disruptive technologies, and with another aspect, the Transformation CTO may need to focus on a holistic overview of changing the overall strategy for the company. In other respects, the role will be integrated as a modified CIO role. This author predicts that the new roles will have major impact on organization structure, human capital, value based organizations, and ecosystem of internal and external relationships. In fact, it is the author's assumption that the Emerging and Transformation CTO roles will take our country, industry, and society into a new and exciting direction to enhance our global competitiveness.

Background of CTO/CIO Profession

In the 1950s and 1960s, many large corporations established beautiful research laboratories at locations remote from their headquarters and manufacturing facilities. The goal was to collect brilliant scientists and allow them to study relevant topics in an environment unhindered by day-to-day business concerns. The director of the laboratory was often a corporate vice president who did not participate in decisions regarding corporate strategy and direction. Instead, his responsibilities were to attract the best scientists, explore new ideas, and publish respected research papers.[57]

By the late 1980s, companies began to anoint R&D laboratory directors as Chief Technology Officers. Technology was becoming such a prevalent part of company products and services that senior management needed an operational executive who could understand it and provide reliable advice on its application. However, executive search agencies, under direction of their corporate customers, continued to fill the CTO position with the same people they had recommended to manage and lead R&D laboratories.[72] Several experiences with these candidates proved that the responsibilities of the CTO were significantly different from those of the research scientist. The CTO position called for a technologist or scientist who could translate technological capabilities into strategic business decisions. Lewis, in the Sloan Management review, expresses this very clearly. "The CTO's key tasks are not those of lab director writ large but, rather, of a technical businessperson deeply involved in shaping and implementing overall corporate strategy."[58]

Though large companies such as IBM, General Electric, Microsoft, Allied-Signal, created the position of CTO in the late 1980s, the position has also played an important role in computer and Internet companies in the late 1990s. Many of these provide products and services that are pure technology. Yes, the CTO role has changed. Yet, a CTO can play a prominent role in directing and shaping their entire business. We are facing a different world.

I have seen some the critical and important changes evolving in my career as a strategist and a CTO, and want to share those perspectives, experience and moments through this comprehensive best practices guide.

Let the journey begin.

Chapter 2

Change and Transformation

Globalization Perspective

We are entering the era of new transformation, and more specifically defined as an era of wealth creation due primarily to Globalization and impact towards our society. Adam Smith accurately said that "natural effort of every individual to better his own condition is so powerful a principle, that it is alone and without any assistance, not only capable of carrying on the society to wealth and prosperity, but of surmounting a hundred obstructions."

To begin, we need to recognize that the 1990s attempted to spoil us, and in fact created a new society of consumers, customers, companies and individuals governed by new processes, values, strategies and rules. This economic trough is a natural part of the business cycle. America just came out of a very prolonged and unusual positive business cycle — ten years when they normally last six — building an information technology and equities bubble as well as unnecessary levels of excess capacity. While we were lulled by the house of cards created by the technology boom, an acceleration of the "globalization" and "exportation" of our economy occurred. The most interesting aspect is that the US economy has fundamentally changed. By the end of the 20th century, most nations recognized that technology is a critical driver of economic growth.

US Government Perspective

This view is presented from the US Department of Commerce. US is very much involved with Globalization efforts. In the 1990s, technology's contribution to US economic prosperity was very visible. Innovation in new technology created US jobs, has increased growth in our economy and helped to make US corporations more productive. According to the Department of Commerce and Department's Economics and Statistics Administration, for example, the information technology sector, over 1996-2000, represented only 7 per cent of businesses in the US but accounted for approximately 28 per cent of overall real economic growth.[66]

US Department of Commerce indicates that:

The United States has long been a leader in technology innovation and development. The 21st century promises the rise of new centers of technological excellence around the globe. Globalization is already a potent phenomenon in respect to the migration of people, the opening of markets, and the linking of national economies. Much the same is also now rapidly becoming a reality for essential activities leading to commerce — such as the research, manufacturing, and marketing of new technology-based products.[66]

In fact, this global marketplace and "technology globalization" is defined as an "expanding roster of nations able to conduct world-class research and development and nations' increased investment in national infrastructures for innovation which presents new opportunities and challenges for US technology entrepreneurs and government policymakers."[33]

According to US Government, US human capital is major and the top element of innovation, eventually leading to economic prosperity. As such, a robust economy depends not only on growing, healthy and open markets, efficient government, innovation infrastructure, a quality education system, but also on an adequate supply of talented and skilled workers. This will be reviewed in a competitiveness report.

According to US Department of Commerce, Canada, France, Germany, Italy, Japan, United Kingdom, and the United States accounted for 67 per cent of the world's Gross Domestic Product (GDP) in 2000, are leading nations in terms of R&D expenditures, and have taken steps to ensure their innovation in technology.[66]

According to US Government and Department of Commerce, Globalization has been reviewed in three perspectives:

Firstly, it has to be reviewed by the supply side, the demand side, and the globalization of work. The supply-side analysis looks at the policies and approaches in-place for the development of the worker, like the primary, secondary, and tertiary education systems in each country. It highlights the "pipeline processes" in each of the seven countries. The demand side looks at the issues surrounding the S&T workforce of the government, business, and university sectors. This includes workforce size, unemployment rates, unfilled positions, and intra-nation mobility issues. Finally, the third perspective, globalization of the workforce looks at the trends and policies in national capacity in terms of immigration and emigration of S&T talent and international mobility.[66]

McKinsey Perspective

According to a recent report from McKinsey (October 2003), multinational companies are benefiting greatly from globalization, innovation and offshore trends. In fact, investment in the developing world opens up new horizons for economic development and for company strategy. McKinsey Global Institute launched an in-depth inquiry into multinational company investment in developing economies. The McKinsey Global Institute's latest report shows that the overall economic impact of multinational investment on developing economies has been very optimistic. Companies are also seeing substantial benefits but have only started to capture the large cost savings and revenue gains possible from operating in these markets. New opportunities in cost savings and revenue generation are opening up for multinational companies. These extensive report findings suggest that there are enormous opportunities for companies to create value by taking full advantage of falling barriers in regulation, transportation costs, communications costs, and infrastructure.[63]

Furthermore, according to the McKinsey report, multinational companies are well positioned to transfer their competitive products and processes, but less equipped to tailor them appropriately to local conditions. Currently, the intermix of industry characteristics, regulatory restrictions, and organizational limitations prevent some companies from pursuing further industry restructuring. However, as a result of competition, liberalization, and new technologies, new possibilities are opening up where a greater degree of specialization is possible. The opportunities for developing economies are significant, and through the application of capital, technology, and a range of skills, multinational companies' overseas investments have created positive economic value in host countries, across different industries and within different policy regimes. According to McKinsey, the single biggest effect was demonstrated through the improvement in the standards of living of the country's population, as consumers have directly benefited from lower prices, higher quality goods, and broader selection. Improved productivity and output in the sector and its suppliers indirectly contributed to increasing national income. Foreign direct investment is already having a dramatic impact on the way companies do business and developing how economies integrate with the global economy.[63]

The McKinsey report goes on to suggest that both multinational companies and developing economies could find enormous benefits through foreign direct investment. It is important to note that the global expansion has its pitfalls as well as its opportunities, and CTO/CIOs, as well as policy leaders, need to fully understand them both. McKinsey states that to find the value, companies need to rethink their entire business process. "Going global" is obviously not a recipe for success in and of itself.

The McKinsey report specifically states that opportunities for developing economies are sizable. As a background, it is important to state this from the McKinsey report:

> Through the application of capital, technology, and a range of skills, multinational companies' overseas investments have created positive economic value in host countries, across different industries and within different policy regimes. The single biggest effect evidenced was the improvement in the standards of living of the country's population, as consumers have directly benefited from lower prices, higher quality goods, and broader selection. Improved productivity and output in the sector and its suppliers indirectly contributed to increasing national income. And despite often-cited worries, the impact on employment was either neutral or positive in two-thirds of the cases. Foreign direct investment is already having a dramatic impact on the way companies do business and how developing economies integrate with the global economy. Investments by multinational companies allow developing economies to share in the considerable benefits of the global economy. Official incentives, trade barriers, and other regulatory policies, though, can result in inefficiency and waste. MNC investment had a positive to very positive impact on the host country. Rather than leading to the exploitation of lower-wage workers, as some critics have charged, the investments fostered innovation, productivity, and an improved living standard. Therefore, government seeking those advantages would be advised to favor policies of openness, rather than regulation, when it comes to foreign direct investment. MNCs were shown to create substantial value for host countries, regardless of whether investments were market seeking, to seek new consumers or efficiency seeking to tap into lower local production costs. In every other case, foreign investment spillover effects stimulated supplier businesses and fostered improvements in technology and skills. Though in some cases jobs were lost through elimination of inefficient local players or streamlining inefficient production operations, benefits to consumers were significant in terms of lower prices, more product choice, and increased productivity, which in turn increased national wealth. Barriers to foreign investment and trade can create a competitive disadvantage for developing nations, rendering the considerable benefits of the global economy inaccessible to them. Governments can more effectively grow MNC investments by putting the basic building blocks of productivity in place, through strengthened power, transportation, and legal infrastructures, and the enactment and enforcement of clear and consistent official policies. Several

powerful factors, from liberalized foreign investment policies to a drop in the costs associated with global operations, are making a convincing case for building truly worldwide businesses. Thanks to an increasingly mobile and connected world, global corporations stand to simultaneously increase efficiency and lower costs by taking full advantage of the growing expertise and specialization in emerging economies. For MNCs to take advantage of these opportunities, they need to recognize what aspects of their industry best lend themselves to globalization.[63]

As a result, globalization has really changed, and new rules have emerged.

This ongoing global expansion allows companies to mine new markets for their products in:

- **Product specialization:** Certain countries or regions take over the entire production process of a particular product.
- **Value chain disaggregation:** Each portion of the supply chain is located in a separate area with relevant expertise within a region. Parts are then assembled in yet another location.
- **Value chain reengineering:** After relocating an activity to a new location, production process can be tweaked by adjusting capital/labor ratio to capture further savings.
- **New market creation:** Successful global value chain management leads to the creation of better products at lower prices, which in turn can be introduced to whole new markets.[63]

It is important to note the following issues related to Globalization. Companies must balance global resources with local knowledge, and companies must recognize that there is no single blueprint that works for every sector in every country.

Information Technology changes around the world are reflected throughout the book. I have a tendency to believe that the Globalization element is very important to the survival of the CTO/CIO role. We will see in the book that companies are moving information technology to offshore locations to emerging markets like India and Russia.

We will also review offshoring as part of a global innovation strategy. I believe that this is a strategy that will change the world. Offshoring is growing at 30 per cent per year and is projected to grow to more than US$200 billion by 2008. Despite widespread concerns that offshoring eliminates jobs at home, in reality the revenue saved through offshoring is being reinvested at home. India is a much needed player for global market for IT talent. India has increased the headcount of thousands of high tech jobs. The emphasis will be on value-added services.

Numerous new jobs have been created, and higher value-added functions have been brought to India and Russia.[63]

Goldman Sachs Analysis Report

Another and slight larger view of emerging markets comes from a recent Goldman Sachs report. It indicates that emerging markets are continuing to grow at a very fast pace. We also seeing a major fundament shift in the world related to global economics. The relative importance of the emerging economies as an engine of new demand growth and spending power may shift more dramatically and quickly than expected. It is important to realize that emerging economies have enhanced infrastructure to deliver services in any geography based on a concept of real value-based virtual organizations.

The growth of new world's economies should reflect on how the firms are taking advantage of global innovation and offshoring capabilities. Indeed, the strategic choices are becoming very complex. Recently, Goldman Sachs, in its Global Economics paper (October 2003), has created a scenario where, over the next 50 years, Brazil, Russia, India and China could become a much larger force in the world economy. In fact some emerging economies, in less then 40 years, could become larger than the G6 in US dollar terms. The article goes further to state that by 2025 they could account for over half the size of the G6. Of the current G6, only the US and Japan may be among the six largest economies in US dollar terms in 2050.[41]

Another astonishing statistic, according to Goldman Sachs, is that as early as 2009, the annual increase in US dollar spending from emerging economies could be greater than that from the G6 and more than twice as much in dollar terms as it is now. By 2025 the annual increase in US dollar spending from the emerging market could be twice that of the G6, and four times higher by 2050.[41]

Being invested in and involved in the right emerging markets may become an increasingly important strategic choice for companies and corporations in United States. Adam Smith has accurately said that "where the inferior ranks of people are chiefly maintained by the employment of capital, they are in general industrious, sober and thriving...and where the inferior ranks of people are chiefly maintained by spending of revenue, they are in general idle, dissolute, and poor." The Goldman Sachs report also indicates a new shift of growth, investments and spending in the emerging economies. Higher growth in these economies could offset the impact of growth in the advanced economies. Higher growth may lead to higher returns and increased demand for capital. The weight of the emerging in investment portfolios could rise sharply. Capital flows might move further in their favor of emerging economies, prompting major currency realignments. Rising incomes may also see these economies move through the "sweet spot" of growth for different kinds of products, as local spending patterns change. This could be an important determinant of demand and pricing patterns for a range of commodities. As today's advanced economies become a shrinking part of the world economy, the accompanying shifts in spending could provide significant opportunities for global companies.

Natural Maturation of Markets and Efficiency

Some people even ponder to say that America is losing its drive, desire and mission to maintain the innovation we once had.

As I was putting my views together on globalization and offshoring, I had a really interesting dialogue with William Sanford from Columbia Strategy, Rustam Lalkaka, Stuart Robbins from CIO Collective, and other members of the Technoogy Leadership Council which really opened another dimension. Can emerging markets catch up with us soon, and can we continue to innovate? In the future section of current economic climate, I describe an "irresponsible optimism" of America during the internet boom. I believe the economic boom was based on speculation, rather than true economics and growth. In fact, some state that Americans may be too much of dreamers to be responsible all the time. As we mentioned earlier, Globalization is a natural evolution maturation in the economics of the world. I agree with Mr. Sanford, who states that "Communication across international entities is becoming more and more widespread, cost-efficient, simple and accepted, while the relative distance is increasingly closing with relatively cheap air travel, global customers, etc. Yet, it may take a 100 years or so until working globally becomes efficient."[79] Other members of the technology Leadership Community and global strategy community agree with this premise, as well.

At one point in his career, he had an idea of creating a database that captures all of the work that anyone does in the company. For instance, Mr. Sanford says "if I developed a java based application that would instantly convert image files and populate a Lotus Notes picture gallery, I would have to complete a comprehensive write up, supply source code and final code, as well as anything done related into a database. This way, if a software engineer in Germany was charged with the same task, he would search this 'intellectual capital' database and find my code and simply use it. The idea is based on the same company and same property."[79] I tend to agree that information needs to permeate through everyone across the globe to become efficient.

We will state in a following section that much of the outsourcing today is for commodity products and services — where the cost advantage is the difference between a profit and loss. In terms of higher level services/ products that can be outsourced, it is becoming a larger challenge, a cultural challenge. There needs to be conformity and understading of thought and beliefs.

As I have traveled around the world, I have seen how Globalization impacts the markets. As an example, European Union Organizations leveraging IT resources and developing applications with their counterparts in Russia. In fact, in a recent Davos Conference of World Economic Forum, former President Clinton mentioned the Importance of Globalizaton.

As we stated earlier, US during the 21st century was the source of most innovation in the world. William Sanford clearly described some aspects of the US Mentality. "There was a certain mentality here that permeates throughout the US in the shape of a 'crazy, lofty and dreamy' culture. Kind of a craziness where we see now boundaries — perhaps often irresponsible." We clearly observe that in Japan, India, China and Germany to some degree, the mentality is almost robotic and it is eroding the human spirit to dream, innovate. Many governments like the Japanese come to US to try and figure out how we keep sparking innovation. Rustam Lalkaka believes that India and China are catching up quickly with innovation and expansion of technology program.

The problem, Mr. Stanford and others believe, is that other nations are being taught to follow the book and make no mistakes, whereas education should be the passing of tools that one can use to build their dreams as their mind wanders. We tend to see that Americans never took too much too seriously, as we have thrived to break rules. That is the mentality that is required to truly innovate and change a culture/ world through product/ service offerings that are value creative across the board.[79]

Mr. Sanford sparked a thought process with me that clearly marks US competitive advantage. This is a key to our success. Our mentality is really required to focus on innovation. For higher level services to become outsourced, there is a lot of maturation that is going to have to occur in emerging markets. As William Sanford states:

> This will include the need to have years of experience in understanding customers, then their problems and only then, begin to dream up solutions. In America, employees are not expected to simply follow rules. They are expected to curtail management and provide a solution to a new problem before management ever knows about it. Many people around the world are just as talented and capable as a traditional American worker, they just need time for their culture to allow them to roam free.[79]

It is globalization that will eventually enable an exponential growth in capabilities of man in creating a global economy.

Competitiveness Issues

As we conclude the globalization section, I would like to summarize important issues related to competitiveness. Very recently, Intel Chairman signaled that our technology innovation is in a challenged state, and we need to act quickly to regain the innovation momentum. Andrew S. Grove mentioned that the software and technology service businesses are under siege by emerging countries taking advantage of cheap labor costs and strong incentives for new financial investment. India's booming software industry, which is increasingly doing work for US companies, could surpass the United States in software and tech-service jobs by 2010, he said. He also said that the software and services industries — strong drivers of US economic growth for nearly two decades — are very similar to US steel and semiconductor industries faced in the past. Grove calls upon a new wave of innovation in United States.[53]

The question is much deeper. Can US compete with the rest of the economic markets? At this point, we are still the most competitive nation in the world .The next section will discuss competitiveness reports. Grove states there are real challenges in the world such as plunging global telecom costs, lower engineering wages abroad, and new interactive design software that are driving revolutionary change. He also states that:

> From a technical and productivity standpoint, the engineer sitting 6,000 miles away might as well be in the next cubicle and on the local area network. To maintain America's edge, Washington and US industry must double software productivity through more R&D investment and science education.[53]

Global Competitiveness Report — World Economic Forum

I am outlining a significant study from the Global Competitiveness Report. This report is published annually by World Economic Forum.[91]

In summary, the global information technology report underscores the growing relevance of information technology (IT) in national economies and the continuing need for an assessment of the readiness of countries to participate in the Networked World. The Global Information Technology Report is the most comprehensive assessment of how prepared an economy is to capture the benefits of technology to promote economic growth and productivity. The report highlights that the use and application of information and communication technologies (ICT) remain among the most powerful engines of growth. Specifically, the Global

Competitiveness Report 2002-2003, which examines the growth prospects of 80 countries, remains the most up-to-date and comprehensive data source available on the comparative strengths and weaknesses of leading economies of the world.

The report states that over the last 12 months, the world economy seems to have been robust and resilient. The report also emphasizes that the global economic outlook remains clouded with tremendous uncertainty. The report outlines that the prospects of a war in Iraq, corporate scandals, the bursting of the IT asset bubble, and the uncertain outlook in some emerging markets continue to weigh heavily on investors' confidence. Considering the potential damage these shocks could have caused, the world economy and the global financial system seem to have proved surprisingly resilient.

This report measures competitiveness — "that is, the set of institutions, policies, and regulations that support high levels of productivity and drive productivity growth and sustained increases in output."[91] Competitive countries can be expected to return to a sustained growth path faster and earlier than those that are less competitive. The Global Competitiveness Report is a five-to-eight-year prospect in a large number of individual economies. The first report focuses on growth competitiveness this year covering 80 countries; the Growth Competitiveness Index (GCI) represents a best estimate of the underlying prospects for growth.

It is also important to note that the Growth Competitiveness Index is based on three broad categories of variables that are found to drive economic growth in the medium and long term: technology, public institutions, and the macroeconomic environment.

Analysis of the Report

The following is a brief analysis of the report:[91]

> In the high-income countries, each new technological innovation triggers yet further innovation, in a kind of chain reaction that fuels long-term economic growth.

> The United States leads the Growth Competitiveness Index, swapping positions with Finland, last year's number 1 and now ranked number 2. Taiwan, Singapore, and Sweden follow. While Singapore has retained its fourth rank, Taiwan and Sweden enjoy a significant improvement of three and four positions, respectively. An even greater improvement in its relative position concerns Switzerland, however, a country that is being ranked sixth this year. The United States owes its position mainly to its stellar performance on technology-related factors. Research

and development, collaboration between universities and businesses, the level of tertiary education, and a sophisticated and innovative business and academic community all contribute to the high ranking of the United States. The United States also receives high scores for its venture capital markets, receptivity to innovation, and leadership in information and communication technology.

Finland also enjoys a very high level of technological sophistication, being ranked third in this dimension of competitiveness. In addition, Finland's public institutions are perceived to be the best in the world. On the other hand, Finland has slipped slightly in terms of its macroeconomic environment. Taiwan's high overall score also results primari'y from its very high position on the technology index, whereas Singapore's strengths are found especially in the macroeconomic area.

As far as e'nerging-market economies are concerned, China and India register substantial improvements in their relative positions, to 33 and 48, respectively. The world's two most populous countries — but especially China — have outperformed most other countries in terms of economic growth in recent years. Much of the countries' overall rankings is owed to their stable macroeconomic environment, although in the case of China, potential risks have been flagged more recently with regard to contingent liabilities for the budget stemming from problems in the banking sector.

Conversely, the overall rankings of Argentina and Turkey decline substantially, to 63 and 69, respectively. Both countries have suffered from severe financial crises that have caused real output to shrink dramatically. Relative to their overall position, both countries do moderately well on the technology dimension. Namibia at number 53, Morocco at number 55, Croatia at number 58, and Haiti at number 80.Tunisia owes its ranking to moderately good performance on macroeconomic environment variables and especially to good public institutions. Haiti, at the bottom, is known to be going through one of the most difficult periods in its history. Its competitiveness suffers from rock-bottom scores on technology and public institutions and only a slighter better position regarding the country's macroeconomic environment.

The authors of the report argue that countries that have invested in innovative capacity look set to become more competitive and achieve higher levels of prosperity. In addition, Porter and Stern express concern that those countries in which innovative capacity lags behind overall productivity are likely to find it difficult to sustain their current levels of competitiveness.[91]

According to Porter and Stern's analysis of the report, the United States continues to maintain the highest innovative capacity.

Current Economic Climate and Changes

General IT Climate
This is an era of change. I recently opened a conference in New York for CTO and CIOs, and declared that we are going through a massive change and transformation. Technology led the world into a period of unprecedented growth in 1980s and 1990s. Technologists and engineers were instantly elevated to star status. They were given virtual carte blanche in the quest to create the newest and latest of everything imaginable. Within corporations, techies were considered a separate and distinct group from the rest of the organization. Elevated by their status, huge salaries, signing bonuses and stock options were offered as incentives for company loyalty. And, as prescribed by their own sub-culture, techies played the role of the "geek" — introverted, analytical, quiet perfectionists who made up in talent what they lacked in management acumen.

Today our economic and business landscape has changed. Investors are no longer impressed with technology and gadgets. Companies are looking to get the most out of what they already have. This means that technologists need to not only understand technology but also how it integrates with the aspects of their business. They need to interact and communicate effectively with people from throughout the organization. Are there IT people in your organization who have great technical ability but lack the people skills required for management? Do you currently have people in place who undermine your goals because of poor management skills? Supervisors who don't interact well with their staffs and can't communicate effectively? Managers who "micromanage" and fail to offer their people the room they need to grow? Leaders who disrespect others and demonstrate a lack of concern for employees?

There is no denying that the nature of the business is changing. The software engineer who enjoyed the craft work of designing a fix and then writing the code is becoming an endangered species, replaced by the more automated process of moving a project through an assembly line of workers who function like cogs in a machine. We are also seeing the concept of Autonomic computing. It is defined as self-healing software and hardware, root-cause discovery, and correction and IT service provisioning. As stated in CIO Insight, according to a new study from Gartner Inc., within the next ten years we will likely see autonomics applied to general purpose grid computing, service billing and service policy managing systems that enable companies to shift IT resources to meet their changing business needs at the lowest cost.[89]

An IT field is involved with massive change. It must distinguish itself with advanced knowledge and the ability to continuously innovate in order to keep up.

Leading thought leaders in the IT world such as Bill Gates and Carly Fiorina have recently stated that innovation and growth will come from "workflow, collaboration, real-time communication" and technologies that "weave systems together."[95]

With the weak economy, global unrest, and lingering skepticism by buyers, tech spending will probably recover to a modest 6 per cent or so next year, and just shy of its 10 per cent historical average in 2005. Will technology rebound? I believe the answer is yes. At the same time, I must say that IT Leaders should continue their quest for innovation by applying their knowledge to building technology solutions that add value to firm's customers and shareholders. On the opposite scale, I hear others say that the information-technology revolution is finished. The industry that has driven the economy and captured our imaginations for years has peaked for good. It's true that after four decades of 10 per cent annual growth, more than twice the growth rate of the gross domestic product, tech spending has dropped for two straight years. Some corporate buyers point to many broken promises in the past. And now, some experts say that IT can no longer provide corporations any more competitive advantage — or growth. "A lot of the core things that businesses do have already been automated", says Nicholas G. Carr, who ignited a firestorm with an article in the May Harvard Business Review entitled "IT Doesn't Matter."[96]

A mere five years ago, demand for IT skills was so strong that many CTOs demanded six-figure salaries, stock options and other perks. But now, IT workers are being compared to the displaced autoworkers of the 1970s. During my correspondence, some people say that high technology today is what the garment industry was in the 1940s and 1950s.

When you look at the numbers for the last few years, technology finance infrastructure remains a mess, with venture capitalists very slow on investing in new ideas. Just 15 per cent of venture capital has gone to early-stage companies this year, compared with 35 per cent in 1995. Corporate customers are wary of buying technology from startups that may not survive. There are also many legal and regulatory issues. "Steam engines and electricity went through one big wave of improvement — and not even one as big as the one for IT", says economist Eric Brynjolfsson of Massachusetts Institute of Technology.[46] Many economists believe IT's productivity benefits fueled much of the prosperity of the 1990s, so it's crucial that advances keep coming for our standard of living to improve. Many IT buyers refuse to purchase anything that won't guarantee a return in six months. "There's a big backlash against technology and a lot of skepticism about what it can do", says technology consultant and author John Hagel III.[46]

In the information industry, technological advancement has radically changed the way we conduct businesses. The change is so drastic that it really needs fewer systems administrators, or complete ubiquity of common platforms that can be tended to in India as easily as in San Francisco or New York. John Scully, a former executive at Apple, states:

> What's happening is that we're going through the commoditization of virtually everything. It started with hardware. It's moved to software. And now it's moving to services. Companies have to find the least-cost way of delivering their products and services, What it means for workers in the US is that they need to keep refreshing and improving their skills. More and more, we're moving toward a system of certified IT workers. Certified in terms of knowing that when you hire somebody, they will be able to do the job you need them to do.[89]

I actually believe blaming the current job market conditions on the structural element of outsourcing job operations and singling out China, Russia, and India isn't entirely fair. Many companies in the US have outsourced their labor forces for the past 20 years. I believe that the reason why the job market is tight is more straightforward. The problem resides in what I call "irresponsible optimism." From the managerial side, poor business planning and over-investing — and from the consumption side, adhering to a false sense of security based on low short-term interest rates, ultimately allowing increasing levels of debt.

The process is picking up speed as companies start to outsource basic design and programming tasks as well to lower-paid workers in India, China and Russia. We will discuss this late in an outsourcing chapter.

Having said the above, we also must agree that technology days are far from over. Its days of maturity may be decades away. The IT revolution that shares similarities with manufacturing and other industries is also different because technologies are constantly accelerating.

An interesting statistic is that the economy depends on the technology industry moving its growth machine. In fact, up to 10 per cent of the gross domestic product comes from tech, which accounts for nearly 50 per cent of all capital spending

Said Intel Corp. Chairman Andrew S. Grove, who has worked in tech for more than 40 years: "The rate of change in technology is as much today as any time in my experience."[46] Technology will remain an important component of our economy.

New Generation and Digital Revolution

We are also experiencing something very interesting. We are seeing the growth of a new generation. It is literarily a new generation of young IT professionals and managers. We hope that this book will be a guide for this next generation group. This next generation group is the first one to be born in an all-digital world. It is developing its own culture and is just starting to impose it on the workplace. This force is formidable because of their attitude toward authority. It will demand some big changes in the way our society, business and individuals interact.

CIO Insight Executive Editor Marcia Stepanek convened a roundtable on youth and the future of the workplace at the magazine. Most agreed the N-generation will change the balance of power on how employees and management will work.[84] It will force today's leaders to forge new partnerships with employees with a focus on the abilities of people and experience to promote change and harness emerging technologies in the service of business goals. CIOs will be at the center of those profound changes, providing fresh opportunities to integrate new ideas and technologies into the values based organizations (discussed in later chapters). This young generation will be a real force to make an impact in our society.

Women as CIO/CTOs

Women CIOs and CTOs are a growing and emerging trend. They may be few in numbers but their influence and achievements are growing. The most prominent women are Carly Fiorina of Hewlett-Packard, Meg Whitman of eBay, Anne Mulcahy of Xerox, Linda Sanford, IBM. All are leaders in high-technology corporations. Based on a business week article, according to Catalyst, just 11 per cent of corporate officers at America's 500 top technology companies are women vs. 15.7 per cent at the largest 500 companies overall. And women lag behind in the competition for seats on corporate boards, holding 9.3 per cent at tech companies vs. 12 per cent-plus for the 500 largest corporations. From 1996 to 2002, the Information Technology Association reports, the percentage of women among IT professionals barely increased, inching from 25 per cent to 25.3 per cent.[11]

Women such as the Carly Fiorinas and the Meg Whitmans demonstrate the importance that women bring to this profession. They also open the minds of girls who could be the next generation of women business leaders. "At the end of the day, it's about individuals", says David Nosal, head of Korn Ferry's global CEO practice in Silicon Valley. At the end of the day, it is who has the ability and track record to build value. In technology, the women on our list have proven that they're up to the job.[11]

Furthermore, the special culture in Silicon Valley has helped women to break through major challenges. Parker, founder and CEO of executive search firm DP Parker & Associates in Wellesley, Mass. said that:

> That's why you're more likely to see women and minorities in senior positions in technology than in old-line, entrenched industries such as insurance, banks, steel, or manufacturing." High tech company's development cycles and cutthroat cultures have helped women succeed. In a pressure-cooker environment, executives are judged on whether they meet sales and marketing goals, or on whether a project is

finished on time, not on who their golf buddies are. Having that kind of systemic approach is a benefit to women.[11]

Are CIOs in Decline?

Chief information officers of large companies are in for some discouraging news:

CIO-CTO Environment and Conditions

There is something in the air. Something unusual is happening in New York and cities all over the United States. People are saying that Chief Information Officers have declined in the role. Their budgets have been cut, their work has been outsourced, their staff has been downsized, and they've been pushed off the executive team. Their status within the enterprise has suffered. We will discuss the role of CIOs and CTOs in the next few chapters. Meanwhile, some CEOs are outsourcing CTO and CIO functions and creating organizations such as Tatum CIO Partners. I recently had a discussion with George Wing, a Regional Director who has enlisted some of the top CIOs to work as CIO on the hire.

Consequently, CEOs and CFOs are questioning why they need a pricey CIO position heading a business function that's been effectively outpaced. Some are very harsh and suggest getting rid of the function and ditching the function head. Some are suggesting that vendor contracts return to CFO, or install a relatively cheap IT project manager to manage vendors. An easy way to end a problem or is this a solution?

What we're seeing, I think, is another iteration of a cyclical phenomenon where enterprises are losing faith in IT as a strategic entity, and therefore assume they can do without a strategic IT leader. The CIO role is in real danger of being diminished. CEOs and their boards are grappling to understand if the location and size of an IT workforce determines the need for a highly skilled CIO. Globalization is also a major factor here. In an ideal situation, CIOs could command a global IT workforce, even if some or most of that workforce is employed by an outsourcer. As Paul Saffo, director at the Institute for the Future, said at the CIO 100 Symposium in August, IT staff will come from everywhere, and so will the CIO.[71]

A very important article came out in CIO Magazine on October 15. Stephanie Overby did an amazing job in documenting a major developing story. According to the story, titled "An Incredible Shrinking CIO", there's a pretty good chance that many CIOs of large companies are already aware of their shrinking status because it's neatly reflected in their salaries, which dropped 16 per cent since 2001.[71]

Overby cites plenty of evidence that CIOs' corporate ascent has hit a wall. There's a 2003 survey that found that 22 per cent of CIOs now report to CFOs — exactly twice the percentage of CIOs that reported to CFOs in a study conducted one year earlier. And there's the dishearteningly horizontal line illustrating the change in IT budgets over the past year. There is also an accelerating industry-wide movement to outsource IT functions to faraway places, and there's the overwhelming majority of CIOs who report that their IT function is considered a cost center.

It may be one of the great and tragic ironies of 21st-century business that as technology plays an increasingly more important role in business, technology people play a less important role. Overby tells us that in many companies, IT strategy decisions that used to be made by CIOs now go to other executive and leaders who will have a final say. So is it over?

The article that CIO magazine prompts goes into the soul of our profession. Technology is at its best when it is invisible. If that is true, perhaps it's also true that technology professionals are at their best when they are completely invisible. Are CIOs going away? Can the role of the CIO be granted to people with non-technical backgrounds? Does it signal a decline? Some believe that running IT would be easy, and they rely upon IT and Management consultants for strategy and implementation. Can the CFOs and other leaders who focus on profits and bottom line run a creative and innovative group in our companies?

However, I do not believe this is the end and that all is lost. CTOs and CIOs have more to play but perhaps a different role. The role and importance has to be emphasized in terms of value to customers, transformation, and change. Most of the CTOs have been observed into CIOs and that is why we position this book to focus on both. There is also growing demand for new IT capabilities and high expectations for payoff but with greatly constrained resources. The threat to CIO exists. CIO have to respond, and lobby their case for value, alignment, a transformational role in a new economy.

I have read and reviewed many books and journals on strategic alignment and strategic planning. This type of planning and alignment is a recipe for disaster for CIOs today. When IT tries to please each and every business unit leader, each and every function head, and those people have competing priorities, there's no way to win. CIOs need to demonstrate value, and fast.

We all know that the only way to be successful when the number of high-value business initiatives greatly exceeds the resources available to deliver them is to get all the business stakeholders to agree on what is most important, and then to agree on how things should be prioritized. This effort must be brought in with substantial customer and shareholder value, and some very sophisticated, well-running governance mechanisms.

In reality, CIO carries a special significance. They really control and focus the innovation in the organization. They also have an ability to identify the problem/solution which goes up the value chain to prioritize, define and communicate goals for the entire enterprise — not just for any one business unit or function, and not just for IT. Second only to the CEO, CIOs are uniquely positioned to view the business in this cross-functional, process-oriented, holistic way. Finally, they are uniquely positioned to think about and lead discussions on IT-enabled strategy and process change.

Overby states that a 25-year Veteran who was a CIO states, "I don't know why anyone would want the CIO job today."[71] This is a powerful statement to make. The same article also indicates that Phil Schneidermeyer, CIO practice leader for executive recruiting company Highland Partners, says that "CIO is no longer the same level of position." He continues to say that:

> Companies are stepping back and saying the job isn't that big anyway. We're making less investment in IT. We have a smaller headcount. We're not going global and doing any mergers. We're done with ERP. We're sending it all offshore. Therefore we don't need the caliber of CIO we may have had in the past.[71]

Another CIO in the article states the following:

> Companies no longer view IT as a profession. It's a no-win situation. And if things don't change, the list of potential losers is long: CIOs, their users and staffs, their companies, and possibly the future of American IT.[71] "As a leadership position, the CIO role had little or no credibility left, and we deserved every bit of it", says Malcolm Fields, CIO of office furniture and fireplace manufacturer Hon Industries in the same article.[71]

The percentage of CIOs reporting to CFOs doubled this year from last year, according to CIO's "The State of the CIO 2003" survey. Yet, reporting to the CFO rather than the CEO or COO is almost always a sign of diminished clout. Recruiters report that companies are looking for low-cost techies and, surprisingly, junior employees to fill the role of CIO. In addition, in 2001, compensation for CIOs at large companies decreased for the first time since 1985 and has slid 16 per cent — from $434,000 in 2001 to $363,000 in 2003, according to IT management consultancy Janco Associates. The increased interest in outsourcing and shrink-wrapped technology strategies have resulted in a diminishing CIO stature.[71]

Furthermore, according to the "2003 State of the CIO" survey, 84 per cent of CIOs said their IT function is currently being budgeted as a cost center that generates expenses rather than an investment center that generates new business capabilities. And as corporations continue to cut technology spending, more and more companies are going for an off-the-shelf IT strategy.

"Put yourself in the shoes of a CEO", suggests Fields. "They're asking, do I really need a CIO, and if I do, why not report it lower in the organization and let the CFO handle it as a cost matter?"[71]

CIO's Responding

Hello World! CIOs and CTOs need to respond. Analysts are saying that CIOs haven't helped matters in the way they're responding to the current crisis in their corporate status. Most of the CIOs and CTOs are either running away, hiding or making excuses. Few lucky ones are holding on for a dear life. In fact, Infoworld Magazine has cancelled a CTO Section due to lack of demand in this market. The attendance at the 2003 Infoworld and SIM events was very light compared to other years. CIOs are in survival mode.

While some CIOs are withdrawing, others are fighting back. CIO Magazine has some suggestions for CTOs and CIOs to improve their image and finally respond.

So, what could CIOs do to improve the image? CIO Magazine believes that they could focus on the following:[71]

- Run IT like any other business unit.
- Put fiscal controls in place.
- Surround yourself with people who have business backgrounds.
- Get out of your office.
- Teach your staff to be businesspeople.
- Make the numbers tell the story you want.
- Work those relationships.
  - CEO Relationship
  - CIOs need to proactively push their value.
    - Business value and competitive advantage with a comprehensive global strategy
    - CFOs think in terms of quarterly earnings. IT is best managed as a long-term investment.
    - Vendor management is one of the CIO's core competencies.
    - Information is the most important asset in a company. CIO has experience to deal with information.

Technology has to be leveraged for competitive advantage. A good IT organization with a sound CIO can be part of a company's competitive advantage if they're closely tied to the business and help it improve processes faster than their competitors. In fact, most competitive advantages have an IT component today.

The article points out that CIOs are incredible resources to mange and minimize amount of business risk.(71)

Finally, outsourcing makes CIO a core requirement since CIO is key to global vendor management and understands key risks in vendor transactions.

Changing Environment in Context

I would like to end this section to describe the changes in holistic terms. I believe that a new individual in this new world is a mix of old CIO, Emerging Technologist and a Prophet of Change. Clearly, we are dealing with a changing environment. America is experiencing a major disconnection with corporate management, the interests of individual customers, shareholders and employees. The corporations rely on the old notion of managerial capitalism. It was a right model for a different time. Success was always what's best for the organization, which often also means what's best for senior managers — whatever makes them money or enhances their careers and reputations. The new world order depends on consumption and employment of a new society of individuals, but corporations and organizations continue to operate according to the notion of managerial capitalism, invented a century ago for different people, different markets, and different needs.(94)

In general, it creates a major misalignment between individuals and organizations that is marked by frustration, mistrust, disappointment, and even rage. There is also an opportunity to leverage the tools, techniques, processes, and models for the creation of the new way of capitalism. I believe that a new CTO will play a crucial role in this. CTOs will play a role in creating a new era of wealth.

Let's review this new individual. The new individual will have plenty of things. As consumers, they ask for treatment and support that will enable them their dream lives. People now have unique visions, desires, needs and wants, but corporations have remained distant and indifferent to the true nature of this change. Our business environment is malignant in that people are chronically disappointed and frustrated by their experiences as consumers and employees. Americans have lost the trust in large brand organization to serve their unique needs. Even at the CTO level, it is clear that we are experiencing a divisive "us vs. them" mentality. Now, after decades of challenges and corporate indifference, individual consumers are making their value known in individual consumption. One of the unique individuals are CTOs who are pushing us toward the next leap forward in wealth creation that Shoshana Zuboff names "support economy."(94)

Once you shift the source of value in the individual and not in the corporation, everything changes. The entire way we think about wealth creation, ownership, and control changes. We compare this shift in thinking to the great political and social revolutions of the 18th century, when people went from being merely subjects to becoming full citizens. We see this as the same kind of revolution — the consumer will no longer be a corporate subject. In this new vision, the individual is now the source of all value and all cash. This distribution of value also means the end of the corporation and industrial sectors, as we know them. It leads to what we call the distributed condition, as it necessitates new ways of distributing ownership and control across what we call federated support networks that are fundamentally aligned with the interests of the individual end consumer.[94]

We as CTOs view the fundamental shifts in the nature of capitalism. There is a major convergence of three forces: new markets, new technologies, and new enterprise logic.[57] There is evidence that those forces are coming together as I am putting together this book in December of 2003. This new highly educated, sophisticated knowledge population is pushing very hard for the rise of new markets for deep support. In fact, we now have a new digital medium uniquely capable of meeting the demand associated with these new markets. Finally, many people including senior management and technology executives today sense that there must be alternative attention to the orientation, purpose, and economics of transactions. Very soon, new value based commercial entities will figure out how to realize the value in the new markets for deep support — everyone who wants a share of the new wealth will follow. Then, we will experience a different world for our customers and ourselves as CTOs.[94]

When we get to the real support economy and value based organization, it will transform us to a new world. We will start exploring where we are less certain because we may not have the necessary techniques, processes and tools. History suggests that it is important not to underestimate the changes. The hope of our civilization really exists in a better understanding of cultural dynamics and interpersonal relations. We will see advances in "spiritual" disciplines that provide future generations with a solid awareness of the process of change. In a few years, our society could emerge into a period of rapid, sustainable, and evolutionary growth. New technologies will come into our horizon at breathtaking speed, but they will not have the same chaotic, transformational effects as earlier technologies. Our support model with distributed capitalism and value based organizations will allow us to handle those technologies at a different level. As a caution, a number of events could hinder this progress: a global war, a major plague, a religious upheaval, an asteroid strike or other environmental catastrophe. However, assuming these things do not take place, humankind could enter into a new transformation.[44]

Outsourcing and Offshoring

We are dealing with a new paradigm — an interesting experience of offshoring with innovation. In fact, offshoring and outsourcing are become mainstream, and clearly effecting the way the CTO and CIO need to work

Changes Leading up to Mainstream Outsourcing-Offshoring Model

To begin, as we outlined in Current Economic Climate, we need to recognize that the '90s attempted to spoil us, and in fact created a new society of consumers, customers, companies and individuals governed by new processes, values, strategies and rules. This economic trough is a natural part of the business cycle. America just came out of a very prolonged and unusual positive business cycle building an information-technology and equities bubble as well as unnecessary levels of excess capacity. While we were lulled by the house of cards created by the technology boom, an acceleration of the "globalization" and "exportation" of our economy occurred. The most interesting aspect is that the US economy has fundamentally changed.

We stated many times that Corporate America is beginning to experience a sea change in its attitude toward information technology. In increasing numbers, routine programming and business processes are being sent offshore to lower paid but highly trained workers in other parts of the world. Technology platforms are being standardized, with fewer IT workers needed to plug-and-play any number of more and more sophisticated systems. There is also a rise in on-demand computing utilities.

Indeed, Offshoring is moving mainstream. This affects IT professionals. In the long run, many IT workers in the US will be retrained or leave the field for something else. Global head count migration will be significant. The move toward offshore has been aided by the telecommunications bubble of the late 1990s. So much infrastructure for high-speed Internet connections was laid, much of it never used, that the cost of achieving high-speed communication plummeted. Deloitte's study estimates that 2 million of the 13 million worldwide financial service jobs will be relocated, primarily to India and Southeast Asia.[100] A Gartner study in July looked at the US computer services and software industry and estimated that one out of every ten jobs could shift to lower-cost emerging markets by the end of 2004. Gartner's report, "US Offshore Outsourcing: Structural Changes, Big Impact", forecasts that 500,000 of the current 10 million US technology jobs could move within the next year. "In our view, offshore outsourcing is an irreversible trend", said Diane Morello, a Gartner research vice president in the IT management sector.[97]

The forces — such as outsourcing, utility computing, autonomic computing — are changing the very nature of IT work.

In CIO Insight, Labor Pain article, a senior executive quoted:

> In a lot of companies developing software is like a craft. An employee is an analyst part of the time and a developer and business process expert other parts of the time. All of this is wrapped up in single individuals. If the development function is taken away, that changes their value proposition and what their fundamental job role is. Peeling those functions out may meet with organizational resistance.[89]

Furthermore, the standard Technology paradigm that CEOs, CTOs and CIOs were accustomed to have stalled in the past years due to the slow down in the US economy, corporate reorganizations, technology shifts, globalization, terrorism, uncertain political situations, the threat of world regional instability, and lower than expected corporate profits. As stated earlier in the book, I have called this problem an "irresponsible optimism." It has to do with poor management, poor business planning and over-investing and, from the consumption side, adhering to a false sense of security based on low short-term interest. And yet, the need remains; sizable reservoirs of intellectual assets and property representing vast amounts of wasted shareholder value go untapped in various parts of the world.

The challenges from previous years, the continuing need for innovation, and a new set of world driving forces have opened the door to a new paradigm, Global Offshoring. This new paradigm allows all of us to lead an "open source" and interconnected life. Although it may be difficult to adjust in short term, it would produce better life and better work for individuals in US and emerging countries. Evidence indicates that offshoring components of the Global Offshoring Paradigm are as beneficial to the US as they are to the destination countries. In my opinion, the concept that I am putting forward, Offshoring /Innovation Paradigm is a powerful new way to redefine the role of the Sr. Technology Leaders from the head of IT operations to executives in charge of global delivery of business services. We will discuss this more in detail in the following chapters.

Clearly areas such as innovation, transformation, and change are clear motivators and drivers to a leadership position in the US Information Technology market space. I believe that the CTO and CIO will have a say in this value chain which requires elements of our society and our EcoNet to have a significant impact and leverage. The Global Paradigm would be influenced by the way we change and transform our economy, and how it is aligned with Ecosystem Networks around the globe.

There is also a trend of autonomic computing, where systems auto configure and self-correct, theoretically freeing up IT workers from routine chores such as system administration. The current trends in computing have the potential to cut IT infrastructure costs as much as 50 per cent, including up to one-third of the IT workforce in the developed world.[89] Autonomic computing, for its part, takes even more people out of the equation through the development of such technologies as self-healing software and hardware, root-cause discovery, and correction and IT service provisioning. According to a new study from Gartner Inc., within the next ten years we will likely see autonomics applied to general-purpose grid computing, service billing and service policy managing systems that enable companies to shift IT resources to meet their changing business needs at the lowest cost.

More common platforms have lent themselves to more modular work, pieces of which can be done by different workers — often in different parts of the globe. Managers can typically choose various combinations of full-time employees, contract workers and projects that can be sent overseas at great cost savings. IT may get more commoditized, and lower cost items will end up offshore. The focus has to remain on high end value-added offshoring functions.

Trends and Figures

This section discusses statistics and trends from various publications and analysts.

ITAA

According to a survey earlier this year by the Information Technology Association of America, a Washington, D.C. trade group, the total IT workforce in the US peaked in 2000 at 10.4 million jobs, then shed more than a half million jobs before bottoming out last year at 9.9 million jobs. While some of those jobs have returned since then, the more robust rebound everyone is hoping for may never come. The survey found that managers have cut projections for adding staff this year in half. The reasons are myriad: the sluggish economy, the dot-com bust, a lingering hangover from the Y2K tech overdose and a growing sense that corporations now have alternatives to the highly skilled — but highly priced — US IT worker.[89]

Companies are also moving more positions overseas, with 12 per cent of IT companies and 3 per cent of non-IT companies saying they have already opened up overseas operations. Large IT companies were most likely to say they've made this move — 22 per cent have already moved work offshore. Additionally, 15 per cent of IT firms say they will, or are undecided about, moving jobs overseas in the next twelve months, while 4 per cent of non-IT firms say the same. Sixty-seven per cent of respondents already outsourcing IT work overseas say that jobs most likely to be moved offshore are programming or software engineering positions, followed by 37 per cent moving network design, and 30 per cent moving web development jobs. The ITAA annual survey placed the size of the US IT workforce at 10.3 million.[89]

Forester, Meta, Jupiter, Gartner

"Outsourcing is an irreversible trend" is an opinion of Forrestor and Gartner Analyst organizations. Recent research from Forrester Research indicates that the percentage of offshore outsourcing for US IT budgets took a leap from 12 per cent in 2000 to 28 per cent in 2003. META Group, Inc. predicted last month that offshore outsourcing overall would grow more than 20 per cent annually.[47]

According to Jupiter, overseas outsourcing has indeed been picking up steam for many years due in part to the array of services that can be had for substantially less cost than the equivalent here in the US.[47]

Forrester research shows that 70 per cent of enterprises that are turning to offshore outsourcing are sending out custom application development work. Sixteen per cent are sending system analysis and architecture planning offshore. Thirty-two per cent are using offshore outsourcing for system administration and support. Cambridge, Mass.-based Forrester Research Inc. projects that more than 3 million US white collar jobs will be lost to offshore outsourcing during the next 10 or so years — a half million of them in IT — accounting for almost $136 billion in annual wages [based on the 3 million jobs]. Offshore outsourcing will continue to grow at a rate of more than 20 per cent annually, according to Stamford, Conn.-based Meta Group, becoming a $10 billion market within two years. Gartner Inc., also in Stamford, Conn., predicts that 40 per cent of Global 2000 enterprises will embrace offshore or near-shore IT outsourcing by 2005, and that more than 80 per cent of US companies will seriously consider outsourcing critical IT services by 2004.[86] Some indicate that approximately 8 per cent of IT work is being outsourced. After surveying IT services vendors, IDC reported that the offshore component in delivery of US IT services may rise as much as 23 per cent by 2007, up dramatically from 5 per cent in 2003.[98]

Unfortunately, the domestic market can not fulfill the need for lower cost labor resources. The reality, and much more then a trend, is that the lower labor costs in Asia, Eastern Europe, and Russia enable services to be delivered at much lower cost than in the USA and Western Europe. I must say that combined with the falling cost of high bandwidth global telecommunications, the financial case for offshore outsourcing is hard to ignore. The statistics to back up this case are also staggering. In Europe alone, according to Gartner, there is a 40 per cent increase in the European market for offshore outsourcing during the year of 2003. And, in the European financial services sector alone, Datamonitor forecasts growth of $240m in offshore outsourcing over the next 12 to 20 months.[99] In fact, Gartner expects the rest of

Europe to catch up quickly and predicts that 75 per cent of large to medium-sized companies across Europe will consider offshore services by 2004.[97]

Offshore outsourcing has become an attractive financial option, according to Gartner. A study released by Gartner states that one out of every ten jobs at information technology companies and at companies that provide IT services will move to emerging markets. It also forecast that one out of every twenty jobs within internal IT departments will shift overseas by the end of 2004. "Offshore outsourcing is becoming a tool for improving service delivery and a source of highly qualified talent in greater numbers", Diane Morello, a research director at Gartner, said in a statement.[97]

American technology companies are increasingly shifting part of their research efforts to countries such as Russia, India, Ireland and China. They are lured there by large numbers of highly trained software and hardware engineers and by lower development costs. The Gartner study cautioned that although outsourcing may lead to lower costs, businesses must realize that it could also lead to a loss of talent, intellectual property and overall organizational performance. Gartner advised chief information officers in US companies to devise well thought-out outsourcing strategies that could lead to new competencies in areas such as service management and business integration. However, it also suggested that they move some day-to-day activities overseas.[20]

Challenges in Offshoring

One of the challenges is to turn developers into business analysts and architects and vendor relations managers. Managers must navigate a successful transition to an outsourcing relationship with trust and confidence. It is important to keep productivity high. Many US businesses are at the beginning of a decade-long transition from IT developed on a company-by-company basis to a future where IT resources are shared and provided on demand as a utility. CIOs need to work with employees and other shareholders to figure out how best to apply technology to further business goals.[89]

This is a god time to discuss two emerging and yet distinct countries in an offshoring market: Russia and India.

Russia

I recently took a trip to Russia, and Russia is an interesting case illustration. It had experienced four consecutive years of stable growth in its economy. With a significant R&D heritage, it is one of the world's best educational systems, and the largest pool of highly qualified software engineers and researchers. According to Ernst & Young, The Russian IT & Telecommunications sectors are experiencing an average growth of 45 per cent and are expected to reach $20 billion by 2005 The country is acknowledged by major US and European companies, such as Boeing, Intel, Motorola, IBM, Sun Microsystems and many others running and expanding their innovative R&D centers in Russia. The true evidence of the country's success in recent years is in the recent achievement of investment grade status by independent Moody's Investment Services for the first time in Russia's history. Russia was also included in the list of the world's 10 most attractive countries for direct foreign investments.

Some indicate that Russia's Golden Age of Russian Offshore Outsourcing is coming with full speed. Most Russian offshore outsourcing companies have doubled in growth in the last two quarters. And for the first time since the IT boom in Russia, new economic stability is keeping Russian brain power back home. And among those who stay, the best and brightest of Russia's scientists and programmers are working in the field of offshore software development.

India

India is another interesting case study. It is a deep source of low-cost, high IQ, English-speaking brainpower which may soon have a more far-reaching impact on the US. *Business Week* recently concluded an analysis of Indian offshoring. "India has always had brilliant, educated people", says tech-trend forecaster Paul Saffo of the Institute for the Future in Menlo Park, Calif. "Now Indians are taking the lead in colonizing cyberspace." The Indian labor card is unbeatable", says Chief Technology Officer John Parkinson, a consultant for Cap Gemini Ernst & Young, quoted in Business Week. "We don't know how to use technology to make up the difference."[54]

India is turning into a fast-growth economy, and it will be the first developing nation that used its brainpower, a driver for a global change. The country has long possessed some basics of a strong market-driven economy: private corporations, democratic government, Western accounting standards, an active stock market, widespread English use, and schools strong in computer science and math. But its bureaucracy suffocated industry with onerous controls and taxes, and the best scientific and business minds went to the US, where the 1.8 million Indian expatriates rank among the most successful immigrant groups.[54]

In fact, India's emergence is fast turning into a globalization giant. By some estimates, there are more IT engineers in Bangalore (150,000) than in Silicon Valley (120,000). Meta figures at least one-third of new IT development work for big US companies is done overseas, with India the biggest site.[54] A.T. Kearney Inc. predicts that 500,000 financial-services jobs will go offshore by 2008. India produces 3.1 million college graduates a year, but that's expected to double by

2010. The number of engineering colleges is slated to grow 50 per cent, to nearly 1,600, in four years. So there's a growing movement to boost faculty salaries and reach more students nationwide through broadcasts.[54]

A top electrical or chemical engineering grad from Indian Institutes of Technology (IITs) earns about $10,000 a year — roughly one-eighth of US starting pay. Says Rajat Gupta, an IIT-Delhi grad and senior partner at consulting firm McKinsey & Co.: "Offshoring work will spur innovation, job creation, and dramatic increases in productivity that will be passed on to the consumer." By 2008, forecasts McKinsey, IT services and back-office work in India will swell fivefold, to a $57 billion annual export industry employing 4 million people and accounting for 7 per cent of India's gross domestic.[54]

India's forte is services — which make up 60 per cent of the US economy and employ two-thirds of its workers. And Indian knowledge workers are making their way up the New Economy food chain, mastering tasks requiring analysis, marketing acumen, and creativity.

Deloitte Research, Gartner, Booz Allen, and other consultants find that companies shifting work to India have cut costs by 40 per cent to 60 per cent. Indian IT market is a $240 billion IT-services industry. Indian players are Infosys, Tata, and Wipro, and Cognizant.[98],[100] A study by McKinsey Global Institute, which believes offshore outsourcing is good, also notes that only 36 per cent of Americans displaced in the previous two decades found jobs at the same or higher pay. The incomes of a quarter of them dropped 30 per cent or more.[63] Goldman, Sachs & Co. thinks India will be able to sustain 7.5 per cent annual growth after 2005. So India is destined to have the world's largest population of workers and consumers.[41] India presents an opportunity for the US which could accelerate productivity and innovation.

Offshoring Maturing

No question, offshoring is taking off like a mainstream business. Many businesses have turned to offshoring as a way to boost profits. Another major issue that seems to be on everyone's mind, especially decision makers such as CIOs and technology executives, is how to stay competitive and obtain reliable up-to-date information and knowledge on emerging markets, and subsequently establish innovation centers and IT outsourcing areas around the world where costs are significantly less than in the US, like Russia. All of these global players, at least most, are aggressively looking to grow their offshore outsourcing.

As we have noticed, we are increasingly facing a completely different world — a world based on the concept of virtuality, trust, values, and globalization. The world of information technology is a perfect example of the progress that we are making as geographic locations evaporate, and working locations have a tendency to be flexible, adaptable and virtual. And finally, the communication bandwidth has increased with infrastructure cost around the world being lowered.

Of course, the next generation of offshore development and outsourcing services will be based on adoption, results and significant processes. It also has to do with major cultural elements and shifts. In fact, offshoring is pushing the world beyond the information economy, and towards global knowledge based economy. In this case, knowledge is being shared and collaborated across the world, and it is becoming specialized into many segments and domains. The core components of Information Technology and Communications are necessary engines to facilitate the push into the new era of Collaborative and Knowledge based economy.

The most forceful driver behind the shifts in IT staffing is the so-called "offshoring" of IT work, which appeals to major corporations and financial companies. A Gartner report forecasts that by next year more than 80 per cent of US executive boardrooms will have discussed offshore outsourcing, and more than 40 per cent of these enterprises will have finished a pilot, or will be outsourcing IT services either offshore or "near shore" — somewhere on the North American continent.[97] Even companies that choose to outsource IT functions domestically with one of the growing technology service powerhouses — among them IBM Corp. and EDS Corp. — end up augmenting the offshoring trend. Many of these service companies operate subsidiaries overseas to provide lower-cost alternatives to applications development or maintenance services, or farm the work out to the growing number of emerging tech markets around the globe.[100] A recent research report by Deloitte Consulting estimated that the financial-services industry will send $356 billion in expenses offshore within the next five years. According to the report, this will translate into an annual cost savings of $138 billion for the world's top 100 financial-services companies by 2008 — an average of $1.4 billion each. "It's not only some of the big players — GE Capital and American Express Co. and Citibank. Virtually every financial institution is now engaged in figuring out how to reduce fixed costs by going offshore", said Chris Gentle, a Deloitte director of research and author of the report.[89]

Some critics have challenged the legitimacy of the offshore outsourcing due to protectionism and job migration to emerging and newly developed countries. Actually blaming the current job-market conditions on the structural element of outsourcing job operations and singling out India, Russia, and China isn't entirely fair. The reality is that offshore outsourcing is a component of a new global paradigm, and it is a lot more complex then simply moving entities and resources in various parts of the world. It already takes advantage of the high skill labor and enormous innovation in the developing and emerging countries. This phenomenon started a while ago with the growth of the developing markets, and the linkages of value chains around the global economies. In fact, many companies in the US have outsourced their labor forces for the past 20 years.

It is already viewed as a viable and economical approach to a wide range of Information and Technology based initiatives. There is also a major reliance and trust factor that has been overcome in which companies in the US are forming mature and long lasting links with Research and Development and Information Technology groups and companies in emerging and developing countries.

The timing for offshore outsourcing could not be better. In today's complex world where cost cutting has been taking charge, it has really enhanced and contributed to the value and success for offshore outsourcing plans. Some may even venture to say that offshore outsourcing has become a mainstream way of doing business. We are seeing some incredible success stories in offshore outsourcing due to a selection of quality vendors, the degree of trust and openness factor, acceptance of virtual organizations, collaborative teamwork, and value driven success and motivation. We also must recognize that the driving forces in the IT outsourcing are speed to market and quality, not just cost of services. A new wave of outsourcing is allowing companies to quickly acquire reliable IT to deploy specialized services and ramp down easily when those services are no longer needed. Moreover, it's enabling corporate transformations, so companies may have more agile and responsive business models. Big pools of cheaper, high-quality offshore talent have made it easier to strike a cost-efficient balance between the desired skill level, exemplified by the skill sets that salaried in-house workers have; and the flexibility of contractors, who can be retained on an as-needed basis.

Risk Management

There are many risks in outsourcing situations. There are serious challenges abound, and they spell potential obstacles to companies focusing on the offshore course.

Security

Companies are outsourcing software development to cheap labor overseas, where there is little or no way to ascertain the security risks posed by offshore workers. One risk is the potential loss of intellectual property and business-process secrets. Offshore outsourcers can copy and sell that knowledge or repackage it and present it to a competitor.

Business Continuity and Political Situations

Terrorist networks exist in the Middle East and Southeast Asia, which are also home to superb IT talent. Companies that exclusively outsource to a third party in a single country are at greater risk that their operations could be disrupted. A political situation, such as armed conflict between Pakistan and India, could shut down offshore operations.

Controlling Customers' Fears

It can be difficult to convince customers that their data will be secure with a company thousands of miles away, in a country with a different language and culture, run by a government whose regulations and concepts of intellectual property ownership may be alien to those in the US.

It is suggested that CIO minimize risks in the following ways:

- Work with large vendors that have multiple regional centers worldwide.
- Break up key pieces of the work being sent offshore, so no one can easily re-assemble those pieces; this process is analogous to encryption.
- If you're big enough, open your own dedicated offshore center staffed with local talent provided by an outsourcing partner. These employees can be managed under the same umbrella as US employees.
- Have detailed business continuity procedures spelled out in contracts, and be aware of a country's intellectual property laws.[35]

What Does It Mean for the US IT Market?

Some people say that the US IT employment picture won't brighten even with the return of a growing employment marketplace. The proponents of this view argue that the growth of offshore outsourcing will remove any new employment demand in the IT sector from the US to other countries such as India. The logic is simple: Application programs can be written anywhere since they're not geographically dependent, and the cost of development (labor) is much cheaper overseas.

However, the argument is wrong. To begin with, the IT employees of India, Russia and other nations can't all be assigned to serve US needs. Europe and Asia have growing business sectors of their own and will be consuming much of the available talent. It's not just US demand that will grow; inevitable worldwide growth will create intense, escalating worldwide competition for the available talent.

Throughout US history, the US workforce has managed to move up to better-paying, higher-quality jobs. That could well happen again. Engineers could work closely with customers, manage research teams, and creatively improve business processes. Displaced technicians who lack such skills will need retraining; those entering school will need broader educations.

One reason IT employment hasn't picked up steam is that, since the end of the 1990s, there hasn't been significant technology advances spurring industry acquisitions of new systems, hardware or software. Those technology advances will occur, and industry will invest. US demand will go up, and offshore outsourcing won't satisfy that demand.

Security is another important factor. Many systems, both those of corporations and government, won't be outsourced offshore because of security concerns. Companies and government alike will be keenly aware of the need to protect and keep safe critical software data as well as hardware and chip advances.

Then there are the demographics issues that we addressed earlier. There are 76 million baby boomers. Generation Xers, born between 1965 and 1978, number about 46 million, so there's a population shortfall of 30 million in the coming generational transition.[101] Clearly, as baby boomers continue to age, the supply-and-demand situation will turn more dramatically in favor of the American worker. Also, in the US, the number of people choosing computer science careers has been rather steadily declining. Offshore outsourcing may be a necessity to simply attempt to cope with demand. In IT, the natural evolution is to marry the technical with the administrative, necessitating the acquisition of business acumen as well as technical skills. Real growth in the field will happen in areas like data management, systems architecture and the merger of IT technical skills with business management skills. These positions aren't likely to be outsourced offshore.

There also are growing new areas requiring IT skills like bioinformatics and nanotechnology. These embryonic growth fields will blossom and create new and strong areas of demand. The world won't turn out enough qualified people to satisfy its technological employment demands. New industries will appear. The generational US population decline will have an effect. The American technology worker will prosper.[56]

According to Mckinsey, Offshoring will allow US to capture economic value through multiple channels:

- Reduced costs — Savings from reduced costs means more savings, which can be passed to consumers or to investors to reinvest.
- New revenues — Offshoring creates demand in destination countries for US products, especially for high tech items.
- Repatriated earnings — Several providers serving the US market are incorporated in America, which means they repatriate their earnings back into the US.

- Redeployed labor — US workers who lose their jobs to offshoring will take up other valued added jobs, which will in turn generate additional value for the economy.[63]

What Does It Mean for CIO?

Offshoring has the potential to redefine the CIO role from head of IT operations to executive in charge of global delivery of business services.

That understanding of how technology can help the business is even more crucial for CIOs and IT managers. As we discussed, IT outsourcing market is driven by speed to market and quality, not just cost of services. It is also enabling corporate transformations so companies may have more agile and responsive business models.

The truth is that successful IT executives obsess about how they can contribute to company growth, profitability and strategic direction. In many cases, they've been constrained by bloated, often ill-equipped IT workforces, which have now been pared down. Big pools of cheaper, high-quality offshore talent have made it easier to develop cost-efficient balance between the desired skill level, with variety of skill sets in-house; and the flexibility of contractors, who can be brought in on an as-needed basis.

As a result of offshoring changes, CIOs are now focusing more energy on hiring experienced project managers and business/IT liaisons, and redirecting their employees to critical roles such as leadership, architecture, business analysis, business enhancement and vendor management.[56]

New Paradigm

This new interesting global innovation/offshoring paradigm is based on the selection of appropriate and strategic technologies, skills, and resources for offshoring and commercialization; the coordination of those individual initiatives into a strategic plan and portfolio for development and innovation; the location of specific global technology ecosystems with the strongest potential and lowest cost structure to move the technologies forward; and the funding of these initiatives through non-traditional and global sources. This model is in step with and complements the concept of globalization. It recognizes how tightly coupled the world's economy is today and fuels additional markets, opportunities and funding sources. For instance, developers in Russia have the opportunity to market their products and services to European and US companies. Unique technologies in South America or Central Asia could be leveraged in the biotechnology incubator of a large multi-national company. Specialty software concepts could be modeled, developed and tested in emerging markets, etc.

The paradigm that was just outlined holds the promise of moving technology implementation and research and development to offshore, as well as commercialization of untapped assets, forward by leveraging advantages that are only possible through a worldview. The driving forces for this new paradigm include:

- Availability of low cost, high quality sources in Information Technology and R&D and the specialization of various regions in specific technologies and skills (programming, bioresearch, etc.)
- There is increased activity with open source community development (Linux, for example), which propels additional growth in emerging technologies.
- Local development organizations and governments around the world are stimulating Information Technology and funding economic commercialization projects to start the growth of new industries in their countries. This provides additional and unique sources of funding from international/regional funding sources and regional economic development centers.
- Investment by the global organizations and multinationals designed to expand and grow and business incubation in various regions of the world.
- Technology Parks have begun to specialize in particular types of companies, technologies and industries.
- Information Technology companies are beginning to spring up in terms of area strength or weakness and/or regional growth.
- Recent years have seen tremendous growth in the number of Information Technology Companies and Technology Parks outside the US, including Russia/CIS.

We are living in a new world, and need to effectively leverage skills, resources and technology in a way that increases the value. There is a consensuse that this paradigm will help to create win-win solutions and ensure that everyone in the US benefits from a more competitive and healthier global economy.

New Economy — Creating Value for Customers

Let's assume your company has outstanding products and services, marketing, and sales and customer support has well-organized data on customer desires and buying preferences, market segmentation, demographics, competitive analysis, etc. You have highly motivated employees, a good track record of innovation and project implementation and a stellar management team. In fact, you may be a market leader. Is this enough to ensure your future? No, it is important to create incredible and long lasting value with customers. The focus is customer participation, involvement, organization changes and passion for creating and sustainable trust. It is important to focus on customer awareness and leadership to support this momentum through technology changes. Leadership must be prepared to transition the entire company in response to customer feedback. It must be prepared to adopt a corporate culture to support customer engagements. Technology must be applied to increase connection to the customer.

Also, nowadays the customer is really in the driver's seat, and technology companies understand the reality. This is a customer oriented value-driven economy which I will discuss a bit later. It also suggests a shift in industry economics and company behavior. Partly, it's because lower prices will give customers more technology benefits and profits. To accommodate these value-conscious customers, producers will outsource to lower-cost providers. In a customer driven world, suppliers no longer can act as sales driven people, but must focus on reliable and customer focused product, technologies and services. We see that technology companies are adopting those new business models.

Let's step back and discuss the new episode of new value based support capitalism that emerges from the complex interplay of a number of forces that supports individual value:

(1) New human yearnings that create a new approach to consumption and new kinds of markets.
(2) They want to be treated as individuals, not as anonymous transactions of a mass consumption and production society. They want to be heard and they want to matter. They no longer want to be the objects of commerce. Instead, they want corporations to bend to their needs. They want to be freed from the time-consuming stress, rage, injustice, and personal defeat that accompany so many commercial exchanges. They seek advocacy, relationships in place of transactions. They want to take their lives in their own hands and they are willing to pay for what we call the deep support that will enable them to do so.

This concept is not new. It is a concept of support and value based economy, and not an enhanced version of conventional customer service.[94] It is an entirely new way of doing business, a radically different approach to the realization of value in which the very purpose of commerce is redefined around the objective of supporting individuals. Deep support enables "psychological self-determination." It produces time for life, and it facilitates and enhances the experience of being the origin of one's life. It recognizes, responds to, and promotes individuality, and at the same time it celebrates intricacy. It multiplies choice and enhances flexibility. It encourages voice and is guided by voice. Deep support listens and offers connection. It offers a collaborative relationship defined by advocacy. "It is founded on trust, reciprocity, authenticity, intimacy, and absolute reliability."[94]

There is a new digital medium whose networked intelligence, flexibility, ubiquity, and complexity make it ideally suited to meeting the demands of the new markets for deep support. This digital medium has really been focused on old consumption, according to the principles of the old capitalism. The new medium has to integrate with "a new enterprise logic capable of liberating its revolutionary potential."[94]

As they say, a lot of components are in the fire. What's needed is a match to move this forward with fast speed. These conditions create the urgent need for a third force — "a new enterprise logic capable" of marrying and integrating the new markets for deep support and the new digital medium with a proper balance. Zuboff calls this a "new enterprise logic distributed capitalism."[94]

It is also worth comparing a "distributed capitalism" with the old form of "managerial capitalism." The key here is where value is located. With the old model, organizations create value on the inside through the production and distribution of goods and services. The organization and its top management are at the center of the commercial solar system. In the new model of "distributed capitalism", the concept of value is totally inverted. Value is not created by organizations, but instead resides with individual end consumers, based on what they require to satisfy their needs on their own terms. The role of the "new enterprise is not to create new value but to realize the value that already sits with individuals lodged in their unique needs. This shift of focus is the crux of the role of a CTO focusing on transforming the organization and it's crucial to understand the support economy.[94] As you see, "The support economy relies upon the new enterprise logic of distributed capitalism, in conjunction with the new digital medium, to provide the deep support that the new individuals really want. The provision of deep support is the new higher order purpose of commerce — more complex because it includes, but goes beyond, the production and distribution of goods and services."[94]

CTO/CIO — Change and Transformation

The demands for a CTO are so diverse that sometimes we could think of a CTO as a superman. "S/he will have strong business acumen, and will likely have spent time in the high-tech business development arena. S/he will also have a proven track record of working successfully with venture capitalists and be able to negotiate complex deals with stakeholders." The CTO will be required to "work with product group general managers and business development managers to determine future technology opportunities."[39]

Companies will face a more sophisticated marketplace and the unique demands of a consumer. At the same time, the CTO's role will shift to include a broader business and financial focus with real returns but provide competitive edge. The shareholders, employees, and customer cannot accept fantasy projects with an unclear path and destiny. The days of real capabilities and real knowledge are in front of us.

We are experiencing a major slowdown of our economy, and at the same time technological changes are occurring constantly and everywhere around us. Everyone is working with a tighter focus and preparing several options to spend a much smaller budget.[27]

As we mentioned earlier in the book, Parker and Associates pointed out that large companies such as General Electric, Allied-Signal, and ALCOA created the position of CTO in the late 1980s. In later years the position has played a very important role in IT and Internet companies in the late 1990s. Over the short history, CTO played a prominent role in directing and shaping their entire business.[72]

By the 1980s, companies appointed research chiefs to CTO positions. Technology was being positioned as a solid building block of a company. Senior management started to rely upon a CTO to provide reliable input on applications, products, and services. In the 1980s, companies began integrating Chief Technology Officers to the top management ranks. Technology was already a crucial part of strategic decisions and future planning. Senior management felt that additional advice regarding the "creation of new products and services with large technical components" would be a step forward for a CTO.[5]

In early 1990's, the CTO position was really centered in IT/Software companies, where this individual served as a bridge between the engineering department and the rest of the business. CTO was partly a technology evangelist, and partly a senior product architect.[27]

Today and tomorrow, the CTO is not really expected to be a senior technologist of the company. The CTO must connect business with technology, and s/he must provide real advice on business decisions involving technology instead of research or concept ideas.[5]

We went through a difficult period of separation from the CIO profession. The InfoWorld CTO Forum and CTOs from Sun Microsystems, eBay, Dell Computer, and other companies contrasted responsibilities as being externally focused while the CIO's responsibilities were internally focused.[82] I believe that the CTO is turning in a different dimension, and becoming a very important and pivotal player in executive management focusing on external and internal issues.

As part of this historical trend, organizations have realized the need for the CIO to oversee internal technology operations which includes billing, computer manufacturing, accounting, purchasing, security, and others systems, including computer systems for accounting, billing, and telephony. At the same time, the strategic decisions of incorporating emerging technology and scouting for new applications have taken a back seat.[55]

The internal/external division of responsibilities created a major gray area and a sense of confusion. In fact, the Transformational CTO will tackle most of the strategic responsibilities of the CIO. The CTO has to step up and accept the broad shoulders of corporate strategy and profitability. We will discuss the roles later in the book in more specific detail.

CTOs are not the first senior executives to face the challenge of inclusion or exclusion from the strategic process. Everyone goes through the drill process and learning the ropes. In previous times, CIOs were also labeled as technologists who could not function as business strategists. However, the days of Techno CTOs and CIOs are far behind us.[55] It is clearly understood that technical skills are highly connected human capital, management strategy. Neither one could be excluded effectively.[55] CTO and CIOs have recently demonstrated themselves as business savvy leaders with sharp business decisions that are effective with other management peers. One paper cites the results of a study of pairs of executives at hundreds of companies that indicated that the business acumen of CTOs was equal to that of their executive peers. A complimentary study of 417 company executives found that 80 per cent of the CIOs in those companies were considered very important contributors of the strategic decision making process.[74]

Clearly, there is a lot to be learned from the holistic drive and experience of CIO colleagues, and how a CTO would assimilate into this environment. Executive management is recognizing that the stereotypes associated with technology focused CTOs are in the days of the past and, having proved an accurate stereotype for the CIO, is starting to push the CTO into a different strategic and change-oriented role.

The next several years will challenge IT leaders to become partners with their internal customers, sharing in the setting of corporate direction and seizing growth opportunities. They'll have to broaden their vision and shift their priority from saving money for the company to creating value for customers. Although excessive costs, process inefficiencies, legacy systems, software bugs, and laggard implementations will remain big concerns, IT's greatest impact will continue to be in finding innovative business uses for technology.

It bears repeating, with the accent on innovative business uses — cutting-edge technology, bigger and faster networks, and more "enabling" devices may or may not be relevant. After three years of cutbacks, what counts is for the IT organization to foster its innovative capability to exploit changing conditions, then to imagine how the business and IT strategies interweave to create value. Examples are support of customer-centric strategies at retailers such as Best Buy, Home Depot, and Walgreen. In a previous issue of Optimize, we outlined the basic skills, tools, processes, and platforms needed to build innovation capabilities. All we'll add for the moment is that staff issues are paramount.

Most top executives already grasp this new reality. They see that the path to greater customer value and competitive differentiation is paved with real-time data and lit by customer insights derived from that data. The trouble is what executives think in their armchairs and what their companies do in conference rooms are often utterly different. And while there are exceptions, the gap still shows few signs of shrinking.

Type of Companies — Focused on Customer Value

There must be an opportunity for everyone involved in our companies that inspires, motivates, and fulfills the internal stakeholders, while also creating a positive experience for the company's external stakeholders. Every party has to win in this scenario.

Our CTOs need to adapt to a new dynamic model — a practical, non-threatening model that is founded on fundamental values to which most people can relate. This pragmatic new approach is not a new way of imposing violent, ethereal "psychological change" on an organization that is exhausted and disenchanted by the frustrations of fighting the win-lose approach currently employed in corporate world today, but rather "a blueprint for helping organizations achieve extraordinary results by addressing stakeholders' needs and getting them to work together in a focused and frictionless manner towards a common purpose that benefits all."[50]

An environment where care and trust are prevalent is an essential precondition for the individual and the community to flourish. This community has to provide consistent win-wins for a growing number of its stakeholders. This is priority for our nation, it is realistic, it is imperative and urgent! A previous section on support economy demonstrated that the current business model is barren, broken and basically unsustainable. Virtually all stakeholder constituencies voice dissatisfaction and loss of faith on a daily basis.[50]

Individuals share values such as love, care, relatedness, freedom, etc. They may not talk about them very often. "September 11 was one of the moments when it became clear that a huge number of people not only hold these values dear, but thirst for opportunities to express and apply them."[50] The key condition for success is a willingness to bring those values into the open and to actively apply them to all business activities. CTOs have the unique position to influence the organization in that direction.[50]

Based on the work of Zuboff and Inzelstein, one belief that is shared by a growing number of people is companies and other communities that embrace a values-based approach will thrive and rise above their peers. The other systems that do not adopt will increasingly struggle under the burden of dealing with unhappy constituencies with no common agenda.

As we have seen earlier in the book, technology executives and managers are seeing some patterns, and are now trying to redefine their roles and demonstrate the value of IT. It is still very important to create a successful leadership style with skills, and nurture them within networks and relationships.

A company called Edizen recently conducted a market research study with technology company executives and others in the industry.[38] The study consisted of interviews with executives representing a cross-section of the IT business landscape — big corporations, mature startups, venture capitalists, and outsourcing firms. The result of the study was a major new focus on development and leadership; organizations that can bring the skills of IT managers in line with their business vision and values. Executives also agreed that collaboration is a very important aspect of technology. People management is a hot priority issue. Technology leaders must have one foot in strategy and one foot in implementation in order to be effective. Edizen participants in the study were quoted as saying that "Leadership in technology today must be far more sensitive to the human element, accepting different work styles and allowing work-life balance. As business leaders, we must get people involved and engaged."[38]

We see a general trend that technical IT managers need to transform to technology visionary leaders. The CTO must be able to able to communicate vision and build value through relationships. All of the participants need to understand business issues and problems. We see a tendency of managers looking for effective facilitators, collaborative decision makers, and caring models of balance. While the Edizen study of participants recognized the need for "leadership", not everyone agrees on exactly what that means.

One thing is certain — to survive in today's challenging business environment means delivering consistent performance over time. We described that we need to move further then revenues and profits and revenue, and demonstrate performance in terms of value. Developing the new skills of IT leadership will go a long way in helping to leverage the value of technology as well as build the bench strength talent needed to move your company forward.[38]

Chapter 3

CTO Priorities

Defined by Media, Analysts and Corporations

This section brings us major issues and priorities surrounding the CTO profession. Those issues take account of some major implications of long-term and short-term spending patterns and recognition of new priorities for a CTO. Priorities are important for us to make certain decisions and define who we really are. I have assembled priorities that are outlined by major media publications, analysts, and corporation.

BusinessWeek's Technology Overview

BusinessWeek[46] indicates that:

> The underlying technologies not only aren't slowing down, they're accelerating. Computer-chip performance keeps doubling every 18 months, and disk-drive capacity and Internet-connection speeds are improving even faster. That's spurring new products, from MP3 and DVD players to Web services for corporations, that are disrupting industries from entertainment to health care. Indeed, the titans of business today, from Dell to Wal-Mart Stores, as well as upstarts such as Amazon.com and JetBlue Airways, owe much of their leadership to using information technology in special ways. Each employs some of the same technologies, whether that's Linux software or servers based on Intel chips. But it's their expertise in deploying and customizing those technologies year after year that gives them a continued. From steadying orders and better-than-expected profits to the rise of promising technologies such as the wireless Internet, Linux software, and digital entertainment, tech's long winter is thawing. To take advantage of these new opportunities, however, technology companies must reinvent themselves — fast. Instead of applying the advances of silicon, storage, and network economics to

hiking performance on existing products for the same old customers, they must turn those forces to making products, existing and new, that are cheaper.[46]

CIO Magazine

CIO Magazine recently had a survey of CTOs and CIOs. It shows, to a major surprise, that, in fact, technology executives' worries have less to do with technology and a lot to do with typical management issues. CTOs are worried about the general management issues like deficiency of key staff/skill sets/retention, inadequate budget, and lack of time for strategic thinking/planning. An annual report also stated that "communication and business savvy are personal skills that are most pivotal for the CIO's success." At the end of the day, CIO/CTO performance and salary appraisal are based on company profitability, CIO/CTO leadership ability and demonstrated value of IT. The CIO's biggest challenges or hurdles have less to do with technology and more to do with management.[18]

CIO Magazine also indicated recently that any cost control will be part of the outsourcing strategy. To keep headcount down and manage budgets, outsourcing is being used to get projects or programs.[22] Another survey and analysis from *CIO Magazine* is presented in the reference section of this book.

Gartner Group

Gartner demonstrates another roach on priorities. Gartner analysts came up with a list of major predictions that impacts enterprise businesses and how those predictions cross over technology, economics, and social boundaries that will morph during the next few years. The deep understanding of those priorities will impact the work and role of the CTO. We must clearly project where technology and business intersect and converge in the next scope of five to ten years.[32]

Bandwidth becomes more cost effective than computing

Network capacity will increase faster than computing, memory and storage capacity to produce a significant shift in the relative cost of remote versus local computing. Cheap and plentiful bandwidth will catalyze a move toward more centralized network services, using grid computing models and thin clients. Gartner bases this prediction on the fact that optical networking improvements are far outpacing growth in computer-related technology. The challenges of the last mile — security, quality of service, and grid economics — are barriers that need to be overcome.

Most major applications will be interenterprise

This means that the evolution of applications and middleware is heading toward more adaptive software architectures that can be reconfigured on the fly with minimal hassle. This concept is the next evolution of the software model that has spawned ERP suites, portals, CRM, and supply chain applications that span across various constituencies involved in an economic ecosystem. This is the promise of Web services, and if they ever mature, we will have more of a plug-and-play capability for configuring applications. But we have already been through eras in which applications would seamlessly resolve into interoperable parts. Initiatives for industry-specific XML standards need to take root as well as other Web services standards.

Macroecomonic boost from interenterprise systems

If most major applications moving to interenterprise comes to fruition, the overall economy would reflect a major upswing into productivity and efficiency. The logic suggests that corporations closely aligned through industry segment or some other value chain should actually see increased productivity that would flow to the macro-economy. The savings and increased productivity that would result would be clearly evident in government adopted business process and technology architecture.

Successful firms in strong economy's lay off millions

Given that productivity improvement from IT improvements suggested in predictions that previous trends would come to fruition and healthy profit margins, Gartner envisions a shrinking workforce. The concept is that like the agrarian industry, technology will reach a point where IT system automation substantially lowers the labor requirements. Gartner's strategic planning assumption is that enterprises transformed by the Internet are 70 per cent likely to have 10 per cent fewer workers by 2005 and 60 per cent likely to have 30 per cent fewer workers by 2010.

Continued consolidation of vendors in many segments

Gartner predicts that at least one major player from most segments will disappear by 2004 through extinction or consolidation. That's not a risky prediction. As more of the smaller com companies evaporate, the major players will consume the smaller fish. At some point our industry will enter a period of oligopoly, in which a few vendors dominate the enterprise landscape, and that by 2007 the innovation and growth cycle will return.

Moore's Law continues to hold true through this decade

Gartner gives Moore's Law, which posits that processor power doubles every 18 months, a 70 per cent chance to continue unabated through 2011. Gartner projects that by 2008 the typical desktop computer will have 4 to 8 CPUs running at 40 GHz, 4 to 12 gigabytes of RAM, 1.5 terabytes of storage, and 100Gbit LAN technology. By 2011, processors will clock at 150 GHz and 6 terabytes of storage will be common. And, there are numerous technologies such as nanotube transistors and spintronics that could jump the next hurdle when CMOS reaches the end of its run.

Large banks become primary providers of presence services by 2007

Presence services can manage your preferences, personal information and experience on the Internet. Gartner considers what it calls "one-click Internet" as essential to bringing convenience and mobility to the Internet. Microsoft (Passport), the Liberty Alliance, AOL, and Yahoo (among others) are vying for a piece of your presence — if not all of it. But Gartner has said that the future belongs to independent companies or financial service provides, such as the banks. Banks have had to deal with security, privacy and issues of trust for centuries, and that legacy is particularly relevant in the digital age. Gartner gives the banks a 70 per cent chance of succeeding in the presence business by 2007. Gartner predicts that the banks will play a major role and adopt something like Liberty or Passport as the underlying framework for the trust broker business.

Business activity monitoring is mainstream by 2007

BAM (business activity monitoring) is one of the hottest buzzwords making the round today. Garner clearly describes this as having automated sensors that provide the relevant information and context that leads to more effective, real-time decision-making. Gartner describes BAM as reshaping decision-making in the enterprise: "In the past, when enterprises made complex decisions, the answers were precooked because the information wasn't available at the point of contact between your business and customers. In the future, decision-making will be pushed down because of more real-time data and business processes throughout the enterprise." This concept fits neatly with prediction 2 — tighter linkage across enterprises and industry value chains. Without BAM, organizations will fall on their faces trying to do business in real-time, which will be a requirement in many areas of business in the coming decade.

Business units, not IT, will make most application decisions

The Gartner take is that business units, rather than a centralized IT department, will make decisions on business applications. By 2007, this trend has a 70 per cent probability of governing purchasing in 65 per cent of enterprises. The downside is that the overall benefits of IT expenditures will degrade. Accounting and business principles will define whether IT expenditures provide the necessary ROI. Applications will be grouped into three categories, according to Garner. First, basic utility applications will keep the business functions. Second, enhancement applications will provide some measurable ROI. And third, frontier applications, although more risky, can give a company a significant competitive edge. Gartner said that empowering business units is a good fit with decentralized organizations and delegated authority. Well-organized, decentralized organizations in volatile markets typically have the advantage of faster decision response time, and result in better business outcomes despite inefficiencies resulting from decentralized IT decision-making. The entire process works best if parties from both camps are involved in decisions and collectively understand the business goals.

Pendulum swings back from centralized to decentralized

Gartner predicts the focus on more centralized IT during this time of economic contraction will shift by 2004 to a more decentralized model. Business objectives outside of cost containment will drive decision-making to business units, where agility is a highly valued commodity and there is resurgence in economic growth.[32]

Morgan Stanley

Morgan Stanley recently released a report where they state that security topped the list of software interests, while storage narrowly edged out PCs as the top hardware priority.[67]

META

Meta also emphasizes that security is a major area of investment due to terrorism and September 11.[25]

CSO Magazine Online

The second issue that appears constantly on the minds of CIOs is how to measure return on investment (ROI). After a major catastrophe, measures can be made, but all IT staffs are dealing with how to measure ROI for security. Tina LaCroix, chief of information security at Aon Cor, indicated that "This elusive packaging of the ROI formula to validate our existence is one that may take us down an endless path."[4]

Top Industry Players

The industry's top players are spending heavily to position themselves for a new economy that is fast approaching us.

Let's now examine what the largest companies are putting together as priorities for the upcoming years. The few top companies with the most innovative technologies and the most aggressive strategies are positioned to increase their revenues and profits with innovation.

According to sources and publications, the large companies plan to revolutionize their own markets and technologies before competition. We are observing that corporate spending on information technology has been increasing. Market researcher IDC estimates tech spending will rise 2.3 per cent this year. For example, the Merrill Lynch index of the top 100 tech companies has increased 38 per cent since the start of 2003. In the 1990s, technology was the glowing engine of economic growth. Tech's share of GDP rose from 3.2 per cent in 1990 to 4.9 per cent at the peak in 2000 — and still accounts for 4.2 per cent. Economists credit tech spending for at least one-third of the productivity gains in the second half of the 1990s. According to David A. Wyss, chief economist for Standard & Poor's, it's contributing to abnormally high productivity growth in an economic slump. Innovation will play a key role in the economic recovery.[45]

According to a 2002 study of US companies during the 1990-91 recessions by McKinsey & Co., the companies with the strongest stock sustainability and appreciation after the recession launched major initiatives during the downturn. Most of their investments were focused on innovations and acquisitions. We are observing that the 10 richest companies hold a total of $130 billion in cash.[102] IBM, Dell, Verizon, Nokia, and Microsoft all are making strategic but aggressive moves. Some companies are trying to transform the industry.

Microsoft

Microsoft possesses $46 billion in cash as it moves into such new markets as collaborative. Microsoft strategy is to get customers passionate about technology again. The company is spending a lot of money into the next version of its Windows operating system, code named Longhorn, due in 2005. As its PC software business slows, Microsoft is moving beyond its mainstay corporate market into new fields such as video game players. This will force Microsoft to become a different company.

SAP

German firm, SAP, is providing a platform for other businesses to build on, and make their own technologies more attractive to customers. It has technology that makes it easier for smaller companies to create innovative applications on top of its basic applications for managing corporate finance and manufacturing.

IBM

IBM is pushing a radical vision it calls on-demand computing. The idea is that it will offer computing power to corporate customers as a service, whenever they need it, with all the reliability and simplicity of electricity. CEO Samuel J. Palmisano is reshaping the entire company around the idea and spending $1.6 billion on research and development this year for on-demand products. Sam Palmisano thinks the answer is to make computing simpler, and to shift the burden of managing tech systems from corporate customers to experts, such as IBM. This concept is called EBusiness on-demand computing. Most of the complexity can be removed by using software to better stitch together applications and computers, and to deliver computing power to customers via the Internet. The focus is to sell computing as a service. IBM vision is very ambitious in this space, and it introduces technologies that enable sick computing systems to heal themselves and that tap into grids of computers, as needed, for processing power and data-storage capacity. If this strategy works out, IBM will be able to get a steady revenue stream and customer lock-in.

Sony

Japan's Sony Corp. is investing around $3 billion over the next three years on new chips for devices in the digital home of the future, enabling a fusion of computing, Web surfing, electronic games, music, and videos on easy-to-use home networks.

Qualcomm
Qualcomm Inc.'s latest chips and software already are focused on the arrival of next-generation mobile phone services, including the ability to shoot videos with cell phones and instantly transmit them to friends or business associates

Nokia
Nokia is putting some of its $11.4 billion to design new mobile phones. It spent $3 billion on research and development in 2002, up 18 per cent since 2000. It is pushing the market with a variety of new products. As an example, one of them is N-Gage, a mobile phone that doubles as a portable game console.

Intel
It is moving to a higher value chain. It is aiming at entirely new markets, such as cell phones, handheld computers, and networking gear, whose much larger volume could make up for their lower profitability. It also has vowed to give each chip wireless capabilities.

Chapter 4

Emerging Technology Direction and Vision

In this section, it is important to cover the new direction of a CTO with emerging business opportunities that we are going to plan for the years ahead. This section of the book will also cover some new and amazing technologies and methods to revolutionize, and spark the growth in the technology world.

Next Generation Consulting Harvard Report

Before we review emerging technologies and trends, it is important to understand the direction and vision of a new consulting model. A Harvard Business School has been looking at the technology management consulting trends for the future. In an interview, the paper's authors, professor Richard Nolan and HBS Interactive Senior Vice President Larry Bennigson, explain their findings.[69]

Professor Nolan and Larry Bennigson believe that there are a couple of major triggers that deal with autonomous computing and "computer-to-computer" communication. In fact, the Harvard Report states that:

> By the end of the decade, more than 60 per cent of computer communications will be computer-to-computer. Computer-to-computer vastly speeds up the pace of business. For example, end-to-end supply chains can be automatically adjusted by point-of-sale computers that are directly communicating with warehouse computers, which in turn directly communicate with manufacturer computers. Manufacturers' computers can then directly communicate with their suppliers' computers. In addition, computer-to-computer communications can track demand and adjust logistic systems in order to automatically direct a product to geographical points of demand.[69]

Future Growth Opportunities and Technologies
Enablers and Drivers and Globalization

Professor Nolan and Larry Benningson further describe some of the major enablers and drivers behind the future growth of the IT consulting industry as well as how globalization has impacted this growth:

> First, innovations in frameworks and methodologies, along with trained professionals, have provided value-added services uniquely available from the consulting firm. For example, the Boston Consulting Group and McKinsey came up with unique conceptual frameworks for assisting management in sorting out action plans for their various lines of business. Newness and complexity have been a second driver. Andersen Consulting, now Accenture, has provided expertise in designing and coding complex computer applications. SAP and Seibel Systems have developed unique package software. They have also provided specialized consulting services in order to assist in the implementation of the package software. A third driver has been the building to critical mass of high levels of expertise that are not economical to maintain in a particular company. For example, computer security consulting requires a high level of expertise, which few firms can economically maintain in-house. By providing these kinds of services to many firms, critical mass can be maintained in the practice group, as well as ensure that the group stays on the leading edge of the subject matter. Related to this third driver is the focus that a separate consulting firm can maintain in managing a highly talented group of knowledge workers. The management and incentive systems are quite different in a consulting firm than in, say, a product firm. Consequently, a product firm may not be attractive to various knowledge workers who prefer to work in the consulting environment. A fourth driver is the demand for process and behavior change that IT implementation puts on most organizations. IT was not just a new technology. To capture the value that IT represented, organizations had to address changes in structure, culture, people, process, and leadership. Many organizations turned to the consulting industry for help in understanding and managing these significant changes. Finally, the IT consulting industry enjoyed an unprecedented frenzy of convergence of first, the adoption of systems such as enterprise resource planning (ERP) and customer relationship management (CRM); second, the management improvements such as Biological and Physical Research Enterprise (BPRE); third, the problems to solve such as the Year 2000 bug; and fourth, new territory to pioneer such as e-business.[69]

Predictions

HBS has outlined some amazing predictions for the future of IT management consulting. Let's glean to the future of IT consulting through the eyes of HBS:

> We believe that the recent restructuring in the IT management consulting industry is at a point of industry transition. That transition coincides with the emergence of new drivers of IT management consulting growth. While the transition is still being played out, we can see some of these new drivers taking shape. By the late 1990s, new applications development had become almost exclusively supplanted by package implementation. In addition, networking and the Internet moved the IT infrastructure for the IBM standard to an emerging environment characterized by open standards. Accordingly, the IT infrastructure became simpler and more complex at the same time, through the innovation of layers and application programming interfaces (APIs). The implication for IT management consulting is a rather complex demand to provide both strategic perspective and implementation savvy on managing the considerable risks of not being able to realize the strategic competitive advantages of computing because of failures to effectively manage implementation challenges. Further, within the context of the management challenges of balancing strategic opportunities with implementation capabilities, there are dampening forces on industry growth. For example, the wave of ERP installations projects is now beyond its peak. While outsourcing is still an established practice, companies have gained experience, and can now do much more for themselves that they, in the past, have looked to outsiders to do. Managers know more about IT, more about the business, more about organizational potential and implications of IT and more about designing their own backbone and architecture. There are forces that will drive new demand. Security is fast becoming a ubiquitous issue. The Internet will experience dramatic growth in Asia and Europe. New applications such as bioinformatics and telematics create new consulting segments. And the adoption of Internet2 will eventually have broad impact. IT consulting, as much as any product or service, creates its own demand. A high degree of industry adaptation in the IT consulting industry will be required in the future. By introducing innovations and educating the market about the competitive benefits of those innovations, IT consulting invents and "earns" its opportunities for growth. This ability of IT consulting to lead and to adapt is key to its robust development.[69]

HBS thinks there are major lessons here for CTOs and CIOs. Let's follow them:

> Many functional and business leaders have become conversant about IT, and many IT specialists have become knowledgeable about the strategic and business benefits

of IT. Companies that encourage and incorporate this integrated and more sophisticated capability within their organizations will have an edge over those that have to rely on outsiders for the integrated view. The rate of change in IT capabilities is a companion to the rate of change that most companies experience in other technologies, markets and initiatives of competitors. We have noted that the successful IT consulting firm must be able to anticipate, sense and nimbly respond to change. This is equally true for operations managers who face the daunting task of implementing new IT capabilities while ensuring that they are also prepared for the next version or generation. The emerging IT environment is at a level of complexity such that efforts to build IT infrastructure and integrated applications require specialized expertise that is often available only in IT consulting firms. Good operations managers will ensure that their organizations have the ability to work effectively with and integrate the value from networks of service providers with a variety of special capabilities. Finally, we think that it is tempting but risky to completely turn over IT initiatives to IT consulting firms. A significant number of your own IT professionals and users should be included in integrated IT initiatives.[9]

The future is very bright and full of emerging ideas and technologies that would be analyzed and properly redirected by a CTO focusing on emerging technologies.

Vance Chan Associates

According to Vance Chan Associates, some important technologies are the following:[87]

- Convergence of data and voice communications and mobile access to enterprise systems
- Networking: wireless, VPN, other options
- Multi-channel customer and management
- E-commerce, m-commerce: payments, security, partner interface
- Supply chain
- Sales and distribution: forecasting, support
- Virtual organization and teleworkers
- Knowledge management

George Washington University and Future of Technologies

Furthermore, we are actually going through a Technology Revolution as described by George Washington University Technology Future study. The futurists at

GWU expressed in most vivid terms how the vision of the new technologies will shape the world and IT. These technologies and innovations will become the necessary components for distributed capitalism and value based organizations of tomorrow.

Science and technology are essentially accumulations of knowledge, and the information revolution is magnifying our ability to create and share technical knowledge. The result is that IT has become a major factor enabling unusually rapid technical developments, therefore accelerating advances in all fields. For instance, science has been transformed as networks of researchers are able to collaborate regardless of geography. IT-enabled research organizations are evolving into new forms that speed up investigations. Major advances in the field of information processing, for example, can have direct effects in others areas, such as managing the huge amount of data flowing from the Human Genome Project. At the same time that technical prowess grows, uncertainty over its social assimilation persists. Technological advances do not occur in a vacuum but are shaped by social forces. For instance, industry recognizes that the acceptance of new technologies is driven by consumer awareness, needs, lifestyles, values, and a host of other market factors. For example, while the Internet continues to expand at phenomenal rates, results from the Information Services field show that we should not expect major changes in IT services very soon. The least conservative estimate — entertainment on-demand — is not expected until late 2000, while half of all goods in the US sold through information services may arrive in 2020. Similarly, while search engine technology on the World Wide Web is advancing, we will not see intelligent software agents in routine use until 2009. Personal digital assistants (PDAs) will not be adopted by the majority of people until 2008. Personal computers may soon be able to incorporate television, telephone, and interactive video but our panel did not see this or a Web-TV with telephone capabilities in wide use until 2005 or 2006.

Software also has a long way to go. Expert systems, once heralded as then undeniable decision-making software for the 1990s, have a major chance of finding routine use by 2010. Computer programs that can learn and adjust their own programming will not be commonly available until 2012. Language translation software has a similar fate, not achieving widespread practical use until 2012. A standard digital protocol that would allow more advanced global networking applications is not expected until 2006. And while citizens are heralding the Internet and the World Wide Web, most people will not have access to the information superhighway until 2008.

In other fields, such as medicine, responses were more optimistic. Computerized medical information systems including provisions for home and self-care could be commonly used in the general population by 2007. Holistic health practices are becoming more accepted and will be well integrated in medicine by 2009. Gene therapy will help eradicate inherited diseases by 2013. Organ replacement strategies will become routine, by growing genetically similar or cloned organs or making synthetic organs, in the years 2018 and 2019, respectively. By 2008, genetic engineering and its accompanying regulatory regime should have changed to allow the routine production of new strains of plants and animals.

As the information revolution proceeds into the 21st Century, major advances in information technology will occur. As the IT fields mature, the effects will begin to permeate all fields and industries. Multimedia interconnectivity will be the theme for the first decade, allowing people to interact seamlessly across information mediums and geographic borders. Virtual reality and large flat panel displays will take the place of the computer monitor, allowing simultaneous viewing of several applications at once, virtual meetings, and group collaboration. On-line communities will have grown from text-based chat-rooms to three-dimensional, real-time realities. Education, entertainment and virtual tourism will enter a new era, and the consumer will have nearly unlimited choices. Electronic commerce and banking will be the currency of choice in developed countries as the cashless society is realized. Sophisticated software will aid consumers and professionals by providing intelligent agents to filter news and mail. Expert systems may finally see routine use as surrogate doctors, lawyers, and other professionals. These systems will be remotely accessed, not bought as stand-alone software, and updated continuously. Software will run on microprocessors imbedded in household products, walls and automobiles. Modular programming and a common language for computer communication will lead to ubiquitous computer-enhanced environments. While the amazing advances in information technology will steal many headlines, medical breakthroughs will compete for the news.

The early 2010 CTO will witness the most striking technological advances in terms of number and scope that our civilization has seen. Information technology will be taken for granted and IT-enabled activities involving working, learning, shopping, publishing, and leisure will become a way of life, much the way automobiles became a way of life a few decades after their introduction. Computers themselves will begin to emulate the human brain in sensory recognition and thought processing. Neural networks, biochips, and artificial intelligence may finally reach fruition as computing speeds and parallel architectures are applied and exploited. The interconnections of technology during this decade will transform developed societies in ways similar to the agrarian and industrial revolutions. Information technology innovations will allow parents to check on their kids, farmers to check on their crops, states to check on their criminals, and meteorologists to check on the weather. Our ability to manipulate matter will change, as nanotechnology becomes the new enabling technology for the remainder of the century.[44]

BusinessWeek Predictions of New Technologies
BusinessWeek — Innovation 2004
BusinessWeek covered the latest trends and predictions:[14]

Voice over IP
JetBlue Airways Corp. has invested in a new technology called "voice over IP", which lets corporate data networks handle phone traffic using Internet protocols. It also allows its reservation operators to take customer calls from home.

RFID
Buyers also are getting excited about newly emerging technologies that promise to make their operations more efficient. Wal-Mart Stores is making a big investment in radio-frequency identification (RFID) chips, which will allow it and its suppliers to track goods all the way from the factory to the checkout counter. Such tracking is expected to reduce theft and other losses, cut the number of people in warehouses and stores who must track goods, and boost sales.

Consumer Smart Phones
Less than 12 per cent of the world's population has a PC, and, even with Net-connected cell phones and Internet cafés, just 13 per cent are on the Web. One example of the new products: smart phones that are in every way computers, with Web connections and cameras. Gartner Dataquest expects revenues from such products to jump 140 per cent this year, to $4.9 billion.

Computing Power and Servers
Innovation is full speed ahead. By 2005, IBM is expected to make a huge leap in performance that will break Moore's Law, stating that chip speeds double every 18 months. That's when Big Blue will unveil Blue Gene, a supercomputer faster than today's top 500 supercomputers combined. And Sun is also working on so-called "throughput computers" that cram the equivalent of eight huge servers onto a single chip — an advance that could boost the power of big Internet servers fifteen fold by mid-decade.

Engineers are creating cutting-edge machines using commodity, industry-standard building blocks. Computer makers have a running start at building state-of-the-art machines. Now, they are able to focus and solve other problems — from developing self-healing computers to packing more power into ever smaller devices — by letting advances in automated maintenance made by its 1,200-person mainframe R&D team filter down to its lower-end machines.

Blade Computers
Companies end up buying lots of Windows base computers, and spend loads of dough getting them to work together. For every $1 spent on new equipment, operating costs run $3, according to IDC. Imagine if all those servers could be shrunk down to the size of a legal pad and stacked inside one console like books on a bookshelf. That's the main idea behind blade servers. This lets companies fit far more computing into far less space, cutting real estate requirements as well as the monthly electricity bill. All told, blades can reduce operating costs by 25 per cent, according to blade pioneer RLX Technologies. Dell and IBM only recently began shipping blade computers, so sales are just ramping up. The market for blades is expected to grow from 150,000 units in 2003 to 1.9 million in 2007.

The first chips will be in the form of a blade server, due out in 2005. The chip may sound like science fiction, but consider this: Thanks in part to Moore's Law, it will be possible to get 500 million transistors on one sliver of silicon by 2005, and 1 billion by the end of the decade.

Grid Computing
Grid technology is designed to make the most of underused computing power. Companies are beginning to use grid software to plug into computing power on the Internet or private networks as easily as electricity can be drawn from the power grid. It's technology management on a grand scale. The software constantly monitors the network, searching for computers that could help run a job that may be overwhelming the company's own computers. It then slices up the job into small portions so all the machines can help.

Throughput Computing
It's working on a new class of computers based on a radical concept called "throughput computing." While most servers are designed to run a single task as fast as possible, Sun's idea is to develop computers that can run far more jobs at the same time. To achieve that, it intends to cram the guts of eight of today's servers into a single piece of silicon. Throughput computing could be perfect for

Internet servers that must handle thousands of requests quickly, from Google searches to music downloads to complex business transactions

Flexible Computers

Among the concepts made possible by Moore's Law is the idea of nearly reconfigurable chips. Today's jack-of-all-trades chips are designed to handle some tasks well, while doing passable work on other chores. These new chips and the computers they would power would be able to morph by the millisecond, depending on what the computer is being asked to do. One such effort is a research project at the University of Texas called the Polymorphous TRIPS architecture. Each instruction received from a program gives hints as to the nature of the task. The chips come pre-loaded with various plans, each designed for a particular type of job. The chip is divvied up into 100 tiny panels, each of which can be programmed to take different forms, say either memory or networking circuits. The computer's software analyzes program instructions as they flow in, arranging the panels on each chip in the best way to handle the task at hand, like a never-ending game of electronic musical chairs. If a video clip is called up, for example, the memory circuits would be reprogrammed as networking circuits. That way, the clip would be sped on its way, rather than delayed sitting in memory.

Prototypes aren't due out until 2005. IBM, Intel, Sun, and Defense Advanced Research Projects Agency (DARPA) are investors in the project, but there's no certainty such chips will get to market. If it works, TRIPS chips could bring supercomputer-class power to everyday products, from game consoles to home medical imaging equipment.[14]

BusinessWeek also demonstrated significant new emerging technology advances.[13]

- **NANOTECH: Molecular Machines.** In the 2020s, we may be able to buy a "recipe" over the Net, insert plastic and conductive molecules into your "nanobox", and have it spit out a computer.
- **Artificial Intelligence.** Superbrains born of silicon will change everything. Previously intractable problems in science, engineering, and medicine will be a snap. Robots will rapidly displace humans in factories and farms.
- **Quantum Computers.** The toughest problems will be solved with a roll of the dice. Physicists hope to use subatomic particles' imprecise nature to answer questions beyond the reach of today's computers
- **Genes: Automatic Assembly of Genetic Pieces in Jigsaw Puzzle.** As biology's deepest mysteries are finally revealed, medicine will be the first beneficiary. New drugs that conquer Alzheimer's disease, vaccines to wipe out AIDS, and crops packing vaccines will be among the fruits of these discoveries.

- **LIFESTYLE.** The nomads shall inherit the airport lounge. The 21st century belongs to the fleet of foot. Technology has not freed road warriors like John Gruetzner from the constraints of travel. It has freed him from staying at home.

Finally, this section shares Batelle Future's predictions, and their vision of top strategic technology areas.[3]

Batelle — The Top Strategic Technologies

- **Human Genome Mapping** and genetic-based personal identification and diagnostics will lead to preventive treatment of diseases and cures for specific cancers.
- **Super Materials.** Computer-based design and manufacturing of new materials at the molecular level will mean new, high-performance materials for use in transportation, computers, energy, and communications.
- **Compact, Long-Lasting and Highly Portable Energy Sources,** including fuel cells and batteries will power electronic devices of the future, such as portable personal computers.
- **Digital High Definition Television.** This important breakthrough for American manufacturers — and major source of revenue — will lead to better advanced computer modeling and imaging.
- **Electronic Miniaturization for Personal Use.** Interactive, wireless data centers in a pocket calculator-size will provide users with a fax machine, telephone, and computer capable of storing all the volumes in their local library.
- **Cost-effective "Smart Systems"** will integrate power, sensors, and controls. They eventually will control the manufacturing process from beginning to end.
- **Anti-aging Products** that rely on genetic information to slow the aging process will include aging creams that really work.
- **Medical Treatments** will use highly accurate sensors to locate problems, and drug delivery systems will precisely target parts of the body, such as chemotherapy, targeted specifically to cancer cells to reduce the side effects of nausea and hair loss.
- **Hybrid Fuel Vehicles.** Smart vehicles, equipped to operate on a variety of fuels, will select the appropriate fuel based on driving conditions.
- **Edutainment.** Educational games and computerized simulations will meet the sophisticated tastes of computer-literate students.
- **Genetaceuticals.** Genetics-based medical treatments will cure or mitigate the effects of various human diseases and disorders, including pharmaceutical treatments for osteoporosis, MS, cystic fibrosis, Lou Gehrig's disease, and Alzheimer's.

- **Personalized Computers.** Your personal computer at home and in your office will be replaced by a very powerful "personalized" computer. It will recognize your voice and follow your voice commands, and it will include a variety of security and service tools to personalize the computer for its individual owner. The personalized computer will be as mobile and versatile as its user, sending and receiving wireless data and accessing information from remote sites.
- **Multi-Fuel Automobiles.** To obtain maximum efficiency and meet stringent environmental standards, vehicles will use combinations of various fuels, such as reformulated gasoline, electricity, and natural gas. Vehicles may carry more than one fuel type, with an on-board computer that will conduct on-going analyses of travel conditions to calculate fuel mixtures for maximum fuel efficiency and performance.
- **Next Generation TV.** In ten years, our television set will be large and flat and will hang on the wall much like a large painting. It will be a digital, high-definition model with clarity approaching that of a movie screen. This TV will be much more than just an entertainment device — it will also be used as a computer monitor capable of networking with other computers as an interactive, videoconferencing device.
- **Cyber Cash.** Electronic money will be used for everything from buying soda in a vending machine to making an international transaction over your computer. Pockets will rarely jingle in ten years as credit card-sized smart cards begin to replace cash, as well as house and car keys.
- **Home Health Monitors.** These devices will be simple-to-use, non-invasive, and relatively inexpensive for use in monitoring health conditions at home. Many physical functions — liver functions, ovulation, levels of cholesterol, triglycerides, sugar, hormones, water, salt, and potassium — may be monitored as easily as weight is now tracked by bathroom scales.
- **Smart Maps and Tracking Devices.** Getting "there" will be decidedly easier with the widespread use of Global Positioning Systems-"smart" maps that will show travelers, boaters, and hikers their exact position and direction. Global positioning systems also will be used to help prevent crime by tracking the exact location of cars and other valuables. People also will be able to track the exact location of their children and even their pets.
- **Smart Materials.** New materials for construction and other uses will be able to give off warnings when they detect excessive stress. For instance, materials in bridges or office buildings could change color before conditions become unsafe. Automobile parts could give a similar warning when approaching the point of breakdown.

- **Weight-control and Anti-aging Products.** Though no Fountain of Youth is on the horizon, new products will make aging a little less traumatic. These new developments may include weight-control drugs that use the body's natural weight-control mechanisms, wrinkle creams that actually work, foods with enhanced nutrients, and an effective cure for baldness. Many of these developments will come from genetic research.
- **Never-owned Products.** Major household appliances, such as furnaces, air conditioners, washers, dryers, and water heaters will be leased instead of purchased. This trend will be spurred by environmental concerns and regulations, cost, and the increasing speed of technology, which causes products to become obsolete quickly.
- **Genetic-based Medical and Health Care.** Over the next 20 years, we will witness an explosion of medical technology originating from genetic research, giving us the ability to detect and correct many genetic-based diseases before they arise- possibly even in the womb. A wide range of new pharmaceuticals that originated from genetic research will come onto the market in the next 20 years, leading to treatments, cures, and preventive measures for a host of ailments. They may range from treatments for life-threatening diseases to psychological disorders to cosmetic problems. Most incredible, some of these treatments will be personalized to meet the unique needs of an individual's genetic makeup. It will really be the ultimate in individualized care."
- **High-power Energy Packages.** Developments such as highly advanced batteries, inexpensive fuel cells, and micro-generators of electricity will make many of our electronic products and appliances highly mobile. Decentralized power sources will be extensive, affordable, and environmentally clean. These new, high-power, distributed energy systems will provide backup if not primary energy sources for appliances, homes, and vehicles. In the transition to fuel cells, we will see further improvements in batteries-perhaps linked with solar power-and small generators fueled by natural gas.
- **GrinTech (Green Integrated Technology).** Global crowding, fears of global climate change, and mountains of garbage will thrust environmental concerns to the forefront of consumers and industry around the world. Technology will provide the answers, with new systems that eliminate rather than reduce waste. GrinTech will be especially important in agriculture, mining, manufacturing, and transportation systems.
- **Omnipresent Computing.** Computers will be everywhere. We will be in constant contact with very miniature, wireless, highly mobile, powerful, and highly personalized computing with network access. Such computers may first appear on the market as watches or jewelry with the power of a computer and cellular

phone. Later, we will have computers embedded in our clothing and possibly implanted under our skin.

- **Nanomachines.** Microscopic machines, measured in atoms rather than millimeters, will revolutionize several industries and may perform a wide range of jobs for us-from heating our homes to curing cancer. Battelle researchers see the medical industry as the most important area for nanomachine technology by 2020. We may be able to develop nanomachines that will go into your body and find and destroy individual cancer cells while not harming healthy cells. Nanomachines also could be used to deliver drugs to highly localized places in the body, to clean arteries, and to repair the heart, brain, and other organs without surgery.
- **Personalized Public Transportation.** The continuing growth of cities will further stress our transportation infrastructure. Yet, Battelle researchers say an aging population with concerns about safety, convenience, and independence will help maintain a high demand for personal vehicles. The challenge is to integrate many individual cars within a coordinated and optimized public transportation network. Technology will help us turn our cars into what will almost be personalized public transportation. New information technology in your car will work with a central traffic control system to guide you through the quickest route to your destination. Traffic jams and road rage will decline substantially as people drive their cars to remote parking areas and take highly advanced-and comfortable-trains into central cities and between cities.
- **Designer Foods and Crops.** Grocery store shelves will be filled with genetically engineered foods that are environmentally friendly and highly nutritious. Through genetic engineering, researchers will develop crops that resist diseases and pests, greatly reducing the need for pesticides and other chemicals. Battelle predicts that most food sold in supermarkets will come from genetically engineered fruits, vegetables, and livestock. Nearly all cotton and wool for our clothing will be genetically engineered. Even lawns could be genetically engineered to need less fertilizer and pesticide and-best yet-grow more slowly.
- **Intelligent Goods and Appliances.** Advances in quantum computing will lead to smaller, more powerful computers and electronics that will add amazing intelligence to appliances and other products. These products will likely include telephones with extensive phone directories, intelligent food packaging that tells your oven how to cook the food inside, refrigerators that help make out your shopping list and tell you where to get the best price on the food you need, and maybe even a toaster that won't burn your toast.
- **Worldwide Inexpensive and Safe Water.** Within the next 20 years, clean drinking water could become an expensive commodity around the world. However,

before water shortages become critical, technology will answer the challenge, with advanced filtering, processing, and delivery of potable water. Desalination of water and water extraction from the air are two possibilities.

- **Super Senses.** One of the hot technologies today is virtual reality. In 20 years, though, we will be marveling over "enhanced reality." Using sensors and electronic or genetic technology, we will be able to implant devices that will allow us to hear better than ever before or see farther or in the dark.[3]

Chapter 5

Strategic and Influential Relationships

Empowering a CTO — A Complex Ecosystem

A CTO is not acting as a solo technology executive. A CTO is part of the community. CTOs view themselves as part of a network with multiple institutions and industries.[5] The CTO can also add value to the company by participating in government, academic, and industry groups in a manner that creates positive influence for the organization.[5]

The CTO position was initially created to insure that senior management focus on corporate technological capabilities.[6] It is important to get the attention and, at the same time, operate as an effective member of the executive team. It requires that the CTO establish solid relationships with a number of external and internal influencers.

Community

CTOs constantly set up adoptable sets of formal and informal networks to implement the policies and to insure that they are aligned throughout the company and industry. These networks are meant to serve as the conduits through which corporate vision and direction can be communicated. There is a lot of evidence that informal networks of technologists can be used to mediate organizational problems that extend beyond the control of operational and business managers. Lewis reports the emergence of internal publications, technical seminars, lists of known experts and knowledge base.[58]

CTOs are often called upon to provide services to government, academia, and professional organizations. These services combine civic and professional duty with the opportunity to convey a positive image of the company and its products.

CTO participate in governmental committees that investigate issues of national and regional importance. CTOs demonstrate tremendous honor and prestige, and at the same time dedicate time, energy, and money. This develops CTOs as sound members of the global community. There are many rewards associated with participating in those types of committees and forums. It is a form of recognition as a leader in the field. It is an opportunity to influence the decisions of the forums and committee on a professional and senior level. There is also an opportunity to meet and interact with very senior leadership. Finally, it provides early and intimate access to the work generated by the committee. Many CTOs maintain a close bond relationship with the academic and scientific community. Those relationships lead to significant alliances and funding opportunities for research.

There are a lot of partnerships and alliances that come out of forums, committees, and academia that could be extremely valuable for a company and stakeholders. A community provides a number of opportunities for a CTO to spend the time and money, but they must be aligned with the corporate strategy. Acting in a community creates a holistic approach for a CTO to contribute to the company's success and competitive advantage. Finally, CTOs are frequently asked to participate in professional organizations and their associated meetings. They also provide an opportunity to project a positive image within the profession and to communicate important messages. Presentations allow the CTOs to tell partners, suppliers, competitors, and customers about their agnostic expertise, products, future strategy, or commitment to an industry. The Technology Leadership Council was set up in parts of the US and New York to connect the CTO as part of the regional and national affinity. Members of the Technology Leadership Council and CIO Collective emphasized that the value based relationships that are built through the professional associations provide significant opportunities with business deals and relationships.

CEO-Executives

The CTO must exhibit a clear understanding and dedication to improving the competitive position of the company. The acceptance of the CTO as a business strategist is an important step. It will determine whether the CTO is treated as an equal member of the executive team or is isolated as an outside source for technical advice and information. A CTO must have superior communication skills and business savvy. "You've got to be an extrovert. You've got to be willing to get out in front of CEOs and the investment community to evangelize", says Phil Schneidermeyer, who heads the IT practice at corporate recruiting company Korn/Ferry, in Stamford, Connecticut .The ability to see the big picture is also critical, according to Estrin.[49] Providing strategic advice to the CEO and the Executive Committee requires the trust and confidence of the CEO. In previous technical roles, the CTO may have earned the respect and confidence of peers and superiors through technical prowess and performance. But, this new position requires business prowess and financial performance.[57] A CTO must be willing to interact on a professional level with CEO and executive management contacts. Providing strategic advice to the CEO and the executive committee is not an easy task. The CTO must earn the trust and confidence of the CEO and other executives. This business sophistication has to be combined with management, operational skills, presentation, communication, and financial performance.[57] Interaction with executive management creates a bond with the decision makers, and creates an opportunity to be treated as other management and executive members of the company. Roberts has conducted a study of the strategic management of technology that indicates that most companies include the CTO on the Executive Committee along with the CEO, COO, CFO, and CIO. In North America 60 per cent of the companies surveyed included the CTO on this committee. In Europe the number was 67 per cent and in Japan it was 91 per cent.[78] In some companies the CTO actually teaches senior management about the importance of technology in their industry. The goal is to ingrain technology as a significant consideration in all executive decision making.[43, 28]

CTOs are not the first officers to face the challenge of inclusion or exclusion from the strategic process. When the CIO position emerged, they too were branded as technologists who could not function as business strategists.[55] This image has diminished as CIOs have shown themselves to be just as effective at making business decisions as their management-schooled peers.

Executive Committee members should also recognize that the technological stereotype that was not accurate for the CIO might also prove to be inaccurate for the CTO. If the CTO is to provide business decisions and advice, there needs to be some measure of the quality of this advice. The CTOs performance should be measured against a plan worked out with the CEO. This plan may include achieving milestones, introducing new products, reducing costs, reducing uncertainty, and selecting the right research projects to fund. Some advocate maintaining and teaching technology within the organization, measuring the speed at which technology is brought into the organization, the rate at which the CTO turns technology into salable intellectual property, and the CTO's effectiveness as the custodian for research and development money.

CIO

Many organizations have a difficult time separating the responsibilities of the CTO from those of the CIO, which can make the working relationship between the two very difficult. At the 2001 InfoWorld CTO Forum, large companies identified their responsibilities as being externally focused while the CIO's responsibilities were internally focused.[82]. However, the Infoworld CTO Forum at 2003 really emphasized a major integration of two roles.

Corporations have realized that they need a CIO to oversee the application of technology to internal operations. This has included computer systems for accounting, billing, telephony, security, and a host of other functions. Prior to the creation of the CTO position, the CIO was the only executive technologist and was often called upon to support manufacturing computerization, the purchase of computer aided design packages, and strategic decisions for injecting technology into products.[74]

The internal/external division of responsibilities is a very useful differentiation, but it leaves significant gray areas that can result in turf wars between the two players. Therefore, the CTO's relationship with the CIO should be based on a more clearly defined division of responsibility. The goal is to create a complementary and supportive relationship that maximizes contributions to corporate strategy and profitability

Kwak cites the results of a study of pairs of executives at 69 companies that indicated that the business acumen of CIOs was equal to that of their executive peers. Another study of 417 construction company executives found that 80 per cent of the CIOs in those companies were considered equal contributors of the strategic decision making process.[7] Therefore, the CTO should be able to learn from the integration experience of the CIO.

Chief Scientist

Chief Scientists are much more intimately involved in the day-to-day execution of scientific and technical projects. Each of these is usually limited to the laboratory, division, or facility in which he or she resides. As described earlier, senior technologists are often very eager to explore emerging areas. But, these explorations should be harnessed to contribute to the company's strategic direction. Earl maintained that a company should not have a separate technology strategy. Supporting this perspective, one study has found that short-term, product-focused R&D is positively correlated with the financial performance of the company, while long-term R&D is negatively correlated with it.[78] This one reason that it is important for the CTO to mentor the Chief Scientists and to direct their focus such that it contributes to the success of the company. Chief Scientists may also have informal networks of technologists that span business areas, but they do not have the official charter to cross-pollinate technologies. The CTO can organize an internal council of technologists to search out and apply the best technologies available across the company.[12] It is a good idea that internal summits to bring leading technologists together to share ideas. It could be a responsibility of a chief scientist to create leverage across many different business groups to identify potential combinations of technology that could become new products or services.

Marketing and Sales

Many CTO that I spoke to are actively involved in marketing products and services. These CTOs recognize that some products are so technically sophisticated that explaining them to the trade media requires a technical representative. The technology leaders are constantly involved in sharing their experiences in trade media events. In fact, they become marketing spokespeople for products and services in organizations. CTOs have an inherent ability to sound natural and be recognized as sophisticated technical experts that explain the technical elements. CTO becomes a de facto member of the extended marketing and business development staff.[36]

As the CTO continues to spend more time with sales and marketing departments, it also connects the CTO to the customer's need of the product. This type of mapping requires regular and detailed interactions with customers and the marketplace creates a much more adoptable and robust CTO. Working with the sales and marketing departments also insures that the CTO remains rooted in the customers' need for the product, rather than the technical sophistication of the product. Making this mapping requires regular and detailed interactions with customers and the marketplace.

This perspective is supported by Michael Wolfe of Kana Communications who says that, "Creating a product is mapping what a customer needs to what you can build."[2]

In front of clients, CTOs are "external-facing technologists" who focus his/her efforts on using technology to provide better products and services to external customers or clients.[5]

Research

Research and development laboratories have been transformed from independent scientists working on challenging but questionably marketable technologies to organizations that are expected to make direct contributions to company profits. The CTO can play an important role in monitoring and directing these labs. Erickson recommends several principles that a CTO should use for directing

R&D. First, R&D personnel should be kept in touch with the company's customers and markets.[31] Few labs can seclude themselves from the market and conduct research for its own sake. Second, the CTO should foster open communications between R&D staff, manufacturing engineers, and the marketing department. Third, the CTO should hold the R&D labs to schedule and budget commitments. If an R&D project is not delivering results, it may need to be terminated and the funds applied more productively elsewhere. Some longstanding projects constantly show great promise and absorb resources, but produce nothing. These projects, though considered "pillars of the lab", must be held accountable and face termination if they do not produce results.[29]

R&D laboratory budgets should be the topic of critical reviews by the executive staff. The CTO should lead initial funding reviews in which R&D projects present the expectations for the project, its applicability to market needs, the position relative to competitors, and a record of past successes. The CTO should also hold in-progress reviews to monitor problems and successes. A CTO can serve as an honest broker in these reviews because he or she comes from outside of the laboratory and is not personally involved in the projects.[60][77]

Values Based Organizations

Earlier, we have touched upon the unique communities that are set up based on the concept of value-based organizations. A community of value based participants could be comprised of various stakeholder groups, direct and indirect. It could be considered as the target audience. Stakeholders are, of course, internal and external. A balance has to be maintained between the need to have early alignment among internal stakeholders (employee and management groups) and an early involvement of external stakeholders who often supply essential input. Customers are an especially important source of early input. Many wrong assumptions and much expense can be avoided with early customer input. An effective way of organizing stakeholder groups for community dialogue is by the process in which they are involved. Other stakeholder groups can usefully be defined by the process in which they participate. After all, they are the customers of the process and provide invaluable input. Investors and analysts are an interesting and vital target audience in the integrity economy of trust. They must also be educated and encouraged to go behind the stage curtain and get a feel for the "heart" of the organization.[50] CTO becomes an important element in the value based economy, and the involvement with stakeholders, customers, investors, employees, and analysts.

Chapter 6

CTO Strategic Roles and Responsibilities

The CTO position is far from being a standard role and set of standard responsibilities. Each company has unique requirements for its CTO and provides a unique organizational structure into which the person will fit. This section describes responsibilities of the CTO. CIOs are being more responsible for the economy, government/regulatory issues, international/political climate, education, workforce, ethics, social issues, and emerging technologies.

First, it is important to outline the skills and competencies of a CTO before we proceed with the complexity of a CTO/CIO role.

Skills and Competencies of an Effective CTO: Technology Summary

Technology
The CTO should have been a leader in a technology that is an important part of the corporate business base.

Strategy
The CTO is a corporate executive dealing with strategic decisions about the future direction of the company. The CTO must make the transition from technical expert to business strategists.

Business Growth
CTOs must make decisions about which technologies are most likely to generate the highest rate of return. The CTO thinks about technology as a moneymaking asset, not as a field of exploration for its own sake.

Interpersonal Skills

All executives, including the CTO, must be able to communicate clearly and effectively with people from all types of backgrounds.

Executive Relationships

It is important to insure that CTO is included in the executive decision-making cycle.

CTO — Leadership and Coaching

It's widely understood that the CIO's job isn't just about technology anymore — it is about leadership with a human element. The most successful CIOs spend huge chunks of time educating, leading, and coaching a wide base of business stakeholders — executive colleagues, board members, business unit managers, supply-chain partners, IT staff, customers, service providers, and external regulators.[52]

This complex array of commitments is changing the CIO's role in the enterprise. Gartner Executive Programs' (EXP) CIO agenda survey said their responsibility is no longer to the IT staff alone, but rather to the business as a whole and to its customers and partners. There are now six imperatives: to lead, anticipate, strategize, organize, deliver, and measure.[52]

At the very top of the CIO's agenda is the responsibility for leadership and coaching across the enterprise. IT executives have to keep an eye on the marketplace and the long-term strategies that will keep them ahead of the competition, as well as the day-to-day operations that satisfy customers, generate revenue, and enable growth. And then they have to bring those insights to key decision makers.

As discussed previously, CIOs must know how to engage their peers at a human level. They must build and sustain personal and positional credibility by knowing their business colleagues as individuals, focusing on their agendas, communicating clearly, and simply helping them achieve business success through timely and cost-effective service delivery. It's important for CIOs to seek opportunities to support the agendas of other executives and collaborate with them. They must have a clear understanding of the key people they need to influence and find ways to support them, which can be accomplished by volunteering for assignments that afford opportunities to demonstrate a business perspective. And feedback is important for education and growth. They should conduct frequent peer reviews and set up formal and informal channels to gather business intelligence.

The leadership role also means guiding the board and top executives on how IT can enable business innovation. Some companies leverage this by increasing IT centralization to gain synergies across the business units and an understanding of how business goals are linked with the IT strategy needed to achieve them.

As part of the leadership role, CIOs need to communicate a clear vision and agenda for using IT to enable the business. It's up to them to help the team make informed executive decisions about business models and business architecture, as well as about IT governance issues for the enterprise. It's not enough just to understand business imperatives, though. CIOs also have to communicate them back to the IT organization. They need to ensure that their staff is fully aware of the enterprise's strategic direction, and link performance metrics and appraisals to that direction. It's everyone's job to effectively prioritize projects and use resources in keeping with the company's strategic goals. Strategizing means taking a more active role in shaping demand and synchronizing business and IT. Every executive has to assume responsibility for helping grow the business; they can all play their part by envisioning ways IT can help achieve growth and profitability. They can help shape the informed expectations of both business peers and the IT organization. If this coaching is done well, it helps build a real partnership between the business and technology sides of the house. That, in turn, will help synchronize investment approaches and funding strategies that support desirable behaviors.[52]

In the long run, a sound business-driven IT architecture will provide the enterprise with the right technical base to scale up critical business initiatives, especially those that cross business-unit boundaries. No strategy is complete unless it considers enterprise wide risk exposure and establishes a risk-management program designed to minimize vulnerabilities and protect the enterprise, its customers, and its shareholders.

Relentless budget pressures on IT make CIO survival dependent on effective supply-side management. This includes organizing multiple sources of supply to get the best value for your money, as well as managing IT's capability to meet business needs. The final three imperatives — organizing, delivering, and measuring — fall into this category.

While CIOs are frequently hired for their business acumen, they're often fired because of a failure — or perceived failure — to deliver on expectations. The message, then, is to ensure that you're perceived as delivering against key expectations. The first imperative is to be a professional services organization that delivers cost-effective services; attracts, nurtures, and sustains people and resources; and manages resources prudently, balancing cost and growth initiatives and ensuring that succession planning is in place:

- Building — or providing access to — well-targeted capabilities for agility and low cost is another key element.
- Set demanding timetables to deliver value. Make sure business continuity and security requirements are in place.
- Implement disciplined and quality-based program and project management.
- Source IT services strategically manage partnerships and alliances effectively.

Every company has its own challenges and markets, of course. The survey identified three business environments, each with a unique CIO agenda: fighting for survival, maintaining competitiveness, and breaking away.[52]

Technology Decision Maker

The CTO serves as the master gatekeeper for external technology. This includes selecting and conducting long-term research consistent with the vision of the enterprise. This is not to imply that the CTO's role supersedes that of the Chief Executive Officer ("CEO"), but that the CTO is the principal technology adviser to the CEO or other Chief Decision Maker ("CDM") member of the leadership team.

Act as the Technical Conscience

Colmen states that "A chief technology officer should be a statesman, conscience and traffic cop."[107] The CTO would, under this capacity, determine the balance between short-term and long-term technology programs. This includes assessing the programmatic needs to assure balance of financial resources between the program elements. This also includes protecting the integrity of the research and development against the demands of technical services. .

Provide Technology Oversight for the Enterprise

The CTO also develops technology metrics for the enterprise. This includes performing technological benchmark studies. This oversight function includes the design and guidance of technology audits. Based on these activities, the CTO prepares reports on the status of the enterprise's technological fitness and makes recommendations to the other members of the leadership team. This also includes advising the leadership team about the technical implications of strategy, policy and programs.[6]

CTO and the Emerging & Competitive World
Monitoring and Assessing New Technologies

The CTO develops and is responsible for tracking both internal and external technological developments which can impact the enterprise. This includes identification and support of advanced and enabling technologies that are threats to or opportunities for the core enterprise. This could be achieved through a technological environmental monitoring system.

A technology environmental monitoring system is a formal system for the collection and analysis of both external and internal technology data including developments, markets, legislation and other factors which may impact the enterprise's technological developments.[108]

The rate of change of technology guarantees that knowledge and expertise gained several years ago will no longer be completely valid. This creates the need for a technologically current person to serve as an advisor to senior executives during strategic decision-making. Paul O'Neill stated that a CTO should be expected to, "identify, access, investigate high-risk, high return technologies possessing potential application within existing businesses or for creating new businesses."[70] Knowledge that is several years old cannot effectively guide this type of assessment. If a company is planning to modify its production process or add new products, it must understand how the latest technologies can contribute to those plans.

A CTO who embodies current knowledge, is networked with company engineers, has years of experience, and has access to executive decision-makers is a valuable resource in recognizing important new technologies and bringing them into the company's strategic decision-making process.

Bert Thurlings from Philips Research Laboratories has arrived at conclusions similar to those of O'Neill and Bridenbaugh through his field studies of numerous CTOs. These indicate that CTOs themselves feel that one of their most important responsibilities is to monitor, evaluate, and select technologies that can be applied to future products and services.[85] A significant investment in the active exploration of all relevant technical areas is required in order to identify opportunities buried amid all of the information available. Internal company managers and scientists are often qualified to perform this analysis, but are so focused on day-to-day operations that they do not have time to study broadly and deeply enough to locate the technologies that will be essential in the future.

These people frequently identify important changes once a competitor has already implemented a similar idea. However, by that time, it is too late for the company to capture the lead in the application of that technology to products, services, and production techniques. Such a company would find itself trying to catch-up to the new leader in the field.

The expertise of business executives, unaided by technologists, would not have been sufficient for identifying such a unique opportunity. Situations like this demonstrate the real contributions that can be made by a CTO.

It is assumed that the CTO has to be very current with the innovations around his group and organization as well as guiding the organization towards making the most efficient and effective use of technology. CTO will have to guide the future of technology in a company. The added responsibilities to review the futures will have to align with the comfort of defining the strategic mission of the company to design a blueprint architecture for any initiative.[7]

The CTOs that depend on the future of emerging technology are actively involved in monitoring new technologies, separating marketing rhetoric from technical facts, and identifying profitable applications for those technologies that can make a significant difference in the organization's competitive future.[5]

Increasingly, as Paul O'Neill points out, the CTO is using the assets to "identify, access, investigate high-risk, high-return technologies possessing potential application within existing businesses or for creating new businesses."[70]

We all know that knowledge is a leading component that marks the success of a company. However, knowledge has to be updated constantly and adopted to the right opportunity to be effective. If a company is planning to modify its production process or add new products, it must comprehend the latest knowledge with consequences to latest techniques and latest technologies to adopt to a flexible plan.[70]

Monitoring new technologies and assessing their applicability to business opportunities is an ideal way to act for a CTO. Through the assessment and applicability, it is possible to influence operational and scientific ranks and CTO's focus changing organizational and financial issues. We have seen in many instances that technology leadership does not possess the latest information and technology to support their opinions, and does not have the influence to impact the higher decisions. Therefore, a CTO who embodies current knowledge, is networked with company scientific, development, infrastructure, engineering, has years of experience, and has access to executive decision-makers is a value added contributor resource in recognizing important new technologies and bringing them into the company's strategic decision-making process.

Numerous research indicates that CTOs themselves feel that one of their most important responsibilities is to monitor, evaluate, and select technologies that can be applied to future products and services.[85]

This type of work requires significant investment in all relevant technical areas to identify "gold seed" opportunities which reside in the knowledge bases. CTOs will need to work hand in hand with engineers, programmers, and scientists that perform this type of analysis on a day-to-day basis. Those types of resources focus on tactical and short-term operations, and may not have the right opportunity to convey the broad thinking of locating the future technologies essential for overall business. The goal is to implement the competitive advantage early on in the process. CTOs must be a critical element in the company to capture the lead in the application of that technology to products, services, and production techniques. Those opinions are shared by CTOs in IBM such as Dr. David Boloker and Dr..Jim Spohrer. In fact, the opinions and experiences expressed by large companies like IBM are echoed by the CTOs of competitive and emerging companies. Both David Boloker and Jim Spohrer feel a very important part of a CTO job is reading and evaluating large amounts of data about new concepts, technologies, innovations, and other sources of emerging information.[8][83]

One of the CTOs in Aspatore's Inside CTO Minds mentioned:

One of the key roles of the CTO is to provide the technical vision to complement the business vision, setting the tone and direction for the company's technologies.

Leadership, in this context, comes from being able to set the technical course and from being able to define what the company's products and technologies might look like in two, three, or more years.[2]

CTO — Strategic Planning and Direction
Development of a Technological Strategic Plan

A technological strategy, paraphrasing Betz [6], Martino [108] and Mintzberg [109] among others, can be stated as: "A formal set of technological enterprise intentions that allocates available resources and sets priorities based on clearly stated technology, enterprise objectives and a perceived environment."

The dimension of a technological strategy expands these essential elements and adds several other important considerations. In formal technological objectives, which are nested within and support the enterprise's system of objectives and mission, no formalized technological strategy will succeed. The CTO interfaces with senior and technology enterprise leadership to develop technology objectives, goals and programs for the enterprise. The position should guide the development of a technological strategic plan for the enterprise. The CTO recommends to the other members of the leadership team the steps necessary to implement the strategic plan both in the short and long term.

In this section we explore the enormous implications of strategic planning towards CTO responsibilities. The rate of change of technology guarantees that knowledge and expertise will not stay constant. In fact, this creates a big demand on the CTO that serves as a value added advisor to senior executives during strategic decision-making.

Infoworld has recently noted that CTOs courageously view their newly gained power and influence which is deeply rooted in a clear understanding of technology's potential to transform every part of the corporate model as we know. This deep strategy is an evolution of value-based organizations and the path of CTOs to transform the organization.[75]

With the Internet revolution, the CTO role has stepped up into a deep strategic position. We have seen that in companies that earn their living by producing and selling technological products or services, or those that are leveraging the Internet to gain a strategic advantage, the CTO will report directly to the top executive and have a value based strategic role on the whole organization with a cross-organizational authority.[49]

The CTO has to carry a strategic hat. The CTO should identify how the organization can use technology to improve the bottom line. The CTO will bring a unique perspective to corporate strategic planning and product strategy. We have already observed that the technology innovation has become essential to running a business. Nowadays, the CTO will ensure that technology is taken into account during all aspects of business planning. This unique individual needs to be able to review corporate current business processes and customer interactions and then identify and prioritize the technology tasks that will make an impact on the business's success or organization. We will discuss further how the CTO contributes significant value to the investment community. The stockholders, investors, and customers clearly need to understand that the CTO represents the important value of technology.[7]

In today's market, companies are looking for a way to remain competitive to establish a base of innovation. It is important to move to new areas as quickly as possible.

Someone who can see how small pieces fit into strategic vision can also impose some level of structure and regime in often chaotic IT infrastructures of very large companies.

Computerworld conducted an interview with several CTOs like Paul Borrill, the CTO at Veritas Software Inc., who said the CTO "is not important for things that must be delivered next quarter." For him this position is evolving into an important one for promoting corporate growth through the use of technology. It's about forming the relationship with the business side, where it then becomes ownership.[59]

The leader in a CTO technology entrepreneurship space, Mario Cardullo, has indicated the CTO changes in strategic planning during a recent March 2003 Technology Leadership Council meeting. Mr. Cardullo has outlined the strategic plan which becomes the important component of the CTO's position. The strategic plan is defined as a formal set of technological enterprise intentions that allocates available resources and sets priorities based on clearly stated technology, enterprise objectives and a perceived environment in which the process is to be embedded.[16] Mr. Cardullo is also featured in the appendix section of the book.

Mr. Cardullo outlined the monitoring system as a formal system for collection and analysis of internal and external technology data in the area of developments, markets, competitors and legislation. The monitoring system has to be aligned with the identification and support of advanced and enabling technologies.[16]

The CTO must drive clear value and commitment to safeguarding and maintaining the competitive position of the company. The acceptance of the CTO as a business strategist is an important step of the value-based economy with deep strategic implications for the organization.

In fact, the CTO has to be capable of translating a complex technology theory and capabilities into strategic business decisions for the organization. The CTO's key tasks can be associated with research and development but of technology business savvy individuals who are recognized for the value and deeply involved in shaping and implementing overall corporate strategy."[58]

The economy expects specific measurements for any job. This deep strategic work undertaken by a CTO has to provide business decisions and advice, but at the same time find a way to measure the quality of the strategic advice. The CTO's performance has to be measured against a plan worked out with senior management. This plan may include achieving milestones, introducing new products, reducing costs, reducing uncertainty, and selecting the right research projects to fund. Some concrete work includes mentoring and teaching technology within the organization, measuring the speed at which technology is brought into the organization, the rate at which the CTO turns technology into a product, and the CTO's effectiveness of research and development projects.

The CTO has to act and portray an image as a strategic thought leader that spends his/her time evaluating how technology can be used internally by the business to 1) enable new business models and business lines, 2) increase revenues, and 3) preempt a competitor's attempts to use technology to disrupt or dislodge his/her company's market position. The CTO's responsibilities often include advanced technology, competitive analysis, technology assessment, prototyping lab, partnering, planning, and architecture standards.[5]

CTO Innovation and Commercialization

Innovation is an important part of the CTO's job. It has to be combined with commercialization.

Chief Technology Transfer Office

One of the basic functions of a CTO is to promote internal enterprise technology transfer — serving as the interface for any external transfer and representing the enterprise at technical forums, committees and other appropriate activities. This functional area would benefit the enterprise by the interaction of the CTO with major universities, industry, government research consortia and other groups associated with rapidly changing technology.

Strategic Innovation

Michael Porter explains that, "companies have to find ways of growing and building advantages rather than just eliminating disadvantages."[40] In some industries, new products based on new technology are the lifeblood of the company. In other industries, core products remain unchanged for decades, but the processes used to create them are continually evolving and becoming more efficient. Proctor & Gamble recognized that their products were mature, but that their scientists had a number of good ideas for improving existing products and creating new ones. The company's CEO and CTO created the Innovation Leadership Team to find and allocate funds to support these new ideas. This program quickly led to eleven new products and a number of innovations waiting to be turned into products, giving Proctor & Gamble a significant lead on competitors.[12] Just as Peter Bridenbaugh learned that emerging technology was creating a new class of competitors for rolled metal products, companies that create commodities must apply technology to improve their production processes and add an edge to their products that competitors cannot match. O'Neill emphasizes that established companies need a CTO or CIO to develop fundamental technologies offering clear competitive advantages for current and future businesses.[4]

A product vision is one of the key reasons for employing a CTO. Ron Moritz, CTO of Symantec, says "One of the key roles of the CTO is to provide the technical vision to complement the business vision, setting the tone and direction for the company's technologies. Leadership, in this context, comes from being able to set the technical course and from being able to define what the company's products and technologies might look like in two, three, or four more years."[2]

Product vision should be based on an intimate understanding of the power of the current technology component of the product and knowledge about innovations and changes that are occurring in related fields. Michael Earl emphasized that investments in technology and innovation must be connected directly to business strategy. In fact, he found that the most successful approach was when a company did not have a separate technology strategy. Instead, the best technology strategies were those that were fully integrated with the business strategy.[29] CTOs are now expected to contribute technology expertise to business strategies, not to create independent research laboratories and strategies that are only loosely coupled to the company's profit engine.

Few would dispute that information technology is an important facilitator of innovation which, in turn, produces solid business benefits. According to the Accenture study, the IT department is the least likely part of a business to be a primary source of innovation. The Accenture study highlights the need for CIOs not only to run effective IT operations, but also to be active participants in the development of the overall business strategy.[92]

Drawing on an independent global survey of nearly 600 senior executives, "The Innovator's Advantage-using innovation and technology to improve business performance", examined the relevance of innovation to global business and the relevance of IT to successful innovation. It revealed that companies reporting a strong record of innovation also reports that nearly two-thirds (64 per cent) of their recent IT investments were successful at meeting their strategic objectives. By contrast, less innovative companies reported only a 28 per cent success rate for IT investments. Indeed, more innovative companies report getting more value for their money from IT and are more likely to see IT as a source of competitive advantage.

The study also confirms that the more innovative companies that see IT as an integral part of their business strategy are far more likely to consider IT to a greater extent when they are developing new business strategies than less innovative companies. In doing so, innovators consider the business capability that IT can deliver, not just the IT alone. Given the crucial role of IT as both an operational and strategic asset, tactical management alone by the CIO leads to a misalignment between the company's strategic needs and its own. The IT opportunities to generate value are lost. The CIO's strategic input is vital. Yet the indications are that even among more innovative companies this particular aspect of the CIO's role needs more emphasis.

The Accenture study supports this, suggesting that one reason why the most innovative companies gain more strategic benefits from their investments in IT is because they spend proportionately less of that budget on day-to-day operations and more on new investments.

In most businesses, greater value is generated when a larger proportion is spent on discretionary investment. Spending less on operations and more on new systems is a clear priority of the majority of executives responding to the Accenture survey. Consequently, CIOs must not only run an effective IT operation, but also be able to communicate the strategic benefits that IT-including newer forms of IT-can bring.

If the IT department is to contribute to innovation across the business, then CIOs need to be proactive and take propositions to the business units about ways to use IT to create new, market differentiating business capabilities. One aspect of this is the increasingly important responsibility of the CIO to identify how existing and emerging technologies can generate business innovations. Innovation and the imaginative use of IT can create significant wins for companies in many different contexts.[92]

CIOs must work even harder to escape the organizational status quo and venture out of their technologist comfort zone to put the plan into action. As we've known for some time, CIOs must keep enhancing their influence by making sure they and their teams understand the strategies of their internal customers and find people who can help them. As better information inevitably shifts market power toward customers, the innovative use of this information will be at the heart of differentiation.[92]

Commercialization

Commercialization is increasingly becoming an important element for the role of a CTO.

Commercialization has a number of steps, and CTOs are actively involved with a number of the steps in the commercialization process. Mr. Cardullo indicates that the CTO has to be a primary liaison to promote internal technology transfer. The CTO is an interface for external technology transfer and an enterprise technology representative for forums, committees, universities, industry and consortia.[16]

A relationship with a VC and investment source is a major area of cooperation for a CTO. A few years ago, the CTO was a crucial element of Internet start-ups. CTOs must also create convincing presentations and demonstrations for venture capitalists emphasizing technology value. The VCs in turn provide the initial capital investment necessary to turn an idea into a viable product or service.

Another process in commercialization is an alliance with a university research center. The CTO is also involved with linkages and partnerships with research centers within universities and academia. Companies participate in those activities because they have first right of refusal to access the results of the research. A prestigious commercially successful and widely recognized industry/academia partnership is the Media Lab at MIT. Another is an incubator within RPI. ACDC Incubator in Georgia Tech. is another impressive technology incubator within an academic environment. As far as Media Lab, it investigates the application of computer technologies to practical social problems. In 2001, the lab received 95 per cent of its $36 million budget from 140 corporate sponsors.[60]

CTOs are also involved in thousands of acquisitions every year. Pre-qualifying, selecting, and identifying the best targets for an acquisition often requires reliable advice on technical issues at the executive level.[5]

Jim Spohrer, the IBM Venture Relations CTO, is heavily involved with the evaluation of new technologies for IBM.[83] Finding and isolating specific gold seeds is a real contribution by a CTO.

Senior technologists are often very eager to investigate new emerging opportunities. It is very important that the technology commercialization strategy is aligned with an overall business and technical strategy. There are several studies that depict that short-term product-focused R&D is positively correlated with the financial performance of the company. The CTO need to spend time and mentor senior engineers and chief scientists, and constantly keep them focused on the overall strategy with contribution to the success of the company.

In some companies, the CTO organizes an internal council of technologists to scout and apply the best technologies available across the company.[12]

In some companies it is important to put together internal summits to bring leading technologists together to share ideas from various geographics in one centralized area. The CTO needs to create leverage across many different business groups to identify potential combinations of technology that could become new products or services.

Medisource Ventures, Safeguard Scientific, CMGI, IdeaLab, Cambridge Innovation, and Lab Morgan are excellent examples of commercialization. I recently had a conversation with executives at LabMorgan Each one of those organizations has a uniquely talented CTO who identifies valuable opportunities and solves local problems. A Global CTO of the holding companies could organize technology summits between technology leaders and portfolio companies.[77]

The CTO is on the search for innovation. A significant part of a CTO job is linked into strategic innovation. It is important that innovation and development of fundamental technologies offer a clear competitive advantage. Walter Robb, former CTO of General Electric Medical Systems, believes that "it is the responsibility of the CTO to push the boundary on risk taking."[77] Furthermore, Michael Earl emphasized that investments in technology and innovation must be connected directly to business strategy. In fact, he found that the most successful approach was when a company strategy is highly integrated.[29] The demands of the environment indicate that the CTOs are now expected to contribute technology expertise to business strategies. At the end of the day, the technology strategy has to be linked to a Profit center.

CTO and the Evangelist

The CTO is constantly involved with addressing the critical issues of technology. Generating enough public attention and awareness is a very important element of a CTO. The CTO is also a valuable tool in addressing the increasingly well-informed media about the products, services, and the future plans of the company. CTOs confidently speak to technologists and can play a role in convincing public relations that the company's decisions have merit and will add significant value for the company's stakeholders.[5]

Public relations are an important marketing element, and demonstrate the success of the company products and capabilities. Although producing information and images for public consumption is primarily the responsibility of the marketing organization, the CTO is heavily involved in evangelizing at a strategic level a market position for the company.

In other organizations, the CTO actually dives deeper to teach and mentor senior management about the importance of technology in their industry. The goal is to ingrain technology as a part of integral and significant consideration in all executive decision-making.[43][28]

The CTO adds critical expertise because the CTO is capable of accurately translating some product and technology details into terms that can be used in marketing and business development. The CTO is heavily involved with the press and media. It is also very important for a corporation to have knowledgeable experts to be interviewed and quoted. Trade publications rely upon statements by insiders and experts who can speak authoritatively and with credibility on a subject. CTOs are critical experts for their perspective companies. These experts are like politicians — they're made, nurtured, and coached.[40] An example of this, stated in an Aspatore book, is of Ron Moritz, CTO of Symantec, who was an expert in Internet security but the media was not aware of his expertise. Therefore,

Symantec's strategy was to turn Morinz into a media recognized and consulted expert.[2]

CTO and Globalization

These new frontiers and the imperatives of international cooperation will raise questions for all societies. Nations will find themselves with increasingly less influence than virtual communities or multinational corporations. World religions may need to seek unity in diversity.[44]

As discussed earlier in the book, I have developed a model based on corporate commercialization/incubation as a powerful concept aimed at driving shareholder value by leveraging existing and emerging IP in the form of startup ventures rather than simply waiting for it to be developed and sold under the corporate flag and channels to market. The traditional model was to package the IP in a form that was attractive to external venture partners and, if possible, locate management talent from within the lab to run the ventures. This model has stalled in the past year due to the slow down in the US economy, terrorism, uncertain political situations, the threat of world regional instability, and lower than expected corporate profits. And yet, the need remains — sizable reservoirs of intellectual property (IP) representing vast amounts of wasted shareholder value go untapped. This year's difficulties, the continuing innovation need and a new set of world driving forces have opened the door to new model — Global Incubation. Global Incubation holds the promise of moving commercialization of untapped assets forward by leveraging advantages that are only possible through a worldview. The driving forces include:

- Availability of low cost, high quality sources of R&D and the specialization of various regions in specific technologies and skills. (Programming, bioresearch, etc.)
- There is increased activity with open source community development (Linux for example), which propels additional growth in emerging technologies.
- Local development organizations and governments around the world are funding economic commercialization projects to start the growth of new industries in their countries. This provides additional and unique sources of funding from international/regional funding sources and regional economic development centers.
- Investment by the World Bank in the Infodev initiative designed to expand and grow business incubation in various regions of the world. Specifically, the three-year program of grants will provide technical assistance to support new international incubators, a worldwide incubation support center, and programs

to support the performance and growth of existing incubators in developing countries. In addition, several United Nations organizations have been involved in supporting incubation initiatives since the 1990s including those in Russia, Poland, Romania, Uzbekistan, Czech Republic, Malaysia, Ecuador, Dominican Republic, Pakistan, and Columbia. Further, global foundations and endowments are providing for economic development funds to support international incubation.

The new global incubation model is based on the selection of appropriate and strategic technologies for commercialization, the coordination of those individual initiatives into a strategic plan and portfolio for innovation, the location of specific global commercialization centers with the strongest potential and lowest cost structure to move the technologies forward, and the funding of these initiatives through non-traditional and global sources. It will be highly integrated into the work conducted by CTOs. This model is in step with, and complements the concept of globalization. It recognizes how tightly coupled the world's economy is today and fuels additional markets, additional opportunities and funding sources. For instance, developers in Russia have the opportunity to market their products and services to European and US companies. Unique technologies in South America or Central Asia could be leveraged in the biotechnology incubator of a large multi-national company, Specialty software concepts could be modeled, developed and tested in emerging markets, etc.[66][33]

CTO — Merger & Acquisition

Mergers and acquisitions (M&A) are an important part of the growth strategy of many companies. These involve important strategies in financing, governmental oversight, taxation, corporate culture, and technological synergy. Unfortunately, after studying more than 5,000 acquisitions, divestitures, spin-offs, equity investments, and alliances, Frick and Torres discovered that over half of the deals resulted in a lower market value for the resulting entities.[37]

Other McKinsey studies in the late 1980's reported that, at that time, more than 70 per cent of acquisitions failed to earn back the cost of capital used to purchase the company.[72] Frick and Torres maintain that there are two major causes of this problem. First, the acquisition becomes an exercise in financial engineering. It focuses on successfully structuring the finances required to make the acquisition possible and loses sight of the strategic objectives of the acquisition. Second, it is a form of corporate ego boosting. Corporate leaders are eager to build an empire or capture high profile products. Frick and Torres contend that, in contrast to these two motives, value creating mergers and acquisitions are focused on the strategic value that can be achieved through the transaction. However, to make this happen, it is essential that the due diligence leading up to the deal includes an evaluation of the value of the technologies being acquired. The CTO's role in due diligence includes evaluating patents, reviewing technical publications, and studying trade data to determine the value of the target company and to rank it against its competitors.

As an illustration, Wayne, Pa.-based Safeguard Scientifics acquires or invests in a company. The CTO at Safeguard has the task of helping to extend strategic relationships. The CTO is very effective in the commercialization/incubator environment, and plays a key role in the investment strategy. In an investment situation, a CTO has to attend a number of social events where some entrepreneurs pitch plans. Another aspect to this job is an actual acquisition of technologies; however, discussion of acquisition is beyond the scope of this book.[48]

CTO — Marketing and Media Role

Media attention to company products and capabilities plays an important role in the success of those products. Constructing the information and images released to the public is primarily the responsibility of the marketing and sales departments. However, technical expertise is required to accurately translate some product details into terms that can be marketed. CTOs must translate technical details into real customer advantages that are superior to those of competing products. Internet start-ups must also create convincing presentations and demonstrations for venture capitalists (VCs).

The VCs provide the initial revenue stream necessary to turn an idea into a viable product. In the early stages of a company, the VCs are the customers and the marketing story is focused on them rather than the actual consumers.

CTO — Government, Academia and Professional Organizations

Prominent technologists are often called upon to provide services to government, academic, and professional organizations. These services combine civic and professional duty with the opportunity to convey a positive image of the company and its products. Governmental committees investigate issues of national importance. Service on these committees is an honor, but it also requires the dedication of time, energy, and money that could be focused on other pursuits. Participation brings several rewards that are an alternative form of payment:

- Tacit recognition as a leader in the field,

- Opportunities to influence the decisions of the committee in a professionally positive manner, and
- Early and intimate access to the work generated by the committee.

Since many CTOs possess advanced college degrees, they tend to have multiple relationships with members of academia. These relationships lead to partnerships and funding for research that is of mutual interest. Companies participating in these activities generally structure the partnership such that they have first access to the results of the research. There are many examples of corporate and academic partnerships that can involve participation or oversight by the CTO. As a businessman, the CTO must insure that money and time spent on such projects is aligned with the corporate strategy and has a realistic potential of contributing to the company's competitive advantage in the foreseeable future.

Finally, CTOs are called upon to participate in professional organizations and their associated meetings. Similar to government committees, these are an opportunity to project a positive image within the profession and to communicate important messages. Presentations allow the CTO to tell partners, suppliers, competitors, and customers about their expertise, products, future strategy, or commitment to an industry. Many CTOs maintain that the relationships that they build through professional organizations contribute directly to their business base.[88][92]

CTO and Company Culture

Previous sections described how the CTO could contribute to strategy, acquisitions, media relations, government committees, and academic research. But, the CTO can also serve an important role in creating the internal and external culture. The CTO should initiate activities and policies that create a technology-friendly culture aligned with the company's business strategy.

Other technology leaders throughout a company may create policies and practices that attempt to attract and retain the highest quality people available. However, if these are not aligned with the corporate business strategy, they may attract excellent people who are not able to contribute to business objectives.

The CTO should insure that policies and practices are constructed to attract the right kind, right number, and right placement of technologists. This will require the establishment of formal and informal networks to implement the policies and to insure that they are aligned throughout the company.[58] These networks will also serve as the conduits through which corporate vision and direction can be communicated.

Informal networks of technologists can be used to mediate organizational problems that extend beyond the control of operational managers. In some companies these networks tend to catalyze unofficial practices that are aimed at improving internal performance. Lewis reports the mergence of internal publications, technical seminars, lists of known experts, and technical expositions.[58]

CTO — Emerging Business Technology Role

We have discussed a number of areas that are critical to the CTO with a focus on emerging business and technology opportunities.

Mario Cardullo indicates the role of the CTO in the emerging technologies is invaluable. The CTO will act as master gatekeeper for external technology and will select and conduct long-term research. The CTO acts as principal technology adviser. The CTO determines the balance of short-term and long-term technology programs. The CTO is responsible for assessing programmatic needs and for protecting the integrity of R&D against the demands of technical services. The CTO develops technology metrics, performs technological benchmarking studies and designs and guides technology audits and reports on the technological fitness of enterprise.[16]

The CTO should combine a broad knowledge of the potential value in emerging technologies, and a very good understanding of how these technologies can affect the company's business and business processes. This person also needs strong communication and interpersonal skills to influence senior executives. The emerging CTO's function is to help the company evaluate different paths to achieving business goals, in addition to being an evangelist for the organization. The value added role is to improve the awareness of innovation and disruptive technologies.[5]

As we have seen, the CTO is heavily involved with technology decision-making in the organization. We have also observed that the CTO is a technology expert in the organization. Clearly, the CTO needs to spend a significant portion of their time monitoring trends and evaluating new technology. The CTO should be identifying and recommending appropriate technology solutions that enables the company to be more competitive, better serve customers and improve the overall profitability of the organization. The CTO is constantly on the lookout for technology trends among your competitors, customers and similar organizations in other industries. Continuous competitive and comparative analysis is an important step in enabling an organization to leverage the customers' technology decisions to the best advantage. The CTO needs to be a strategic thought leader supported by the company and industry. This leader will manage a technology organization and technology initiatives in the company. The CTO will set priorities and provide full project life-cycle management including the quality assurance and implementation of the internal development projects. The CTO will be responsible for partnerships. Partnerships could take advantage of new and emerging technologies without the challenges of developing and maintaining those systems internally. The CTO should recognize the opportunities and be willing to build and manage external relationships and alliances. The Chief Technology Officer becomes the public relations voice of technology for your company. Converging strategy, technology and leadership expertise into play, the CTO will help identify the major opportunities and win and avoid the obstacles and bottlenecks that are inherent in chasing the technological trends of the "new" digital economy.[7]

Furthermore, the CTO is responsible for determining how technology can be used to implement the business strategy. The "technology visionary" aspect of the emerging CTO is the most important aspect of the role. However, the CTO must have an excellent combination of both business and technical skills in order to successfully design the functional and technical aspects of the business strategy and then build the IT organization to execute its components. The CTO must always be on the lookout when technology innovation outstrips the organization's capacity to manage rapid change. One of the great challenges of this CTO is to balance work that is centered in product research and innovation while accommodating solid business requirements necessary for building a successful company. CTOs must focus on emerging areas, and must also connect a complex set of relationships among other assets (human, social, knowledge, and financial).[5]

As a CTO focusing on emerging areas, it is very important to develop the strategic technology plan for the organization by identifying, tracking, and experimenting with new and potentially disruptive technologies. The goal is to project and assess technologies' impact on the corporation and its customers.

As far as the organization, the emerging CTO would have a relatively small group of people with responsibilities that may include technology research & development, technology transfer and change management, intellectual property, knowledge management and/or best practice management, and advanced specialized technology centers. In addition, the CTO is usually responsible for ensuring that best practices for exploiting key technologies are shared across the organization's front line with its customers. The CTO may have a strong reputation with the senior executive leadership team, ecosystem partnerships, clients, and external public perception. The CTO's success comes from a position of influence as a key advisor to the executive management. It is difficult to measure the sphere of influence of this type of CTO. A CTO will serve as a strategic advisor on major decisions or changes in direction for the company.[5]

CTO — Change Agent Roles

We have presented significant amount of analysis and research pertaining to a changing role of a CTO. This new role deals with transformation of the organization and our industry. The CTO must have business acumen, strong academic credentials, a broad interdisciplinary background and a solid record of technical accomplishments. CTOs should have successes in commercialization demonstrated by publications and/or patents. CTOs must also demonstrate experience in operations and/or general management somewhere earlier in their careers. Being able to understand the perspective of the operating management of a strategic business unit is considered a major advantage for a CTO focusing on transformation. In addition, an international experience is becoming a valuable asset for a CTO. This book has covered the element on how CTO serves as the technology advisor to the CEO and has involvement with acquisitions, strategic partnerships, joint ventures and other industrial, government or academic alliances. The CTO with a transformation experience has to become a senior member of the management team, and should also have the business attributes sought for general management. These include a strategic/conceptual orientation, excellent verbal and written communication skills, sound judgment, high energy, flexibility, motivational and empowerment skills, and total dedication.[72]

Parker indicated several key strong leadership characteristics that would be valuable for the important role of a transformational CTO. This transformational CTO must have strong strategic/conceptual skills that can bridge the gap between the technologists and all of the business functions of the company. The number one characteristic that companies are looking for in a CTO is leadership ability. A CTO leader is generally an individual who can define a direction, facilitate change, inspire teamwork, make decisions quickly, and has a take charge personality with a strong work ethic.[72] Key characteristics of a CTO would be:

- A broad interdisciplinary, technical background
- Operations, marketing and/or general management experience
- An international assignment
- A strategic/conceptual orientation
- Experience evaluating and negotiating partnerships, joint ventures, acquisitions
- Superior communication skills
- A persuasive personality[72]

Mr. Cardullo defines technical leadership as the development of technology objectives, development of technology goals, and development of technology programs. The recommendation includes the leadership team members as well as the short and long-term technology implementation steps. The transformational CTO oversees the technological strategic plan, is involved in the technology environment monitoring system, and has a technology decision-making process. In making the decisions, the transformational CTO provides technology oversight for the enterprise, acts as the technical consciousness for the enterprise and is responsible for the technological benchmark studies[12]

This new CTO, reflective of this age, must work in a position of influence — as opposed to direct control like the line manager. This CTO will have a strong reputation with the senior executive leadership team. Furthermore, this CTO must demonstrate the ability to influence and work effectively with key senior executives to consider new information or different paths to accomplish key goals. This CTO is given to formulate a long-term innovation, broaden the strategic horizons of the company, and envision future paths. The CTO must have the freedom to think out of the box, and wait a longer period of time to develop innovative ideas into reality.[5]

Another important element of the transformational CTO is to create a value for the CTO profession. Vance Chan Associates demonstrate the value advantage by understanding strategic goals and being aware of top concerns of his/her counterparts in marketing, sales and customer management. It is the ability to communicate concerns to the rest of the management team.[87]

Jim Sphorer, CTO of IBM Venture Relations and Director of Research of Almaden Services Research, has stated that the transformational CTO has to have a technology road map with specific headlights to all relevant technologies. CTOs must demonstrate thought leadership. The CTO must be outwardly focused, as well as able to provide an ability to work with key leaders on a strategic, leadership, and tactical level.[83]

In terms of culture, CTO serves a very important role in facilitating the internal culture to initiate activities and policies that create a technology-friendly culture aligned with the company's business strategy.

The CTO position must use its leverage to appropriately attract senior management's attention and spotlight for corporate technological capability.[6]

Being part of the transformation in a company means both attracting the attention and operating as an effective member of the executive team and requires the CTO to nurture and build relationships with a number of people and groups internal and external to the company.

A transformational CTO must be involved with three components for value based organization: communication, projects, and processes. The communication aspect will go through a new communication paradigm, called community dialogue. Community dialogue is "A framework for effective, empowering and aligned communication that creates a work environment of vitality, cooperation, fulfillment and abundance for all."[50]

The transformational CTO has to deal with command and control. The chief technology executive is in a high-visibility role, serving the technology needs of "customers" inside and outside the organization. The CTO must be able to focus on expectations. Company executives must play a part in defining the roles of a CTO with real performance expectations. Leading-edge companies tend to be willing to take risks with technology and business strategies. Middle-of-the-road adopters of technology tend to support proven, cost-effective IT initiatives where the competitive advantage or market differentiation is clear. Trailing-edge companies tend to adopt technologies and new economy business strategies defensively. The role and expectations for the IT executive are shaped by the aggressive, moderate, or defensive attitudes companies have toward technology. The challenge for the CIO/CTO in moderate to defensive type companies is that technology is often seen as a disruptive force rather than an "enabling force, a transforming force." CTOs must be in position to identity organizations that are highly accepting or adaptive to new technologies and expects CTOs to know the business that they're in, the business that the company should be in, and also all the market forces. They expect, basically, a CTO who's a CEO, who understands the opportunities that information technology and telecommunications can provide. A CTO must have a seat at the table. For most companies, the role of the CTO is one that is primarily responsible for what happens within the walls of the organization. This often translates into being a member of the company executive committee and a direct report to the CEO or president of the company. The driving forces behind the elevation of the CIO/CTO role can be either external or internal. One is fueled by the recognition that a fundamental change in business demands a technology response; the other is fueled by the recognition that technology can capitalize on a market opportunity. CTOs need to be able to communicate technology issues in plain English to the business staff, while gaining the respect of the IT staff with their knowledge of the limitations and opportunities of technology. In fact, there is growing evidence that the CTO with the right mix of business and technology background and experience is in transition to becoming a CEO. In fact, a transformational CTO is "a CEO in training", either for the business they work for or one they will work for. The CIO or CTO role is becoming more transformational and competitive.[30]

Finally, this book demonstrates that businesses respect, and harness the power of technology to change and drive the bottom line. CTOs have emerged as the transformational force behind this change. CTOs oversee the convergence of the technology and business and hold the power to make change. A CTO is a real executive that brings invaluable assets to the table that guide the enterprise's direction, from setting the company's strategic vision to finding short-term solutions, achieving long-term goals, and bringing in partners who can change and enhance the company's revenue model.

Influence at the CTO level is the power to transform business as we know it. CTOs are the real change agents determining the direction of business tomorrow and convincing others to join them on a technical journey when the road is not clear.[75]

CTO — Chief Creative Officer: Latest Trend

Is there room in the IT organization for corporate creativity? Jeff Mauzy, the author of Creativity, Inc.: Building an Inventive Organization, thinks so.[62]

Mauzy believes that we need creativity in today's business-technology environment. He says that:

> We tend to look at what I call "big C" creativity-like, have we invented the new G4 lately, or are we knocking the socks off our competitors in the market with something new and exciting. Everybody's looking for the big breakthrough. Meanwhile, they're going about their lives, making up each day as they go along, as the market shifts, as the office environment shifts, as the politics in the office shifts. And they're applying "little C" creativity all the time. But they look at this "big C" breakthrough and think, "I've never done that; I'm not very creative", and they lose heart. Instead, if people can learn to focus on the small stuff, they'll recognize themselves as creative beings and creativity as being a part of everything. If we recognize that, just like fitness, this is all the time, everyday, then when it comes time to apply creativity toward major change, we're more fit and able to do it.[62]

In his book, Mauzy distinguish between creativity and innovation:

> Creativity is the ability to get ideas and to be flexible and open to your environment. Innovation, on the other hand, is the application of creativity. It's trying to change the world, whether it's a little world or a big world, or simply a change in your office. Change and action come from the act of innovating. So innovation is one of those things that gets into the world and the world accepts.

Creativity doesn't necessarily mean you have to innovate, but it's from creativity that ideas are born before you can begin to think of innovation.

It seems all the energy in IT for the last year or so has been less focused on innovation than on simply cutting costs. Mauzy believes that creativity is important, and is occurring all the time:

> On the small level, creativity is going on all the time. We're looking for ideas on how to cut costs, and that takes creativity. Getting the company to embrace them is going to take the collective processes and constant application of creative new ideas and actions that build up into innovation, even to make a cost-cutting measure. So creativity is embedded in all of those. When we're trying to get an innovation and change the world, we're talking about an innovation that we all recognize and that the market recognizes. Sometimes there's a lot of creativity involved. All of these things are important; all are innovations, but some require more risks, and some take a collection of many more creative frameworks being broken all at the same time.

Business goals may change, but the need for creativity remains constant. Mauzy says that:

> For example, if a company realizes its strategy isn't working or that its cost structure isn't profitable, then we have to create ideas that might change things, try them out, experiment to find out if something will work. If it doesn't, we create an alternate solution, whether a small change or big change. Then we work on that. So we are constantly looking at our environment and trying to understand how it works and how we can respond to it. That's the process of, on the one hand, creating these new possible solutions and, on the other, increasing your learning. The more flexible you are, the easier it is for you to say, "I can get a solution. Let me spread my attention and look at this from different perspectives. Let me tolerate the ambiguity of not knowing something a little longer," rather than having to get a quick answer. These are all psychological operations that underpin what we call creativity.

There are several things that business-technology executives can do today to start making their groups more creative:[62]

- **Take risks yourself.** Serve as a model. When you think of how cultures change — because that's what you're doing if you want people to increase their own creativity — you have to change the climate, the risk, and the perceptions of people. By beginning to take your own risks, you say, "I am ready to take a risk in front of you."

- **Listen to the staff.** I mean everyone on the staff, not just your favorite people or the people who report to you. If someone comes in with an idea, let them know you hear it, that you understand their idea. Paraphrase the idea as you understand it. Talk about why it might be a good idea. Every idea has positive aspects, so acknowledge them:
- **Increase the autonomy of the people** in your department. Instead, little by little, start giving more freedom to your people. Let them take on the whole problem. Instead of saying, "Here's the problem, and this is how I want you to address it", say, "Here's the problem. Can you get a solution for me?" This challenges people to bring out their own creativity. It will also challenge you to hear their solutions and accept them more.
- **Recognize the risks people are taking.** Recognize that people are doing good work and they're taking risks and wrestling with the unknown.
- **Failure could be acceptable.**

Chapter 7

Conclusion

Companies began adding Chief Technology Officers to the executive ranks in the 1980s because technology was becoming an integral and influential part of many strategic decisions and future planning cycles. The world is different today. The good mix of CIO and CTO are providing strong expertise on the internal application of technology. But, senior managers needed expert advice regarding the inclusion of technologies in existing products and the creation of new products and services with large technical components. A new agent, CTO, or newly created name for this role that is actively involved in monitoring new technologies, separating marketing rhetoric from technical facts, and identifying profitable applications for those technologies can make a significant difference in the company's competitive future. The CTO can and must add value to the company by participating in government, academic, and industry groups in a manner that creates positive attention for the company.

Technology companies are involved in thousands of acquisitions and strategic parterships every year. Selecting the best target for an acquisition or strategic parterships often requires reliable proven advice on technical issues at the executive level. The CTO is also a valuable tool in addressing the increasingly well-informed media about the products, services, and the future plans of the company. CTOs can speak as peers to other technologists and can play a role in convincing the media that the company's decisions are sound and will add value for the company's stakeholders.

It is critical and important that the CTO not become the senior technologist of the company. Instead, he or she is the senior business executive, a transformational agent with a focus on technology. In the CTO position, senior management is not looking for enthusiastic advice from a research scientist, but sound and proven advice on business decisions involving technology. We hope this role will keep evolving into something very meaningful and valuable to our companies, society, and our future. CTOs and CIOs really focus on progress and innovation of our society, and we need to move forward.

Depending on the environment in which your company finds itself, now is the time for new era of CIOs and CTOs to broaden their role and assume a new set of responsibilities in the new world society.

The Sections Ahead: CTO Thought Leadership and Best Practices

The next section of this best practices guide offers a glimpse of exciting thought leadership, best practices, and best practices of some of the most exciting and influential C level Executives in the Industry such as Bowstreet, PeopleSoft, Sybase, Perot Systems, Stapes, and more.

Final Few Words

Thank you for allowing me to share this knowledge with you. I hope this book gave you some insight on the best practices and thought leadership for the changing world.

As Technology Leaders, we have a responsibility to human kind. We are there working hard to increase competitiveness and innovation for our employers, investors, customers, families, friends and selves. We are creating a roadmap, and setting our destiny for the future ahead.

We are part of a single global community, and we need to continue to collaborate and share knowledge to continue to evolve this world as it adopts to incredible changes a better place to live and work.

We will raise to a new level in the value chain. It will take patience, support, trust, hard work, and persistence, but we will get there.

Part II

Part II

Chapter 8: Opportunities for Large and Small Software Companies for Today and Tomorrow

Chapter 9: Software Savvy: Taking and Keeping Your Place in the Software Market

Chapter 10: Basics of the Business

Chapter 11: Closing the Gap Between What Technology Can Do and What People Want It To Do

Chapter 12: Creating and Enriching Business Value

Chapter 13: Bridging Business and Technology: Keeping Things as Simple as Possible

Chapter 14: The Art of Being a CTO — Fostering Change

Chapter 15: Keep Your Blade Sharp

Chapter 16: Intelligent Enterprises Everywhere

Chapter 17: The Changing Face of Technology

Chapter 18: Major Dilemmas Facing Privacy Practitioners

Chapter 19: Managing Privacy

Contd...

Chapter 20: The Myth of Privacy
Chapter 21: Starting From Scratch
Chapter 22: Relationship Management
Chapter 23: Finding the Right Fit
Chapter 24: How to Make Every Customer a Repeat Customer
Chapter 25: Best Practices For Offshore Software Development Outsourcing

Chapter 8

Opportunities for Large and Small Software Companies for Today and Tomorrow

Michael George

Automating Change

It is interesting to me that even over the last one hundred years the concept of automation has existed in almost every industry: from making automobiles to building houses. You can buy a pre-fabricated home today. And the automobile industry is the greatest example of factory automation.

The one area that you think would be most driven by this type of advancement is the software industry, and it is not. We have millions of software programmers out there who take a piece of scrap paper and start to build software programs. It seems absurd. It's an area that should be the most automated, and yet it is the least automated.

Developers still change software manually, and the ripple effect introduces errors and delays that add huge costs to IT projects. Lack of automation makes change one of IT's worst enemies.

But change is inevitable, and keeping up with changing requirements poses one of the biggest challenges to IT groups today. Application software has become a liability and maintenance nightmare from the point of view of change. What you build today immediately becomes tomorrow's legacy — obsolete.

And change will continue to play a large role in IT, whether caused by new customers expanding functional requirements, companies merging and consolidating, replacing and updating legacy systems, or an increased user load forcing application redesigns. To make matter worse, companies are also dealing with other constraints, such as developers leaving or being reassigned to different projects and reduced budgets.

Change can be your enemy unless you have the tools to implement it automatically.

Until now, the software industry has not focused on enabling change, but instead, has focused on providing rapid application development (RAD) tools. RAD tools help you build your application code today, but fail to address how you change or branch your code tomorrow.

Over the past 5 years, the software industry has focused on providing service and component architecture for distributed re-use. Today's RAD tools make it relatively easy to build applications out of re-usable services and components. But this creates a big problem: RAD causes code proliferation and an inability to effectively implement change from that point on. Using RAD tools, IT groups create applications relatively quickly, but the resulting code is static and brittle.

When a component, service, schema, HTML page, or other referenced object changes, all the applications that use it must be changed manually. This introduces errors, delays, and high costs, resulting in change gridlock. What's needed are software companies that enable mass customization of the structure, functionality, and behavior of applications.

Technology Has United

Wind the clock back to 1998 when you had companies that were engineering their own applications based on their specific framework and solving their own unique problems. The customers for those products had to buy SAP to handle their supply chain and manufacturing, PeopleSoft to handle their HR systems, and Siebel for CRM. They required all of these different, disparate application sets to meet their business needs in each application area. All of those products had their own application framework. There was a tremendous amount of disparity in any sort of cross-functional requirement that may have come across any one of those application areas.

If I were a CFO, I wouldn't want to see just how we were doing in manufacturing. I would want to know the up-to-the-minute head count, cost for employees, and CR customer acquisition costs. I would like to see all of the things that might come as a compilation across all of those disparate systems.

The days of customers pouring millions of dollars into buying and customizing these "stovepipe" proprietary enterprise applications is giving way to a new environment: companies are building composite applications that provide interaction with their various backend systems to their employees, partners and customers. Technology has united to make the development of these applications possible.

Enterprise application vendors are breaking down their previously massive applications into a set of low level, standards-based components, which can be combined into customized applications that leverage data and functionality from disparate back end applications.

Much of the value of these applications comes, not only from providing centralized access to applications, but providing it in a customized, role-based manner, which creates a highly tailored experience for each user. To build these applications using traditional software would be time consuming, error prone, and difficult to maintain as the application grows or changes. Traditional software simply does not lend itself to building dynamic, role-based composite applications.

The industry is moving towards "Adaptive Software", which is the key component that makes it practical — for the first time — to build composite applications that adapt to various user roles or application contexts, allowing any aspects of the application — including the data, the processes, and the presentation — to be customized, on-demand, for individual employees, partners, and customers.

With Adaptive Software, companies with heterogeneous environments of enterprise applications, infrastructure software, and portal software can take advantage of the trend towards componentization and standardization to increase efficiencies, lower costs, and improve customer loyalty, by more fully leveraging the systems they already have in place. Software companies and enterprises alike are talking about e-business on demand and the adaptive enterprise.

A Lasting Company

Often, technology is innovative, and there is a demand for it, but unless a company's management has the ability to adapt and change its offerings, that company will not survive.

Look at companies like General Electric, General Motors, or IBM. Today, IBM is a leading technology company with a significant portion of its business in software, but they began with weighing scales, typewriters and various electro/mechanical business machines. Companies that can adapt to changes, as IBM has done, have the potential to exist 100 years from now.

Bowstreet's growth and early successes were based on understanding how companies intended to conduct business with other companies, and enabling systems to accommodate the dynamic change that would be required in such an environment. For companies to stay competitive they needed to develop application programs that allowed them to interact with third party company computer systems to obtain information and services. This was the beginning of Web services, and Bowstreet is appropriately credited as having invented this technology and created this important category.

Bowstreet was born on the premise that it could help create XML-based standards and other industry standards, so that rather than having to integrate all of those different applications, we could enable an end user to benefit from all of them as though they were in the same application framework, but without the cost of integrating them. They could spend a fraction of that and get the same amount of interoperability across those applications using Web services.

Bowstreet initially realized tremendous success in this market, and raised a record amount of venture funding to lead this category. But Web services failed to materialize once market spending was suspended in 2001 and the company focused its energy on finding new markets for its innovative technology.

Bowstreet saw a growing opportunity in the application development space. In particular, the need to rapidly build and change portal applications had a growing importance in this new economic landscape. Portals were becoming more sophisticated and were being used to connect various, disparate backend applications. As the use of portals developed, it became clear that out-of-the-box portlets would quickly fail to meet customers' needs. Developers starting looking towards customized portlets to tap into legacy data and other backend systems. But these portlets were not easy to create, and of equal importance, very difficult to change. IT groups had to look to J2EE experts, who spent long hours developing these portlets. Bowstreet saw the need for development tools that would simplify the creation of portlets with dynamic change capabilities, and significantly improve the end result.

Bowstreet introduced Bowstreet Portlet Factory in Q4 2002 as a dedicated portlet creation tool that addresses the challenges faced by application vendors that need to build portlets. Portlet Factory's ease of use and advanced development features dramatically streamline the entire portlet development process, enabling developers to deliver highly flexible, configurable portlets in a fraction of the time and at a fraction of the cost required today.

Unlike portlets created with RAD or "clipping" tools, Bowstreet-powered portlets are dynamic, robust J2EE applications that can be easily modified by customers in real-time, to meet their unique business requirements. By eliminating the need to write code that handles the various customer requirements, Bowstreet Portlet Factory simplifies the development and change management process, saving application vendors time and money, and freeing developers to focus on more important, strategic work. The importance of this innovative technology is demonstrated by the fact that IBM, as well as other industry leaders, now sells Bowstreet products on a worldwide basis.

Bowstreet has remained agile in order to thrive on change. We have been able to modify ourselves to meet the requirements of a shifting market with unique, patented software, and a basic technology that has not fundamentally changed. We have adapted this technology around a new and unique model, and adjusted the way we promote this technology to the marketplace.

If we had not adjusted, it is quite possible that we would not be around today. There are many companies that were not willing to or were unable to adapt to changing market dynamics that don't exist anymore.

Risk in the Marketplace

To be an innovative company, you have to take risks. Let me be very clear to separate putting your customer at risk versus taking risks. In order to be a lead innovator of technology, you have to experiment and invest. We are funded in a way that affords us the opportunity to look at investments in a three- to five-year cycle. We have no expectation of getting a return on the money that we invest in software for as many as three years.

We have a three-year technology investment strategy we call "seed, succeed, and standardize." In our first year, we purposely go out and seed the market as a loss leader. In the next year, we focus on customer service and concentrate on making all of our customers very successful with our product. By the third year, we expect to have set an industry standard with our technology and customer service.

When companies begin to standardize on our products, we begin to change the economic equation in our business model. Few companies are funded in a way that allows for such investments over extended periods of time. Private companies by and large are not, and we have had the good fortune of raising more money privately, than most companies raise in public offerings.

We take some risk in how we develop applications. We study potential trends in the market place, and we invest and try things that other companies might be less likely to do. Ultimately, we are active participants in XML standard bodies, as well as the new portal development standard called JSR 168. Rather than leading our customers out on a proprietary tangent, we make sure that anything that we produce is in line with industry standards. We have either helped establish those standards, or we have studied them and participated in the development of them in a way that puts us on the forefront when they do emerge.

I would say that we have a tendency to be aggressive in how we progress in the development of software, but conservative when we ultimately produce the product for our customers because our customers are generally conservative. They are large financial institutions, insurance companies, and manufacturers such as AIG, MetLife, General Motors and General Electric. These are companies that want to be early, but don't want to be first. They don't want to be, and don't need to be, on the bleeding edge of technology changes.

Since we either establish or adopt industry standards, we are probably through an 18- to 24-month cycle from the time the product was originally conceived until the commercial product is produced. That has been typical for us. We introduce point releases through out the cycle in order to provide updates. For example, we recently released version 5.6 of Bowstreet Portlet Factory. Typically we produce major new version of product every 18-24 months.

The Customer (and Therefore Customer Service) is Still King

In the business world, there is nothing more important than customer service. The best customer is not one that we never hear from, but one who, if they have a problem of some sort, will come to us. We are often the glue between lots of disparate systems. Databases change, workflows change, vendors change, and products upgrade, so eventually customers will run into a situation that requires our assistance.

We like to be, and ultimately want to be, measured on the way that we service our customers. It is our goal to make sure that all of our customers are 100 per cent successful with our product. We use the term internally that they are 100 per cent "referencable." Only then do we feel like we are fulfilling our end of the bargain and meeting the needs of our customers.

Public *versus* Private Companies

As a private company, we are not under the scrutiny of the public market, where you can't afford to take risks and make those kinds of investments in your customers. Bowstreet probably has more money than most public companies have ever raised, but we don't have the scrutiny of having to meet short-term (quarterly) objectives. We have an opportunity to make long-term investments in our customers and, therefore, in our future.

It is more difficult for private companies starting out today. The days when a small company could raise a couple of million dollars, build something interesting, field an enterprise sales organization, and start to achieve momentum are gone.

Publicly traded software companies today are up against a very scrutinizing, very difficult market. It prevents them from investing in their customers because the financial markets will punish them for it.

Skills in Highest Demand

Only just a few years ago, there was a large market demand for developers skilled in enterprise applications such as SAP or PeopleSoft. As a result, many developers rushed to learn these enterprise products and the technologies (such as ABAP) required to customize and extend them.

Today, the tide has changed. The demand for developers skilled in proprietary application frameworks is over. This is due in part to industry consolidation and open standards. I believe that the market is going to come down to a handful of vendors. Microsoft and IBM will clearly be part of that exclusive group. If I were an individual today looking to build a career path around software development, I would try to hone my skills, not with some unique, off-brand application framework, but with technologies that are at the heart of IBM's roadmap, or meaningful in the IBM ecosystem, such as third-party software tools that compliment IBM's strategy for selective market dominance.

Bowstreet is investing heavily in expanding our developer community, since we have a rapidly growing number of application software developers who use the Bowstreet application development tools. We want them to be well trained, well educated, and to have access to the best tools and resources available.

To develop using Bowstreet tools gives a programmer a unique set of advantages working inside of the IBM model. We have a community portal for developers, and we have a dynamically growing list of people who are adopting our tools, not just because they are Bowstreet tools and Bowstreet developers are in such high demand, but because they are IBM tools as well. IBM is re-selling our tools supporting the products and the developers who use them, and companies in the new economy want skills that are IBM-based.

That is also true for Microsoft. Developers with skills specific to companies in the Microsoft ecosystem are far more attractive than off-brand products. They have, for instance, far more marketable skills than if they were the once sought after PeopleSoft programmer skills.

Developers are far better served by going out and acquiring skill sets for industry leaders such as IBM and Microsoft, and the companies in their inner circles.

No Advice — Sharing Experiences

I don't like to give advice, but I am happy to share my experiences with people, so they can learn from those experiences and apply it to their own particular circumstances.

Running a software business is a complex challenge. There are no silver bullets. You need to have a long-term view and maintain good metrics around your business. You have to make a successive series of smart decisions, and a little bit of luck doesn't hurt either.

People complain about the behemoth software companies, and that there are no more opportunities for smaller vendors. I disagree. Young software companies starting out today have some tremendous opportunities. Without the burden of needing to satisfy existing customers, young vendors are free to architect innovative, flexible solutions and technologies. Further, larger companies are typically slower to react to market needs and have difficulty being innovative. As a result, there will always be the opportunity for smaller companies to correct the deficiencies of larger companies and to fill in the 'holes' or gaps in their offerings.

The late 1990s were full of unrealistic expectations for many companies and the people who worked for them. Companies were easily intoxicated by the false successes brought on in this era, and frankly, the hangover is lasting longer than most had predicted. Rapid innovation and change is great, but remaining grounded and focused on fundamental business principles is essential to the long-term success of any company.

Biography

For Michael George, the road to his current role as CEO of Bowstreet, a pioneer in adaptive Web applications, began many years ago with his natural technical ability, business savvy, and entrepreneurial spirit.

While a student at Suffolk University in Boston, Massachusetts, Michael established a video game arcade to help fund his education. Making the most of what was becoming a national sensation, Michael grew his business to include seven arcades in New Hampshire and several "Game World" arcades on Cape Cod. He sold the business during his junior year at Suffolk University.

Through his rapidly growing business venture, Michael caught the eye of inventor and fellow entrepreneur Dean Kamen, now internationally famous for his Segway Human Transporter. Faced with the choice of completing his degree at Suffolk or joining Dean Kamen in his new ventures, Michael decided to accelerate his studies, and graduated one semester early with a bachelor's degree in Philosophy.

After graduation, Michael joined Dean Kamen's creative "invention center", and worked on many projects, employed by DEKA — the medical electronic R&D center, Michael led the purchase and repurposing of textile mill buildings which still house Dean Kamen's operations, and the purchase and operation of a helicopter company where Michael took pilot lessons.

Still in his early twenties, Michael decided to apply the knowledge he gained from working closely with such a brilliant thinker, and strike out on his own. His undertakings were varied both in geography and scope, and included endeavors with an auto leasing company, various technology based companies, an overseas manufacturer, and an importer of unique gifts. Armed with the lessons learned from both the successes and failures in his enterprises, Michael was both economically and spiritually ready for a change by the late 1980s.

Michael joined TALX Corporation, a small voice-processing company in the mid-west, and led the company's sales initiatives over the next four years. The company grew to become the leader in its industry. As an officer and one of the largest operating shareholders of the company, Michael greatly contributed to and benefited from the company's IPO in 1996.

Michael went on to found Interlynx Technology, the first Web-based provider of employee self- service application software. The company's early years were met with great success, since it had created a new category of software and had the unique ability to fulfill it. However, as the market became more defined, newly formed and well-financed companies emerged, making it difficult for the self-funded operation to compete. Michael eventually raised a modest $3 million in early 1998, a time when new companies in the space were raising in excess of $50 million.

In order to succeed, Interlynx needed to employ its entrepreneurial roots. While its competitors were outspending the company on everything from hiring to advertising, Interlynx remained frugal, but resourceful. The company garnered top industry awards for innovation, and earned the business of over 100 companies such as GE, Allied Signal, Safeway Stores, and Office Depot. With modest outside investment, the company was acquired in December of 2000 for $60 million.

After his success at Interlynx, Michael decided to spend a year with his family and renew his love of sailing, while maintaining a modest schedule of board commitments. Michael was honored by Suffolk University with the "Alumni of the Year" award in 1999, and became a class of 2000 graduate of the prestigious MIT Executive Management Program, "Birthing of Giants." Michael also continues to pursue his passion for traveling and participating in competitive sports. He is a USCG licensed captain (100 ton — Sail Master), two-time Boston Marathoner, and an active trustee for Suffolk University and the Boston Classical Orchestra.

Chapter 9

Software Savvy — Taking and Keeping Your Place in the Software Market

John Chen

Basics of the Software Industry

The software industry is built on programming applications on computers and hardware. Software is meant to reflect creative ideas and processes and is probably the most flexible component of the IT world. And because of the intense intellectual property aspect of software, it's hailed as the highest margin business — the most profitable business — if you have a good idea.

The biggest negative of the software industry is the barriers of entry are not high, resulting in strong turbulence. Of the top ten software leaders of ten years ago, probably only half of them either exist independently or are still in the top ten. Software is a game for a lot of newcomers, with many intellectual property and creative challenges. It also tends to have a winner-take-all mentality.

Because so many new ideas keep surfacing, we go through more waves of innovation than probably any other industry. Ford stopped making the Model T about 100 years ago, but we still have luxury cars. In the hardware industry, the cycles for new waves of innovation span between five and ten years. You can be a winner in one wave, but if you blink and miss the next wave, you could be a dog.

The software industry is now a very integral part of the US economy and US productivity.

Pushing to Create a Niche in the Marketplace

Innovation has to be the cornerstone of the industry. Continuous investment and focus are needed. You need to keep pushing to make sure your customers are happy not only with your services of today but with the potential of tomorrow. We talk about standards and compatibility and serviceability. These are the reasons that you are in business and that the customer wants to buy your material and stay with you.

We spend a lot of time innovating not only from the technology perspective. The claim to fame of Sybase is mostly on technology, and we own a lot of technology. We "early lead" on a lot of innovations, including wireless. Those are really the results of many years of investing in research and development and many years of investing in market research. This is a hard business to stay put in. Sybase tries to go after certain niches. To guard against becoming obsolete, you have to have a corner on the market. We focus on doing just that at all times.

Small companies are a little more focused, a little more versatile, and very nimble. In our business, where things happen so fast, those are distinct advantages. The disadvantage is that you typically have little muscle in the market or the channels.

When the economy is in a downturn, the ability to generate cash and make money is of paramount importance. If you don't have that, you can't invest in new technology or new generation. Size matters: You want to be small when the market is good and large when the market is bad.

Building the Customer Base

The consumer space is basically a volume game. You have to sell a lot or make a thin margin. The enterprise space, however, is very different. Enterprise is based on reliability and serviceability, and once you are in the door, unless there is a good reason to remove you, typically you don't get displaced very easily. We tend to stick there, providing good service and solid future road maps.

In this business, there is no economic value to your customers to move from your products to somebody else's products. As a vendor or provider, all you need is one interruption, and you are in trouble. Your ability to back up your customer, recover his system losses, and fix his problems quickly, professionally, and accurately are key cornerstones to your customer support.

Software has a lot of bugs, principally because there is so much code generated every day. My software needs to interact with the software of many other companies, including the software being generated by my customers themselves. You often don't know what is connected to you. When your customer has a problem, you have to dive in and figure out what is wrong and fix it because your customer's business could be at risk. It's critical that you're able to do that. If the use of your software shuts down anyone's business, your reputation is at stake. A loss of reputation is very tough to recover.

It is not impossible, however, to move your system up, especially if a newer idea comes along. The customer is always confronted with keeping the platform stable with good support or moving to something else that is a little more innovative and less expensive.

Typically the inertia of an incumbent is the best account protection. If my customers buy my software, use it day-to-day, have their people trained on it, are happy with my responsiveness, and they understand my road map, and if I've kept up my research and development with my competitors, then even if I am a little late, they will still wait for me. They like doing business with me, and that whole chain ties to robust customer support. Not only is that the most lucrative part of the business if your platforms are stable and your products are good, but it is also the strongest connection bonding you to your customer.

Software is a people business. People buy from people in this industry. It's extremely rare that you have such an innovative idea that you are the only one who can provide it and customers will buy from you even if they don't see you.

We are definitely not in the mail-order business. Our products are complicated, and it takes time and energy to explain them, to help put them to work, and to map into our customers' needs. That is where much of the margin and the "stickiness" come from. You have to be there for your customer and look them in the eye. They have to know you are trustworthy, that you have a good plan for the future, and that you won't come and go on them. Trust and loyalty take time to grow. Personal contact is the key in this business.

It follows, then, that the most profit-rich area of software is customer support — the service and maintenance part. It reflects the degree of stability of your product. Customers continue to pay you to make sure you are responsive, and because you are a more stable platform, you don't need to spend much money to fix the same problem many times. That makes service usually the most lucrative piece.

Making and Marketing Good Ideas for Software Products

In creating a new software product, your aim most of the time is to offer a more efficient way of getting something done. If your customer has ten people managing three systems, your product should provide a better way to run the business. The product you offer can collapse your customer's three systems to two, reduce the ten people to six, run the business faster, and improve your customer's interaction with his customers. That is a more efficient new software product.

Coming up with a way to replace, condense, or simplify some of the things being done today by other IT systems and processes gives you a winning product. That is evolution. Every so often our industry comes up with some revolutionary ideas, the Internet being one of them, and commercializes it. Those revolutionary products have a longer shelf life.

The product cycles in our business run 12 to 18 months at the longest. If you come up with something truly new, very exciting, and evolutionary, you will probably be able to sell it in a reasonably profitable way within 12 to 18 months. If you miss that cycle, it is best to move on because nobody buys older technology. Occasionally, we have truly innovative ideas that have a little longer shelf life — maybe three to five years.

When you have an idea for a product, you try to sell it, and if you don't already have a base business, you try to sell it through partners. When you reach a certain number of partners, you make next-generation upgrades and try to sell it yourself.

This is a gradual process. It gets you closer to the customer so you can get a lot more market research. After you have done that for a while, the next step is to grow by pushing your business overseas. Then you battle against your competitors in the new space.

In product marketing, you have to speak to the needs of the market and follow its trends. Establishing yourself as an innovator, providing products and services to help customers do something more efficiently than they could before by reducing the number of systems, staff, or other resources, is normally how software is marketed.

The industry moved off mainframe to prepackaged applications to get through the year 2000. Now the needs are for integration solutions to enable all those packages to talk to each other and use the Internet to best advantage. The next step will be having wireless, the Internet, and broadband collide, followed by a move toward intelligence.

Software Business Financials

Normally if you are in the mature part of the curve for the business, your pricing is dictated by the market — supply and demand and how other people price. If you have an innovative idea and you are a market leader, you can dictate the price. You won't stay market leader for long, though, because the market is very turbulent, and you always face challenges by new startups. Then the prices start shifting. After a while the product matures, and you price as everyone else prices. This is the early lead cycle. You are the first one there, and you can actually take a lot of the margin off the table.

In a mature, non-Internet-based cycle, you price on number of users. If it is Internet-based, you price on number of systems because with the Internet, you can't count users. Early entry always gets the lead in the price war.

Depending on the company, expenses run typically as follows:

- Research and development costs between 15 and 20 cents on a dollar of revenue.
- The Q & A cost is between 8 and 10 cents.
- The sales and support infrastructure are between 25 and 35 cents on the dollar, depending on the kind of company that they channel. If they sell through partners, it will be lower; if they sell direct, it will be higher.
- Your marketing costs are 10 cents on a dollar.
- Your costs of goods is typically between 5 and 10 cents, depending on whether you make all or some of the components.

If you add this all together, you have 20 to 30 cents per dollar left, and that is your profit. Your predominant cost is for people. Our business is very people-intensive, or brain intensive. We typically have a high percentage of people supporting and people selling — and a very high percentage of people doing engineering work.

The costs of our products are not high. If you develop your own software and don't resell other people's components, you don't have to pay royalties, so you can run a margin business in excess of 80 per cent. On the other hand, we spend a lot of money on R & D for innovations — very big numbers.

It is easy to see how most of the well run software companies make 20 to 30 cents net on the dollar before taxes, depending on how pervasive they are in a certain market. It is a highly lucrative business and that is why so many people jumped in.

Skills in Highest Demand

The most important skills in the software industry go back to the product side, the engineering and innovations. Today, a lot of people can program, but whether they can program reliably and turn those programs into a product is the big question. They must be able to have a great idea, to develop it, and — most important — to develop it in a commercially viable way, linking it back to customer support. That skill is paramount.

The secondary skills are in the people who can actually take such complex equations and map them into something customers not only understand but see that they need. Those are the two most important roles: creating a product and creating a demand.

The software industry will continue to evolve to a higher level of intelligence. In the past, software was used for programming, for mimicking certain processes and parallel orders of things, how factories are run and how certain businesses are run.

In the future, a number of high-potential software applications will be based on intelligent systems — software that can actually learn and adapt and heal itself if it runs into trouble. It will self-diagnose, recover, and alert people. The wireless phenomena will drive software intelligence and will be ubiquitous.

Approaches to Risk Taking

There are two components of risk. One is risk management. The other is risk taking.

Risk taking depends on the time. Ten years ago, when the market was searching for new direction, it was best to be a little more of a risk taker. If you fit only on the old paradigm, you may have missed the entire wave. The penalty for missing a wave is very high. It could almost cost the company.

You have to take a certain amount of risk. That is what a good management team does. You take the risk, and you monitor the progress of new ideas and new components. You know you will win some and lose some, but you're confident that you are knowledgeable enough, with fast enough reactions and reflexes, that you can pull back from potential loss and continue to be a winner.

The other component is risk containment, or risk management, which is extremely important to our business. So much of our business is people-based, wrapped up in the building of intellectual properties. Managing that risk and making sure we can restart with maybe the same set of talents somewhere else are concerns to which every software company pays a lot of attention.

Risk in terms of managing for business continuity on such a high intellectual property-based business and people-oriented basis is a little more challenging. Because of the turbulence of our market, we do need to take risks and manage them to continue to be innovative.

Ensuring the Longevity of Your Company

Diversification is a good way to think about a successful company. I have a very stable, mature business that makes money. I have various stages of incubated business, and I continue to have that pipeline of businesses and markets on which we've focused and built some technology know-how and technology innovation and barrier of entry.

Right now, I have four major businesses. My database business is very defendable but is not a high-growth business. It is a good cash generator because customers like us and stay with us. However, I have an integration business that has been growing 30 per cent to 40 per cent a year.

You have to pipeline your future opportunities and always look ahead. What are people buying? Who are they buying from? Why should they buy from you? You can't focus on one business and bet everything. Pipelining different stages of opportunities into the market ensures longevity and success.

Staying on Top of Technology

There are three ways to stay on top of new technology.

One way is staying close to your customers. Customers are constantly being pitched to about new ways of doing things and new technologies. You know their demands and what they are thinking about, and you can make sure you move along with them.

Another way is through standard bodies in the industry. The industry has many standard bodies in various stages of maturity. You need to be in the industry making sure you listen to what other people are doing and what industry standards are driving toward, and you stay there.

The final way to stay on top of technology is to be associated with universities to capture some early potentials. You need to keep an eye on what they are doing and figure out how you can apply it later in your business. You have to filter the ideas.

Biggest Upcoming Changes in the Industry

A fundamental shift coming soon in the business involves how people pay for software. There will be a divergence of methods — people renting some software, paying as they go, which is different from the way it's done today. There is a lot of discussion of software as utility. What it all boils down to is a different form of pay-for-it-as-you-go software. All the software companies have to pay attention to that because it will have a profound impact on the business.

The economic aspects of your business can change dramatically, depending on who you are and at which point in the food chain you enter. In the next five years, that will change. Today, because of the choices and the economy, customers have the ultimate power. Five years ago vendors had the power because if the customer did not buy their software, they could not keep up. Now the pendulum has swung the other way, and we have to listen to how they decide to spend money. That will be the biggest change in the industry.

I could help buffer myself by continuously trying to reduce my cost base. That is why you see a lot of outsourcing activities. People try to do things a little less expensively. It has a profound impact on your primary strategy and your acquisition strategy. Because of the turbulence in the software industry, there have been many combinations, some of which were for technology reasons and some of which were for survival reasons.

The only competitors in software for US companies are in some niche areas in Israel, Canada, and Europe. The top ten list today is dominated by US companies. But if you want to stay in the software game, you need to be highly adaptive. Our society and our industry are very fluid and dynamic and are certainly used to changes. This flexibility has made the United States a leader in the industry. The key long-term issue as the industry matures is to maintain that competitive edge and also have enough talent to fuel the growth engine.

A principal reason the software industry does well is that they essentially have no government regulations, other than the same regulations of accounting and so on that all businesses are subject to — but not in terms of how the industry works. Much of the software industry was built on the enthusiastic encouragement of R&D tax credits the government issued some 15 or 20 years ago. These are important logs for keeping the fire going. That is why you find a long line of software companies very close to and interested in public policy. Such a big part of our growth and a big part of our business is overseas. Typically you will find software companies who are mature having at least half of their business coming from overseas.

No Rest for the Leaders

Once you understand the turbulent nature of the business and you compare the lists of top ten companies of yesterday and today, you know you can't sit on any lead. There is no comfort zone. You have to be in constant paranoia. That piece of advice comes from a lot of well known people in the industry. You have to keep moving.

I also try to point out to people that there is no perfect way of doing things. The industry moves too fast for perfection to develop. You have to challenge the status quo. That is how the margin of business is built.

Biography

John Chen, Chairman of the Board, chief executive officer, and president of Sybase, is known widely as an IT industry leader and technology visionary, a corporate turnaround specialist, and a clear, well-informed voice in matters of international trade and US — China relations.

Chen is recognized in the IT industry as more than a clever tactician. He is a visionary leader both in the development of new technologies, and conceiving the real-world uses to which new technologies will be put into practice. His education, a Bachelor of Science degree from Brown University and a Master of Science degree in Electrical Engineering from the California Institute of Technology (CalTech), enables him to understand both the inner workings of technology and the business needs it can address.

John Chen is also a recognized expert in engineering of a different type— corporate turnarounds. In 1997, when Sybase's corporate fortunes were at their lowest, John Chen was recruited as president to restore growth and profitability. Since then, Sybase has reinvented itself and posted nineteen consecutive profitable quarters, made significant acquisitions, including AvantGo and New Era of Networks, launched successful subsidiaries — including iAnywhere, holding a dominant position in wireless software, and Financial Fusion, the top facilitator of online banking — and captured sizeable market share in key segments, all while accumulating substantial cash reserves.

As few other executives of major American corporations, John Chen is deeply focused on international relations and trade policy, particularly as it relates to Sino-American relations.

Born in Hong Kong in 1955, Chen hears and understands the voices of China. He is known for taking thoughtful and highly regarded positions on matters of interest to strengthening international trade and US — China relations. Chen was among the first American business executives to argue in favor of permanent normalized trade relations with China, testifying to the US House of Representatives Ways and Means Committee, and for American support of Chinese membership in the World Trade Organization (WTO). Often through organizations such as the US Center for Asia Pacific Economic Cooperation (APEC) of which he is a member of the Board of Governors, the Council of Foreign Relations, and the Board of Directors of the US Chamber of Commerce, Chen has worked tirelessly to build the U.S.-China relationship. He has spoken widely on intellectual property rights (IPR) protection, market openness, and policy and trade issues.

Chen is also vocal about the experience and contribution of Asians in America. He is vice chairman of the Committee of 100, a group of nationally visible Chinese Americans, which promotes understanding of issues faced by Asians in America.

Chapter 10

Basics of the Business

Gerald D. Cohen

Our company is in the sector of the software business that involves delivering information. We're in two sectors of it: one is what is called business intelligence, where we deliver information to human beings; the other is the application integration business, where we deliver information to other processes (that's sometimes called middleware). In all cases, it involves the delivering of information.

We're an established company; we've been in business 28 years — we started in 1975. No one is writing books about how companies continue to stay in business. Most of the business books talk about how to introduce a hot new product and get it to catch on. We started when the world of computing was in batch phase, moving to time-sharing; it was called host-based computing. We introduced a product called Focus, which was the first fourth-generation language. We are the inventor of fourth-generation languages. That, for many years, was one of the hottest standards around, and everyone wanted to use a fourth-generation language for their information systems. The theory was, why would you want to write a COBOL program, for example, to generate a report? You'd have to get a programmer and explain to him and it could take weeks. You just want to get your information. So the Focus program created this category of fourth-generation languages, and we sold Focus all around the world to companies with mostly large IBM mainframes. Eventually, when UNIX came in, we put Focus on UNIX and other machines.

We've been with the information industry through all of its phases. We started with host-based computing, and then went to time-sharing, then to minicomputers, then to PCs, then to client/server, and now it's the Internet. Our flagship product today is WebFOCUS, for example, and our integration product is called iWay Software.

We're basically doing very much what we were doing years ago. Organizations need information to run their businesses. That's the way things happen; it's not a new fad. The main thing that has changed is the form of delivering the information. Years ago, a lot of information was delivered on green screen terminals. Today a lot of information is delivered via your browser, or perhaps you get it through your e-mail. The second major change within the business is whom we deliver the information to. Years ago, the only place you delivered information was to someone who worked in the company; you had an ID on some machine, you logged in, and you were able to get information. If you were outside the company — a partner or a customer — you didn't share that information. Today we're delivering information between companies.

We're in a high-tech world. We sell software to companies under the expectation that they will use it to do several things. First, they will make their existing processes more efficient. Second, they will be able to save money some way internally. And, third, they'll be able to use it for competitive advantage; that is, they will do something that will attract new customers or solidify their customer base.

The marketplace changes. A few years ago the market was all about competitive advantage: "I want to get out there and do something on the Internet before the next guy." Today, a great deal of the emphasis is on using technology to save money. These things go in cycles. The challenge to us as a software company is to show companies how they will save money, become more efficient, or gain a competitive advantage.

Making money is a matter of scale. There is an investment cycle to build a product. Before you can sell it, it has to be useful enough that someone can use it productively. So there's an investment process — it's not a matter of just a demo. Demos are good for attracting investors, but by the time you're out to sell it, it has to really do something useful. And software is not a single investment; it's a continuous investment. It's an intellectual product and intellectual products are easier to augment. It's easier to have new releases and add features to it. If you buy, for example, a camera, and then two months later the camera manufacturer comes out with some slick new feature, you're out of luck. In software, however, you can call up the manufacturer and there's a maintenance counter and it ships you the new software. There's a more continuous upgrade. You don't really get obsolete in software. What that means is that there is a flow of money that comes in from selling upgrades. So a software business model is that you first invest in building products, you find some method of selling it, and you get both direct revenue and maintenance revenue from upgrades. That's the business model of all software.

The difference between larger and smaller software companies is mainly in the channels they use. Microsoft really doesn't sell directly; it sells through Microsoft agents. You buy from a local supplier of Microsoft products. IBM, in contrast, will mostly sell to you directly through the company's own sales force. So you can either sell direct or indirect. The pricing can be either that you buy it one time and pay maintenance, or you buy it on a subscription basis — Microsoft, for example, allows you to pay so much for Windows XP over the next two or three years, then you sign a new contract.

We sell using all those models, depending on the marketplace. In the Internet marketplace, if it's for Web Focus, which is for human beings getting information, we might sell it based on the power of the machine. If it's for a larger machine, we'll charge you more money. We may, in some occasions, sell it based on the number of users on a machine. For example, if the application is for internal people, we can measure users. If it's an external application, we can't. So, it's usually sold by the power of the machine, the number of processors on the machine. The user either pays for it by subscription or pays one time.

Profits and Product

The software business eventually builds up a substantial maintenance base, but the profit is really in selling new products. The maintenance base is nice to have and keeps you running, but when you have a product that's selling like hotcakes, then you make money. This isn't a fashion business, but it has a certain element of that. Everyone wants a hot product that lots of other people want. The other aspect is that you want to get there first. The company that gets the hot product first usually gets most of the market and most of the profit from it.

Being on the cutting edge is a double-edged sword, however. Not every customer is a cutting-edge customer. Not every customer wants to buy the latest and greatest. In fact, today in particular, people are holding back, waiting to see what technology is really going to survive.

Software marketing is a bit different than consumer marketing. In consumer marketing, I want everyone to know that I'm making a camera because consumers buy them, and I'm going to advertise on television. In the industrial marketplace that we sell into, you're not going to see us on television. Occasionally software companies do advertise on television, but it's quite rare. We use technical marketing channels such as technical publications, for example, or technical trade shows and conferences. In these places, we get our name out. Also, we provide Web information, so people get on the Web and learn about the product remotely. Plus, we have salesmen knock on doors, and part of their challenge is to educate customers about what software we provide. We have a direct sales force that goes out and builds a relationship with the customer directly. We mostly sell to the business-level user. For a local application, a departmental application, it's the business user who needs a solution to meet his needs. Sometimes we sell to IT management for more of an enterprise solution or something they can use in many locations. So, we sell both to the CIO level and to the departmental level, depending on where the solution is used. Today, many people are educated about computers. Years ago, we only sold to IT management, but today everyone uses computers, so you'll find people who are running a trust accounting or a purchasing department who very often are capable of putting out a system, installing it, and getting it run themselves.

We only sell to a CIO if it is a strategic system that is very important to the company. Not every system is CIO level; many of them are pedestrian things. So, if it's a strategic system, you're selling higher up. There's more interest in picking the right thing because it's a more important decision for the company. If you're selling a departmental system, it's usually lower priced and gets a lower level of attention in the company. Obviously, if you're selling higher up, you're going to put more effort into it because those are bigger sales. The basic strategy is to show the buyer that you have a product that they can use easily, that is going to do the job that they want done, that will grow with their needs as time goes on, and that is going to be the best long-term solution for them. It's a very fundamental set of things that we sell in software.

A good software product should live up to the promise that it has made: do the job as advertised — economically — for the buyer. It must be easy to use, because otherwise the user has a lot of expense to keep it running. And we keep it up to date for him, so his investment is preserved.

Life Cycle of a New Product

We've been selling these similar products for years and years, and so for us, starting a product may be a bud off a tree. For example, when you're in front of a browser you have information pulled to you. But let's say you're not in front of a browser. You might just say, "Every Monday morning send me an e-mail with this information in it." In that case we're pushing information to you. What happens there is that perhaps at night we're going through all the data and generating all the information and sending it out in e-mails. Recently, we had an idea that not everyone wants the information pushed out in e-mails; some people want to take this information and put it into an archive. For example, I want to know what my cash flow report was in February 2001. It's not available now; the data is gone from the database, so you have to go to an archive. If the archive is up on the Internet for you, you can very easily pull it out of a database and look at it on your browser. So, we said, while we're doing the preparation of people's e-mails, one of the options, instead of putting it into an e-mail, would be putting it into a database for archive purposes. That's a new product idea — it's a bud of an existing product, but it's a new product idea. So we'll research what customers want in that area. We'll ask them what they do in terms of archiving. They'll tell us, "I don't only want to archive what you produce; I have a lot of other things. I may want to archive other things like my Web site." What if you want to look at what a still-existing Web site looked like three years ago? You'd archive it. Now we'll archive it for you. So customers will come along and say they want archived reports that we produce, reports that other people produce, Web sites, and so on — and they tell us that. So there's a certain information gathering stage about what would be the useful features of a product. That comes from customers telling us and our own analysis and observation.

The second phase would be to build a prototype product, then go back and show it to a few customers and talk to them about it. When we have something that's working, then the issue comes in about how to price it. We look at the competition, we look at what's available, we look at the value of it, and we come up with a pricing schedule. Then we go out and we introduce it with a rollout.

From there its profitability depends on sales. It becomes profitable if you sell enough. If you guessed right and enough people want it, then that bud on the tree becomes a profitable entity itself. Now, if this were the only thing I produced, then I would have to depend on the sales of that archiving product. A larger company like ours can say that maybe that product is not profitable on its own, but people buy our entire information solution because they like the fact that we can also do archiving. We're looking for products that have large-scale usefulness for customers, and this is one more area of usefulness. It might not even be profitable, but it contributes to the profitability. We know we have a good product, and anything we add to it may be incremental. You have to differentiate between the smaller companies that survive on that niche, versus those who are in the broader area.

Expenses and Growth

Most of the expenses in any software company are people's salaries. Software companies do not have elaborate machinery. Yes, we have computers, but we don't have big plants or warehouses with lots of inventory. We just have people who sit down and write software. What's the expense of a software firm? The programmers, the QA people, and the product managers. Then there are the marketing costs. The two expenses of software firms are the programming and manufacturing of it — which is all intellectual property creation — and the marketing of it. Marketing is also, to a great extent, the people cost, but there are also other expenses involved.

There are several ways to grow the business. You could add salespeople. If you add more salespeople, you get to a larger share of the market. You can add new types of sales activities; for example, you could start to sell through other people, which is called selling through channels. Occasionally we'll sell through channels. Sometimes we'll build a vertical. We'll say, "This product is very good; we've built systems in the healthcare area." So, we'll try to sell into the healthcare market, which is a new vertical. We're always looking for new niches, new methods of selling — whether it's new channels, new reseller deals, or systems integrators — or more direct sales. That's principally the way we sell, and I think many software companies have similar methods. You could also sell on the Internet, but you have to get people to know you're there, so it's really a marketing/advertising activity.

Another way to grow is through acquisitions. The advantages of acquiring another software company are that you pick up products that augment yours or products that your sales forces can do a better job with. Or, you think the people would fit into your organization very well. If you give them the opportunity, they'll invent nifty things for you. That's one of the advantages of buying companies. The disadvantage is if you make a mistake — if, in fact, the product doesn't fit so well, the people don't mix so well, the market turns and you made a poor decision. That happens.

In terms of potential acquisitions, we're always looking for good management and smart people who would fit in. We're looking for product that would either augment our existing product nicely or would be a submarket that we can do a better job in. We look at a company's market penetration, how many copies they sold, who they sold them to. We look at the bottom line, of course, but we're interested more in the influence they have had. We want to know who bought the product, how they like the product, what influence the product has. So it's not entirely a financial situation, at least for us. We're not buying big, huge companies; we're just looking at little, tiny ones.

Everything we do has a risk factor. Every time we put a price on a price list we're saying, "Maybe it's the right price; maybe it's the wrong price." Every time we open a sales office, every time we make a deal with a new agent or a new distributor, we're taking a risk. Every decision we have carries a risk. There's nothing ever guaranteed to us that's going to be the right decision. It's a matter of scale; some decisions are a little bit bigger than others. It's not very often that the life of your company is at risk with these decisions. That's very rare.

Changes in the Marketplace

There are a couple of golden rules in software. First, take care of your customers. They go away very quickly if you don't. Customers are quite fickle if they're not taken care of. Second, keep your products up to date, otherwise there's always that competitor right behind you. There's always a competitor in every sector. Don't think you're the only one. That's a big mistake.

If you are a brand new software company, you had better figure out how you're going to distribute your product. You may have the world's greatest mousetrap, but, today, you'd better figure out how you're going to sell it. The doors are not so open to everyone that you can go in and say, "Here's my great mousetrap. The world will come to me." That's not the way it works. Most new software companies start out with stars in their eyes: "I've got the greatest product. You can't live without it." That's just a small part of the question. The real question is: How are you going to distribute the product? That's where the attention should be put.

Every software company is always reading the tea leaves. You're reading the analysts' reports, you're talking to your customers, you're going to trade shows. You just have to be out in the market. If you're out in the market, you get the drift of what's going on. That's how software works — just like any other business. If you can anticipate changes in advance, then you can have a product available that rides the wave.

Our strategy for the future is based on a number of things. We're not going very far out in the future. If someone asked me in 1994 to give them a five-year plan, I would have been 1,000 per cent wrong because no one would have predicted the Internet. Everything changed when the Internet came in, so everyone's plans were wrong. You can't plan too far ahead in technology because there are too many uncertainties. But you do plan ahead some length in time because you do see trends of where things are going. We're always reading the teas leaves, figuring out where things are going, and we're trying to position ourselves to be there. But it's not more than a year ahead. Two years ahead, yes, we're thinking about it. Five years ahead — no.

I remember when we first started in 1975, I was talking to an executive who asked how it was going. I said, "We sold our first system last month." He said, "There's a huge difference between zero and one. You have no idea how far ahead you've moved because of that difference." I always think about that. It's so true. In some sense, that's my advice. When you can sell something that's ready to be sold, it's a huge step forward.

A lot of people will show you prototypes, but they just talk a good story when they never have anything to sell. Their demos are always nice, but they never get the product to the point where people really can sell. That's why there is such a huge difference between things that are saleable and things that are demoed. There are a lot of demos in software that we called slideware: "I'll show you my presentation in PowerPoint." I want to see a working product that is saleable. That's a big difference.

Right now times are much harder; people are not spending their money so easily. My advice is probably directed to what you have to do to get people to open their pocketbooks more. In the software business you have to know what you're selling; you've got to know your product inside and out to represent it and sell it. That's a piece of advice I always give, even to the salespeople. You really have to know what you're selling. The days of just being a spiel artist are over.

When I started this business in 1975, there were no stores that sold packaged software. In fact, when we would go to sell a product in 1975, potential buyers would say, "Why would I want to buy software? I have programmers." It was later, particularly when PCs came in, that you could buy software at a store. The industry had already matured by that point and they knew that to get software, you go to the store and buy it, not programming it yourself. The newest thing is buying software over the Internet. That's just another way to buy software and I think that has enlarged the market. The total marketplace has gotten bigger, but the fundamental difference in buying software occurred much earlier. It is just that the method of distribution has changed by being able to get it on the Internet. You can download it yourself in many cases. It's a little easier to use; there's a lot of emphasis on making it easier so people don't need as much help.

There is no doubt that software is going to invade many products in which you can just see the tip of the invasion. Cameras, for example, are going to get a lot smarter now that you can put so much information on a chip. I think we're going to start to see very much smarter gadgets. Everything is going to be smarter. They're already starting to put chips on all the items in a store instead of tags. The tags will have chips and the way you do inventory is you turn on a machine and tell it to read all the tags in the store. Then, boom, you have your inventory. I think the area of computers invading our everyday life is just starting. We think of computers as being that big box under our desk. When I was a kid, my parents and great-grandparents had radios the size of the refrigerator. In ten years, people are going to look at computers from today and say, "Look at that big computer!" We're going to think of them as really strange things because computerization is going to be in everything you touch. Computers will be down to the size of a tiny card or CD. You can put gigabytes of storage on your fingernail, practically. Yes, you need a place to put cards and such, but by and large, as these things get standardized, computers will not only be little things that you have on your desk; they will be in everything that you do. It's starting already. Slowly, we are beginning to see the computerization of everything. We've got all the factors: miniaturization, huge storage capabilities, very cheap chip production, a communication course of practically down to zip. We're going to see all kinds of computer invasion in our lives.

Biography

Gerald D. Cohen is President and CEO of Information Builders, Inc., the global leader in Web-based business intelligence, and CEO of iWay Software, an Information Builders subsidiary specializing in enterprise integration. Information Builders was founded in 1975 to provide an innovative way for people without formal computer programming skills to work with information systems. Since then, the company's solutions have been used to construct business intelligence systems for tens of thousands of leading companies, universities, and government agencies around the world, and to help them leverage existing systems to meet new business challenges.

Mr. Cohen is a frequent speaker and published writer on the topic of information technology. In 2001, he was named one of the 'Most Powerful Leaders in IT' by Enterprise Systems. A native of Manhattan and lifelong New York City supporter, Mr. Cohen serves as the chairman of the New York Software Industry Association and has been honored with the prestigious New York Academy of Sciences Mayor's Award for excellence in technology.

Chapter 11

Closing the Gap between What Technology Can Do and What People Want It to Do

Dr. Carl S. Ledbetter

CTOs get to help make the future, and most often they do that by explaining what technology can do. I'm a scientist by training, education, and nature, but my background for that is probably a little unusual. I was a philosophy major throughout most of my college years, and my family upbringing wouldn't have suggested a career in technology. My father was a minister, a preacher — and a very scholarly one, the kind who had degrees in ancient Greek and Hebrew and church history. His sermons, which I listened to every Sunday until I left home for college, were always on abstruse, arcane subjects out of the Bible, such as the translation of a particular word from Hebrew and how it applied to the topic of his sermon that day. Interestingly, though, about midway through every sermon I ever heard him preach, he would depart briefly from his scholarly presentation to perform a magic trick in the pulpit. The tricks were all different — I never saw the same one twice — and each of them illustrated by some kind of a topical reference the point he was trying to make in his lesson, something that made the very technical, intellectual, academic subject come alive in a visual way that people would remember. The result is that his congregation was always packed, and people were sitting on the edge of their seats until he did his trick.

What that taught me, almost intuitively, instinctively, is that the way you make difficult subjects clear to lay people is by using analogies, stories, and references to things they know and understand. If you amuse them, entertain them, make them laugh, you also make them understand what's important, even if what matters is otherwise very difficult, complicated, even beyond ordinary understanding. In my case it's technology I'm trying to explain, rather than religion (and I note that my subject is far easier than my father's), and the task is to render accessible to lay audiences what is technically difficult — to show them the heart of the matter as it applies, or will apply, to their lives and interests, without resorting to all the techno-babble that many technologists in the industry fall into instinctively. Such mumbo-jumbo obscures the real issue behind technical language you don't really need to know to understand the main themes in the evolution of technology and what it can do. So because of that lesson my father unknowingly taught me, I have always stood with one foot pretty comfortably in the technical arena and the other in what you'd have to call marketing — by which I mean the ability to explain what the technology is about, how it works, why it's important, and how to use it in a way that doesn't require the listeners to have a Ph.D. to understand. I look for ways to do that and admire it when someone else does.

For example, recently I was in Toronto at a huge conference on e-government. E-government is a catch-all phrase for how you use the computer and the Internet to interconnect everybody to everything they want or need to do with the government. Canada's vision is quite stunning; they call it "One Window, No Wrong Doors." You log onto the Net and go to Canada. You want a fishing license, you get a fishing license; you want a driver's license, you get a driver's license; you want a passport, you get a passport. It's a matter of indifference to the citizen that the fishing license is issued by a local jurisdiction, the driver's license by a province, and the passport by the Canadian federal government. The Canadian government realizes the citizen shouldn't need to know which jurisdiction is responsible for which government activity — it's likely even the government can't keep it straight. So Canada's idea is a wonderful concept, but even better is that they would present this to Canadian citizens in the "One Window, No Wrong Doors" format. This invites citizens to come to the Net to work with the Canadian government, without confusing the issue with a lot of unnecessary complications. This approach says, "Just look in the window the government provides, and we'll get you to the right place, even if you're not a computer expert." So when I went to Canada to explain Novell's role in this new way of thinking about the Net and how Canadians will be able to use it for government services, I needed a way to make this approach clear without being overly technical.

My way of explaining how this would happen, being faithful to the technical potential without exposing all its complexities, was to take up a Rubik's Cube. (I actually wrote the solution book to that more than 20 years ago.) I tossed the Cube into the audience and had people scramble it up, and then during the course of the speech, I solved the Cube in front of them, using it as a prop to make clear how a hard problem can be broken down into easy-to-understand-and-execute phases, and then I tossed it back at the end of the speech completely restored. I doubt that anybody will ever forget the demonstration, but more importantly, they will remember the parable. What I did was a way of saying, "Here's why it's hard. Here's how you attack it. Here's how you do it." If you attack the Cube in some random fashion, you're never going to solve it — it would take you, on average, 1.8 billion years to finish it if you did it that way. And learning the technology — the mathematics of group theory — to solve it on your own is a daunting multi-year effort for math majors. But we solved it in considerably less time than the speech, of course, and the analogy to how Canada can solve the problem of creating e-Government access for all Canadians within four years was clear. I joked that I wouldn't take too long to solve the Cube because I didn't want them to miss lunch, and their politicians didn't want to take too long to provide Net access to the Canadian government because they didn't want to miss reelection.

Overcoming People's Intimidation by Technology

People are intimidated by what they don't understand, and more so if they believe that what they don't understand is important to their success. The difficulty in getting people to feel comfortable around technology is what C. P. Snow called the problem of two cultures — for him these were the scientific and the literary cultures; they would probably be better described as the technical and the non-technical now. The real issue is that scientists and engineers think things are important if they're technically interesting. But most people think things are important if they're useful. And those are not the same thing at all because frequently being technically interesting means being inaccessible to those who are not technologists.

When I became president of the consumer division of AT&T, one of the first things that happened was that someone from marketing brought me an ad they had been working on before I arrived, something they were very excited about. The advertising agency was coming to show me this wonderful new creative piece to get the buy-in from the new president of the division. The ad was part of what AT&T called the "You Will" campaign. It was a vignette of someone on the beach, holding a computerized slate, similar to what we would now call a PDA. The ad said, "Have you ever received a fax from the beach?" And the tag line was, "You will." My answer to the ad executives was, "Gee, I hope not."

What that ad did was confuse what we can do technologically with what we want to do in real life. Why in the world would you want a fax from your boss at the beach? The issue is not technical; it's sociological. What exactly is the protocol when your boss wants to get you, when he knows he can reach you, when he can even confirm that he has reached you, that you have the message, but you won't answer him? You're on vacation. You don't want that fax. What exactly do you say to him? What's your excuse for not responding? There has to be a sociological convention for this; having the technical capability to send faxes to the beach is not the same thing as wanting it to happen.

If you look far enough back in time, you can find an industry that has gone through the phase we're in now in the computer industry, and beyond it, so you can see the effect. Look at the turn of the century — the last one, the early 1900s. The automobile industry was at a nascent stage; it had some interesting things going on, with Ford Motor Company, in particular. I often ask technical audiences when I'm giving speeches to engineers, "What's the most important invention in the history of the automobile industry?" And I get all kinds of interesting answers: internal combustion engines, independent suspension, automatic transmission, radial tires, even tubeless tires sometimes if someone is really thoughtful about what was going on back then. But I think the answer is none of those, and it's not limited slip-differential or fuel injection, either.

The most important technical inventions in the history of the automobile industry are the electric starter and the enclosed cab. Those inventions meant you didn't have to be an engineer or a hobbyist to use the car anymore. Because of those innovations, the wives of the hobbyists (they were almost all men then) could, and would, ride in the car. Because of those innovations, the automobile was transportation instead of engineering. Only when you didn't have to crank the stupid engine outside to get it started — you could push a button to make the machine run, and then get inside the relatively comfortable cab to go somewhere — was the car useful, and therefore interesting, to non-engineers; the electric starter made the automobile accessible to the masses. Because they could ride inside the cab, where they wouldn't get their hair blown into a mess by the wind, the automobile became comfortable to use for ordinary people, rather than a hobbyist's plaything. In other words, it wasn't a really big technical breakthrough that made the automobile industry economically successful, and it wasn't a technical innovation that made it acceptable for large groups of non-technical users — it was something that made the car easy to use for the average person.

The most important insight I think we've had today in the technology industry is that our computers are plenty capable enough technically; they're just so damned hard to use that they're infuriating! I've been using these machines since 1970-something — before my kids were born, and they're 22 and 20 now. I used to think that every good software development kit had a soldering iron in it. But even I can't do that anymore. If I install some new software application, or some Microsoft upgrade, or a new system utility on one of my machines, everything breaks for weeks. I just can't stand it.

We cannot have that if we hope to take the industry to the next stage. The most important thing we have to understand about what will happen in the technology industry is that we will be successful only when we stop designing things for engineers — we have to start designing them for my mother.

I started taking PCs home to my mother about ten years ago. I set the first one up for her, so she could do e-mail with her six kids — I got her a PC, a modem, an ISP connection, and the right software, and made sure it worked, showing her how to use it to send e-mail. She was delighted. But after a few days or a couple of weeks, I'd stop getting e-mail from her, and when I'd go back to visit, every two or three months, the thing was out in the garage. "What's the problem?" I'd ask. "Well, I was using it just like you said, and I got this blue screen, and something said I had a 'fatal error,' so I figured it was dead, and I put it away." All she knew was that it didn't work anymore, and she didn't have a clue how to fix it. She couldn't use it. The instruction manuals were useless — they were a foreign language to her and didn't tell her what she needed to know to bring the machine back to life. "I can't even understand the Table of Contents or the Index", she said. "How can I figure out what to do?" And it's not that she's stupid; she's just the way everyone else in the world is, except the handful of us who are basically geeks.

When my son was about 13, it was time for him to go out and get his own first software program, one that he would buy with his own money, so I took him down to the software store for what turned into a two-hour session. He had to look at every box in the store, of course, all the games, and then he bought the one he liked best. He brought it home and put the disk in the drive (this was in the days before CDs). There was a great big, slick manual in the fancy box, and it immediately went over his shoulder into the pile of blue jeans and t-shirts, never to be seen again, and he started hammering on the mouse. I said, "Don't you want to read the instructions?" And he said, "Dad, instructions are for wimps." And he was right. That's what people do. If you can't figure it out by looking at it, you're not going to fool with it, and that's the most important lesson for technologists and engineers to learn. Even online instructions are a mistake — making instructions and help files more accessible is dead wrong; what we need to do is make them unnecessary.

I was riding in an airplane a few years ago and saw what was probably the single most important instruction guide I've ever seen — I understood what this industry's problem was in a heartbeat. I was on a flight to Europe, where they pass out those little foil-wrapped packages of lotion-saturated tissues to clean your hands with after a meal. This one was called a Wet-Nap. As I was fumbling with it, I saw the directions, which read, in their entirety, "Directions for use: Open and use." That's it. Open and use. No other instructions necessary. If we could get this Wet-Nap interface into what we do technologically, we would be winners. Almost all the innovation and brain power that will be applied successfully in the next three to five years in this industry will be used to close the gap between what technology can do and what people want it to do, and to making it easy, which is to say obvious, to use.

Defining Success as a CTO

Ultimately to be a success as a CTO, you have to make the company successful by aiming it in a direction that will be fruitful for the development of technologies that customers will want to pay for. At the end of the day, I work for a company, so I work for shareholders, and it's my job to help make the company successful. But that task is really one of choosing main directions and grand themes, to seek out the right path for a time two or three years down the road, rather than next quarter.

To do this successfully, CTOs of the major technology companies have a responsibility greater than to their own companies. That responsibility is to help the industry, the governments that regulate it, and all the other components that are associated with that enterprise aim in the right direction and think of things in the right way.

For instance, we're all now very interested in what we generically call "security issues" on the Internet. But I think that largely we worry about the wrong things. Encryption technology — the worry about whether your credit card number gets stolen — that's really not as big a problem as people generally think. The SSL link — you don't even need to know what that is, but it's basically secure server technology for transmitting your credit card number, for instance — is sufficient for most purposes. I'm not worried about handing my credit card to Amazon.com over an SSL link. I'd be a lot more worried about handing my actual credit card to the 18-year-old kid who just graduated from high school who's the waiter at the restaurant I went to last night. He can take my card to the back of the kitchen and make a rubbing of the number a lot more easily than anyone can pick it off from Internet traffic.

The real issue to consider in Internet security, for everything we do, in commerce and in the very important things that are emerging in health care and government use of records, is the privacy of those transactions and records once they are securely transmitted. Privacy is really about the management of a trade-off between the risk of giving others information about yourself so you can make things you want to do easier to do, and the risk that the information you supply in this way will be misused or abused in a way you don't want, by someone you don't intend to have it or isn't authorized to use it. This privacy issue is much more of a boogeyman than what we call the security issue.

A year-and-a-half or so ago, someone in the press found out and revealed that some Internet sites were parking special kinds of cookies on your disk. Cookies are small collections of information that are stored on your disk to remember certain things about you to make it easier to navigate and transact on the Net; they overcome the limitation of the fact that your transactions on the Net are stateless — every page, every hit is new news to the site you're on, unless there is a way to remember something about who you are, what you have done there in the past, and where you came from. Cookies are very intrusive in and of themselves, but the penalty for not permitting them is that you really can't use the Internet for most useful kinds of commerce, and even having your machine warn you when they are being parked on your disk is an unacceptable annoyance, especially when most people don't even know what cookies do or understand what accepting them means. Go look on your browser at the file that contains your cookies; you'll likely be stunned at how many are there and where they came from.

But some sites were doing worse than just putting cookies on your machine: They were also watching what you did while you were out at other sites on the Internet, collecting that information, and sending it back the next time you landed on the cookie's originating site. Horrible! They were spying on you, and they were using your own PC to do it to you, without your consent, without even your knowledge. And they were both using the knowledge about where you went for their own purposes and also selling that information to people and businesses whose sites you probably would never have visited. It was intrusion of the worst possible sort, invasion of privacy that is wholly and entirely unacceptable. Now, these companies, when caught, promised they wouldn't do that anymore, and I hope and expect that these particular sites do not. But others might, and do.

The real issue with this is that there are ways to intrude on your privacy that you would neither tolerate nor permit, if you knew about them, which can be hidden by the technology, and they are still being exploited on the Net. We have to be very vigilant about these kinds of intrusion and ensure that people are made fully aware of what is at stake.

And there are other kinds of intrusion that are, if not as explicitly unethical, at least as objectionable. There are sites that force what are called pop-ups, or, worse, pop-unders. These are windows that are spawned by an originating window you've opened, either on purpose or accidentally, and parked either on top of the original window or underneath the one you're looking at, and which may continue to generate a storm of other windows being opened, essentially taking over your machine by launching windows faster than you can close them. This technique is like nothing so much as a door-to-door salesman who not only knocks on your door to sell you something, but kicks in the door, forces his way in to your house, and trashes the furniture, even when you've told him no. The industry has to drive this kind of behavior out of existence. It's one of the few places where technology needs the government to protect users from the abuse by its misapplication.

Even the issue of "opt-in/opt-out" I find infuriating. These terms refer to the two ways that have been proposed to handle the most common of the intrusions computer technology enable, the creation of mailing lists that can be used to solicit us with e-mail. The worst offence is spamming, the widespread practice of sending out thousands, even millions, of e-mails to a long list of addresses, to solicit something, but even more targeted mailings can be objectionable. Opt-in means that you get such e-mails only if you explicitly request them; opt-out means you get them unless you explicitly tell them not to e-mail you. In my view, the opt-out approach is hideously burdensome. It's like saying anyone can force you to waste your time figuring out how to get off unwanted mailing lists. The advocates for the opt-out make the argument that opt-out is the better technology because it is better for business and is closer to the laws that permit junk mail. But, of course, consumers hate junk mail, and the analogy is flawed because there is at least a barrier to junk mail in that it is costly to produce and deliver, much costlier than the e-mail equivalent. Almost all consumers would prefer opt-in, getting advertising materials, e-mails, solicitations, information, only from sites and about subjects they are interested in and have requested. I don't mind having Mountain Tools or Black Diamond Equipment send me information on their products because I'm an avid mountain climber, and I like receiving information from them. I sign up for their catalogs; I shop at their sites; I give them certain information about myself because I want to. But I don't want to be inundated by information about insurance, how to make a million dollars at home stuffing envelopes, chain letters, and worse. That stuff is just infuriating. And it's hard, and time-consuming, to figure out how to get off their lists, and sometimes it's essentially impossible — just sending them an e-mail telling them to quit it is difficult to do and may even generate even more unwanted e-mail because sending a reply, even if it's to say Stop! has the unintended effect of confirming that the e-mail address is a legitimate one that can be sold to others. The only acceptable technology is to require opt-ins, rather than permitting opt-outs, but I predict it will be a long battle. These junk e-mails, and spamming in general, ought to be prohibited by law and excluded by technological means when possible.

Those are the kinds of issues we need to be worried about. CTOs in the industry need to make sure we're talking about them in ways that will help the government and members of society who are not technologically inclined understand what is at stake, so they can make the right choices and force the right legislation.

Exciting Technologies in the Works

I travel all over the world, and I do so, essentially, with two documents: I have a driver's license for use inside the US and when I'm getting on airplanes, and I have a passport that will get me into most countries. So I can cruise across almost any border in the world, and I'm able to identify myself and transact whatever business I want when I'm traveling by using just those two documents.

When I'm on the Internet, it's a very different thing entirely. The Internet is supposed to have made the world smaller, to have eliminated borders, and to a large extent it has, but it hasn't made it much easier to do business while you're out there. The problem on the Net, as it turns out, isn't access, it's identity. I don't even have one name on the Internet. I was actually looking into this for a speech I gave recently, and I counted all the names I had in my various relationships on the Internet. I found I had 36 different ones — not different passwords, different names. Sometimes I'm Carl Ledbetter; sometimes I'd have to separate my first and last names with an underscore; sometimes I have to use a space; sometimes my names are concatenated; and on and on. I've even learned there are several other Carl Ledbetters in the U.S., so sometimes I have to use my middle initial to distinguish myself, and there are even four other Carl S. Ledbetters, so I have to use my full middle name or some other differentiator, and with all of these I have the underscore, space, concatenation issue to contend with. When it's all added up, I have so many names I can't remember which one I am on any given site, especially the sites I visit only infrequently. When you add in the more than 70 different passwords I have, there are nearly 2,500 different user name-password combinations that are possible from among the ones I actually use. And the passwords change all the time, so my big yellow sheet of paper is all scratched up and hard to read. It's a wonder I can do anything at all on the Net. So I do what all of us who are concerned about computer security tell people not to do — I put the user names and passwords I use on a big piece of paper and tape it to the side of my monitor — where they can be seen by anyone even mildly interested in stealing my identity, thereby compromising the security provisions that protect me, to be able to get to those sites at all. What a nightmare.

Recently, I was trying to get on to a service that handles my kids' tuition, and it asked me for my user name, so I could check to make sure the deductions had started. I tried three or four times and couldn't get in, and then, because I had made the maximum number of attempts permitted, I got locked out. I had to make a phone call to get help at the service, and you know how harrowing a process it is to get a live person these days. That company spent a lot of money, and I spent a lot of time — and was pretty irritated while I did it — just trying to make sure I could pay my bill. How dumb is that? They made me fight to pay them money — all because I didn't know my own name on the Net. So I can't travel around the Internet the way I do around the world because I don't have the right to my own name and can't remember the information I need to authenticate my identity.

What we really need is illustrated in a great line from a movie several years ago, *The Adventures of Buckaroo Banzai Across the Eighth Dimension* — "No matter where you go, there you are." That's what happens when I travel the world with my passport: No matter where I go, there I am, and I know my name, I have credentials to transact business, and my identity can be authenticated reasonably well by whatever gate-keeping authority is checking. I want to do the same thing on the Internet. I want to be able to make a claim about my identity and to have as many identities as I want — because I may have good reason for having several different personalities or roles that I want to distinguish. I want to make sure the agency of authorization can identify me correctly and that I'm authenticated by reasonable means at some level of assurance that may vary by purpose and mechanism of authentication. And then, now that I'm on the Internet, I want to be able to move around without being pestered over and over again for the identity and authentication credentials I've already presented. From the time I'm in and authenticated, almost all the dot-coms should accept me for who I am. If the authentication is at a high enough grade — maybe just knowing my password is good enough for some purposes, but knowing other information, having a smart card, or presenting biometric information like a fingerprint or retinal scan could be required for other more sensitive and secure applications — there ought to be a secure-certificate technology that makes sure my identity and authentication, with all the rights and privileges of access I'm allowed from that, gets handled correctly and handed off as I instruct, so I don't have to do it again. My one-time authentication ought to be enough to allow me to navigate around the Internet's electronic world, just as my passport allows me to travel around the physical world.

I think the thrust of the next five to ten years will be to make that vision a reality. No matter where you go, there you are, on the Internet. The industry will create software components that make this happen without forcing customers to jump through a lot of hoops or know a lot of things.

Positioning Your Company for Change

One of a CTO's most important roles is positioning his or her company for changes that are likely to happen. The CTO is an internal evangelist, as well as an external spokesperson. You have to rally the engineers and the business people inside a company to understand the big scene: Why is this market going to make it? Why is it productive for us to spend resources in one arena, rather than another? What technology choices should we make, and what will that technology do to solve a real problem that matters, that has economic value?

There's a story that Warren Buffett used to decide which companies to invest in by listening to what products his wife and her friends were talking about — what was going on in the grocery store and at the shopping mall. That's a very important part of the issue: What is actually happening in the real world, as opposed to what technical things are the engineers interested in?

We spend far too much time looking in the mirror, thinking we're seeing the rest of the world. We're not watching what other people — non-technical people — are doing. Amazingly, technical people often argue with others about what they should want to do with technology, surely a losing argument every time it occurs. It's the same problem the automobile industry had when it was still making cars for hobbyists instead of their wives. We have to figure out how to make machines for people who don't care how the technology works.

I saw one of the most brilliant technology advertisements ever a few years ago, for a satellite TV service. It was for Hughes Direct Broadcast Satellite TV, which was one of the companies that started that whole industry. In the commercial, an actor came out and started talking about "Direct Broadcast Satellite" — using that technological word, "satellite" — but then he immediately stopped talking about the technology and asked, "You like movies? We have 250 movies, ready at any time. You like basketball games? From Gonzaga University?" When do you ever get to see Gonzaga University play on TV, except maybe during March Madness? Are you a displaced Broncos fan, living in New York, who wants to see the Denver Broncos play Seattle when they're showing the Jets against Miami where you live? With Direct Broadcast Satellite, you can use an easy little index to choose what you want to see, and you have hundreds and hundreds of choices. Then the actor said, "How do we make all this happen?" He started to turn around, and behind him, an old-fashioned green chalkboard appeared and filled up with a bunch of equations — real ones — any technologist would recognize the Schroedinger Wave Equations, Maxwell's Equations, some phase-shift calculations, things that really do matter to making the technology work — but the actor looked back at the camera and said, "I have absolutely no idea."

The supremely important subliminal message there is that some very smart people who understand this technology were back there working on this. They got it to work. But you and I don't need to know how they did it. What you need to know is that you can watch Gonzaga play basketball on TV tomorrow if you want to, or see Gone With the Wind, and all you have to do is push a few simple buttons.

That's the technology story we have to get to: Make the technology easy to use for people who don't care about technology, and then technology will succeed. Try to make technology for the geeks, and you'll satisfy only the geeks. The job of technologists is to make technology invisible in any application. The way to make it useful is to make it disappear from view. Almost everyone drives a car in this country, but almost no one can tell you what kind of transmission is in it. What are the gear ratios? How many quarts of transmission fluid? My point is that this is a good thing. Transmissions are crucial for automobiles. Once they were the subject of important engineering innovations on the leading edge of automotive technology. But they became most important when they disappeared from view, when they were not only automatic, but also invisible.

Taking the Right Technology Risks

With one very interesting exception, the only real judgment that can be applied to taking risks is, Will the product be commercially successful? If you're in business, you're in business to make money, and the shareholders are owed every effort to make a business economically successful so they can be financially successful. So you have to tune the technology risk correctly to get the right thing done for real customers who will want to buy the products and services you offer.

The exception to this is in the realm of public service. Often we learn a lot about how to make successful products by doing something for free in the public interest — things like the Internet grid that attempts to "Fight AIDS at Home." It is perfectly plausible that hundreds of thousands of PCs working part-time when the screen savers are up can actually find some drugs by using the molecular modeling software that pharmaceutical companies use or by searching through the genome information that's now becoming publicly available. We'll actually find some things just by brute force by exploiting the idle time of machines that are temporarily or intermittently under-employed, and I think that's a useful thing for the industry to support, endorse, and find ways to enable. But principally, companies won't be around to help in those kinds of projects unless they make money with what they do, and you make money only by finding markets that go beyond the early adopter phase. And to do that, you have to create technologies that make non-technical people capable of something economically valuable, in which the enabling technology is so good that it disappears.

Best Business Advice

When I was a young, second-line manager at IBM, I made a major presentation to my boss's boss's boss's boss on a big project I wanted funded. It was a big deal for me, and I worked a long time on the presentation. I thought it was absolutely terrific; it was slick; it was right; and it was the right thing for the company to do. But I was running against a tide I didn't really understand at the time. IBM was having a rough quarter, and there were some political issues afoot, and I couldn't get the full attention of the division president when these other things were on his mind; he was too distracted. He liked it, but he wasn't going to fund it just then because he couldn't afford to put it in the budget. So I got sent home to do some more work and more study, and come back in six months to see if we could do it then.

I was bummed out by this and probably a little surly in the next few meetings I had that day, and I was a little distracted myself. The next morning, I was a little overly curt in a meeting with my staff. My secretary at the time had been with IBM for 25 years, so basically I reported to her — she knew more about the company than I did. She had worked for a lot of very senior IBM executives on their way up through jobs like the one I was in, so she knew everybody. After that morning meeting, I went back to my office and was working on some e-mails, when she came in to ask if she could talk to me for a second. When she had my attention, she looked me right in the eye and said, "You have 120 people reporting to you. When you have a bad day, they all have a bad day. Knock it off." And then she left.

Hers was exactly the right advice. People who are in positions of leadership and authority have a duty and responsibility far beyond what they feel like personally. There's a continuity issue associated with it: Leadership requires that you stay on your game all the time. I used to joke with my wife that every time I'd go with her to the mall in blue jeans on a Saturday morning, I was absolutely certain to run into someone I knew from work. There's never a private moment, and that's an important business message. You're always on.

Managing in a Turbulent Market

I think there is an interesting sense in which people are always over-optimistic at the same time they are also over-pessimistic. I've said often that the Internet is the most over-hyped technology in the history of the world, but it's also the most under-estimated. Not only does the market swing from extreme to extreme, but also people's sense of what's going to happen swings from extreme to extreme. And there's a kind of counter-intuitive way you should manage particular technology investments because of that.

When things are just blowing the lid off, like during the go-go days of the dot-com bubble, rather than going out and hiring like crazy and making more investments in wilder and wilder things, you should start to pull back, start inspecting everything you do with a much sharper eye, start cutting back programs, and be much more skeptical about what's going on.

Conversely, when everything is in the dumps, pour on the coal. Now that the Internet bubble has burst, it's time to hit hard with investments in technology. Things are cheap. Innovation has slowed. What we do now has a better chance to win because it's not as obscured by clutter and nonsense, if we're doing smart things. You need to be counter-cyclical to the way the world thinks things are happening. This is the very best time to invest in the market. It's the very best time for venture capital, the very best time for technology.

People will be successful in this market — just not this month. But this is the time decisions are being made, technologies are being developed, investments are being placed on things we'll be talking about in three years. It doesn't happen over night. Nobody invents something as complex as the things we're working on now in an afternoon. What's being invented now will be suddenly important when they are mature, and it will look like an explosion of creativity and innovation again, but it is really happening very quietly right now.

Becoming a Technology Leader

Although I learned a lot of things at IBM that were very important, this is something I learned that was wrong, and knowing that it's wrong is one of the most important lessons I ever learned. IBM at that time had a particular philosophy of professional management. They believed that management was itself a discipline, so if you can learn to manage something well, you can manage anything well. I think that's not true. My advice to anyone who wants to be in an important role, whether in technology, or finance, or sales, or marketing, or whatever, is that within your general discipline, you need to be really good at something. It doesn't matter what it is — but you do need to be good at it, and it has to be something of substance, something that's hard to master, something that matters. You have to have earned your credentials, made your mark, gotten your stripes, from having been at the very top of some important subcategory of the discipline you're in, or else you can't possibly understand how to manage things that are on the cutting edge of the larger enterprise you're going to lead.

In my case, as a technologist, I have a Ph.D. in mathematics; I studied computer architectures; I had a very, very successful machine program at IBM; and there are other successes I've had in my career. I've earned a kind of credibility as a result of these successes, with the engineering community, both within my company and in the industry in general, that cannot be won in any other way. It's a kind of a union card, a secret handshake that marks me as a member of a certain society. When I walk into a room full of engineers, they all know who I am and what my background is. Because they know I am a technologist, they think I understand what they're talking about, even if I don't. I can ask unbelievably stupid questions as a result of that, and that's a very important skill. And I will not accept an answer that has any of the technology mumbo-jumbo or acronyms that the computer industry uses. "Enterprise application integration?" What the hell is that? I don't have a clue, and anyone who uses these terms is probably masking a lack of real understanding behind industry buzzwords. No one ever challenges those kinds of things unless they're confident they understand the technology they're working on. It's important to be good enough at something that you're not worried about looking stupid.

About 1994, I was talking to some very senior AT&T executives, trying to explain what was going to happen with IP — the Internet Protocol — and ATM — Asynchronous Transfer Mode, a cell-switching network standard — which are underneath all we do on the Net. I asserted that it would become a substitute for voice, and anybody who was going to be moving bits around on big backbones was going to get ranked into a commodity vendor, which is exactly what has happened to AT&T in the last seven years. During the course of this explanation, I was talking about the difference between circuit switching, which is the way telephone calls are completed, and packet switching, which is the way the Internet moves packets around. I said IP technology and ATM were going to be alternatives to the way telephone companies switched voice, and that was a threat to AT&T's entire enterprise because anybody who moved bits around would become a commodity supplier of pipes.

During the course of this brief monologue, one of AT&T's most senior executive interrupted me and said, "Carl, this is all very interesting, but we still don't understand what automatic teller machines have to do with telephony." He thought ATM meant "automatic teller machine", the machines that dispense cash at your bank. A senior executive in the largest telecommunications company in the world didn't know the technology that was about to clean his clock. He has since gone on to another telecom enterprise, which has failed miserably, and I don't doubt why. He doesn't get it. He didn't have enough technology — specific expertise to make good decisions or to understand what was going to happen to telecommunications technology. He might have been a great manager in another industry, but not in this one. The skills are not transferable.

You cannot understand this industry if you don't know certain things about the technology that underlies it. You don't need to rub people's faces in technology; you don't need to have the customers understand it to be successful — in fact, that would be an impediment. But you have to have that union card. You have to be credible. You have to know enough about how things work that you can make reasonable decisions about the way the technology will go. You have to be really good at something.

Keeping Your Edge

I read constantly. I use the technologies constantly. And believe it or not, I watch other people constantly. In my kids' dorm rooms in their first years of college, I watched them play with their computers, and I noticed the things they did. I noticed, for example, the rise of the Napster phenomenon and of peer-to-peer sharing of files because they were doing it. I watched instant-messaging technology because they used it and said it would be killer. The kids keep these windows open on their desktops all the time, carrying on interrupted two-way conversations with a dozen or so people at one time, while they're sitting there doing their homework. That's a very different way of thinking about the world, and unless you actually see it happening, you don't know how it works.

You have to get out of your own environment. You have to watch what real people are doing. And you have to make sure you're drinking your own brew, that you're away from people who are like you. It's sort of like the story about Warren Buffett's wife: Find out what your spouse is doing, rather than thinking that the world is like you.

In the October 1878 issue of Scientific American, there's a story written by a very knowledgeable science writer of that time. It was the first month after the commercial introduction of the telephone from the new American Telephone & Telegraph Corporation. The writer talked about what he and the company thought the main uses of the telephone would be. I was dumbstruck when I read it. He thought the major application of the telephone would be managers of large companies talking to their employees on the assembly line, giving them pep talks and company information. The manager would be up on a balcony overlooking the assembly line, and each of the workers would have a handset. Or people would subscribe to opera, so they could sit around the phone in their home and listen to a performance, or to the broadcast of a baseball game during which they could chat amongst themselves as if they were in the stands.

What the article missed was that telephony was a brand-new means of private two-way communication that meant that two people who were not in the same room could have a conversation no one else could hear. There was no paradigm for this at all at the time. The paradigm that did exist was the new radio broadcast technology, so this new telephony idea was inappropriately shoehorned into that format in the speculations of even pretty savvy observers. Who would have thought back in the late 1800s that there would be billions of telephones in the world today? There was no way to think of that, no experience that predicted it.

What we often miss with new technologies is their eventual real use and importance. The way to stay sharp is not by studying journals, but by watching what people do — observing the sociological implications of technological change.

The Golden Rules and Skills of the CTO

The most important skill a CTO can have is to be able to understand technology well enough that you can explain it to people without having to go into acronyms and mumbo-jumbo. You should be able to do it with metaphors and analogies in a way that makes technology clear not only to the people who are not technologists, but also to technologists who are in related areas but are not themselves experts in your specific field of reference. You should be able to give people a sense of confidence in understanding how the pieces all fit together. This is so important. It's what distinguishes a CTO as a public spokesperson from someone who is a great development manager, for instance, for software or hardware devices.

You can do those other jobs and be able to talk about XML and TCP/IP; you can't do a chief technology officer's job if that's all you can do. You have to be able to make it sing for people who don't know the tune. They may never know the words, but it's important for them to be able to hum it.

But you also have to have that union card, that fundamental indicator of credibility. Engineers love it when a technical person succeeds in business. That's why there's something approaching hero-worship of the geeks who actually make it to the top of a business enterprise from the engineering community. It's fun for them to see someone who comes out of their world succeed in a different way. But the reason some can do that is that they can find ways to articulate those technology visions that take the technology off the front burner and make it recede into the background.

As a chief technology officer, you also have to keep your head up. Go back to the 1960 presidential debate between Kennedy and Nixon. A major bone of contention in that debate was the fate of Quemoy and Matsu, two little islands out in the China Sea. The moderator posed that question, and these two guys who wanted to be President of the United States of America got down to the nits and bits about these two tiny islands — and that was the last time those islands were ever an important issue in world politics. They basically just didn't matter.

It's way too easy to get caught up in a specific, right-now contention or technical issue and get your head down into those details, with your nose in the dirt, where it doesn't matter. We CTOs have to keep our heads up, so we can see where the ship is going for the long haul. I think we too often get far too embroiled, for instance, in which standard is going to succeed, and that's not what matters. What matters is what the standard is trying to be used for, so we can figure out where the whole enterprise is going. I think the most important golden rule is to keep looking five years out.

The Future of Technology

The single most important issue for technology will be privacy because as soon as people actually understand what's happening to them, there will be outrage and a period of retrenchment and all kinds of regulations; in fact, the government will get into it in ways that we don't want them to. They'll handle it even worse than the industry does today.

Here's another important issue. Human beings are extraordinarily efficient receivers of information. Even when you're sitting around like a couch potato, watching "Ally McBeal", you're getting the equivalent of millions of bits per second because you're seeing a TV picture. We're extremely efficient machines at seeing something and picking out of it what's important, almost without any conscious effort. And we're pretty tolerant, in ways that machines are not, of moderate errors in that. For instance, if there's one bad pixel on the screen you're watching, you probably won't even notice it; you can ignore that input. So we're efficient consumers of high amounts of bandwidth because we can afford to ignore most of the data that's going into that bandwidth. This marvelous brain of ours allows us to figure out what's important and what's not.

So in five to ten years, we're going to have access, everywhere we go, to a six-megabits-per-second continuous stream of information that we can look at. We're not very good at generating information; it takes us a long time to type a document of a few thousand bits. So we don't send very much up individually, but we sure do suck a lot down. The other big technological imperative of the next decade is going to be getting the bandwidth connection secured to be able to get those six megabits everywhere we go. We'll get it wirelessly in many cases. We'll figure out ways to make the investments and to develop the right business model to get that done, so we can look at anything we want to look at, anywhere we want to go.

We bought our kids an encyclopedia when they were around six years old. My kids never looked at it. They don't even look at the dictionary. They look everything up on the Internet — essentially, the new library of Alexandria. We're going to be able to get that everywhere we go. Our kids will carry these tiny devices that will give them information they need anytime they need it, anywhere they are. Six megabits appears to be what it takes to put full-blown, razzle-dazzle, blow-your-eyes-out, full-motion graphics and video onto the device you're looking at. So getting six megabits everywhere is probably all I'm going to care about for a while. And the one piece of dream technology I really would want to help create is one that would let me get those six megabits through the air by a private subscription channel — emphasis on private. I want a completely secure, private mechanism for finding any piece of information in the world, wherever I am. It's the combination of access and privacy in a secure environment that is the greatest technology this generation will produce.

Biography

Carl S. Ledbetter is chief technology officer and senior vice president of Novell, Inc. Joining Novell in 1999, he was chief technology officer and senior vice president, Business and Corporate Development of Novell, responsible for leading Novell's move to a one-Net services approach and championing Novell's open-standards, cross-platform development efforts, including software architecture, strategic partnerships, technology evangelism, and Novell's Venture Fund.

Dr. Ledbetter's experience includes roles as chairman and chief executive office of Hybrid Networks, Inc., an innovator in the wireless broadband industry; as president of AT&T Consumer Products; as leader of Sun Microsystems's PC networking business; and as a principal of Decision Point Consulting. Before joining the computer industry, he taught mathematics at Wellesley College and Clark University, and was academic dean and professor of mathematics at California State University, Sonoma.

Dr. Ledbetter earned his Ph.D. in mathematics from Clark University, his master's degree in mathematics from Brandeis University, and a bachelor's degree in mathematics from the University of Redlands.

Chapter 12

Creating and Enriching Business Value

Richard Schroth

The CTO is one of the key technology leadership positions in many organizations. This position can be defined in many different ways but is most commonly associated with the efforts to advance the technology of a company and to communicate the difficult task of strategic business and technology positioning. The CTO is generally seen as the key individual who helps establish or influence the next generation of technological products and services of the organization.

The title of CTO is being established in more and more organizations as the newest of the senior leadership positions, and generally the CTO serves as a direct report to the CEO. In that regard, I view the CTO as an individual who has the responsibility to help shape and influence both the strategy and processes of the organization, to enrich external client relationships and business value through the smart deployment of technology to solve business problems, and to understand the basic elements of the technology deployed by the organization, both globally and locally.

The CTO must focus on and execute three primary areas of the responsibility. First is understanding and influencing the business strategy and value system of the corporation. Second is continually trying to understand and put into conversational perspective the evolution of the technology as a whole. From this position, the CTO should be able to provide guidance to the company with that knowledge. The third primary responsibility is watching the business processes of the company, both internally and externally, and forming a directional strategy on how to introduce those technologies that will have the most profound effect on aiding in developing new business value and enhancing the business delivery process.

There can be an additional role for the CTO, depending upon the organization and the products or services it provides to the market. Directing the research labs or research activities of an organization is often a significant effort led by the

CTO. This is especially true in technology product-driven companies where proprietary technology innovation is a cornerstone for the evolution of products to the marketplace.

Typically in this role, the CTO spends more attention on the science of the technology and becomes an influencing figure in the work of the laboratories and early product development cycles of the company.

Differentiating the CTO from the CIO

There are clear differences between the CTO's and the CIO's roles and responsibilities. Most of the differentiation is centered on the fundamentals of where they direct their focus, the degree of direct internal and external customer contact, and the planning horizons they hold critical to the business behavior. Typically, the CIO has the overall responsibility to manage the infrastructure of the corporation and deliver the day-to-day technical operations of the corporate needs and the applications that run throughout. Most of the time, the CIO is responsible for the telecommunications and information technologies and the operational service levels that support the entire technological functioning of the corporation. For the most part, the CIO is focused on the internal customer and the electronic linkages between the organization and its business partners.

In contrast, the CTO should be expected to contribute to a broader technology perspective for the company. Additionally, the CTO should play a key role in the overall management team of the company for helping set priorities and directions. When the CTO is an officer of the company, execution of those elements that involve technology or those processes affected by technology are all part of the purview for change by the CTO. Relative to the CIO, the CTO should clearly reflect a more definitive position on the business marketplace, the financial wherewithal and capabilities of the company to acquire or divest, a strong sense of technology's impact on the market drivers of the business, and the product offerings involving technology innovation that are going to affect the market segments in the industry segment.

While the CIO is managing the central IT infrastructure elements, and in many cases some of the application areas, the CTO is working in conjunction with the CIO to help bridge the elements of the business and the research facing elements. An active CTO has a large presence with all types of customer groups inside and outside the company's walls to develop relationships, bridge the technology to large industry plays, gain and test external perspectives, and build back into the company those linkages that connect it with the CTO's network of individuals, companies, and corporate clients.

Defining CTO Success: "The Theory of Three"

I was taught a long time ago about the three-trip/three-month/three-year theory as the most accurate tool to predict the success of the CTO. The three-trip/three-month/three-year theory is all about the relationship of the CTO to the business units of the organization and the value that they create. The theory is based on whether or not you, as the CTO, can engage an executive of the company in a project that requires you to visit three times in three months, and then repeat that frequency for at least three years to report progress of that and other initiatives. If you can go back to that same executive, or the successor, after the three-year period and share the same energy to repeat the relationship, then you are probably on the road to succeeding. If you can repeat the three-trip/three-month/three-year theory with all the divisional heads, and achieve an equally supportive relationship, then you have probably become a critical element of the executive team and would be considered a success in any organization.

It's a simple test, but it's surprising how accurate and difficult it can be. The three-trip/three-month/three-year theory sorts out a CTO's people skills, value creation and contribution methods, technical savvy, change management skills, and, most importantly, devotion to doing the best things for the company.

The Varying Role of the CTO

The concept of a CTO varies widely from company to company. The title of CTO has gone through quite an evolution and continues to evolve. Some of the traditional roles of the CTO still exist in many companies today. Thought of as the deep technology guru of the company, CTOs were sometimes scientists, engineers, or computer science specialists with skills primarily focused on product development, R&D, and possibly a few specialized application areas requiring highly notable skill sets.

Evolution has reshaped this early description and is converting the role to require an understanding of not only the technological implications, but also the process implications brought on by the use of the technology. This evolved position is one of the hardest to fill in organizations today, and the CTO perspective is one of the most sought-after — that of a combined deep understanding of business, business processes, and technology. Adding the ability to communicate to executive audiences increases the rarity substantially.

One of the key drivers of this shift in the role of the CTO is that the business process is starting to integrate more and more technological elements into it, so that it is almost impossible to differentiate the process understanding from the technological capabilities. Under these conditions, the CTO is no longer focused on the application or the technology but attempts to understand the fundamental relationships between the two and the required changes in both to move the company to the next generation of thinking. A bridge has to be developed between a division that is trying to execute a new application and the other elements that it has to go through to change its fundamental process. Some still call this reengineering. My thoughtful and learned colleague, James Champy, one of the inventors of the re-engineering concept, now thinks of it more as X-engineering.

The CTO is also playing a more active roll in the specialized areas of mergers and acquisitions. I find that strong CTOs in many organizations are clearly involved in the acquisition and merger decisions, much more so than a CIO would be. The CTOs go in sometimes as part of the due diligence process. CTOs performing in these capacities are clearly people who have networks and knowledge that can enrich the perspective and the business proposition of the deal. If the deal structure does not appear to create the business value anticipated, they may also propose relationships and alliance structures on behalf of the company. In my mind, the CTO must have the senior business executive skills to shoulder a broader responsibility for the corporate well-being.

The CTO as a Horizon Filter

As the CTO for Perot Systems Corporation, I initially look at things with two very different lenses. These two perspectives are formed around my role to provide service to the corporation and service to the clients with whom we do business.

In filtering the horizon inside the company, I believe that keeping a perspective from 18 months to two years is quite sufficient to allow the corporation the time it needs to prepare for new generations of initiatives. Even with some of the far-reaching technology breakthroughs on the horizon, most corporations will not tolerate significant planning horizons beyond that period. To accomplish longer-range initiatives such as this, I've always believed that research and development, or horizon planning, is done by facing the market, partnering with willing partners, and developing prototypes. Interestingly, real-world industry partnering and implementation can validate directionally and isolate the critical problems from more than one perspective. As you grow the products and technologies externally, and you find that the market has validated the functionality, there's always money for further research and development to take the next steps forward. Stand-alone, self-funded technology research and research and development projects are slowly fading into the distance, becoming the exception in creating business value. Open and partnered projects with longer horizons are always under enough scrutiny that they generally establish the right set of circumstances to make the project ready for the market.

The second filter for looking at the horizon is from the market's perspective. Generally, you should keep a list of five or ten technologies you think are profound. Going into an organization and asking about the most significant technologies an organization believes will affect them gives you a relatively clear sense of what they believe are truly the technologies that are affecting their business. Generally, the two lists match closely. Most of the time, one or two technologies will differ and create an opportunity to explore viewpoints.

A ready-to-go list of the "Ten Most High-Impact Technologies" is a great tool to have in many different situations. These list elements give you a place to start exploratory conversations about business initiatives and technology evolution and serve as a barometer to establish just how much tolerance an individual or organization has for the future and how their perspectives get framed. In using the "Top Ten List", you normally do not start with the list itself but try to establish a set of business conditions that represent the drivers, economic constraints, and value propositions. Once those are established, forming a perspective on how they're going to grow and how their markets will change creates the stories that are needed to frame the fantasy. (No one actually knows the reality, even though they may claim they do.) Bets with world-class "guessers" can bring accuracies up, but the market is the only final determiner of reality.

As you begin to list the technology reformations (the Top Ten List), it becomes very evident that you cannot talk about them without telling a story of some of the marvelous implications that will shift mankind's thinking. If you concentrate on the evolving physics of the technologies over the next generation of its Moore's Law cycles, the size of the shift starts to take on a new reality. But translating the physics into business opportunities is clearly one of the art forms of the CTO.

After the CTO makes these types of translations for many years, the art that actually becomes most useful is the final translation of the technologies into the improbable process changes that can appear somewhat unthinkable. Carefully, the CTO must figure out a way to translate what may seem to be almost a fictional glimpse into a story with a solid market presence and a business value proposition. Unfortunately, the dot-com companies used up a significant amount of credibility for such stories. As a result, many business leaders are exercising a significantly higher level of caution about any predictions they may have to absorb, and their energies for risking such change have dropped considerably.

The second level of screening the new horizon is to understand the relationship between the physics of the technology and the management science of the process. I have given this theory the name of "Process Physics." A basic theory about the evolution of business processes continues to perplex me but has served me well in trying to understand the change business faces on the horizon. I am firmly convinced that when I look at new technologies, I see an interaction between the physics of the technology and the business process itself. When Gordon Moore started to evolve his Moore's Law theory, he laid out the fundamentals of the physics process pretty close to being correct. If this curve continues to track as accurately as it has in the past, we will continue to be able to capture a curve that has a high degree of accuracy in its predictive modeling. From that we can predict a lot of the availability of bandwidth, switching capabilities, or computing power. What he didn't anticipate or didn't focus on was that we would integrate those technology changes much more closely into the business process. In some ways the process itself was a function of the technology.

As a result, the technology shifts that are occurring at these exponential levels have started to push business change to occur at some form of a curve that has a direct relationship to the physics of Moore's Law. If you can isolate fundamental breakthroughs in technology that will occur at these focal points; you can begin to understand processes more completely. Process reinvention is no longer a duplication of the same business functionalities on an incremental scale, but represents a fundamentally new type of re-alignment or restructuring of the business process. This non-incremental opportunity is a direct result of the stage we see occurring in the exponential cycle of Moore's Law.

It is at this predictive juncture of physics and business that the role of the CTO gets much larger and becomes one of a process change agent. Ideally, the relationship the CTO has established with the operating divisions, as well as the staff functions of the organization and the senior leadership team, provides a vantage point for creating change in the organization. At this juncture, the role of the CTO must shift to a business strategy perspective, involving discussions among the senior leaders to begin thinking about the possibilities of change they must confront. It is also at this juncture where the Theory of Three comes into play, as trust and credibility become critical tools for organizations to make progress.

These reinventions of the company's thinking and approaches keep the company competitive and become a defining differentiator between the early job of the CTO and the new, evolving role. As time goes on, these curves will become steeper and steeper. Process has a defined relationship to the physics of technological change.

Pivotal Technologies

There are many pivotal technologies evolving in industry today, but one particular piece of work that has been evolving at the MIT media labs is of particular interest to me. What impresses me the most is not the technology, but the approach to the technology. The approach is to bundle a group of technologies under a functional theme. In the case of this particular research project, the labs have given it the name of "Things That Think."

Defining pivotal technologies under a larger functional umbrella is a significant step forward in understanding the much larger ramifications of their impacts. In this particular case, when you begin to think about the ability of items, from clothing to fixtures, to monitor their environments as well as ours, everything we have around us takes on an interesting importance. The idea that at some point those things can talk back and "think" back is going to be one of our most incredible uses of technology for getting our organizations to the next level of performance.

For example, look at something simple like a shoe that is being experimented on by a number of sports organizations, in particular the NFL. The new shoe is "wired" to provide information about performance. The ability to analyze the performance of athletes in new ways boggles the mind. Impact, speed, performance, distance, and efficiency become new vocabulary words for watching the Sunday NFL games.

Taking this work a step further, some of the biggest breakthroughs in the area of "Things That Think" are occurring in the material manufacturing groups. As of this writing, a small group at Georgia Tech was making significant engineering progress on a wireless shirt. This shirt has the capability to monitor everything from blood pressure to other types of physical features of an individual. The ability of various healthcare organizations to take advantage of such data and begin real-time monitoring of people and their conditions is phenomenal. It's the next generation of what we might expect to see in new forms of remote health care and preventive medicine. Moves like these begin shifting our organizations to more far-reaching concepts, such as "real-time" business.

The other aspect of "theme" technology is the ability to combine various types of evolving technology into an integrated concept. The wider you can find an integration concept like the one above, the better the opportunity to develop a point of view around the conceptual integration. Seeking principles that apply to the opportunity becomes the next level of task. As the principles are derived, the opportunity allows the business leaders to explore their deep concerns about highly relevant management issues that otherwise would never have surfaced. Taking the opportunity to involve the senior leadership whenever appropriate in such planning exercises also allows them to develop an evolving sense of the opportunities that technology and business may present them. This technique also allows them to begin to grasp the complexities that have a high probability of accompanying the process changes needed to support the technological capabilities.

As technology continues to evolve into more complex and efficient propositions, there is a need to ponder the end state for the foreseeable future. Two of the most interesting questions are, "How fast and efficient can we really run a business? Where do the profound possibilities of combining more information-dependent processes and the Moore's Law effect of technology lead us?"

It is at this point that my stake stands in the ground. It is my belief that this is the guidepost for filtering what's on the horizon. The primary thesis that drives my long-term thinking revolves around how companies will begin functioning more and more in real time.

Challenges on the Horizon

Many companies claim they function in real time and that they are real-time companies. From what I can tell, certain elements of companies may have closer to real-time concepts functioning, but we have yet to see the entire company and its surrounding business partners function in real-time in any well coordinated manner. An example of one strategic move that a company might make in real-time business would be to breakthrough the barrier of closing the corporate books in real time. When we can close the corporate books instantly, with accuracy and accountability integrated into the entire process, we will have truly achieved a new milestone in understanding the new directions of business process and technology.

The concept of "real-time business" has as one of its strategic drivers the active role of auditing, as well as revenue tracking, expense management, and inventory control, and all other asset and liability components of the company, so they can be reconciled at any point in time. If that ever occurs, and companies do have the capability of reporting to Wall Street their earnings information in real time, a whole new set of questions will find their way to the corporation's big investors, shareholders, and management — questions such as, "Do we want to trade our companies on an instant basis?" and "If Wall Street rewards that type of trading and behavior, what will companies do that are not capable yet of even thinking like that?" The concepts of "Things That Think" and "Doing Business in Real Time" are two of my ten biggest value themes that enable me to attempt to understand the technologies that are important to deploy both externally and internally and provide a measure for me to gauge how the horizon should be approached.

The Execution of Technology

Perfect execution of technology initiatives and an equally thoughtful effort in the creation of the corresponding business value propositions associated with the execution are the two most important goals an individual or a corporation can have when unlocking the power of an implementation initiative. As a rule of thumb for most corporations, cutting-edge technology deployed in open business environments is a recipe for disaster.

The execution has to do with the level of customer service that is both measured and perceived. Incidentally, lower levels of customer service sometimes established under SLAs never work or are always found unsatisfactory in the long run. Customer feedback (scorecards), the use of constantly monitored feedback mechanisms (dashboards) generated from the system, and employee feedback from those actually doing the work (project review and evaluation discussions) become the cornerstones of good execution and support of major and new technology.

The bottom line on the execution of technology speaks volumes over and over again that nothing less than consistent 100 per cent perfection is the only acceptable way to view the development and deployment of technology. Short of this performance, almost anything can be questioned, be put down, or otherwise fall short of expectations from the user's perception. Interestingly enough, the senior executives who have grown up in an era of some of the first- and second-generation technology deployments find it toughest to bring this level of performance to the foreground and hold company performances to nothing short of perfection. Secondly, this expectation level is also required in reality as we evolve the "real-time business" because, again, a true "real-time business" has no tolerance or latitude for systems that fail, as the majority of system elements are dependent upon 100 per cent uptime.

Privacy Issues

Privacy and the security of information are two of the most significant technology theme elements corporations will face in the next ten years. I think the events leading up to the September 11th bombings and the events after this willful act of terrorism will raise the level of consciousness around the world about accessed information and the information security marketplace. This will especially be true around more and more personally driven elements, such as our individual movements. When I talk about things like the wireless shirt, camera traffic enforcement, or even something as commercial as geo-positioning car navigation systems, the scary thought of "Big Brother" looms ominously in the foreground.

The reality about many of these ubiquitous monitoring systems is that they all are fundamentally information tracking and monitoring tools. Unless the area of privacy is buttoned down much better than it is today, our society will never be able to evolve a certain sanity check for feeling free.

Additionally, no one knows for sure, at any time, where the information really resides, especially when it goes on the Internet. And even with all the attempts to encrypt and protect the privacy of individuals, there are many sloppy systems that have significant flaws. Unfortunately, since these flawed systems exist, records of personal information can permeate the Net without anyone's awareness once the crack in the armor is found. Global presence of networks, including the Internet, now presents surreal catacombs of places to hide and create mischief. Inasmuch as there is no guarantee that the information is riding the network in the US or in any country where it might actually originate, deep and forceful laws are virtually impossible to mandate and enforce.

Protection of individual privacy is something that corporations are doing a moderate job in representing and enforcing. Generally, I believe companies that rally around the concepts of accountability and privacy protection will find that doing so will strengthen the brand more and more over the next couple of years. At this junction lies the problem of execution we just discussed. For example, banks recently have issued privacy information to their customers. The leaflets basically explain the privacy laws and how the banks will handle them, and then ask customers to decide whether to stay at the bank or leave.

People are confused. I would guess that 99 per cent of the people just pick up these position statements and throw them away. No matter how we reach out to the individuals, as long as they're not being directly affected, privacy is not a high enough priority for them to read the legalese that must come with those things. But the minute they're personally affected by it, the idea that they gave up their rights raises their consciousness. It is a dichotomy right now because the information is replicated, gets sold, etc. It's just too overwhelming for people. I think the integrity of the business becomes the great and important differentiator as stories of privacy situations are told.

As another example of this position, if I gathered all of the data on how my financial providers handled my personal privacy, I'd probably have at least 15 different types of privacy areas just around my finances. I would have to read the legalese that would probably exceed 100 pages of privacy information. I can't do that. I put a tremendous amount of trust in those banks to not lie to me and to treat me in an upright and fair manner. I think the CTO of an organization has to be sure the company he or she represents is clearly conscious about the branding issue and understands that security and privacy have to be kept at the highest level of authority and conduct as possible.

Leadership

Personal integrity and a strong ethical attitude, combined with boundless enthusiasm, great business savvy, a strong understanding of finance, an unyielding respect for people, a love of technology, and a passion for free markets, create the most interesting leaders as CTOs. In my experience at the "C" level of an organization, especially around technology decisions, most decisions to go forward rely on a personal trust situation. Basically, the CEO, the leadership team, and the board need to know that you will stand with them and that you have the integrity to make your recommendation succeed. Once that level of comfort can be established, everything else seems to distribute very naturally in the organization. Leadership is about "gut checks."

I believe one of the key elements around leadership for the CTO is to be able to understand the business, be compassionate about the people, understand the financials of the organization, and understand the company's past and its drivers for the future — then put himself or herself in the same line as an executive partner of the company. CTOs should never be technology geeks. They should always be thinkers on behalf of the business, with a technology bias. If they represent themselves as a technology geek, they will never be allowed to have the gut check with the C level individuals; it's just not permitted. But if they are business partners, and they understand the working and value propositions of the business, then they will be invited to participate at the most senior levels.

The Golden Rules of the CTO

The first golden rule is to place personal interests aside as much as possible and make the decisions that tend to be the best for the company. Above all, you must try to remove yourself from the vision of how decisions will benefit you.

The second rule is to bring the integrity of your office to bear upon your resources, your network, and everything you stand for when you are ready to play.

The third golden rule is to be committed to helping the corporation evolve itself in the way the collective corporation sees fit, but with the caveat that honesty and fair play must always be present.

Finally, an element of giving back is one of the most important contributions we all make as leaders. The most successful CTOs contribute to the communities around them, the ones outside the business. Such contributions truly keep us in touch with the realities of life. When we take this particular step and make these types of commitments, CTOs truly demonstrate leadership for their companies and serve a larger purpose, as well — improving our society.

Changes in Technology in the Future

The biggest change we'll have to face in the future is the increasing focus on privacy and security. I think the second major focus will be on the pace at which business continues to change and the acceleration to find the new business value propositions. Third, we will tend to support more individual intrusion of technology. We will bring technology into our daily lives, and that intrusion will occur with increasing speed.

I think another impact that technology will have is that the ubiquitous nature of technology will continue to flourish, which will cause more stress and conflict between work and personal life. Most of us have no concept of what we're going to do with the speed at which we'll be able to find and do things. Our level of tolerance for things that aren't fast, accurate, and integrated is going to quickly diminish.

I think the next generation of individuals will come into the business world, look at what we've done, look at the current generation and say, "You've brought together the foundations of technology, but we actually understand how to use it and integrate it better in our lives than you did. After all, we've never known a world without Internet access. We're now going to change the directions of technology to be more reflective of new life-functioning ways."

This positioning by the next generation will become almost as unimaginable for us as we move into our elder days as our current technology revolution has been for our parents. The future we will receive from the next generation will bring with it all of the principles that we somehow created. Let's hope that we paid as much attention to thinking about people as CTOs as we paid to thinking about the technology.

Biography

Richard Schroth, as Perot Systems' chief technology officer, has added a strong focus on the market-facing elements of the company's technology efforts, further enabling Perot Systems to assess and lead our customers' visions of technology and business process, especially at strategic levels.

Dr. Schroth, who joined Perot Systems in 2001, is regarded as one of the most sought-after independent technology strategists, thought leaders, and international presenters on management issues and the application of emerging technologies.

He has more than 23 years of experience directing strategic use of technology and is well known for his work in business strategy and emerging technology development. He has served as a trusted advisor to a wide range of top executives and companies throughout his career, both domestically and internationally.

Before founding Executive Insights, where he provided private advisory and speaking services, Dr. Schroth served as senior vice president of research and advisory services for Computer Sciences Corporation (CSC). There he co-founded Vanguard, one of the most successful, advanced technology advisory services in the world. While at CSC, he was also involved with four of the largest outsourcing engagements in the industry (General Dynamics, Hughes Electronics, British Aerospace, and J.P. Morgan). Before working at CSC, Dr. Schroth served as chief technology officer for Marriott Corporation, where he reported directly to Mr. Marriott.

Dr. Schroth has a doctorate from Indiana University, a master's degree from the University of Illinois, and a bachelor's degree from Western Illinois University. He has also served as a Senior Visiting Fellow at the Wharton School of Business and was a member of the Executive Education Faculty at AT&T for five years.

Chapter 13

Bridging Business and Technology — Keeping Things as Simple as Possible

Mike Ragunas

The Role of the CTO

My role as CTO at StaplesDirect.com is to focus on developing and delivering e-commerce technologies in support of all of our different e-commerce ventures, including Staples.com, StaplesLink.com, Quill.com and BusinessDepot.com, our Canadian site. My focus is on how we deliver customer-facing and support technologies, and how to deliver them in a way that is best aligned with our business objectives.

I see myself as a bridge between our technology delivery capabilities and our business strategy. It is important to really understand both sides of that equation so that I can make sure we are delivering the technology that best matches our strategy. We add value to the business not just by building solutions, but by also bringing forward technologies and ideas that we think should be considered as part of the business strategy. I also partner across the business to help identify things that we can do to serve customers better.

I measure our IT organization on how much value we deliver to the business. We are here to help the business drive the top line and the bottom line — sales and profitability. For the last three and a half years since its inception, my team and I have been 100% focused on developing our Internet channel. Our success has been clear — we have built our e-commerce business from effectively zero in 1998 to what will be approaching a billion dollars in revenue in FY2001. The business has also begun to turn a profit for us, so we have achieved that rare feat in Internet business, to grow rapidly and deliver profitability at the same time.

Customers as Co-developers

We are in business to serve our customers. Never losing sight of this fact is a major driver in the technology we select. By serving our customers as best we can, we are able to maximize their value at Staples and make them more loyal customers. We don't just go out and develop a project based on what we think might work or if we think it is a "cool" technology. We are focused more on what we know about our customer, what we think they want, and how to understand better what they want. We, as a company, focus a lot of attention on gathering information about our customers, talking to them, testing things that we want to do with them, and making sure that those things are understandable and deliver value to them. We look to our customers to be co-developers with us. What we are delivering, from a technology perspective, is exactly what our customers need and want; things that they will use and will have the most benefit to the business overall.

Keeping it Simple

We have a general philosophy here to keep things as simple as possible. That manifests itself in terms of trying to minimize the number of different technologies we are using. This keeps our environment simpler. It also allows us to be much more flexible and nimble in flowing technology resources into areas where they are most needed. This allows us to deploy our technical talent more broadly across the board, rather than pigeonholing people into a particular technology space that is providing a narrow set of benefits to the company. We also look to select technologies that we believe have "legs", ones that we expect to be around and supported down the road. As a Fortune 500 company, we assess the long-term value of technology very carefully — when we put in a technology, we need it to scale and we expect it to last. We are growing very rapidly and have to make sure that things that we select today are going to meet the needs of the business several years down the road, not just today. That is sometimes difficult to do when you are growing rapidly in the dot-com space, where the technology is often immature. We are still using things that we built three years ago, but we have had to regularly update them to meet the changing current and future needs of the business.

It is easy to get caught up in looking for the most elegant technical solution for a problem, not realizing that the best technology may not provide the most value to the business. I believe in standardizing and picking technologies that may not be the most technically elegant, but that can be applied broadly to do multiple jobs well and that we know are going to have very strong vendor support down the road as well.

When we do a new project, we always look first at the technology we already have in house. Even though another technology may have a slightly higher degree of fit to our requirements, we will not bring in a new technology unless we have a compelling business case to offset the increased support and complexity costs of adding it in.

Being Technologically Nimble

Being technologically nimble means being able to respond quickly to new requirements and needs, and being able to support change on a rapid basis, even large scale changes. Being nimble involves both a philosophy of how you select, implement, and use technology, and how you manage your team of IT professionals behind it. Standardizing is important because we need to minimize the number of different technologies we have to manage. This links directly back to keeping things simple. As we build new things and put new systems in place, we work to do it in a modular way so that we allow ourselves the flexibility to change solutions more easily in the future.

Much of what we do is provide systems that support our customers and associates out in the field, as well as here at headquarters. One of the biggest challenges you have in a corporate environment in an enterprise like we have is integration of new things into your existing environment. We focus a lot of attention on how we can minimize the touch points between different applications, and make sure that we are able to bring in and out different pieces of the application at different points in time. From a technology perspective, a lot of our focus here is on how we can use middleware technology in between our applications to create a buffer that allows us more flexibility as we make changes around the business. Again, we always focus on simplicity, trying to keep things as simple as possible so that it is less complicated when you are faced with needing to make modifications. It is then easier to understand what is going on in the environment and identify places where you need to make changes and then implement those changes.

Staples has made a conscious effort as we've built out different parts of our business to refrain from building anything twice. If we already have something somewhere within the organization, we are going to try to leverage that as much as possible. A good example in our dot-com business is that we already had a delivery and catalog operation that had customer service and distribution fulfillment. Rather than going out and creating a separate instance of that for the dot-com part of our business, we built the dot-com part to be just a new order acceptance vehicle that could get orders into our existing customer service and distribution infrastructure. That has benefited us because we are able to then provide for our customers a single view of the company. When they call the Staples call center, they can ask about a catalog order they placed or a dot-com order they placed. We have also integrated the dot-com part of our business into our retail stores through in-store Internet Access Points (or kiosks), as a way to order products from our online inventory while in the stores. Again, rather than building something new to take an order in the store, we have adapted Staples.com to the store environment, leveraging the Staples.com infrastructure.

We focus on knitting all of our systems together into a common set of services to our customers across all of our different channels. Being nimble is a key part of implementing and further developing our multi-channel business to serve customers however they want to shop with Staples. This is our way of doing business now and in the future.

To Build or Buy

Building a custom solution versus buying a packaged solution is a question we deal with continually. Our bias is generally toward buying solutions where we can. In those cases, we are going to get the advantage of a vendor producing a solution for which the vendor can leverage their resources across a lot of different customers. If we built it ourselves, we would have to maintain the same kind of team that the vendor would have just to keep the application going. Where we think it is feasible, we are going to buy a solution and then modify it only where absolutely necessary. We particularly focus on buying packaged solutions for back office applications such as financials and human resources systems. These systems are critical to the operation of the company, but are not considered competitive differentiators.

Our approach will be different in places where we feel we have a strategic imperative. Some of our core customer-facing areas in particular, such as e-commerce, catalog order management, and retail point of sale, are where we are going to focus most of our in-house and custom development. These solutions are either fully custom or heavily modified packaged solutions. In the case of our e-commerce businesses, these are highly customized solutions because we feel it is important to offer exactly what our customers need, but also offer a differentiating experience with Staples that is really tapping into all that we have to offer within the company.

There is also another big question based on using internal resources for custom development versus using a third party. We base this decision on a number of factors. Do we have the appropriate skill sets internally? If we do, are those resources available, or are they committed to another project? Are there other benefits we can get from using a third party? When we first built a number of our e-commerce businesses, we did much of the work with third parties, but always kept our team plugged into the development process so we could pick up the application once it was completed. At the same time, we were building our own internal team to do follow-on releases and development of those products. In general, we are only going to bring in third parties for custom development when we have a need for the particular skill or when we have a project that we don't have the resources internally to do ourselves. In those cases, we either outsource the project entirely, or we put together a joint team of our resources and a third party resource to develop something.

Executing Technology Projects

One of our key areas of focus is predictably delivering the value that we need to deliver to the business. One of the general challenges around technology projects is figuring out how to make sure that you will get them done on time and delivering the value that was expected. We focus very heavily on the project management process within technology projects. All of our major projects have assigned project managers who work very closely with our counterparts in the business to define exactly what it is we are trying to do and make sure we are all clear about what we are expecting to deliver. We also make sure that we keep the deliverables organized into manageable blocks that have fairly short timelines associated with them. We generally don't do long term projects in which you don't get anything until the end of the project. We are very focused on figuring out what we can do in a matter of weeks or months to deliver some initial value and then build upon that with follow-on releases to continue adding incremental value. With all of our e-commerce properties, we are very focused on defining clear and manageable sets of functionality that we can deliver, focusing on the ones that have the highest business value and doing them in a way that allows us to deliver that value in a short period of time and then move on to the next deliverable.

For us, serving customers comes down to looking at how our customers want to interact with us, and how we can offer those things in a way that provides the best shopping experience for customers. For example, in our e-commerce businesses, we offer a variety of ways in which you can interact with us. You can work with us over the phone, over email, or even through a live chat solution right from the website. In all of those cases, you are dealing with the same set of call center associates who are servicing phone, fax, and other ordering channels. These associates therefore have access to all of your orders and can help you with any question. Technology enables us to provide customers different avenues to shop with us, and then letting the customer choose which way is more convenient and appropriate for them. We don't push one over the other. Some companies will hide their 800 numbers because they would rather have someone send them an email. We put our number right out there on every page of our website, but we also put icons to email us or chat with us, because some people might prefer to use those mechanisms. We track very closely our handling on all of those things. We make sure we are providing response levels to all those different channels that our customers would expect.

I look at my team as having customers directly, as well, such as our internal customers with whom we partner to bring these things to the market. It is very important to think about what we do in the technology space as providing a service for our own customers, and it is very important that we live up to their expectations, because like anything else, it is very easy for a customer to lose confidence in you if you are unreliable. From our perspective, "delivering reliably" is extremely important because it allows us to be partners in building the business and delivering that value, but to also make sure that the business can count on getting the value that we are expected to deliver at the time it is needed. We can then bake those benefits into our business plans and use them to drive profitability and sales in the business.

We are also very focused on managing and communicating expectations for our team. For example, we publish a scorecard weekly that tells all the people around our business how we are doing on delivering the projects that they are expecting. So we can tell them very quickly whether we are on track or not, what we are planning to spend, and when we are planning to deliver these things. We do that for every single project we have that has any kind of expectation set. We make sure that everyone is one hundred per cent aware of what we are doing and how we are doing, and then we measure our entire team on how well they deliver against those expectations. We also distribute the scorecard to everyone on my team, so they know how they are doing as well and what we are telling the business about their projects.

Focus on Strategy, Not Technology

The CTO's focus should be at least as much on the fit of the technology organization and strategy to the business as it is on the fit of the technology itself. There are lots of good technologies out there, and there are many technical solutions that will work equally well to solve any given business problem. It is unusual to find a company where the technology they have cannot meet the needs of the business, from a pure platform perspective. What is more important is understanding the alignment of the technology organization with the goals of the business and how well they are using the technology they have. You will run into more issues from a lack of alignment of IS or IT objectives with the real strategies and objectives of the business, and a lack of partnership between technology and business, than you will from people implementing technology that is just not going to work.

In assessing an IT shop, it is easy to figure out what technologies are being used and where they are being used. It takes more time to get a sense of whether the organization is aligned well. It also takes longer to understand whether the applications in place have been developed with a view toward supporting the future needs of the business. You must look at how the applications were developed, how they were architected, and how they are set up to allow for and support change in the business, as opposed to dealing with a particular need at a point in time.

The Future of Technology

As technology is getting more complex, it is also getting more intelligent. One of the trends that I have seen is that technology professionals are spending less and less of their time actually coding technology, assembling the bits and bytes. They are spending more of their time configuring and implementing technology in direct support of business needs. Successful technologists must become more and more business experts and understand how to deploy technology in support of business objectives. They need to be less focused on knowing a particular bit of technology. Technology changes so rapidly that we need to be flexible in what technology we use to solve a business problem. The days when a programmer could spend an entire career working with one programming language are over. What is going to be most valuable and get to be more so going forward is people who understand how technology provides value and can understand the needs of a business and be able to figure out the right technology to put in place, and how to do it most effectively.

We look at all of our technology decisions in the context of our customers. We try to avoid jumping on technology bandwagons. An example is wireless. We look at wireless connectivity to our customers as an example of something that we just don't see a great driving need for in our business right now. A lot of companies went out and spent a lot of money on building wireless interfaces into their business, and nothing came of it. In our case, we are going to really focus on the things that might not be as glamorous, but things that will move the lever in our business, which is based on understanding what our customers are really going to use and need.

The future of technology must increasingly consider the people interfacing with it — customers. Our company focuses across our business on usability. This takes the form of talking to our customers, understanding how they think about things and interact with us, and making sure that the things that we bring to market are things that we are going to get the full value out of because we have usability tested them. We are using that concept across our business now and doing usability work on internal applications that just work with our own associates. We recognize that in a company like ours, with 50,000 associates, we can't afford to go out there and train all of them on how to use an application. It has to be intuitive. It has to be something that people can understand just by looking at it, and it also has to be able to conform to common standards about how people interact with technology. It is best when people can pick something up and understand it right away. That concept applies with our external customers as well as internally with our associates. Our key drivers are really focusing on technology as very easy to use and enabling tremendous value in the businesses.

Golden Rules of Being a CTO

One of the key rules as a CTO is to understand at least as much about your business as you do about technology. You need to be clear about what your business is there to do and how you, as CTO, can support and help drive the success of that business. Particularly at the CTO level, it is important that you spend as much time learning about your business as you do technology. Having achieved CTO level, you probably know enough about technology already; however, you may not know enough about your customers or your business to maximize your ability to contribute.

Don't assume that you personally represent your typical customer. If you are developing technology for non-technical customers, you are most likely not going to be able to think like your customers. Your products must be developed with your customers' needs in mind, not your own. We rely very heavily on usability experts in the design and development of our products. You have to understand how your customers are going to interact with your products and not allow your own biases as a technologist to come into play when you are developing a product that is going to meet a customer need.

Keep things simple. Try to minimize complexity. No matter what you do, you will end up with an environment that is more complex than you would like; whatever you can do to keep it simpler is always going to put you in a better position to be nimble. Don't deploy a new technology without a strong business case to support it. Every technology you add to your environment will add complexity and support costs; make sure it's worth it.

Make sure your team is working on the things that have the most value. As a business grows, there is a tendency for that focus to get diffused sometimes. I make sure that my team works very closely with the key leaders in our business to identify the things that have the most impact, and to make sure that we are focusing as many of our resources as possible on those things. We pick a small number of key initiatives that we focus on "nailing", and then deliver those things on time with everything that was planned in order to make sure that we get the full business benefit of the original idea.

Another big focus for me is building the team, getting the right people on the team, hiring well, and making sure that the team has the right support and training to do the things that we ask them to do. We have to make sure we have the right team and that they have the right capabilities and equipment to deliver maximum value consistently.

The Holy Grail of Technology

I have always been fascinated by the "replicator" in Star Trek, which is the device that fabricates anything you ask it to make, seemingly from thin air. Today the field of nanotechnology is focused on developing this same type of solution, in which materials can be manipulated at the molecular level to make microscopic machines, or to produce larger objects molecule by molecule. I am by no means an expert in this field, but the potential applications of this technology — both good and bad — are mind-boggling. It is fascinating to think about what would change in the world if everyone had a machine that could make anything.

Biography

Mike heads development and implementation of e-commerce and related technologies for Staples.com, the e-commerce business of Staples, Inc., the $11 billion retailer of office supplies, business services, furniture and technology.

A 15-year veteran of Staples, Mr. Ragunas was formerly director of strategic technology and systems architecture for the company, where he managed the selection and use of leading-edge technologies and led the initial development of Staples.com. He was recently named one of InfoWorld magazine's Top 25 Most Influential CTOs.

Mr. Ragunas is a graduate of Harvard University.

Chapter 14

The Art of Being a CTO — Fostering Change

Rick Bergquist

The responsibilities of the CTO vary widely from company to company because of the varying needs of each organization. At PeopleSoft, the role is for an individual who understands technology and how it can be applied for business solutions, and then sees that it gets applied or convinces people that the company has to change to use the new technology going forward. It requires an understanding of technology, an understanding of what is possible, and an understanding of the business, because, at the end of the day, we're driving forward to make businesses successful and to fit into that whole strategy.

My job is to consume vast amounts of data and distill it down to manageable amounts. It's a job for which there are no shortcuts. You're always looking for that one nugget of information to give you insight into a new way of doing things.

Success, Leadership and Teams

You must have the ability to avoid getting stuck in time. You have to be able to envision the possibility of the way things could be. The key to success is a willingness to change; otherwise, you are just reinventing the old wheel. On the other hand, you must have grounding in the principles of your organization — you have to know what makes your business successful, and you have to reinforce those things. You have the freedom to do things differently, but know that what you do differently should be aligned with the organization's values. If you can't align with the organization, either you will tear it down, or it will resist the change.

To be a leader, you have to make the right analysis and fight for the right thing. Leaders in technology understand how something could be different; then they work to make it so. Sometimes it just takes persistence to get things done. In the end, it is the ability to say, "Let's make this place better", that creates the change. Then, if your track record is good, people will believe you the next time around.

I think I am successful because successful people surround me. I have the opportunity to represent thousands of developers at PeopleSoft. It's all about us working together.

To be successful, you need good communication skills, so you can articulate your ideas. You have to be a sharp listener to pick up the nuggets of information you get from the people around you.

It is also important how you relate to and seek out diverse opinions. Dysfunctional organizations often have a running feud between the sales and product staff. As CTO, you have to bridge these groups by putting yourself in sales' shoes to understand what they are trying to do and how they hope to overcome obstacles. You have to ask yourself what the salespeople are complaining about. Is it a product deficiency, or is it that they do not understand how to position the value of what you are offering? What does the sales force see on the front lines that your developers do not see? You have to have the ability to transcend your own job role to understand someone else's point of view. You have to break down these barriers to be effective.

I think you need to understand enough technology to appreciate the different pieces and how they all work together, and then synthesize them to the essence of what this new technology can give you. You have to understand what it has now and what it had before. Then you have to have the ability to apply that toward your business. That leads then to convincing and working with other people to affect change. When you combine all of those things, I think you will be successful.

Common Threads of Technology

Technology enables you to do things differently.

Let's take the Internet. We're out of the hype of the Internet bubble, which claimed, "Everything about your business has changed." Some things haven't changed — commercial enterprises still care about revenue and profit. Those that didn't are out of business.

What has changed fundamentally? The Internet was and continues to be a profound technology whose potential is just beginning to be realized. To see how our company has harnessed the changes in technology through time, let's look at our own technology as a case study.

As a startup, PeopleSoft envisioned two things:

Simplified User Interface

Client/server systems could make a vast improvement in the user interface — the prior generation of systems was mainframe systems that used a character-based

3270 display. The whole interface revolved around code values that required operators to undergo long periods of training to master. Navigation revolved around memorizing "transaction codes" to move from one screen to another. With the emergence of the Windows environment, we saw the possibility of deploying systems that could use menus to allow for simple application navigation, and the Windows user interface that no longer relied on code values, but rather let users interact with the system, naturally selecting options without requiring codes. This great user interface enabled many more people to interact with systems without having to attend extensive training classes to learn arcane navigation techniques and memorize code values. Mere mortals could now use applications.

Quickly Adaptable Systems
Mainframe systems were unable to adapt to business changes quickly. They had been built using large amounts of COBOL code that was inflexible and unable to adapt to change. Every IT organization had an infinite backlog of system change requests. With a quickly adaptable system, you could make changes at the speed of business changes — your applications became business enablers instead of being boat anchors holding you back.

Recognizing the two fundamental benefits that the new client/server technology could solve provided the basis for the products that our company produced. It was this technology that enabled our company to become a successful startup company and mature into a billion dollar organization.

Yet, when the times change, you have to be prepared to walk away from what made you successful. In our case, the client/server technology we pioneered was just an enabler to create business applications that enabled our customers to run their organizations more efficiently and effectively. The client/server applications were our roots — they were our legacy. But if we hadn't been prepared to move on, they also would have been our demise.

We recognized that a new paradigm was being created by the emergence of the Internet. It was a technology that enabled a universal method of accessing business systems — available to all employees, all customers, all partners, and all suppliers. And best of all, it was a technology that was ubiquitously deployed — it didn't require anyone to install applications for their use. This technology would allow us to create whole new business solutions that could be deployed to a much wider audience than we had reached before.

Yet this was a risky adventure: We had to be prepared to say that all of our applications were obsolete — that they all needed to be replaced. We had to convince the naysayers in our own organization that the new world was going to be a better place. We had to answer such queries as, "We've been working on this technology for 12 years and have perfected it. Why are we moving to an unproven model that puts our applications on the Web — a technology known for intermittent performance and questionable security?"

Working with the visionaries within our organization, we were able to tackle these objections one by one — to prove the technology could stand up.

We tackled security by showing how the new Internet technologies could replace existing technologies. Encryption provided by the browser was used to protect confidential data. Directory servers allowed the users to have single-sign-on capabilities enabling them to have one user ID and password to access all systems. This improved security because users had only one password, which they could memorize and not have to write down. This reduced costs because IT had only one repository to maintain, not dozens.

With respect to performance, scalability, and reliability, we saw the future as being the deployment of not only hundreds of internal users, as client/server systems had been, but thousands of partners or suppliers, and tens of thousands of customers. We tackled performance and reliability through a server architecture that was efficient. As user demand increased, you simply added hardware to match it. Reliability was provided by having redundant servers that could take over when any other server failed.

We revisited the whole user experience and realized we had two choices: The cheapest one was to simply port the Windows look, feel, and functionality over to the Web. Or we could reengineer the user experience to match the Web metaphor. We choose the second alternative. We reasoned that the value of the Web was our ability to deploy our applications out to everyone — every employee, every partner, every supplier, and every customer. To deploy universally meant that the user experience had to be intuitive to users whose everyday experience was the Web. Applications had to require no formal training courses. This meant a complete rewrite of the applications to be pure Internet applications, not "Windows on the Web", like some of our competitors.

Our company spent $500 million to make these fundamental changes to our technology. We raised our R&D spending to 27 per cent of our revenues in an arena where our peers spend 8 per cent to 15 per cent on R&D. What enabled us to be bold enough to bet the company on this strategy? This action came about because all the organizations within the company got behind it: The sales organization saw the competition as the emerging startups that were Web-based; the product strategists saw this as an enabler to change basic business processes with ubiquitous access; our customers saw the possibilities for lower costs because supporting a browser was 90 per cent cheaper than installing code on a client.

Ultimately we had a good understanding of our mission as a company. History shows that companies that don't really understand their business miss evolving as technology changes. For example, the railroad companies thought of themselves as railroads and didn't realize they should have been thinking of themselves as transportation companies. They missed out on these possibilities and didn't transform their business. At our company we realize we are in the business of delivering technology-enabled business solutions — we are not a client/server company. We also learned from history — none of the vendors that were predominant in the mainframe era made it into the client/server era. They didn't have the will to change. The new way to do business solutions in the new world was to do it on the Internet, and we had to get there.

Maintaining a technology lead is the delicate balance of establishing how the technology can change your business and having the vision and will to completely transform current practices. This requires working with all of the parts of your organization and crafting a common vision of the future.

A CTO's most obvious sign of success is keeping his or her job. The criteria involve asking basic questions: Are we staying current with technology? Are we perceived as a leader with our product and our technology? Are we moving forward, or are we becoming a legacy player? Are we working more efficiently? Do we have better products that meet the needs of our customers? Are we enabling people to thrive in business with the technology that exists today?

Changes in Technology

The Internet is the broad new wave of technology, and we're just at the start of a ten-year cycle. The Internet has changed our ability to communicate and interact with people. We're just beginning to understand how that will change business processes and the interaction between companies and their customers. There is a very bright future ahead. You can do things differently, but it's a freeing experience. It's scary for some people, but it's a good thing.

Our pure Internet architecture has given us a 24-month lead over our competitors. Client/server lasted about ten years, and its major features were effectively limited to a better user interface and the ability to adapt faster. We saw the potential of the Internet as even broader:

- The Internet lowers the cost of doing business by reducing the cost of deploying applications. It is a lot cheaper to deploy systems over a browser than to install code on client.
- The Internet provides universal access to business that enables organizations to work collaboratively with their customers, partners, and suppliers. The most

profound change of the Internet is that we now have an environment where clients, partners, and suppliers all have the same infrastructure to access systems as easily as consumers can access anything over their browsers, such as Yahoo! or Amazon. Businesses have the ability to change business processes and have access to information they never had before. Customers can place orders for products and report problems using self-service features. You can provide your partners with leads, and they can track them down.

A common problem for many businesses was that with channel partners to sell their products, there was little visibility into potential problems. The ability to expand the access to systems via the Internet can help run a more efficient business because it gives the decision-makers insight into what is really going on. Businesses are changing their processes. The Internet is the enabler for it. A simple example is FedEx. They gave you the ability to access their Web site to find out where your package is. For you it's a benefit. You can do it yourself. You don't have to worry about someone entering the number incorrectly. FedEx cut their costs dramatically by not having a staff call center. This is an example of a win-win, where the business process changed to give both parties better information on a timely basis and reduced costs. We're just beginning to see how processes can be changed to do this. It really does follow the macro trend. Companies no longer try to do everything themselves. Vertical integration went out with Henry Ford. You're now using partners or outsourcing, or you're doing virtual organizations that are doing things. But to be effective in those virtual organizations, you have to have access to the core information so people can make informed decisions so you don't lose things during translation. That's what the Internet enables products to give you. You can deploy the applications in a universal scheme.

Business processes are being enabled as Web services to reduce the cost of setting up collaboration. The drive for universal access is being aided by the development of standards to allow business process to be seen as a set of services that can be more easily accessed than the stiff interfaces that have been present in the past.

New devices are emerging; the reign of the PC as the dominant device for accessing the Internet is declining. Mobile workers want mobile access, whether it's by taking their data with them or accessing it via wireless technologies. People are demanding access to information from more convenient devices, such as PDAs and phones. These new types of devices will form an adjunct to the PC of today and will allow access instantly. By removing the barriers to information systems, a whole new class of users can be served, and their work can be made more effective.

Privacy Issues

The first problem we have with privacy is the definition — we don't have a full understanding of what it means and what we're trying to achieve. On one hand, we say we don't want anyone to have too much access to our personal information. The problem is if you want a promotion in a corporation, you want every one of the higher managers to know about you and everything you have accomplished. In this case, you want fairly wide dissemination of data. What you have to understand about privacy is that you must ascertain whether you want certain people to see your data and what you want them to see. You have to establish the criteria. The real issue is often reaching a common understanding of what we are protecting and from whom.

Technologically, I found I can protect any of the information using pieces of it, but the challenge is to ask yourself, "What is the end goal?" There are times when we want a wide dissemination of data and other times when we don't. For instance, in marketing, if you disseminate information about your likes and dislikes, then companies can actually get rid of a lot of junk mail to you because they'll realize that you're not going to buy anything anyway. Do you see that as a positive or a negative? Do you want to sort through all the junk mail? The material is a lot more targeted to you. I think the challenge that society has to face is finding out what the mix is between those two, so that information can be used by both parties, but it doesn't get abused by either one.

Challenges

The biggest challenge I face is getting people to think about what could be, as opposed to what is. People like to continuously fine-tune the way things are. Enacting change is one of the hardest things to do. Machiavelli pointed out that change is the hardest thing to bring about because people always have a vested interest in the way things are.

If you have an organization that is used to change and that embraces the concept of change, then you're going to make changes for good business decisions. You have to be an evangelist. You have to identify the problems, enumerate them, and then identify the vision to make it better. Businesses can evangelize about making more money by solving the customers' needs.

Staying Technologically Nimble

In the proliferation of technologies that are emerging today, the key question for a CTO is, "What is just cool as opposed to what is profound?" I generally try to solve this riddle by envisioning the effects of the new technology. Will this reduce the cost of applications? Will it reduce the cost of doing business? Does it enable companies to do business in a completely different way? There have been many things I thought were really cool, but in the end, I don't know how well they would have been accepted and don't know how they would have changed everyone else's life (remember PointCast?). In the end, you can't stand behind technology if it's not growing the business or cutting costs. You just have to let those cool things go by. Maybe some other day you can envision it a different way, but if it doesn't meet the test of transforming or growing the business, or reducing costs, then it's just an interesting anomaly along the way.

To be successful both individually and as an organization, I think you have to have a vast appetite for taking in information. You then have to have the ability to dissect it and separate the good ideas from the ones that are just curiously interesting. You have to be open to a variety of sources. I haven't found one single source that I could read and say, "I've found everything I need."

Information comes from a multitude of sources. It can come from your customers and from fellow employees. It certainly comes from the media who expose what other companies are doing. You get leading-edge ideas from professors who are writing books. You get information from all of these different sources, and the challenge is to turn that raw data into information that's relative to your organization. You depend on people to synthesize that information and bring it together into a vision of where you're taking your company. Each individual has to figure out what sources to deal with to make himself more effective in his individual job. Each organization has to have in place a culture that is accepting and thriving on change.

We want to make sure we're current with technology to enable us to do business differently. That's why an organization has to have a culture. Those will be the thriving organizations that tolerate change, change the rules, and promote people for bringing out new ways of doing things. In some ways it runs counterintuitive to the order of the world, where people like things to be steady. People say, "I'm all for progress, as long as you don't change anything I have to deal with." You have to have a culture where, once in a while, things are done differently. What you have to promote is not change for change's sake, but change for the business' sake.

Companies are better suited for change when they have a culture that thrives on information interchange. Look at the things you've hoarded. If they were gold, you'd have a whole stockpile of gold, and then you'd be rich. This attitude has pervaded the thinking that information is something that should be hoarded. The cultural change that companies have to realize is that information is not what's valuable — it's the exchanging of information. It's what people do with the information that's actually more valuable than the information itself.

The most effective organizations think about interchange of information among the people in the organization. They think about being willing to share it with your partners and suppliers and others. Even if there's a risk of information getting out to a competitor, an organization that can share and act on information quickly often has an advantage. It's what you do with information that has value in today's economy. That's the cultural change that will determine the ultimate winners from the losers.

Building a Team

Execution from a technology standpoint is really no different from any other endeavor. First, you have to agree on the vision — the goal you're going to achieve. Then you have to build a plan to achieve the goal. It has been said that the difference between a hallucination and a vision is the presence of a viable plan to achieve the vision. You have a process for identifying the goals of your organization, although the way to go about this is not always clear, as the means that each organization uses are diverse and often subject to personalities and company practice. But no matter the process, the common thread will be the ability to lay out what can be and why it is in the organization's interest to do it.

The process is no different from everything else. It's a project management execution strategy, where you lay out the goals, the milestones, and the steps you need to accomplish those milestones and the resources you need. Then you have to have the diligence to monitor and control those elements.

Ultimately though, I've always found the most important resource is your people. No significant endeavor ever gets done by one person — you need to build a team that comprises people with the right skills to accomplish the goals. Recognize that not all people are experts at everything. You need to match your people with the skills that are required. Some of the best execution people have no vision. Some of the people who have vision have no execution skills. Think of it as a football team. A successful football team will have a great quarterback, a great line, receivers, and so forth. But you wouldn't expect the quarterback to be on the defensive line. Identify those skill sets required to execute the project. Make sure you have the right alignment to achieve the project goals.

Goals

Setting goals is definitely important, and you can measure progress against them by product release cycles and penetration of your product in the marketplace. This is important because without measurements toward goals, it's all practice.

The challenge in many places is that people have always had calendar cycles — quarterly or yearly planning. Technology doesn't move according to those cycles. You have to set up goals that match your fiscal calendar, but then you have to be willing to change the goals if the ground rules change, or the marketplace or economy has changed. If you're smart, you'll recognize when an external occurrence has changed and invalidated the plans you have made. Then you set up new goals.

Be aware of the external factors you counted on, and as soon as they change, reexamine your premises. Prepare a new set of goals. Don't just march down the same path. Make new plans and new MBOs when it's appropriate.

Taking Risks

A risk to me means you're willing to try new things that can be accomplished in new ways. A lot of questions emerge when you're envisioning what could be. Will this work? We may not be smart enough to see the unintended consequences of things. You need to take risks in an organization; if you don't take risks, then you won't move forward.

There is definitely an advantage in being the first one with a new product or a new technology. You reap the rewards before anyone can catch up. You have to try a number of things. You have to pick your risks wisely. You have to "go boldly where no man has gone before", and if it's a morass, you have to deal with it. It's a tradeoff, like everything else.

We generally look at risk from a business case perspective. We look for what it's going to cost so we can foresee the consequences if we fail. We see risk in different things. In some places, you take low-risk ventures, and in others, you might take high risk, but you don't bet the whole company. There were times when our company took a risk on the Internet. In essence, it was about the company approach. We knew if we weren't on that new wave, then we wouldn't be in business. You have to size up each of the risks. What are the risks of doing something? What are the risks of not doing something? Often the risk of not doing something is greater than the risk of moving forward.

You have to be willing to express your opinions on those issues. You pick the things that make big changes, and you become a proponent. I think you have to be able early on to build a set of allies who say, "This is how we can complement what you're trying to do." You're really trying to make the whole organization successful. I think when we work it from that perspective, then people will help you deal with things. You must be working toward a shared goal.

Selling Your Vision

There are many different ways to sell a vision. One way is articulating your vision to people to see if it resonates. A corporation is not just technologists. You have to interact with the other parts, as an engine has to hit on all the cylinders to run well.

If I have an idea for the way things should be, then I go to the sales organization and see if they can sell it. I'll talk to our customer base to see if this meets a pain point they have and if it would solve the problem. I'll talk to our support people to see if this will solve a problem where they're hoping someone will have a solution. You can't just sell your vision on a technology basis. It has to meet the needs of the market and show that it will be good for your organization as a whole.

Interacting with Other Groups

My belief is that you often learn a lot just by being around the water cooler, listening to problems other people have or hearing about innovations they've done that no one else has thought of. Part of what you want to do is connect the right people who are doing similar things. The role of a management team is to foster innovation by connecting people. It's my belief that, in the end, organizations don't do anything — people do. So if you get the right people, you'll be amazed at what you can accomplish.

Our sales organization has early insights into what prospects are looking for because everyone who goes out to buy a product has visions of what they're trying to solve. You'll get a different set of insights from your customers because they're not really focused on the future, but on taking what they have and getting it to work really well.

Managing during Turbulent Markets

Our Company has a set of traditional values — we always believe revenues and profits count. Those values align us with the values of our customers — we're making them more successful, more profitable, and able to grow their organizations. These principles count, whether the marketplace is expanding or contracting. What does change is the focus.

In an expanding market where the focus is growth, companies must decide how to grow at a rapid rate. In a more challenging or declining market, the question is how to cut costs to survive. Both of those are present in all the solutions we deal with. We are an organization that's aimed at profit, and to get that profit, we have to provide a superior solution that people are willing to pay us for. It's understanding the customers' level of pain and how we can make their lives easier.

Best Skills

The ability to learn and do new things and change are the best skills to have. Everything we do in technology has a very short shelf life. I can look at my career and see that. The languages have all changed since the beginning of my career, and they'll change again. If you have the ability to surf the waves of change, you'll do well. You need to have the ability to be good at something, to learn it fast and to understand what's different about it and make use of it. Don't get so stuck on it that you miss the next big thing that's there. It's a skill of lifelong learning. It'll keep you fresh, and it will keep you challenged. I think you need all of those things to be effective in your job.

Be prepared to change and be prepared to foster change. There's the old prayer asking to let me change the things I can, accept the things I can't change, and know the difference. I think that's what the CTO role implies. You're not there just to identify with the status quo. You're not there as a caretaker for what is. You're expected to ask where it can be.

The rules for technology will change, too. What's cool today will be passé in a few years. Like everything else, if you wait around for the future, you won't accomplish anything. Find out the best alternative today; make use of it; and when there's something better, change your goal and switch.

Best Advice

My first boss, John Grillos, said, "Pick your battles." The criteria for picking them are straightforward:

- They have to be important.
- They have to be winnable.
- They have to be few.

We all have more opportunities to change things or to take on different battles, but you have to know how to choose them. You don't want to be fighting all the time; otherwise, nobody will want to deal with you. Pick things that are important because they will have the longest-lasting effect. Avoid causes that can't be won to conserve your resources for things you can change. If you can examine the battles facing you by these criteria, you generally come out ahead.

Whatever you do, enjoy it. You're going to spend a great majority of your life working at it. Most of us don't have jobs you leave behind — it doesn't end when you walk out the office door. You think about it later, even if you're home. If you enjoy what you're doing, and you're in the backyard thinking about it, that's fun. If you don't enjoy your job, go find another one.

Dream Technology

My goal is to make sure that every day we are working toward the dream technology. At our company, that technology is to make organizations run more effectively. To enable this, we need to make people more effective. When we get this right, the technology will fade into the background but be ever present. The technology will capture data at its source without anyone thinking about it.

Business processes will flow seamlessly across customers, partners, and suppliers. Information will be available for people to do their jobs effectively through intuitive interfaces. And change will be accommodated quickly. Systems will automatically suggest changes to optimize the business, based on continuous monitoring. Alternatively, people will be able to call up information easily to enable them to use their own creativity to foster change. I see a symbiotic world where the judgment, creativity, and innovation of people are matched with the speed, accuracy, and predictability of computers.

Biography

Rick Bergquist, senior vice president, chief technology officer, Technology and Applications Strategy, is responsible for PeopleSoft's long-term technology vision. In this position, he is responsible for identifying new technologies for deployment within PeopleSoft products in areas such as the Internet, data warehousing, knowledge management, and object-oriented technology.

At PeopleSoft, Mr. Bergquist was one of the original PeopleTools developers and has previously managed the PeopleTools development and strategy teams.

Before joining PeopleSoft, Mr. Bergquist was with American Management Systems, Inc., most recently as a senior principal in the product development group. While at AMS, he supervised the development of the company's application packages for retail banking.

Mr. Bergquist completed the Program for Management Development at the Harvard School of Business, and he holds a bachelor's degree in computer science from California Polytechnic State University.

Chapter 15

Keep Your Blade Sharp

Jeff P. Van Dyke

Define (and Redefine) Success

From the time I founded VanDyke Software, I have measured our success by asking the questions, "Are we better off today than we were a year ago? Is the company more real today than it was a year ago?" The definition of success has really been about building a company that would last. For the first year I was running the business out of a house I was renting by myself. After about one year I had one employee and a small office. To me that was success! We had more of a business after one year than when we started. After three years we had a bigger office, nine employees, and three products. Each year we've been able to look back and say, "This business is more 'real.' This business is more substantial than it was a year ago."

Each year we've added employees, increased office space, launched new products, improved infrastructure, and added benefits. One of my initial goals was to provide our employees with the same level of benefits they would receive at most technology firms — from a 401(k) to paid health care — the same basic benefits you would expect to receive in Silicon Valley. Here in Albuquerque, this is quite unusual. For people who have put down roots in New Mexico, this makes VanDyke a very attractive prospective employer, because it is above the norm. It's equally important that this benefits policy allows us to attract those bright individuals that might otherwise leave Albuquerque for other parts of the country.

Some of my measures of success are very old-fashioned. We are committed to annual financial growth, but we are also deeply committed to sustained profitability. Over the long term, as the past couple of years have shown, you need a business plan that has a clear path to profitability. VanDyke Software has been profitable every year. We've done this by growing slowly, organically, and with purpose. As part of this growth we've taken hiring very seriously. We value our employees and work hard to keep them. I'm proud that in the entire history of the company, only a handful of employees have moved on, and for reasons other than dissatisfaction with working at VanDyke.

One of the most enjoyable sources of feedback on our success comes from our customers. Most of our employees have an opportunity to engage our customers every day. Whether we're closing a sale because our product does what the customer needs, or we're receiving feedback about how our technical support exceeds expectations, the feedback we receive from our customers is an ongoing and gratifying measure of our success.

Engage Your Customers

I think the things that have made me most successful within the technology world are embodied in VanDyke Software's core values. In Built To Last by James C. Collins and Jerry I. Porras, the authors discuss the importance of having core values and sticking to them. VanDyke's core values include learning, being customer-oriented, and building quality software. Since day one these core values have guided my decision-making, and I believe they will continue to serve us well into the future. We still have these values today, and we see them as one of the keys to our success going forward.

My first learning opportunity came when I started the company. I had just left a start-up that had failed to ship a piece of software after two-and-a-half years of effort, and I started VanDyke with the commitment to ship a product quickly and learn from the experience. I didn't necessarily assume that the business would be successful, but I knew I would learn a great deal. Since there was just me, and I had committed to shipping a quality piece of software, I realized it would need to be a small product. To this day, we continue to focus on building small, quality products.

Once I'd shipped the first release of the software, the real learning began because I started receiving customer feedback, and this allowed me to exercise another core value — being customer-oriented and engaging the customer. As an example of our customer-centric model, our employees write individual responses to every piece of e-mail we receive that needs a response — usually the day it is received. We deliver presales support at the same level as after the sale and have liberal upgrade policies.

We have made a point of engaging our customers and have created a feedback loop with them that is an essential part of how we develop and improve our products. In addition, we have consistently embraced open standards, which we believe benefits our customers. Every product we've delivered is based on open standards documented by either Internet RFCs (Request for Comments) or IETF

(Internet Engineering Task Force) drafts. By adhering to these standards as they are developed and after they are ratified, we can provide our customers with interoperable solutions.

The Internet has played a key role in how VanDyke has executed on these core values. From the day we shipped our first product in 1995, we have had a Web site and used e-mail to communicate with our customers. We've never shipped a boxed product or printed a conventional manual. Instead, our products have always been available for immediate download via the Internet. Today e-mail and the Web continue to be our primary media of communication.

The business model from the outset was to leverage the power of the Internet for delivering our products, supporting our customers, and communicating with them. But, unlike many of the dot-coms that blew up, our products were actual, not virtual, and were more than just a Web site.

Find Opportunities That Fit Your Focus

One of the most important ways we find our opportunities and discover where they exist is by maintaining and growing a dialog with our customers. In Seth Godin's Survival Is Not Enough, the author talks about the idea of conducting small inexpensive experiments, testing the results, taking the resulting feedback, and integrating it into your business processes. I believe this is very similar to the approach we have always taken with our customers. We constantly solicit our customers for input and then implement changes that meet their needs.

We often send these engaged customers incremental releases to see if we've met their needs, and if we've been successful, we include those features in a future public release to a broader audience. It can be hard to predict the future in terms of where opportunities will be, but by consistently listening to your customers, you can identify many opportunities that have serious potential to translate into measurable results.

Another way to stay close to customers is by being customers. We tend to focus on developing products that individuals within the company can use on the job every day. This is often referred to in the industry as "eating your own dog food." One of our goals when we work on a new product or a new release of an existing product is to get it to a "dog food" stage, where we can use it internally, day-to-day. Many of our employees have backgrounds that closely resemble our customers'. For example, many of us, including me, have at one time or another worked as network administrators. By making sure every product meets our own standards for usability and reliability, we're better able deliver something our customer will be satisfied using and confident recommending.

Our biggest opportunities have three things in common. The first is alignment with what we do well. We deliver our products directly to the customer over the Internet. We develop small products built by a small team of developers. At times we have had a product literally developed by one person. Most of our product development has occurred with teams of fewer than 10 people. We will not take on projects of a certain size. We will focus on the small. We will focus on products that can be marketed directly to our customers. We will stay in areas where there is a corporate focus. We don't contract with one customer to do one piece of customer software; instead we focus on developing a $30 or $99 product that we can sell thousands and thousands of times to different companies and individuals.

The second thing our biggest opportunities have in common is that our projects tend to be built on ideas our employees are passionate about. Our second product, AbsoluteFTP, was written by an employee whose number one reason for coming to VanDyke was so he could write an FTP (file transfer protocol) client that would be significantly more usable than anything available at the time. He turned down an attractive counteroffer from his previous employer and left a secure position with a more stable company to build a piece of software he was passionate about.

The third is that we are always looking at what we've already developed. When I look at the history of our products, I see that since we released our second product, every product we've developed has leveraged some component or portion of an existing product. By building on the effort we've put into existing products and integrating some or all of that work into new ones, we're able to get an increased return on investment and reduce our development time. And these products tend to fit the needs of the markets where we're strongest. Every year we reevaluate the opportunities we see for the next year or two, but our product roadmap is drawn on those factors.

Getting back to the notion of small projects, we like to go from committing to an idea to putting something in our customer's hands in three to nine months. Then we start that feedback. The product might be small. It might not have every feature they want or can envision, but it allows us to get the feedback and focus on those features that are most important to the majority of our customers, as opposed to those we imagine might be useful. We recently introduced a new tag line for our company: "We Listen. Then We Make Software Better." I think it sums up our approach nicely.

In discussing how VanDyke Software tries to find opportunities in technology, I can't help considering the impact of our core value of getting employees to think like an owner. When every employee thinks like an owner, in terms of both trying to satisfy customers and looking for growth opportunities, we're more likely to find those opportunities. One of the things we encourage is something called bootleg projects. This is an idea borrowed from 3M. At 3M, employees are allowed to spend 15 per cent of their time pursing ideas or projects that don't currently have an official status or budget, without management approval. The idea is to create opportunities for employees to explore new ideas and create some momentum prior to pitching their bootlegs to management. Within VanDyke, we occasionally have a "bootleg Friday", where individuals or small teams can spend the day working on such projects. This gives each employee an opportunity to explore some of the new technologies they are encountering and learning about. On more than one occasion a bootleg project has been used as a prototype for the development of a full-blown product.

To capitalize on these opportunities it is imperative for us to focus on what we do well. With a new product we concentrate on identifying critical functionality, building rock-solid quality software, and offering the product with a price and level of service that ensures it is perceived as a good value in the marketplace. We won't deliver a terminal emulator that has every feature including the kitchen sink. Instead, we'll deliver a product that has the key features that the vast majority of our potential customers need.

When I think in terms of software in particular, one of the big untapped opportunities is in interaction design. In The Inmates Are Running The Asylum, Alan Cooper makes a clear argument why programmers shouldn't do interaction design. This design discipline includes the graphical user interface, but goes beyond that to include any behavior or interaction with the user. Cooper's argument is that programmers will gravitate to the simplest solution possible, but this orientation often doesn't lead to the most usable product. This appears to be a fairly new opportunity, in part because very few schools teach interaction design. I think this area has a huge potential for growth and eventually will influence any successful software company. The software companies that shine in future years will be those that do interaction design well.

The last area I'll mention as a good source of opportunity is our membership in organizations such as The Internet Society (IOSC). For the past several years we've been involved with the Internet Engineering Task Force (IETF) and have actively participated in shaping the future of protocols such as Secure Shell. IETF working groups focus on a wide range of issues, from Public Key Infrastructure (PKI) to calendar standards to Secure Shell. Each of these working groups can be working on one or more drafts that may become an Internet standard. That a draft comes out of a working group doesn't guarantee success in the marketplace, but our participation provides an opportunity to get involved and get a sense of what the future might hold for the Internet. And we have an opportunity to help define what that future may look like.

Reduce Risks with Customer Feedback

We are focused on developing customer-oriented solutions. We have tried to make it clear to our customers that we want input from them. Therefore, much of the research we do, the opportunities we see, and the risks we choose to take are based on that feedback. While I'm not suggesting that customer feedback is the only place a company should conduct research, it is the number one source for VanDyke.

Because we're a fairly small company with a small budget for doing classic market research, we've come to depend on low-tech, low-cost solutions. This includes reading lots of books and periodicals. Everyone is encouraged to read, read, read. This includes reading the USENET newsgroups and surfing the Web. Early on we were able to find potential customers and beta testers online. By reviewing the newsgroup articles, we found individuals who were asking for help in finding solutions. We were able to contact those people and say, "We have a piece of software that we believe solves this problem. Will you try it and give us your feedback?"

By reading Web site reviews on both our products and our competitors', we've been able to identify new opportunities for both feature enhancements and entirely new products. And we've tried to remain flexible. When our CRT 1.0 terminal emulator first shipped, it didn't include any support for printing. In fact, I think I recall saying (or at least thinking), "Printing over my dead body!" However, once 1.0 was delivered, I realized this was a huge mistake. The customer feedback flowed, "CRT is great. It is just what I need to connect to our library system, but I need to able to print out the results of my book query." Within weeks of the official release of CRT 1.0, the beta release of CRT 1.1 shipped with printing support.

Embrace Change

To position your company to thrive on change, you must build an organization where change is the norm. We do this by instilling the notion in our employees from their initial orientation that the only constant at VanDyke is change. We reinforce this message constantly, in company-wide quarterly meetings and in smaller gatherings in between. We continually solicit ideas from employees, from the receptionist to the director of sales and marketing, about how we can improve the company and make VanDyke a great place to work. We publish these ideas on the intranet for the entire company to see, and this in turns generates more ideas. Each quarter we review these ideas and determine which ones should and can be acted on. Generating more ideas is always a good step in trying to generate better ideas. In our meetings we regularly use a technique called affinity sessions to brainstorm. It is amazing how many ideas you can generate to answer just one question when you give people the right tools and environment.

A second way we prepare for change is by investing in our employees. I think training and reading play a key role in making sure individuals are prepared for the inevitable changes the future holds. Different groups in the company regularly have a book they are reading and discussing. This invites discussion of what we're doing, what we could be doing, and what changes we need to make. By involving employees at every level, you create an organization built for change. We don't necessarily know what changes the future will bring, but by reading, keeping abreast of what is happening in the industry, and identifying trends as they develop, we can be better prepared as a company.

Finally, I can't say enough about giving employees the training they need and want. By making sure employees get training in new areas and in foundational skills, such as project management and communications, we're better prepared to adapt to change when it happens.

One of the biggest challenges is to continually communicate with your staff throughout the company. You need forums to make sure effective communication occurs all the time. One of the things we have used with great success over the past 18 months is borrowed from the agile development methodology Extreme Programming — the concept of stand-up meetings. When our developers get together at 9 a.m. for 10 to 15 minutes, they stand in a circle. Each developer in turns reports on what they worked on yesterday and what they plan to accomplish today. It is a good mechanism to make sure the whole team is on the same page. Without this kind of effective, continuous communication, change is almost guaranteed to be more painful and slower than it needs to be.

Plan as a Team

Setting clear, measurable objectives is the first step in trying to plan a successful outcome. But other important steps often get skipped. For consistent success, you must start by clearly identifying and articulating the goals. Then make sure everyone understands the guiding principles and brainstorm about what ideas are possible. Also get as many people involved as possible, so you get a rich set of ideas to choose from. After you organize those ideas, you finally come up with a set of action items or tasks.

I think we often fail to execute when we don't do a good job of tracking our actions, or we don't break those actions down into small enough steps. One of things we try to avoid is accepting coarse estimates like, "I think that action will take me a week." We prefer to break a week-long action into smaller steps, preferably each less than two days. We try to make sure we have a mechanism to track the progress of those individual steps. By doing this, we create a feedback loop that allows us to improve our process incrementally as we progress. Software development by its very nature is difficult to estimate, so you need to calibrate how good your group is at estimating and apply a factor to the estimates. For us, this factor is simply the actual number of hours required divided by the estimate. As the group gets better with estimating, the factor should approach one.

As we've applied this technique over the past 18 months, we've found we are getting increasingly consistent results. There is always room for improvement, but by making sure the goals are clear, making sure the guiding principles have been articulated, making sure we've brought in enough ideas that we haven't prematurely tried to choose a course of action, and then making sure we track that action and have a feedback loop to identify when we fall short, we are able to execute consistently.

When planning your company's strategy for the future, it's my opinion that the process your team uses to develop the strategy is more important than the plan produced. The process needs to include wide participation from throughout the company, and titles need to be left at the door, so everyone feels they are on an equal footing and can be candid. This is best done off-site to eliminate day-to-day distractions and provide a neutral ground. To maximize the productivity of the process, you must create an atmosphere of open brainstorming and constructive debate about ideas, without any hidden agendas or defensiveness.

One of the key parts of this process is to build consensus within the group for where they want to take the company, looking out five years. In 2001 we adopted a new approach for developing our strategy and began working with Paul Bradley from the Bradley Group. I was first introduced to Paul's method when I took a seminar in early 2001. His process for developing a strategic plan had a number of aspects I thought would help us. The first was that our management team met with Paul off-site and drafted a one-page document titled "Ideal 2006." We projected what VanDyke Software would look like in 2006 if everything went as planned, and if we could achieve our goals. Paul shared with the team how companies and organizations have used this technique successfully. One company in Minnesota decided their ideal would be to relocate to Florida. So this isn't just about financials: It is about things that would make a difference to the management and staff. We painted a very vivid picture of our future through 11 bullet points, ranging from "A growing international company with multiple offices and development groups" to "Ensuring company-wide participation in financial success by focusing on long-term ROI."

The second step in this process was for this same group to write three scenarios of what the future might look like from a perspective outside of VanDyke. We looked at something that was of critical importance to us. Most of our growth has been from products based on the Secure Shell protocol. But there are competing security technologies, such as IPSEC (IP Security Protocol) and TLS (Transport Layer Security) in the market. We drafted scenarios of what the future might look like with the demand for Secure Shell-based solutions dropping off, staying flat, or growing rapidly. Based on these scenarios, we tried to identify signs or tip-offs to determine which one of these scenarios might be unfolding. We did this about eight months ago, and we've since found it very useful. Individuals in the company have become more aware of what is happening in our market, what is happening with IPSEC, and what is happening with VPNs (virtual private networks), as well as what is happening with Secure Shell. They are looking for these tip-offs, and we've already identified several that are indicators of how the future may be unfolding.

Finally, there needs to be a process in place to make sure the team executes the strategy. Having a good process to develop the strategic ideas and creating a plan doesn't mean you're going to be successful. You can significantly increase your odds of success by using active mechanisms for tracking the plan's progress, including the necessary follow-up and the inevitable course corrections.

Articulate the Vision

Getting your employees to buy in to your vision is critical to long-term success and requires consistent attention. My vision for VanDyke is to build an organization that can sustain itself over time, one that outlasts the founder and the employees we have today. As part of realizing this vision, I continue to emphasize our core values and how they can be used to build an organization that can stand the test of time. I work to consistently articulate the values, which include everything from building quality software to making sure this is a great place to work. I think in general those are values that almost anyone in this industry buys in to, so I don't think this is a hard sell. The challenge is to make sure that as things progress, as we add new people, as projects succeed, as projects fail, we reflect on those values, and we keep talking about the vision and the values. It is easy to say we want to make this a great place to work, but on occasion we put in policies or procedures or have projects that take away from that. Someone has to say, "Wait a minute, that isn't the way we do things here. We need to change that. This isn't consistent with our values." And, especially for new people, this can come as something of a surprise, because they might not understand the vision or the values as well as we thought they did. There is definitely some repetition to it. For me, I have managers buying in, but I need them to consistently articulate the values with their staff. We do it as a group in company meetings, but it needs to be done on a daily basis as we interact with our staff.

One of the key core values in building an organization is that we focus on long-term return on investment. Getting employees to think long-term is important. It can manifest itself in many ways. We spend money on books, training, software, and good tools our employees need. The first year I realized I was willing to spend $2,000 on a new monitor, but I was hesitant to spend $700 for a new desk. The reality was that the desk would last longer, and I needed a good desk to hold that heavy monitor. Today the monitor is dead, and we're still using the desk. Make sure employees understand what it means to think long-term; most employees haven't seen it. They are often used to working for companies that are focused on the current quarter. But once they get it, thinking long-term can be a powerful component of empowering your management and your staff.

Another key element of realizing our vision is empowerment. We have recently adopted the unit president concept, which I learned about through the American Management Association's Course for Presidents. The unit president concept is an effective way of defining a manager's or an employee's "sandbox" — the scope of their work. The boundaries of the sandbox are defined by their job description, performance standards, a budget, procedures and policies, and legal and ethical guidelines. This concept introduces the idea that where there are shortcomings, coaching is needed. Where there is a desire to expand the sandbox, mentoring should take place. The unit president concept has been an excellent vehicle for discussing where an individual's boundaries are — i.e., where their empowerment starts and stops. In addition it allows us to be flexible and work at moving those boundaries when employees want to expand their areas of responsibilities.

Build Success on Values

As a company that has grown from a one-person start-up six years ago to a staff of 27 today, making sure we execute has definitely been one of our challenges. It is something we continue to work on every day. Day-to-day communication about progress and setbacks is important. Constant, consistent, and clear articulation of our core values with the staff is also critical, allowing individuals to make good decisions without getting bogged down in bureaucracy.

From the very beginning we've tried to establish a performance culture that expects a high level of competence without any of the usual command-and-control nonsense. We have instilled a cultural impatience for sloppy work or lack of professionalism. In our employee orientation we like to say, "We have a casual work atmosphere, but we aren't casual about our work." At the same time, we accept mistakes and failure as part of the norm because we encourage employees to experiment and try new things. As long as we're learning from our mistakes — and our successes — we're growing as individuals and as a company. We're making progress and learning how to execute better.

Clear communication is a key element. When decisions are made, it is vital that all the people affected by those decisions are informed in a timely, effective manner. Before decisions are made, we make sure the people who have input or the potential to be affected are involved in the decision-making process. We try to publish decisions, plans, and progress updates regularly by e-mail and on our intranet. Equally important is how we communicate our successes throughout the organization, large and small. We make sure everyone knows when a sizable new order has been processed, and the customer support staff is encouraged to share customer feedback with the staff via an internal mailing list.

Finally, I also think the strategic planning process I described earlier has been a key factor in changing how we look at execution. We have identified the key success factors for companies in our industry and made considered decisions about what we will do to ensure we execute in those areas. Part of executing well is making sure you execute on the right things. The new strategic planning process we adopted a year ago has helped us focus on executing on those things that matter most to achieving the goals we have set for ourselves.

VanDyke Software has been built around leveraging the continuous experiment of the Internet to create a development, delivery, and customer service mechanism that engages customers in constant dialogue. Engaged customers guide us to create rock-solid products aligned with our strengths and passion, taking advantage of our current technology wherever possible. Incorporating the best strategic planning and communication ideas provides the foundation to capitalize on opportunities, and the company's culture of constant learning keeps us evolving at the intense pace of technology change.

Biography

Jeff P. Van Dyke is the founder and president of VanDyke Software. He formed the company in 1995 to develop small TCP/IP applications to be distributed over the Internet. He has more than 15 years of experience in such diverse fields as retail management, network management, teaching, and programming. Through 1996 Mr. Van Dyke was the primary developer of the company's first product, CRT. Since then his focus has shifted to developing and leading an ever-growing team as the company expands into new products and markets.

Before founding VanDyke, Mr. Van Dyke did C++ development as a research scientist at the University of New Mexico and for Object Science Corporation, an SBIR (Small Business Innovation Research) funded start-up. During this time he also taught courses in computer architecture and UNIX system administration for the University of New Mexico.

Mr. Van Dyke received a BS and MS in computer science from the University of New Mexico.

Chapter 16

Intelligent Enterprises Everywhere

Arun Gollapudi

Technology: The Ultimate Means to an End

About a decade ago I read a book that had a profound influence on my thinking and how business could be revolutionized by strategy and technology — it was called The Goal. Eliyahu Goldratt's book describes the journey of a plant manager who turns his company around through a series of steps that all aim at finding and removing bottlenecks within the company. When I set out to create my company, I looked at technology as a tool one could leverage to help businesses solve their problems. I envisioned that automation and information used productively would lead to businesses achieving greater and greater efficiencies, adding more value to the marketplace and what they can offer to their customer base.

When pioneering decision support systems were created 10 years back, I focused my energies on these systems, as they had provided insights into businesses and supported intelligent decision-making. My company has focused on and specialized in business intelligence from the very beginning, because we have known the potential benefits to the business from business intelligence solutions.

Tom Peters has been another big influence on my thinking. I believe he captures a unique, entrepreneurial vision in his lectures and writings. His idea of a network of "consultants" working together and relying on each other for specific expertise is something I have always believed in. In fact, the result of my MBA thesis project at UCLA was the initial cornerstone of Systech. We were tasked with blueprinting a successful entrepreneurial company, and without knowing it at the time, many of Peters's hallmarks for a dynamic business were in there. When my partner and I cofounded Systech in 1993, we drew from many ideas. We knew from our own business experiences that democracy often encourages innovation in a way that strict hierarchy cannot.

The Three Key Functions of Consulting Firms

Fundamentally, information technology firms and the solutions we provide fulfill the following three considerations:

- Empowering businesses to be more effective at doing what they do best
- Making access to information immediately available, ensuring the systems required to run the business become easier to use
- Extending the reach of business solutions by providing access to business systems from a multiplicity of locations and devices

Let's take empowerment first: There is a dramatic need by businesses today for flexibility. The larger the corporation, the greater the need to be nimble in the face of challenging market conditions. As firms like Systech evolve the range of business-driven technology solutions for corporate America, companies are recognizing the great potential in those solutions for speed and autonomy. Empowerment of management and staff is key for the CEOs I speak with — leaders recognize that if technology can automate time-intensive tasks and suggest possible courses of action, the company as a whole is enabled to act and react in ways that suit them the best and allow them to be competitive in the marketplace.

Next, look at the issue of ease of use. Capability enhancement solutions have evolved significantly over the years, from database programs to enterprise systems like ERP (enterprise resource planning), CRM (customer relationship management), and business intelligence. The full degree to which easier access becomes a vital business element can be seen in the way ease of use and breadth of reach affect an enterprise. In ease of use, solutions have radically developed in just a few decades, from punch cards to character-based terminals, and then to GUI and video game-like interfaces in some industries. For example, a cockpit of the latest military or commercial jet uses this type of cutting-edge application, as pilots use virtual instruments on a screen that looks very much like the real instruments of yesterday's aircraft. These interfaces make it easier for people to intuitively use incredibly complex computer systems.

The third aspect of application development addresses reach, where we have gone from operator-based systems to client server, to Web browser, and now to wireless-based access. The Palm wireless and Blackberry devices represent the latest evolution of such solutions that have a widespread use. Today you can connect to a corporate Web site through a wireless Palm or Pocket PC computer. Blackberry devices have revolutionized the way businesses access their corporate e-mail. You don't have to be connected to a network computer to get access to corporate e-mail. Blackberry devices allow access to the e-mail over wireless, providing access to e-mail whenever or wherever you need.

Historically, every generation of solutions is a little better than the previous generation in having more capability, providing an interface that is easier to use, and extending the reach of the solutions.

Ideation and Methodology at Systech

For my company to be successful, I try to make sure all the ideas in my organization are given visibility and explored to find out if the idea is useful for our business plans. Ideation is encouraged at both the individual and the group levels. We have a highly successful Round Table forum about once a month, open to all levels of the company, in which developments and ideas can be voiced.

Most of my time is spent identifying potential problem areas and business ideas, making sure a knowledgeable person is handling them, and then moving to the next problem area. I try to catch up with my employees whenever possible, but also I follow an open-door policy in which any employee can walk into my office and ask questions. At Systech we often do things the MBWA way — Management By Walking Around, or trying to assess project and strategic situations firsthand as they arise. Systech employs people who are good thinkers and able to proactively follow up on their ideas. We have sought to maintain flexibility within the company, and this includes the willingness to stay open-minded, take suggestions, and admit mistakes. Ultimately, success comes down to challenging employees through opportunity and ideation. If you offer the best and brightest an impossible task and foster the conviction that a project team is only as good as each team member, a business thrives and even excels.

In a networked organization that delivers cutting-edge solutions to businesses, adoption of new ideas gives us a tremendous competitive edge. The new ideas we adopt need to be communicated throughout the organization. As a leader, it is my role to make sure the ideas we adopt to move us forward as a company are communicated throughout the organization. I do this by involving people in planning our implementations to make sure people take true ownership of the processes to be implemented.

To be effective I want to focus on things that are most effective in producing results. I split my time by spending 15 per cent of it on the future, in alignment with my vision for the company, and 85 per cent on the present and near-future. I have been able to carry this methodology into the organization in such a way that each department has its own principle of success, where 10 per cent of time is spent on the future, 30 per cent in the near future (three to six months out) and 60 per cent on today. This 10-30-60 split is informally referred to as the "Triangle of Success" within Systech. Take, for example, our Advanced Technology Group, which is a team of senior consultants responsible for bringing new technology into Systech and ensuring proper internalization and evaluation. Systech's triangle methodology extends to the technology group's time management of spending 10 per cent of their time on exploring cutting-edge technologies; 30 per cent on preparing training regimens and conducting training for Systech consultants in satellite facilities; and 60 per cent on supporting our project teams at critical points on client projects.

Ultimately, a consulting company depends on its people. My ideals come down to what we can do collectively, how we can innovate more as a group. When we talk about Systech's momentum, it is because we are constantly seeking new solutions, new paradigms. The thrill we get from devising solutions, taking them to market, and watching them succeed — there's no thrill like it.

On Entrepreneurship

Is entrepreneurship for everybody? Certainly not. Implicitly, entrepreneurship is for the individual who is willing to work hard, give everything he has to make the business successful, and still risk significant failure. The key is to become an entrepreneur in the early part of your creative life, when you are at a mental place to provide sufficient passion and endurance to grow the company.

It's a quirky example, but look at Jerry Jones when he bought the Dallas Cowboys. He sold everything else he had. He burned all his bridges, so there was no going back. He sank all his wealth in the Cowboys, and consequently he had to give a wholehearted try to make it successful. Regardless of what else you might say about Jones, success can be measured in his three championship rings. Perhaps Systech's story is similar in the sense that my business partner and I did not have any other place to go but forward. We plunged into an arena that we felt passionate about, but also made it the core part of our ambitions and dreams. Opportunities are always there for those who push themselves, take responsibility, and do what it takes to succeed.

Intelligent Enterprise: The Present Future

Businesses are focused on doing what they always do — actively seeking ways to better serve their customers and stay ahead of their competition. At Systech Solutions we are focused on the concept of the "Intelligent Enterprise", which is a framework within which corporations can simultaneously become agile and incredibly robust.

Some of the important trends in the past few years in the software industry have been encapsulated in three-letter acronyms: ERP, CRM, SCM (supply chain management). But the key to the near future, through which all of these trends flow, is business intelligence. The ability to glean knowledge you can act on from raw data lies at the core of the business technology revolution. Over the past decade corporations that have adopted business intelligence have discovered a flexible, durable, and invaluable tool for managers and executives involved in day-to-day decision-making.

Paradigm Shift: Immediate Need to Renewable Resource

Thus far, the common misconception is that BI products need to be custom programmed for corporations to receive benefits from them. As business intelligence is applied widely across a variety of industries, the marketplace is slowly shifting to realize the current business intelligence vendors are providing a product that is not a one-stop solution, but instead an endlessly renewing platform product. As IT dollars for expensive custom data warehousing have decreased, an inverse reaction has also occurred: Corporations are beginning to see BI as a reusable resource. Businesses are recognizing that solutions built on existing data warehouse products can be seen as end products with infinite variation, using the core BI product as a platform the way Oracle is a platform for databases. In short, business intelligence has come to mean paying once for a platform with any number of previously unforeseen applications across the enterprise.

At Systech we have seen this trend coming for some time. Our own suite of BI solutions has gained traction, especially in the complex world of consumer goods manufacturing. Many of the examples in this chapter come back to situations very familiar to me over the years, as we have started to see this trend of a self-sufficient, empowering BI platform take hold. Our vision of the Intelligent Enterprise framework stems from this realization: With BI at the core of an organization, every element of the enterprise maintains an ideal balance of mechanical automation and managerial autonomy.

The Problem with Tradition

Within the Intelligent Enterprise framework, a company can quickly see past the traditional bias of BI solutions as obscure analysis requiring a decision-maker for execution. In the traditional view of BI, managers are burdened by a deluge of reports created for their perusal. The line workers and system processes (programs running on a company's computers) are outside the influence of the BI solutions, as line workers are supposed to follow instructions, and the system processes follow the rules that have been programmed into them. Through Intelligent Enterprise, business intelligence platforms are considered as much a part of the business intelligence solutions as operating systems and databases.

Within the perspective of the Intelligent Enterprise framework, the first main difference is that BI solutions penetrate into the line worker and systems level within the enterprise. For example, we have a line worker at a raw goods warehouse. Trucks are queued, and they off-load at the dock on the first-come, first-served basis. In this scenario occasionally a shipment is extremely urgent, and a manager or shift supervisor manually intervenes to expedite a truck. This expediting requires precise coordination and simultaneously disrupts an entire chain of processes.

Now magnify the situation. From one warehouse we now have 10: A major manufacturer of toys maintains five raw materials factories, two sourcing plants overseas, three distribution centers nationwide, and cross-docker/consolidator issues at the borders. An unexpected rush order comes through for Wal-Mart, and because of the size of the order and a desire to maintain good customer relations, the item is pushed through the supply chain. How many orders of this sort can go through the system before efficiency begins to break down? Will half a dozen orders for different retail chains provide enough of a margin to offset the lost orders that arrived late due to push-backs in the chain? In today's real supply chain environments, managers and line workers are rendered vastly less effective in the face of increasing order complexity, and corporate profits plummet.

Integration Is the Key

In an intelligent enterprise exceptions and the chaos of rush orders are accepted as the norm. Success lies in the close integration of business intelligence with the organization and the warehouse management system. Inputs are provided based on what actually passes through checkpoints along the supply chain. The warehouse management system, for example, is fed the information that Store 144 will run out of certain SKUs far more quickly than usual; also, the system knows a truck is on its way to the warehouse with the inventory required by the store. In Intelligent Enterprise, BI would have forecast the demand, and based on predefined business rules, would recognize the truck as having critical inventory for Store 144. A work order produced from the BI system would then put this truck at the top of the list of trucks waiting to be processed and mark the truck's goods as urgent. The shift manager would schedule the truck to be processed ahead of the 15 to 20 vehicles waiting to be processed, thus creating a small delay that saves hours on this critical delivery and maintains the best balance of exception and profit.

A BI-integrated warehouse management system would produce a work order for the dock worker that indicates the pallets containing the inventory for Store 144 as urgent and would instruct the dock worker to put the pallets in a cross-dock instead of in stock. This series of processes would then cause the critical inventory to be delivered to Store 144 within hours instead of days. And this will happen every single time, as opposed to only when a supervisor gets involved in manual handling of an extremely urgent shipment.

In an Intelligent Enterprise highly disruptive processes that were manually expedited on occasion are now executed every time without disruption to the system. All of this happens without the manager or line worker receiving any special training on report interpretation or decision-making.

Similarly, system processes will be fully integrated with the BI systems, designed now to follow dynamic, rather than static, rules. To understand this better, consider the work of the dock worker in the previous illustration. With the warehouse system fully integrated with BI, the scan gun the dock worker uses is programmed to enact special handling of a pallet being off-loaded from the truck. As soon as the dock worker scans a pallet that is meant to be expedited, the BI business rule will cause an audible beep and a message to flash on his scanner, indicating the pallet has to be sent to the cross-dock area. As soon as the scanner in the cross-dock scans these pallets, the warehouse management system realizes the shipment items are complete, and the next truck out can be loaded with the inventory for Store 144 and expedite the process of delivery.

Has Anybody Seen My Company? An Executive Perspective

At the executive and management level, Intelligent Enterprise provides vital input to an executive in terms of knowing where the company is. Intelligent Enterprise solutions extend this traditional model that focuses on profitability to include analysis of opportunity — that shows an executive where the company can go or what the company can achieve. The opportunity analysis is done on a snapshot of a company's current data and shows an executive the opportunity that exists within a business to increase profits. Opportunity analysis is the recommended way for a company to start implementing a solution. Using the opportunity analysis, a business can determine the greatest potential for revenue and then act swiftly. By understanding the profit-generation possibilities and the potential benefits to the bottom line, an executive can calculate the value of implementing a solution that allows the company to improve the bottom line. The executive can also calculate the lost opportunity cost in not implementing a solution. Armed with these facts, an executive can now decide with confidence the budget for a solution that is implemented to address this opportunity. This process allows companies to get out of the vicious circle for ROI justifications for major software-based initiatives that often fail when the solutions implemented do not address the biggest opportunities within a company.

As an example of what can be achieved when we analyze a company with 150 stores and $26 million in reserve, Systech was recently able to show from the customer's own data that there was a $7 million opportunity in their underperforming store sales. The amount of savings that could be realized pointed out to management that they can focus their time and effort on building processes and systems to improve sales performance.

Breathing Room: Exception-based Reporting

Intelligent Enterprise will streamline the process at the management level to allow more effective day-to-day operations. To my mind, this is the very near future — without the adoption of exception-based reporting in the growing sea of corporate information, corporate managers will fall prey to inefficiency through an overwhelming paper crunch. In traditional data warehousing systems a manager is faced with hundreds of reports that are available to him, and most managers end up using a select and trusted handful of reports to help in daily functions. This leads to a manager ignoring a report when it should be looked at.

Financial departments of large corporations are a strong example of the type of user group best served by exception processing. A manager who is made to look through 80 or more reports will quickly begin to ignore reports that are normally irrelevant to day-to-day operations. Say that one report, analyzing customer payment patterns, shows a weighted average of how many days overdue a customer stands on total invoice remittance. A number of 15 to 30 days may be acceptable, but a pattern of 45-plus days two months in a row may imply the customer is in some financial trouble — and the manager may need to take action to ensure the company is not taking on a significant risk in supplying the customer. Exception-based reporting through an Intelligent Enterprise allows a rule to be established so that the customer entries that have more than 45-plus days for two consecutive months are automatically sent to the manager for a follow-up. With this process the manager's time is freed up under normal circumstances, and when a customer needs his attention, an exception-based report ensures that he is alerted to the situation.

In this way, Intelligent Enterprises have started to complete this data loop: Data -> Information -> Knowledge -> Action ->

This loop is key to a process of continuous improvement that companies have to embark on to stay competitive in today's world.

Complex Technology to Streamline Decision-making

The most important trend that will continue in the future is that applications will get more and more complex in functionality, from a business and a technology perspective. What this means is that the business analysis and customization configuration activities will take up more time than low-level programming (construction). This trend makes sense because businesses are different from one another in their pursuit of a competitive advantage. Moreover, they require flexibility in the software solutions implemented for them, and at the same time would not like to see the lag that exists between thought and action.

Applications will move toward application construction by using business widgets (like billing widget, order entry widget, etc.). These widgets will be able to collaborate to form systems using flexible interchange protocols. We already see the first generation of this collaboration in XML-, SOAP-, and UDDI-based solutions. This will allow for a very rapid development of applications, already quite evident in decision support, where you started with canned reports with custom programs to database-centered decision-support systems. In these systems a report can be created in days or a week. Today BI reporting systems take only minutes to produce a complex and effective report — the near-future business view is increasingly one of self-reliance for managers to run their own reports.

Another trend that will appear is the introduction of new paradigms of computing technologies into mainstream business. Technologies such as recursive, neural network programming and genetic programming that exist in video games and simulation today will probably mature in five to seven years. There is tremendous momentum in ease of use and reach, also. Intelligent devices, kiosks, smart cards, etc., will make access to this technology ubiquitous and easy.

Cutting-edge and futuristic companies have started using some of these technologies. In one of the applications I have heard about, genetic programming is being used to predict stock prices. These types of systems do not necessarily require someone to write the program logic for the entire system, but instead are using "self-learning" technologies that grow based on inputs provided and the program's ability to arrive at the output.

As you can see, the cutting edge of empowerment technologies is quite a bit ahead of the mainstream, and the envelope of technologies and solutions available is expanding at a rapid pace.

Biography

Arun Gollapudi is CEO and cofounder of Systech Solutions, Inc., a Southern California — based systems integration firm. In eight years he has seen Systech grow considerably; a testament to that development is Systech's ranking as L.A.'s fastest-growing company in 2001 by the San Fernando Valley Business Journal, and as one of the fastest-growing private companies in America by Inc. magazine in 2000 and 2001.

Well-versed in a variety of fields, Mr. Gollapudi has an extensive background in business intelligence, CRM, and e-business solutions for industries ranging from apparel, automotive, and finance to healthcare, entertainment, CPG, and others.

Chapter 17

The Changing Face of Technology

Tom Salonek

A Peek into the Future

Ten years ago I left West Group, a legal publishing firm, and started my own technical consulting practice. Today I am the founder and CEO of two successful businesses — go-e-biz and Intertech. Go-e-biz does e-business consulting services. For the past two years we've been on the Inc. 500, and we've won numerous awards locally for being one of the 50 fastest-growing firms in Minnesota.

Intertech provides three- to five-day hands-on workshops for enterprise developers. We teach programmers how to program. Our customers include Lockheed Martin, NASA, and the Mayo Clinic. Basically, we work with groups that have high-tech staff who build mission-critical software. In the beginning these two firms were together; we did consulting and training. A couple of years ago we spun the consulting services into its own offering, go-e-biz. Ten years seems like a short time, but in the technology world, a lot can happen in a short period of time.

Technology changes constantly. To stay competitive in this changing climate, there has to be a strong interest and desire to be in this business. This interest doesn't have to be particular to technology. For example, after we made the Inc. 500 one of our customers, who is with United Way, sent an e-mail I thought was a good summation of what we had been through. He said, "The growth you've had, and your ability to stay together, is a testament of your ability to get along with people." No one is inspired to work for someone who manages them instead of leading them.

When it comes to customers, there's always adversity, and technology provides an additional interesting wrinkle for both our businesses. We're dealing with something that's constantly changing. In sales, for example, there will be some amount of diversity if you're selling something, but with technology every three to five years there's such a significant amount of change in what you're doing that it's hard to keep up. It's just a whole new variable that makes trying to be consistently good or consistently great challenging.

In the next few years wireless and mobile will be significant. Today they're not, because every company is obsessed with what the return will be. This is tough: With new technology it's difficult to assess the potential return.

Another area that will be significant is Web services. In short, interconnected devices are the future of technology. For example, I have a cell phone that uses the same address my desktop PC would use. It will make talking between devices, as well as talking between companies and systems, possible. And http, XML, and the other protocols that go along with those will integrate devices, companies, and systems.

I think the Internet will continue to proliferate to small wireless devices. Data will become more centralized, meaning that we won't have a copy of our address book on our desktop and a copy of our address book on our phone; we'll have a central, secure place where that data will be stored. We'll be able to access it from our desktop or from our phone. The use of wireless technology will become faster and more consistent, but that will only occur in areas that are dense enough in population to support the infrastructure required to have fast, reliable wireless data access.

After the Dot-com Crash

There are two things we've had to deal with since the dot-com crash. The first is that we have to work a lot harder to get the same results. We had 50 per cent to 100 per cent growth for four or five years in a row. When you have that much growth, you make a lot of mistakes — at least we did. When things slow down, the benefit is that we have a reprieve to consider our actions: "We were spending $8,000 on this ad alone. Was it a good idea? Was there a return on the investment?"

The second thing is accountability. Now we have to ask a lot more questions about why we are doing the things we do and whether these things are working to our benefit. There are many more hard decisions that need to be made. When we were growing and starved for talent, it was really easy to say, "This prospective employee doesn't really line up with the value we have of our company, but let's bring him in anyway because we need someone to do X." Now there are hard decisions to be made about people who aren't fitting with us or aren't providing value. We just can't keep them around.

In technology there is just too much caution now. We have to face the reality that e-business will not go away. There was a heightened sense that what we were doing was going to change the world; that's where we were two and a half years ago with regard to technology and e-business. Now we're down in a trough of disillusionment, where we're scratching our heads and asking, "Where will this technology lead? What will technology mean to us in the future?"

The key thing that made the Internet so accepted during the dot-com craze was that we had e-mail. E-mail was an application that made sense to everyone. It made sense to mom and dad. It made sense to Fortune 1000 companies. It made sense to small business. It was the concept that if I want to get something to you, I can fire it over, and it just shows up in your inbox. That is without question the killer application that made the Internet the common network backbone that connects us all.

Today we don't have a similar application on wireless and mobile devices, but I think there will be something. What that something is today, I don't know. But I believe our devices will get smaller and cheaper. PCs have gone through something similar, where the hardware has more power and is cheaper. A similar thing is happening to the hardware in wireless and mobile devices. Cell phones were a big invention. The Internet is also a powerful technology.

Wireless is a combination of all these things coming together. But the missing piece today is the e-mail equivalent — the killer application for wireless that will make wireless and mobile technology something people can't live without. Checking weather and checking a stock quote on your mobile phone is the closest we've come to creating a universal tool for people to use. But that's not what people want. They aren't going to flock to that technology like they flocked to e-mail. We're still looking for that one technology that will equal e-mail, and someday we'll find it.

Making the Sale

When we approach prospective clients we begin by telling our story. Especially in today's market, we explain our roots to people. We want them to know that we're not new to the business world. We saw a lot of groups start out four years ago that went through the roof. Those people are not around anymore. We have a history of staying power. We also have a staying power both in our training ability and in our consulting business, so we'll talk about those successes and the A-list of clients we have as an organization.

We'll then talk about where we're going in the future. For example, a partner in our business, Andrew Troelsen, is a number one, best-selling author on .NET, which is Microsoft's latest technology. We have people at national conferences who present on cutting-edge topics, such as Web services. We also do instruction at a local university, which is the fourth-largest graduate business school in America.

We show clients that we have a solid past but that we're not looking back. We have technology thought leaders who are guiding our way into the future, and ultimately, guiding our customers in the projects and the training we're giving them.

Planning and Executing in a Changing Marketplace

What helps us succeed in the ups and downs of business is that we have an extensive planning process. In our planning process, we do SWOT (strengths, weaknesses, opportunities, threats) analysis, which involves reviewing our strengths and weaknesses as an organization. We find the opportunities and threats that exist. In the marketplace in Minnesota we've had a state worker strike and a budget shutdown. We'll talk about everything that's happening with competitors, customers, and the government, which happens to be one of our clients. We'll talk about our strengths and weaknesses as an organization. We find what we're good at and match those strengths with some good opportunities in the marketplace. Those are the things we'll try to leverage.

Then we look at our risks. What are the things we can do to mitigate or control those risks? We'll factor each risk: If the likelihood of its occurrence is small, and its impact will be small, we won't spend time worrying about it. I would say we avoid risks. We haven't gotten to where we are by taking huge, uncalculated risks. We've gotten here by taking an honest look in the mirror to see where we are. We take honest looks at the market and the overall conditions. We then devise a fairly straightforward plan that we can execute and that can allow us to be successful.

Our planning process reflects our mission — what we're trying to accomplish. For Intertech, our mission is to be number one in America as determined by total profits, the number of workshops we offer, and the number of bookings we have with the people who author books for us. This allows us to have goals. We work backward from our larger goals until we reach our 90-day operational plan for the business. This breaks down into 90-day individual goals. Every quarter we assess what we should be doing. This gives us a fairly simple model to operate within. Operating on a 90-day plan allows us to see our mission clearly. We can see the big picture and how all the changes we go through affect our overall goals. We know if we're going to be successful we will have to make changes. This has been extremely effective for us.

Once we have our plan in place, we do several things to make sure our company executes. One of them has to do with our 90-day goals. These goals are distributed down to the managers. Each manager is responsible for different things. For example, let's say I am the vice president of sales. I am the one who is accountable for sales. I will take my 90-day goal and break it down to key result areas and distribute it to my direct reports.

The second thing we do is to hold weekly hour-long meetings to talk about our progress toward our goal. Tied into those key result areas are work plans. So if I've said I'll have something done this week, before we get together on Monday, I'll say whether it's done according to plan. If not, I'll try to verbalize the problems I'm having and pinpoint the areas in which I need help.

The third aspect of our executing process is huddles, where every day for 15 minutes everyone dials into a conferencing system, including me, and we give updates. If I'm a new salesperson and my 90-day goal is to make 100 contacts per week, when I dial into my daily huddle, one thing I am going to share is that I made 21 contacts. For me and for the business, this is wonderful. We know we're meeting our objectives, right down to how many contacts each salesperson is making, and we're measuring that on a daily basis.

Daily huddles allow us to see if we are not executing. The definition of non-executing is having six consecutive data points going in the wrong direction — for example, 20 contacts that go to 18 to 16 to 14 to 12 to 10. If we have six of those lining up in a row, we have a trend. This hinders execution. And by sampling that often, we're able to correct problems quickly. If we were sampling weekly, we'd find out in about a month what was happening. And if we were sampling monthly, it would take half a year before we'd be able to figure out we weren't executing the way we should be. The efficiency of this process helps us execute successfully.

Addressing Problems in Execution

When work gets done, problems occur. This is a lesson I learned from my father.

When in college I worked on weekends doing odd jobs for money. Cutting wood was one of those jobs. On a Minnesota winter day, I was in the woods cutting trees into firewood. One of the trees was large and needed to be taken to a clearing before it could be cut into logs. I tied the log to my father's pickup with a log chain. I jumped in the pickup, put the truck in gear, and pushed the gas pedal. Nothing happened. I revved the truck. Still nothing. Finally, there was a loud snap. Puzzled, I looked down and noticed the parking brake was engaged. I had broken the truck axel.

Walking home through the new-fallen Minnesota snow, I went through my options: run away, cry, plead for mercy. In the distance was my parents' farm, my father walking through the yard. When I approached, he asked what happened. I told him. He paused and looked down. Then, looking back at me, he said, "If you do nothing, you'll make no mistakes...Let's go look at the pickup." It's a lesson that I've applied to our business.

We have five guidelines we use to deal with problems:

- When you bring your manager a question or a problem, bring along a few possible solutions. Be ready to tell your manager which solution you think is best and why. Don't use the manager's time to think through the problem if this is something you could do beforehand.
- Prepare your manager for bad news early. This allows your manager time to help you, defend you, or prepare other parties for what is to come.
- Take blame. This shows your character in the fires of a crisis. Skip the sackcloth, ashes, and flogging. Once you've owned and defined the problem, cut quickly to finding a solution.
- Listen. Seek first to understand, then to be understood. When you sense someone is upset, or miscommunication has taken place, listen without reviewing in your mind what you plan to say next. If appropriate, make sure you've understood the issues by restating what the person said.
- Act with character, be committed, and divide and conquer. Adversity tests character and shows others how we are "wired" at our core. Behave with character and be committed to solving the customer's problem. If you lose heart when adversity comes, your only strength will be weakness.

Profiting from Creativity

If we have a development team working on a system they're trying to build for a customer, or if a salesperson is trying to secure a project or training deal for our overall business, they have a great deal of latitude in terms of how they can get it done. And while we do have processes and procedures for how we accomplish our goals, we also give individuals the ability to make those day-to-day choices so they don't feel micromanaged.

Also, for the key result areas I mentioned, there are things specific people need to do over the next quarter to deliver for the business. For a salesperson, that means selling. For a consultant, that means getting in billable hours. But in addition to that, people will have projects they'll come forward with and say, "During the next 90 days I will generate X number of hours of billable time on these different projects I'm working on, and I have an interest in pocket PC development. I'd like to spend time to work on a class or a special project."

This dialogue allows us to formalize some of the creative things employees want to do. They have full control over how they'll implement them and get them done. This dialogue also allows us to recognize the benefits creativity brings to our business. It allows us to see the positive results. It also allows us to reward people for their creative endeavors. For example, if someone does creative work on a pocket PC, which is added to the portfolio we show customers daily, we'll recognize that person for that accomplishment. This, in turn, encourages others to be creative, and it keeps our business on the cutting edge of technology.

Steps to Building a Valuable Future

To ensure our company has a future, we have a planning pyramid. I learned about this through a program called "The Birthing of Giants", led by the founder of YEO (the Young Entrepreneurs' Organization), Verne Harnish. We begin by talking about our values and core business beliefs. We realize when we hire people or do anything in our business, there's some framework of values we have as an organization. We begin by having a very clear understanding of these core values.

But back to the planning process: We have a mission based on an objective. We hold ourselves accountable to that objective. We work backward and ask ourselves the following question: "If that's what we want our business to look like in 20 years, what do we need to look like in five years?" From that, we go back to our one-year set of goals. We have to make our one-year goal equivalent or on the same track as our five-year goal. Then we take a step back from that and ask ourselves, "What do we need to do in the next 90 days that will allow us to achieve what we want to achieve in the next year?"

Tied into the 90-day company goals, we have an overall theme. For example, the theme for Intertech was keeping our numbers up in a market where a lot of our competitors were losing money. To achieve this we put together a collage that's about as big as a person, with faces of all our core competitors on it. Whenever we book a student in the class, we put a big "X" on it, and after this thing has been filled up, we have a group reward we'll all share — we go to the lovely Mall of America here in Minnesota and have drinks and goof around for a day. So we have a theme that's tied to the overall company goals, which then get broken into 90-day key result areas for managers, who will then distribute it to their direct reports — and what that really gives us is alignment.

At our company meetings, held on the second Wednesday of every month, we provide an update on how we're doing this quarter in relation to the big theme as well as those key results we're going to achieve. Our communication people post what we are trying to accomplish on the entrance to our offices. We want everyone to see it.

Finding and Empowering Employees

You have to have the right people to be in this business, so empower your employees. The way to empower someone is to give them not only the full responsibility, but also the full authority and power to assign who will work on each project and how it will be done. Executives and managers need to know I won't micromanage them, but they will be held responsible for things that go either right or wrong.

The way to "disempower" people is to set limitations on what they can and cannot do. Recognize when they do a job well. It doesn't cost anything to give someone a pat on the back, and when we interview top-notch talent to come join our firm, even though the pay is good and the benefits are good, we find that people don't come for those reasons, and people don't stay for those reasons. One major reason people quit jobs is that they don't feel recognized for the job they're doing. Part of empowering people is to recognize them when they've done well. Don't be threatened by it. Recognize and reward people who are doing phenomenal work. It's as simple as that.

How do we find these high-performing individuals? Without question, referrals are a very important aspect of hiring. It's very easy for people who have personality flaws — the kind of person who'll fly off the handle and start screaming four-letter words at people in an effort to motivate them — to hide those personality flaws during an interview. But if you know someone who has worked with that person, they will give you a good window into what that person is like and how easy it is to work with that person. That's why referrals are so helpful to us.

To qualify people the first step is a screening interview to determine whether a person is a good candidate for the position. The second step is an interview where we talk about our values. It's important to understand that by the time people are of working age, their personalities are usually set for life. Unless faced with some life-altering event, adults don't usually change their values. As an organization we've been around for 10 years, and we probably won't change, either.

We let people know the key values of our business. We try to learn what their core values are. We give them a skills test on the area they are applying for. For salespeople we have an online exam that seeks to determine whether they have the strengths that will make them a good salesperson. On the technical side, for our development people who do training for us, we have a technical exam.

We ask people to assess themselves on the front end. We ask them how good they are at specific tasks they will most likely face in their job here. We ask them to rate themselves on their knowledge of specific elements of the job — "10" if they wrote the book, down to "1" if they can't find the bookstore. This gives us a very good idea of how well they assess their own skills versus where they really are.

The last step is a meeting in which the potential new hire will meet with people he or she would be working with. The people have to unanimously agree that this person is fit for the business; if they don't agree, we don't extend an offer.

We need to share the same fundamental values to build a team that will last. I am a big believer in commitment and hard work. There must be core values for the company, as well. The team needs to share those core values. Obviously, there has to be enthusiasm, passion, and excitement, because great things don't get done otherwise. A final thing would be great communication. For us to be able to work together effectively as a team, we need to have a plan, and we need to be able to communicate to each other changes or new things that pop up between one another in the loop. Solid communication skills are a final key ingredient.

The 12 Commandments of Communication

When the economy is white-hot and going through the roof, communication keeps everyone working in the same direction. When times get tough, communication stops rumors and controls chaos.

Our communication is a mix of words, delivery, and non-verbal communication:

- 7% of communication is through words
- 38% of communication is through voice, tone, rate, and inflection
- 55% of communication is through face and body language
— Harris/Osborne 1975

Keeping the above in mind, we've developed our "12 Commandments of Communication." The first day someone new joins our firm, we address the way we communicate. Our rules are simple, and they work:

1. Engage in direct communication. Venting to a third party doesn't change any situation and can disrupt office harmony. Address concerns, criticisms, and wishes to the appropriate members (those who have the power to make changes to policy or guidelines) of the company.
2. Remember that physical barriers inhibit dialogue. If you are sitting at a desk, place your chair on the same side of the desk as your visitor. Sit comfortably and keep your eyes on the speaker.
When negotiating, try to agree on something, however small, within the first five minutes if you are going into a meeting with the purpose of reaching an agreement with a new customer or client contact.

4. Always know your outcome, whether it's a meeting, conference call, or phone call. Not knowing your outcome is like getting in a car and driving without knowing your destination.
5. Remember "I don't know" is okay, especially when teamed with "I'll find out." This is much safer than bluffing. It shows you are honest and won't panic in the face of a challenge. If you follow up with an answer quickly, it shows you are responsive.
6. More successful negotiations occur over lunch, dinner, and in the hallway after hours than at a conference table with one side pitted against another. Reaching agreement requires trust. Trust doesn't get built without work and understanding. Invest in the relationship, and get to know the person with whom you will be working.
7. Think and speak solution. If the focus is on us, our hurt feelings, what happened in the past, gossip, etc., time ticks away as laundry lists of bad feelings build and emotions boil. Meanwhile, the solution is still waiting to be discovered.
8. Use "I" statements. "I" statements make our thoughts clear to our listeners. "I" statements make us focus on relevant experience instead of sharing opinion or advice not based on know-how.
9. "You" statements imply blame. Don't take it upon yourself to represent the concerns of coworkers. Each employee is responsible for stating his or her own concerns and suggestions.
10. Act the way you want your team or others to act. Attitudes are contagious.
11. People cannot control your emotions — only you can. If you are upset and not sure if you should say something — don't. Rarely will people think you acted unprofessionally if you say little or nothing.
12. Don't accept a "gift" of anger. In line with controlling your emotions, don't respond in kind when someone is angry. Your not accepting their gift of anger keeps it with them.

Success in Technology: Step-by-Step

The best thing I've learned in this business is practicality. I've seen things that haven't worked — it's new technology, it's a new team, it's a huge promise made that you can't deliver on. There are so many unknowns and so many new things that are factored in. It's hard to say with any certainty what the outcome will be. Being practical with technology means we need to do things in phases. If we're talking about some big thing we're going to deliver in a year and a half, we won't deliver that one big thing a year and a half from now. We'll deliver a lot of little things in one- and two-month increments.

When we approach a problem, we look at the technology we're putting together that will allow us to program or build this solution. Technology for technology's sake is worthless. Technology must allow our customers to do something for their business — the outcome has to be practical; it has to make sense. And if there's a difference between three years ago and now, it's that whole concept of being practical, which in business terms means we'll have an ROI on this thing we're doing.

We need to remember that when we do things for technology, it's never for the sake of the technology itself. There must be some end result we're trying to achieve. And so, for example, if we say the purpose of our system is "to streamline operations", at the end of the day, we're allowing our customer to handle the same amount of volume with fewer people — and then take those people who have been freed up and put them in some other part of their organization. The choices we make as a group should be driven by the positive effect they have for our customer and for their business.

Practicality is one of the golden rules of technology: If it makes sense, it works and gets adopted. If it doesn't make sense, people won't use it. When I look at technologies that haven't worked, I always see a reason, often as simple as, "It didn't make sense." For example, Pets.com, back in its heyday, sold dog food at a negative gross margin, and they would deliver it to my doorstep for less than I could buy it for in the pet store. It didn't make sense. It was a good thing for me as a buyer, but it wasn't a good thing to invest in, and it wasn't a business concept that made a whole lot of sense. A technology that does make sense is e-mail — the ability to connect us all through a common network backbone, so messages can freely flow between individuals.

The second golden rule relates to Jeffery Moore's concept of "Crossing the Chasm." This rule states there will be a period in which the technology you're developing is new and experimental — so much so that you won't be able to pay your bills with it. We see this often in the training side of our business. When we come up with a new training session or a new book, too few people need it in the beginning to be able to support a business. Moore referred to the idea as "crossing the chasm." It means there's a gap between early adoption and mass adoption. As a business, if you're just trying to be a pure-play company on the early adoption technologies, and you don't have money or the rest of the company behind you to support your journey into mass adoption, you won't be in business for long.

People I have seen who are successful outside of our organization say it's hard work, and that nothing great ever comes easy. Shortcuts don't allow you to build something that is great or that endures. Obviously, being smart is a good thing. Unlike with hard work, you can't teach someone to be smart.

Yet to me, the most important attribute is attitude. Even though it seems like a new-age concept, we control what we think about. We can think about all the things that are wrong, and all the reasons the economy is not going the way we think it should. We can think about all the things that can be bad for us — my brain can spew forth a ton of ideas, facts, and statements that are negative. But we can also turn things inside-out and say, in light of this, "What can we do? What are the things that are possible?" My brain can come up with that list, as well.

So the biggest thing is having a positive attitude, and in an organization attitudes are contagious. So if there's a doom-and-gloom mentality, that's contagious — but if there's belief that anything is possible, that will be contagious, too.

Thinking at the Speed of Tech

How do company owners and managers plan for the future when the future is already upon them? Strategic planning can seem almost quaint when you're in quarter-to-quarter survival mode, just trying to stay ahead of the competition and keep on top of rapidly evolving technology. As e-business becomes woven into the fabric of business, technological strategic planning becomes crucial to achieving the overall company mission.

Before you can determine where you're going, you must first understand where you are — as an organization — today. MIT economist and researcher David Birch found that companies exist in plateaus. Between the plateaus are chasms — those perilous places where companies languish or perish because they don't scale to the next level. To progress to the next plateau, companies must solve key technology challenges, address operational or management issues, and focus on new financial indicators. The table on the next page shows a breakdown of typical issues faced by companies at different stages of development.

Understand Where Technology Is

In technology planning, change is constant. This makes developing a 10- to 20-year mission that describes "how" impossible. For example, who had Java as part of their technology plan 10 years ago? No one. The Internet software language didn't exist. Now it's ubiquitous. However, not every technology will be as useful or as widely adopted as, say, Java. Therefore it is important to understand at what stage in their life cycle technologies are located.

Size	% of Companies in US	Technical Challenge	Operational Note	Key Indicator of Company Performance
1-3 employees	96%	Phone systems	You need more office space.	Revenue
8-12 employees	< 4%	Accounting system	Founder must learn to trust a management team and make transition to CEO.	Cash
40-70 employees	.4%	System integration	Competition begins to notice you.	Gross margin
$40-70M+			Execution is handled by others.	Profit on quarterly basis

GartnerGroup has developed the idea of the Hype Cycle to illustrate the stages within a technology's life cycle. There are five distinct phases, each corresponding to the following events:

1. Early adopters experiment with technology and identify new uses.
2. If one of those applications takes hold, the technology gains mass support. If not, it falls off the radar.
3. If it gains mass support, hype develops.
4. Technology does not live up to billing, resulting in disillusionment.
5. Practical technology application eventually emerges out of disillusionment.

A good example of this process is e-business. According to GartnerGroup, today we are in the "trough of disillusionment" — the post-hype stage — where fear and uncertainty obscure the technology's true value. Recognizing and placing the technologies you are considering within one of these stages may pay dividends, as it can help you time the implementation and rollout.

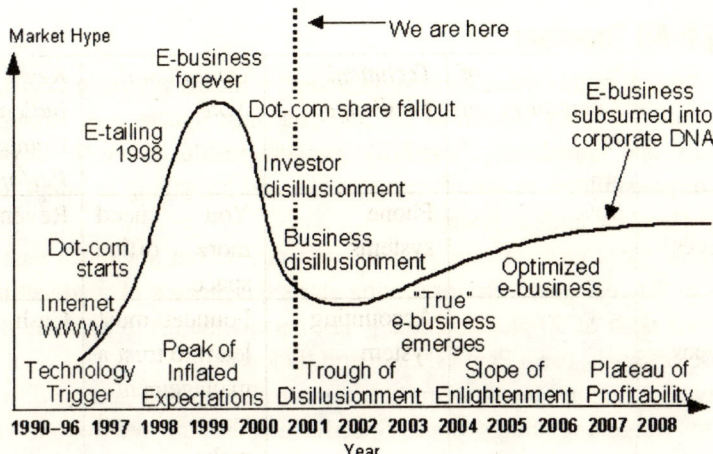

Source: GartnerGroup

Mission and Technology Alignment

Once you have managed to come to a better understanding of both your own organization and the technologies you're considering, it is time to make sure any initiatives you undertake complement your firm's mission.

While often overlooked, missions have a huge impact on the success or failure of a growing enterprise. The mission determines which direction you'll travel when you set out to expand your company. Therefore, your mission should be specific enough to drive certain actions and encourage specific behavior. Consider the following missions:

1. Our mission is to be the first provider of legal research services on the Internet.
2. Our mission is to be the number one provider of legal research services on the Internet, as measured by total number of state jurisdictions, complexity of search conditions, and ease-of-use, as measured by customer satisfaction.

In the first mission every decision — from marketing agreements to how systems are programmed — is governed by choosing rapid solutions over complex, more time-consuming activities. In the second example of a mission — something that takes longer but will result in a deeper and richer experience — specific criteria are chosen over speed. The technology mission aligns with the business mission and drives organizational behavior.

Putting It All Together

So what does all of this mean for your business? It means you have to project your planning out five years instead of 20, and you must update your strategic plans consciously and consistently; carefully measure results every 90 days; assign specific responsibilities to specific employees; and be willing to adapt to change regularly. Here's a quick overview:

Five-year goals provide trajectory mission targets but are much easier to set than 20- or 30-year goals. Brainstorming starts the process of goal-setting. After you've built a list of 50-plus potential goals, narrow the list to no more than five. To help select goals, use a Pain vs. Gain grid (below).

Ninety-day Actions focus on rolling up our sleeves and getting down to the nitty-gritty of getting things done. Specific actions are tied to one-year and, possibly, five-year goals. When the result for the 90-day period is being defined, it should be further broken down into actions that take a week or less to complete. This approach forces thought and focus on the front end. And this level of detail helps define interdependencies, clarifies resources, and creates a more accurate timeline.

Key Result Areas (KRAs) align team members with 90-day actions. KRAs define a detailed work plan, and, like any good goal, are measurable and tied to a date. While they require work, 90-day KRAs create clarity, definition of expectations, and, again, alignment with your mission.

The Bottom Line

In building a business or implementing a technology project, alignment is difficult, and execution is key. To execute at the speed of technology, make your plan result in focused action. It's a plan to succeed.

Pain vs. Gain	
Area	*Rating*
Business Gain	L = Low, customers haven't indicated this is important, questionable tie to mission, not a new product or significant improvement to existing systems *M = Medium, some customers indicate important, positive but not direct tie to mission, represents some enhancement to existing system *H = High, multiple customers have indicated important, direct tie to mission, represents strong enhancement to existing system or a new product or distribution channel
	Contd...

Initiative Pain	L = Low, "minimal" cost at least one order of magnitude less than medium-level initiatives, has minimal cross-department impact
	*M = Medium, modest cost, at least one order of magnitude less than high-level initiatives, has some cross-department impact
	*H = High, thought to be expensive, would require multiple business areas to change how they operate — operations, sales, finance, accounting

e-Do's and e-Don'ts
The 7 Elements of Highly Successful Technology Initiatives

"More people have ascended bodily into heaven than have shipped great software on time." — Jim McCarthy, *Dynamics of Software Development*

When I first read the above quote, I thought it was humorous. After years of being committed to delivering software on time and on budget, our customers have reassured us that shipping on time with intended features is the exception.

GartnerGroup estimates that approximately 75 per cent of e-business efforts fail due to lack of technical consideration or poor business planning. Why is it so hard? What can be done? I've seen a set of elements in every project we've shipped:

1. Selecting the right partner
2. Defining the problem
3. Working effectively together
4. Communicating frequently
5. Working smart
6. Constantly improving the process
7. Understanding the end game.

Miss one or two of the above, and you join the 75 per cent majority.

1. Selecting the Right Partner
Ninety-seven per cent of organizations have outsourced or used consulting services for some part of their e-business initiatives at some time, according to VARBusiness/Reality Research. Obviously, choosing the right partner is key. Without question, the market space of providers is crowded — most having come into existence over the past several years. When looking for a partner:

- Take time to pick a good provider. Ed Yourdon, an author and software methodologist, stated the difference between a good and bad programmer is tenfold.

- When interviewing prospective vendors, see the work and meet with the people who will be involved with your project. Don't fall for bait-and-switch — meeting with a ringer on the sale and working with a junior staff member on your project.
- Look at the long-term track record of the firm. Many new firms have sprung up, and old firms, previously entrenched in Y2K work, are touting e-business expertise. Firms coming from a client/server-centric background are more likely to have the skill sets required for shipping Web-deployed software.
- Make sure you're comparing apples to apples. Unlike cars or detergent, there isn't always a clear way to make sure you are getting the same thing — make sure the work up front includes time for changes to the prototype, design, testing, and staged quality assurance steps, as well as follow-up support.

2. Defining the Problem

There's an adage that a problem defined is half solved. This applies to software. An IBM study by Felix and Watson found well-defined objectives were the number one factor in successful projects. When we work with a customer we have several methods we use to define objectives:

- *Project plan:* This high-level document defines the project vision, critical success factors — what the project must deliver to be considered a success — and areas of responsibility.
- *Functional design specification:* This document is built in conjunction with a prototype and defines what the system does.
- *A prototype:* While not containing any actual business functionality, this creates an interactive way to design the system. Using the prototype, all flows of the system are defined.
- *Technical design document:* This document has multiple parts. It defines logic, data, and infrastructure and how they fit together.
- *Gantt chart:* This timeline states who, what, and when, and defines interdependencies. As the project progresses the Gantt chart is updated. The Gantt chart can also show "what if" scenarios — "what if we remove a person" or "what if we add a feature."

Beginning without the above is like building a house without a blueprint.

3. Working Effectively Together

Expect small teams, phased releases, and frequent deliverables. An ideal project team is fewer than six. If the project is large, it should be broken up into features and tackled by feature teams: project teams of fewer than six.

Working with an outside vendor introduces challenges. All are manageable. To work effectively:

- Define clear lines of responsibility. To stop turf wars before they start, clearly define the role of your vendor and communicate it to your staff.
- Clearly state expectations. The documents shared in Defining the Problem (#2 above), puts everyone on the same page.
- Choose a central point of contact. This should happen on both ends.
- Clearly state priorities. When fleshing out the functional requirements, prioritize features. When the releases are being defined, it is key to know what is a "go" versus a "no go" feature.
- Constantly communicate.

4. Communicating Frequently

In working with an outside vendor, because they may not be physically at your location, you can wonder what they are up to or what roadblocks they might be encountering. Expect regular updates. At a minimum, expect weekly updates.

In fast-moving environments — most companies today — daily huddles can keep communication consistent and effective. At go-e-biz.com, we use huddles. In huddles, which take no more than 15 minutes:

- Each team member gives an update. This streamlines communication and reduces the likelihood that one person will have to retell his or her story throughout the day.
- The daily number is shared. This is a number that measures the bottleneck. The number changes throughout the project. For example, in beta testing, this could be the number of outstanding bugs. Six data points make a trend.
- Each team member shares a stuck item. Sharing a stuck item brings up issues early and often, and allows fixing before they become unmanageable.

It can be tempting to forgo communication tools like huddles when you're in the end game and ready to ship. This is when you need them most.

5. Working Smart

IBM built an empire on the word "think." Thinking is key to deploying applications on time. To get people thinking:

- Encourage team members to constantly ask, "What could be done today that would have the greatest impact on future development?" For example, I've seen expensive developers without computers because a manager was "too busy" to order them a few weeks back.

- Keep meetings, including daily huddles, focused. Set meetings for first or last thing in the day or right before lunch. Cut off talkers. Honor time.
- Don't let meetings make more work. Make decisions on the spot.
- Remember that 12-hour workdays aren't 12-hour workdays. If projects are being shipped because the modus operandi is ongoing 12-hour workdays, the work in the day will cease to be 12 hours. People will still need to eat, have friends, get their clothes cleaned...Don't have crunch time be all the time — it loses its meaning.
- There is no silver bullet. From business process reengineering to object-oriented programming to code generators, there isn't one thing that will make development easy or simple. Rather, like anything, it is a set of things consistently done well by the management and technical people to produce a great result.

6. Constantly Improving the Process

As e-business becomes business, a significant number of business initiatives have an IT spin. Because this isn't the last one you'll be delivering, or the last version, you need to:

- Be prepared to change. Good software doesn't die; it just changes a lot — the next version of MS Word will be release 10.0. Good e-business software requires business objects, well-defined customer profiles, clear business events — these are focused efforts, not by-products. Sometimes this will cause differences in the original cost, making one vendor appear a lot cheaper. Factor in ongoing maintenance and changes.
- Follow some process. Before we can improve something, we need to understand what it is. Follow a process prescribed by your vendor; then make it your own and constantly improve on it.
- Encourage reviews in the business and technical communities. No one has the corner on good ideas. Even if you are moving fast, get buy-in and check-off.
- Make sure you have documentation, all of the code, and it meets your standards. Programmers and vendors leave. When your project is wrapping up, make sure you have all you need to make changes to your e-initiative.
- Do a post mortem. Don't blame. Ask, "What could be done to make it better?"

7. Understanding the End Game

The End Game, the time right before the software ships, can be difficult. It's manageable if you follow a few simple steps:

- Keep teams on track. Tell them to turn off e-mail and voice mail, and stay focused. Beyond the huddles, hold off on other meetings that may be "fluff."

- Keep the site in a known state. With multiple people making multiple changes, expect full builds of the site daily.
- Everyone should ask, "Will what I'm doing help us ship?" This may mean skipping helping out with interviews, sitting through all company meetings, etc.
- Does the bug need to be fixed? Sometimes bug-fixing introduces more bugs. Can you live with the bug, or is it critical?
- Alpha, Beta, and "Soft Launch" releases are not the time to solicit features. It's the time to shake out bugs and ship.
- If a date needs to be changed, don't change one bad date for another. If a revised date is set, get the team involved in setting the date, and hit it, no matter what.

Celebrate and recognize when the project is finished — whether it's formal or a beer out with the team. Napoleon said, "I've found an interesting fact — men are willing to die for medals." Recognition results in heroic acts.

While the list of things that are required day-in-day-out is much larger than seven, I've never seen a project missing one of these seven elements ship on time, on schedule.

Biography

Tom Salonek has founded two successful e-business consulting and software training companies in Minnesota since earning a bachelor of arts degree in computer science from the University of St. Thomas in 1989. Before founding Intertech-Inc. and go-e-biz, Mr. Salonek held software development positions at Control Data and West Publishing. He is responsible for 23 software product releases for the healthcare, medical, insurance, and retail industries.

Mr. Salonek has attended the University of Minnesota's MBA program. He is a graduate of Birthing of Giants, a three-year business development program at Massachusetts Institute of Technology. He also serves as an instructor for the University of St. Thomas Mini Masters in e-Commerce program in Minneapolis.

Chapter 18

Major Dilemmas Facing Privacy Practitioners

William B. Wilhelm, Jr.

Deciding on Choice of Law

The scope and direction of privacy law are changing so rapidly that the dilemmas facing a chief privacy officer or other privacy advisor are numerous. Some of the more significant issues facing privacy practitioners are in the area of choice of law, as well as the practical challenges facing those engaged in the development of corporate privacy policies.

When first addressing privacy compliance matters, it is essential to determine what law to apply. The basic question of choice of law is significant because it identifies the proper legal framework to apply to a compliance question. In many cases lawyers apply the law of the jurisdiction in which a transaction occurs.

The problem with electronic transactions is, of course, that there is often no physical location where goods are sold or documents signed. If, for example, the officer of a Delaware corporation buys goods from a vendor in France and electronically "signs" documents while on vacation in Germany, seeking delivery of the goods in Peru — what privacy law applies to the transaction? The analysis is further complicated by the fact that this information may be stored or carried by Internet service providers in other countries. If the officer submits personal financial information as part of the transaction, and she did not consent to the disclosure of this information to third parties without prior approval, can the Mexican ISP processing the transaction for the vendor nevertheless aggregate her information and sell it to others? If so, is the action a breach of contract, a tort, or some other claim? In answering these questions do you look to the law of Delaware or New York? If the state laws afford a right of action for violation of the officer's privacy rights, are those laws preempted by a Federal statute or the law of another country? Further, can the bill of sale determine the privacy rights of the officer, or are the contract provisions superseded by the rules of a particular regulatory body?

While these questions are of significant interest to large law firms, law professors, and their sleep-deprived students, the proliferation of overlapping and conflicting laws is of little comfort to the thousands of large and small companies that would otherwise find electronic commerce a compelling and rewarding business medium. There is little doubt that despite the dot-com flameouts of the 1990s, electronic commerce is an extraordinarily efficient and compelling distribution channel. While the medium has created an extraordinary opportunity to collect, efficiently process, and harvest information, in my experience most companies are genuinely interested in complying with all of their legal and regulatory obligations concerning the use of this information. The current lack of legislative and judicial focus on choice of law doctrine for electronic commerce transactions has unfortunately made privacy law compliance an unavoidably complex and cumbersome endeavor for even the most knowledgeable practitioners.

Setting Corporate Privacy Policy

In addition to questions of choice of law, there is frequently a considerable dilemma when a lawyer or chief privacy officer must confront a first draft or revision to a corporate privacy policy. In addition to the work involved in first identifying applicable privacy laws, most practitioners are quickly confronted with drafting choices that highlight the tension of both trying to be a good corporate citizen and also satisfying marketing, sales, and legal department guidelines. This tension is further exacerbated by either the absence of any specific privacy law requirements — which can cause marketing and sales staff to exert undue or unhealthful influence in the privacy policy drafting process — or by the imposition of significantly burdensome privacy law requirements, a fact that can impose cumbersome and costly procedures on data collection and sharing processes. This tension, not surprisingly, is at the heart of the legislative debate concerning privacy regulation. Federal and state legislators are grappling with the tension between freedom of speech and the public outcry over unseemly corporate data sharing and collection methods. In the United States, for example, federal legislators are struggling with whether to require opt-in or opt-out privacy schemes. In an opt-in framework, a person's information cannot be shared unless he has expressly authorized disclosure. In an opt-out regime, collected personal data may be shared unless the data subject opts out of collecting and sharing practices. In the absence of formal legal requirements, a corporate privacy officer faces the dilemma of making these and other policy choices on her own.

In creating a privacy policy, one of the worst things a company can do is to develop a policy that is not well thought out or that the company doesn't have the capability to properly implement. It is a dangerous misconception that a privacy policy can be drafted with much forethought but no follow-up. In truth, it is better for companies to avoid creating voluntary privacy policies if they have no intention or ability to self-police compliance.

To resolve these issues, most privacy officers would welcome, in the first instance, clear guidelines on what privacy laws are applicable to any given transaction. More specifically, where two inconsistent legal frameworks could arguably apply, it would be most helpful to easily determine which laws are preempted or how inconsistent laws are to be harmonized. In the absence of clear statutory rules, the highest courts must provide greater guidance. While recent decisions on choice of law have been encouraging, there is still no clear legal test to apply to every case. Most companies, large and small, want to do the right thing regarding customer privacy. The absence of clear rules governing choice and conflicts of law severely complicates compliance efforts.

In addition, there has to be a greater education effort on privacy law issues. Trade associations, federal and state regulators, corporate law departments, and outside counsel all have to be proactive. In our experience, fast-growing technology companies are eager to learn and apply privacy laws, and as a matter of course, we are constantly educating clients on privacy developments. There is no doubt that privacy is a rapidly changing field, and for that reason more than any other it is critical to have a chief privacy officer and perhaps other individuals tasked with staying current on legal and privacy policy developments, although a chief privacy officer himself cannot ensure compliance. Human resources, marketing, sales, legal, and other staff need to be educated — not only about legal requirements, but also about the company's own internal policies and guidelines. Further, one person alone cannot be held responsible for all corporate privacy compliance requirements. Compliance must be a decentralized, shared responsibility and should be given to various departments, disciplines, and geographic locations.

Furthermore, it is critical that companies think holistically about privacy and privacy policies: Corporate privacy practices are not just legal contracts; they are public relations statements, marketing documents, legal guidelines, statements of business practices, and corporate culture. In this regard it is critical to understand several overarching principles when drafting privacy policies.

First, it is critical to acknowledge that privacy policies are not just consumer marketing documents. Privacy policies affect not only interactions with retail customers, but also relationships with third-party vendors and suppliers, as well as other corporate customers. For example, many corporations and government buyers will refuse to do business with vendors or suppliers that do not abide by fair information practices. In this context, the failure to create, understand, implement, and enforce privacy principles will adversely affect individual purchasing decisions and may also have an impact on millions of dollars of government or corporate buying. In some industries, such as healthcare and financial services, vendors and suppliers may be required to have privacy policies; in other cases where legal requirements are not directly applicable, industries may be subject to such scrutiny that they place a substantial premium on information practices. In the final analysis, it is important to acknowledge that privacy principles affect buying decisions.

Second, it is critical to understand that a privacy policy is not just a set of binding legal guidelines for information sharing and disclosure. The policies are also statements of corporate image, governance, and identity. As a result, these policies must be viewed as more than legal documents; they should also be forward-looking and should clearly contemplate future developments, as well as present data collection and sharing requirements. The failure to carefully contemplate current and future information-sharing practices can result in legal complications when companies confront the difficulty of obtaining retroactive consent to share data. Moreover, companies may find that they face public outcry when they make retroactive changes to their privacy policies. Often, these situations could have been prevented with some forethought. Companies have to carefully consider their business reputation and marketing practices when developing or changing policies.

Misconceptions About Privacy

Misconceptions with regard to privacy laws are many. First among them is that in America individuals believe they have a greater right to privacy than they are actually entitled to. Unlike elsewhere in the world, generally speaking, Americans place great emphasis on freedom of speech. As a result, our government is restrained constitutionally in its ability to limit others from "speaking" about us, unless such speech is false. Indeed, if we willfully provide others with information about ourselves, outside of certain limited situations, there is little we can do to prevent the disclosure of that information to others. Although legislation promises to gradually expand our privacy rights, these rights are currently rather circumscribed. To many this does not seem fair; it's a betrayal of the first degree when a survey company that called us for our "valued opinion" on foreign policy shares our personal information with telemarketers or for other purposes we didn't originally intend. Notwithstanding our sense of betrayal, absent carefully tailored laws designed to protect our personal information, such sharing is rarely illegal in the U.S.

Individuals should realize their personal information is a valuable commodity. All too often individuals are too eager to disclose personal information about themselves without recognizing the consequences. Recently people have become more aware of the value of their personal information by way of spam, junk mail, telemarketers, and identity theft. All those occurrences have started to make individuals realize we pay a price when we disseminate our personal information.

Given our limited privacy rights, I have great concern about how the scope of our Fourth Amendment privacy rights seem to be contracting further with the advent of new technology that permits others to peer into our homes and offices, listen to our conversations, or read our correspondence. Our increasing dependence on technology has certainly made our hectic lives more convenient — but it has also made our behavior and communications more susceptible to oversight.

Recently there have been numerous legal decisions that have focused on new technology, and, in particular, the privacy rights granted to individuals using it. We are all aware that we have a reasonable expectation of privacy when we have a telephone conversion using a wired telephone, but recently legal decisions have narrowed these rights. For example, one no longer has a reasonable expectation of privacy when conducting cordless telephone conversations, nor do they have privacy from electronically-enhanced telephoto lenses. There are also limited privacy rights when you are chatting with another using an instant messaging product. Moreover, the US Patriot Act allows government the ability to more easily intercept certain electronic communications. The scope of our privacy rights in the use of new technology is currently being narrowed by the courts and by Congress. Since our legal protections against unreasonable search and seizure are partly dependent on our expectations of privacy, judicial and Congressional narrowing of our rights will undoubtedly lead to even narrower individual expectations of privacy.

The other significant misconception is that privacy laws and privacy policies are economically stifling and disadvantageous. I think several developments suggest otherwise. First, citizens of Canada and European countries have much greater protection of their personal information than Americans. Companies in these jurisdictions have had to contend with data and information regulation that far outstrips any comparable American scheme; yet this regulatory regime has not led to the collapse of these economies. Companies in these jurisdictions remain competitive both in their home countries and in America. Furthermore, data regulation will become a reality — if American policymakers don't demand it, European regulators and the globalization of world economies require it. To this end, American companies that do not immediately confront privacy issues will be competitively disadvantaged, either when they expand into regulated countries or when — as I believe will occur in the next several years — information collection and sharing practices become regulated in the United States. Indeed, companies that collect customer information today without express customer consent run the risk that future legislative and regulatory outcomes will require them to either expunge this valuable data, or they will be forced to retroactively obtain customer consent for the use of this data.

Finally, while it is largely true that the Internet itself is unregulated, businesses and business transactions and personal data flows are increasingly subject to regulatory oversight. The lack of uniform privacy regulation in this country is actually impeding both online commerce and the adoption of new technologies. The obligation to comply with the patchwork quilt of state laws is cumbersome, if not impossible. In the absence of uniform rules, I believe the operative consumer assumption is becoming that personal information will be collected, used, disseminated, and otherwise sold to the highest bidder. The evidence that this chills commerce is more than anecdotal.

Currently, when it comes to privacy in America, we don't have a standard set of rules for the road. Today, we are largely unaware of how our information will be used, what will be collected, how it will be shared with third parties, and whether any current privacy policy might change unilaterally without notice. Although some efforts have been made to develop industry standards, there is currently no default privacy rule. The absence of uniformity is chilling individual and corporate adoption of technology that could increase productivity or otherwise improve lives or industry.

When someone goes to the therapist, for example, they might be concerned about what information their insurer will share with their employer. This situation might make them hesitant to seek treatment. By having a standard set of rules that apply to privacy, society can address the privacy concerns of individuals and companies efficiently. This would provide individuals greater daily comfort when presented with situations where information must be disclosed.

Developments Affecting Privacy

Although some technological developments, such as Platform for Privacy Preferences, or P3P, hold promise, the privacy landscape will be most significantly affected by the passage of any one of the numerous federal privacy bills currently under consideration. A number of different versions have been proposed, and they differ in many respects. One of the key issues being debated in the context of proposed privacy legislation is whether state law will be preempted. This is a particularly stormy topic, since many states have proposed more restrictive privacy regulation. Although Federal preemption would reduce administrative burdens, it would also eliminate the states' ability to regulate commerce within their borders.

A second issue affecting privacy is whether privacy legislation will adopt an opt-in or opt-out approach. Some bills under consideration right now propose a mandatory opt-out policy, meaning that a customer, once he or she provides information to a company, will have the opportunity to preclude that company from sharing the information. The other option is a mandatory opt-in, which is much more restrictive and would require companies to proactively obtain the consent of the individual before sharing information with a third party. Also proposed is a hybrid approach, where opt-in policies would apply only to "sensitive information", including financial, medical, and other types of information. This hybrid approach is currently used in the telecommunications industry, depending on whom information is shared with and under what circumstances.

In addition to legal shifts, technologies such as P3P will be extraordinarily useful in helping implement any new legal privacy requirements. Right now people are frozen with indecision on privacy matters; businesses and consumers find privacy a complicated issue, partly because global economies don't have a default rule. No one knows when they log onto a particular Web site if they will be given opt-in or opt-out rights. Furthermore, an individual needs to read every privacy policy if they want to fully understand information-sharing practices. This situation is not particularly efficient or helpful to online commerce. P3P should enable individuals to quickly and efficiently identify information collection and sharing practices.

Technology will continue to create more privacy issues. Technology is obviously increasing the capability to gather and disseminate information, capabilities that are generally positive developments as our need to collect data, identify trends, and anticipate demand increases. What concerns most individuals is that this computer processing power can be used for purposes not intended by the party providing their personal data. Arguably, as a society, we need to not restrict technologies' ability to collect this information and disseminate it or to use it in fascinating new ways that benefit our lives. Instead, we need to be able to feel secure in the information that is gathered by these devices. We haven't let the genie out of the bottle yet; we do, however, need to develop greater legal guidelines on how information is collected and used. Technology should be allowed to continue along its developmental path, but legislators, judges, and lawyers must quickly develop laws to contain the collection and distribution of personal information contrary to an individual's wishes.

There has been an enormous debate about privacy over the past few years. It is somewhat amazing to me that it took the Internet revolution to get people to focus on privacy issues. Having engaged in this societal debate, I'm certain we will see some privacy legislation that gives consumers and businesses some knowledge and control over how personal information is collected and shared. This legislation must include an individual right of redress if it is to be effective. I also believe these legal changes will drive a host of new technologies, whether P3P or something else, that will allow customers to inventory and keep track of their personal information and make sure it doesn't go where it shouldn't. My guess is as good as any — but I foresee technology and law coming together to give people a greater sense of comfort with respect to information privacy.

Privacy Advice

I went to a Jesuit undergraduate institution in New England. During my time there I took a business ethics class. In the morning we read the front page of a major newspaper, and the professor, a Jesuit ethicist, expounded on various business ethics issues that were related to the paper and the stories we read. At the end of the course he imparted the best piece of privacy advice I have ever received: "Don't do anything you wouldn't want to read about on the front page of the Washington Post the next morning."

In today's environment, where we don't have clear privacy laws, that is really the best piece of advice I can give to both individuals and companies. It is important for individuals, because without specific legislation, there is a limited level of comfort that your personal information and information about your activities won't be disclosed to third parties without your consent. With respect to companies, they may very well have the right to collect personal information, disseminate it, use it for commercial purposes, change your privacy policy without notice, and sell collected personal information to the highest bidder — but just because you can do it, doesn't mean you want to confront the outcry associated with the exposé on the front page of The Washington Post. For both individuals and companies, it is good advice to step back and look your intended activities before undertaking them. For individuals this means working under the presumption that information you disclose may be shared without your knowledge. For companies this means looking at data collection practices and understanding both the legal and ethical repercussions of sharing or marketing this information.

Once a company considers undertaking a privacy policy, it is important to make sure they are committed to implementing the policy. In the absence of a specific requirement, too many companies are eager to adopt privacy policies without ensuring that they have the internal mechanisms to enforce them. Also, all too often companies are not realistic with respect to the resources and the effort they will need to employ to make sure they can implement those privacy policies. Having an effective mechanism to implement a privacy policy involves committing time and resources. Development requires input from marketing, human resources, and legal, if not other departments. It also means ensuring that the sales teams, legal department, human resources group, Web site administrator, and others are all aware of and in compliance with these privacy guidelines. Furthermore, the company must make sure it has an ongoing mechanism to audit those various divisions. The risks of not having a privacy policy are great. But the risk of having a policy that is not implemented correctly is even greater.

In considering who should handle privacy matters, I would suggest the responsibility be shared at different levels within a company, with one person performing oversight — the CPO. The chief privacy officer should be exclusively focused on these issues. Further, the CPO should have the authority to participate in decision-making on legal, marketing, and human resource issues, because privacy intersects with each of those areas in an organization. Marketing input is important to the development and enforcement of privacy practices because information is collected, sold, and disseminated through marketing processes. The legal department should be included in this process, as well, because various contracts (either vendor contracts or contracts with third parties) may address issues related to information collected or information shared about customers. Obviously, human resources needs to be involved because a company may have sensitive personal data concerning employees, and this data may be subject to separate employment privacy laws. The choice of the people to lead corporate privacy initiatives does depend a lot on the size of the organization, but it also depends on the organization's desire to address privacy issues and its commitment to incorporate privacy considerations throughout the sales, marketing, contracting, and hiring functions. Above all, good privacy officers must spot issues and implement solutions.

For individual companies that do not have a chief privacy officer, it is very difficult, if not impossible, to stay on top of all the new developments in privacy. One good piece of advice is to focus on the issues that are specific to the company's particular industry because, in the United States, much of our privacy legislation is directed at particular industry segments. Also, privacy audits by independent third parties should be conducted on an annual basis. Take a look at your existing privacy policies and contracts, and make sure your internal mechanisms are sufficient to ensure compliance with those policies. If you can't keep up with every new rule, turn to third-party providers for advice.

Biography

William B. Wilhelm is a partner in the Washington, D.C., office of Swidler Berlin Shereff Friedman. His practice specializes in the representation of telecommunications, Internet, and technology companies offering products and services that leverage software, computer hardware, or telecommunications networks. His counsel includes advising companies on domestic and international privacy laws, telecommunications regulation, and telecommunications and Internet transactional matters.

Chapter 19

Managing Privacy

W. Riker Purcell

Task 1: Making the Privacy Program Work

Gramm-Leach-Bliley (GLB) put tremendous pressure on financial institutions to get their privacy statements written and to start delivery to customers by July 1, 2001. To create an effective privacy program in such a short period of time, most people in the insurance industry knew it was vital to put a workable program into place with the intention of tinkering with it after the initial frenzy. As this company started to comply with GLB, there was a lot of mailing and passing of information as we tried to figure out how we do business, what the risks are, and how we would get the rules of the game and the policy statements themselves distributed through our branches, as well as through our agents who issue our insurance policies. We then had to make sure our own internal audit department put our program onto their list of things to check for when they conduct their audits. These and other early actions were aimed at making the program satisfy at least the minimum requirements. As soon as that was done, though, we began to get solid, practical questions from the field; we spotted some gaps to fill and delivered some clarifying instructions.

In the title insurance industry, in the early stages, every company was on its own. Everyone thought the best way to do things was to read the rules, make a plan, survey the field, talk to management, and make a good-faith effort to comply. When I give anyone else advice, it is to make your very best effort to come up with a genuine good-faith plan. Sometimes we seek expert advice, and sometimes we make critical determinations ourselves. But we always try, in good faith, to comply with all of the requirements. The privacy officer has to be diligent in asking difficult questions and making sure that the company's answers will hold water.

My impression is that the regulators are going to look for good-faith compliance. They won't look for perfect compliance, and they will not be too critical of small deviations and errors. Instead, companies that seem to have thought the issues through and seem to be making a continuing effort should be okay. Companies that fall under GLB have to understand the entire picture as completely as possible, try to put a good-faith program in place, and keep it working.

The privacy officer must know the rules and the reasons for these rules, and know how to distribute these rules and reasons to the people who can implement. In a company like ours, with about 8,000 employees, I think this means literally keeping a list of names of people in the field who are willing to be concerned about privacy compliance. Again, we should aim for instinctive compliance. People must know the reasoning for the law.

There is an important detail in the care and feeding of insurance privacy compliance programs. Although most state legislatures and insurance departments wound up with laws and regulations that are close to the federal standard, some states have adopted laws and regulations that take a different turn. For instance, a couple of states have adopted, and other states are considering, an opt-in standard instead of the more conventional opt-out standard, so that an insurer or insurance agent would need affirmative permission for certain types of sharing. When managers pose questions about a new plan or program, the privacy officer has to slow down and resist the temptation to give the answer based on the prevalent standard. Instead, the privacy officer should look at the sections of any state privacy laws that could govern the particular issue raised. The statutory and regulatory language differs, and because of this, it's easy to make a mistake.

In the end, I think that continuing, good faith efforts will satisfy regulators. We are not as concerned about private lawsuits because GLB and most of the state laws that follow GLB do not provide a private cause of action for violations — that is, only the state can prosecute a failure to comply. There is some risk of private lawsuits, especially class actions suits, based upon the theory that violations of privacy laws are unfair trade practices under state insurance law. However, as long as companies exercise caution, the potential plaintiffs should have trouble proving they have suffered any damages.

Task 2: Education

There are two levels within the company that must be constantly aware of privacy issues, constraints, and laws: senior management and front line employees. First, it is important that senior management understands the company's privacy limitations. In our company several practices or behaviors could be identified as tempting, but risky. Senior management has to recognize those behaviors and agree early in the game to avoid them. Every time a privacy issue comes up, I am confident that senior management will respond according to the rules. They know what they can and cannot do. I have tried to make them understand where our greatest risks are and why we have to adopt a policy that protects information, rather than disclosing it. If senior management doesn't understand the issue, then a lot of energy is wasted as managers create information-sharing plans (or plans that have information-sharing as a by-product) that have no possibility of coming to fruition. This could be a plan to sell customer lists or a plan to arrange for software maintenance. When members of senior management are educated about privacy issues, they can recognize problems that arise and tell someone "no" early enough in the game.

Second, we must also focus on those employees who actually deal face-to-face with customers. They must understand the rules, so when they confront an issue, they know instinctively what information should be protected. There aren't many people in between these two levels who can actually mishandle information, although mid-level management can certainly hatch ideas that would, if unchecked, lead to trouble.

Beyond that, the challenge has been to get everyone in the company to understand the spirit and the intent of the law. Everyone, but especially senior management and front-line employees, needs to know what kind of information and which documents are supposed to be protected, so they can instinctively conform their behavior to comply with the law. That, to me, is the greatest challenge — we need people to understand the spirit of this law well enough that they don't have to stop and think very hard, and if they do have to stop, they will quickly know the answer. Furthermore, when the insurance examiner comes to check on our compliance, our employees should know what they are supposed to do and demonstrate that they understand the rules and that they are actually complying. The greatest challenge is making sure that everyone who is supposed to know the rules does in fact know the rules.

Title Insurance Industry Initiatives

Because my company is mainly in the business of performing real estate settlements and issuing title insurance policies, there is a body of information we have to obtain from the public records, and also a body of information (deeds, mortgages, releases, easements, etc.) we have to put back into the public records. In 1982, when the first insurance privacy laws appeared, we thought everything we handled was public information. We would search the public land records and put the information we found into the title insurance policy. We then would handle the closing, and we believed the only thing we ever touched was public information.

GLB, however, forced us to look at everything more closely. We realized there were some surprising things in the title insurance policy that technically were nonpublic personal information, even though the information would not normally be considered sensitive. This meant, though, that we had to take extra care to prevent the policy from getting improperly into circulation because of the possibility that some bit of nonpublic information would be shared.

Also, in the context of the closing, we do receive a quite a bit of important information. The title insurance business helps make sure a real estate closing goes smoothly. We deal mainly with real estate information, but also with some financial information. We don't ordinarily have access to income figures, but it could happen. We could get our hands on a credit report, but most of the information in our system is real estate information related to the real property that the customer is buying or mortgaging. We often get nonpublic personal information we don't want or need. GLB has caused us and a lot of other financial institutions to ask questions about the contents of our files and the protection the information deserves. Obviously, a well-tuned document retention/destruction program is an important part of a successful privacy program.

Currently we are trying to make all of the pertinent information fit into a database so the information is entered one time, allowing the system to generate documents and make calculations without the necessity of further re-keying. We would also like to create a database that provides those people who are parties to the transaction access, but only to the information they need, so they can check the progress, as well as add to the posted information.

Privacy concerns will affect the way we implement this goal. We obviously must worry about granting database access to the right people while ensuring that each person can read only the appropriate information. Not everyone involved in the transaction needs access to every piece of information. For instance, we might want the person who supplies the appraisal for the real estate closing to be able to confirm that we've received it, but that person obviously doesn't need to know the loan's interest rate. So our concern becomes making sure they can get into the system but retrieve only the information they need.

Technology is a versatile tool. It allows us to collect, sort, and retrieve information and documents. It also allows us to open the files to interested parties, while blocking access to certain information. In some very important ways, privacy policy is implemented by electronic means.

Technology Trends

There is no doubt advances in technology will lead to more opportunities for sharing. More computer programs and marketing firms will promise to describe the consuming public by name — who the consumers are, where they live, and what they want to buy — for a variety of marketplaces. On one hand, computers will make all of this information more available. On the other, computers will also make it theoretically more possible to screen and block out information in compliance with the laws and regulations.

My guess is that these two trends will go hand in hand. Privacy demands and technology will develop together. As the business people who are responsible for making decisions actually determine how to slice, dice, and share information, they will also have a growing capacity to screen, block, and protect. This means technology will allow companies to individualize privacy protection. If a consumer indicates he wants more information about the types of products he has already bought, but doesn't want to hear about other, unrelated products the company may offer, the company should be able to use technology to deliver only the information the customer has indicated. In a perfect world, the legislatures would pick up this trend and pass laws that call on industry to tailor their programs to individual preferences. Companies that lack the hardware and software to tailor their programs will simply have to limit or eliminate any sharing.

Two things we can't predict are consumer tolerance and legislative concern. I don't think anyone truly knows how the consumer in general feels about having his or her information sliced, diced, and shared. That is an unpredictable element. If consumers become furious about the way their information is shared (as a result of technology, mainly), then they may complain in large numbers to their legislators. This is a high-profile topic now. At least for the moment, consumers can get their legislators' attention. There's a question whether legislators will continue to be interested in the topic of privacy. For example, as a result of the September 11 terrorist attacks, Congress passed laws that favor the collection of private information over privacy concerns.

Is privacy one of those concerns that remain for decades at the forefront, like civil rights, or is it more like antitrust enforcement, which drifts in and out of legislative favor? I would say most people don't mind getting some junk solicitation via the Internet, by mail, or even over the phone. They don't mind getting the junk as long as it doesn't contain references to really private information. A cautious company will think about this before delivering solicitations. A very few people are adamant about the entire topic: They don't want anything mailed to them, and they want their information completely private.

There will always be some of those people, and their concerns need to be addressed.

It seems to me that technology makes it possible to individualize the protections. Legislatures will ensure that virtually all information can be blocked upon consumer demand, so businesses must weigh their ability to protect the rights of the adamant few. If a business doesn't have the technology to block a customer's information, then that business will probably have to abandon any plans to sell or to share information.

In summary, technology will put powerful tools into industry's hands to collect, sort, and retrieve information and to share or limit access to that information. The course of privacy will not be determined by that growing capacity, but by consumer concerns and legislative interest.

The Personal Privacy Dilemma

Privacy issues often go deeper than many people realize. For example, our company is a self-insurer for health insurance, which means we have to comply with HIPAA (Health Information Portability and Accountability Act), as well as with GLB. I am not sure every employee understands how much of their health information may be stored within their employer's files. Every time they take medical leave, it is part of a company's records. If the company administers a flex-spending account, the records are right there in the company. I am not so sure employees stop to think about that, but at the same time, most companies wouldn't dream of doing anything with the information. This is a single example. The point is that most of us don't spend time thinking about where our sensitive, personal information is stored or who may be transferring that information.

I think most people are not very concerned about personal privacy. Certainly almost no one is bothered by the release of a lot of demographic information that has been purged of personal identifiers. If you subtract the name from the information, it becomes completely non-personal. It makes a lot of sense to me for everyone to get used to having their buying patterns monitored, but without their names being involved.

I am, however, personally bothered by all sales of individual customer information. I don't think it is anyone's business to know personal buying habits. Even the sale of customer lists irritates me. Fortunately, I do not buy anything that embarrasses me, but I can certainly imagine that it could happen. I am very opposed to all sales of personal customer information.

On the other hand, I have tremendous confidence in the medical and financial establishments. Perhaps the confidence is misplaced, but I don't believe they are selling the information I really care about. I am irritated, but not angered, by the sale of my name and address. However, it would bother me greatly to think they were selling my account size, my income level, or the prescription drugs I might be using.

If I could make the law myself, I would prefer a system that allows all sharing necessary to accomplish the customer's purpose and to prevent fraud or unauthorized transactions. For this sharing, no particular customer permission would be required. Any company would be allowed to share information with affiliates or even non-affiliates, as long as they were taking care of the business the consumer had brought in the first place and preventing fraud. This is pretty much the standard established by GLB and state laws. However, a company that means to use the information for any other purpose, such as marketing, or cross-checking files (except to prevent fraud), would have to get the consumer to opt in.

I believe a company should be able to do everything it needs to do to handle the transaction and prevent fraud, but it shouldn't be able to use the information for marketing or other purposes unless the consumer consents.

One frightening scenario that motivated the US Congress to pass GLB was, in fact, permitted by the final law. Recall that GLB was not a privacy law, but instead was intended to replace the Glass-Steagall Act and other Depression-era laws that prohibited the common ownership of different types of financial institutions. Before GLB a bank and an insurance company could not fall under common ownership. After GLB, a lender and a life insurance or health insurance company may be owned in common. When you go to the bank for a business loan, the lender can check with the life or health insurer to find out your medical condition. Your loan application could be rejected because you are being treated for depression. The bank knows of the illness because their affiliated insurance company told them. Gramm-Leach-Bliley doesn't prevent that because affiliated companies can share information freely. And yet that is exactly what the legislators were trying to guard against. This is one type of information-sharing I wish GLB had prohibited.

In some ways GLB has done a good job of protecting personal information. In some ways, it has failed. It should make consumers aware of the business use of their information, and over time, the legislatures will react to public concerns. At the moment, I do not see an overwhelming level of public concern.

Privacy Trends

The widespread use of Social Security Numbers creates genuine problems for individuals, and I expect more direct protection of that information. California has adopted a law that prohibits many uses and transmissions of Social Security Numbers, and this law may become the model for laws in other states. In this regard, the problem of identity theft looms large in the public and legislative eye. Specific protection of Social Security Numbers is one probable legislative reaction, but other measures, similar to the more general GLB protections, will be enacted. These measures will touch every business operation, including retail establishments.

The California law has a feature that could signal a direction for privacy legislation. It prohibits any requirement to transmit a Social Security Number (employee or customer) unless the number is encrypted or the site is secure. This type of interplay between privacy and electronic security will be a part of privacy legislation, and again it suggests that businesses have to invest in a certain amount of electronic hardware, software, and expertise.

"Customer relationship management" is a currently popular marketing theory that has achieved modest buzzword status. Each time a consumer has contact with a company, the company collects some information about the customer's buying preferences and patterns. Theoretically, the company can interpret all of that information and offer the customer the exact product or information he or she wants. This customer relationship management will be affected by privacy issues, as well. Companies that make an investment in hardware and software will be able to practice relationship management, while those that don't make the investment will be prevented. But beyond that, if privacy rules do trend toward individualization, then the laws may permit individuals to tell the companies to leave them alone. Then a company's computers will need to be able to cut that customer out of the program.

The privacy provisions of GLB pertain to the intentional sharing of personal information. GLB also has security provisions that relate to the susceptibility of our information systems to intrusion. The security provisions of GLB are an issue in the insurance industry at this moment because state insurance departments are adopting regulations that conform to GLB. This development directly affects only people who work for the insurance companies that will adopt new security measures. I mention it here because improved security enhances consumer privacy, and those who work in industries that have information to protect can expect to see more security measures adopted.

National security interests in the form of the recently enacted U.S.A. Patriot Act compete with privacy interests. This law expands an existing requirement that banks and securities dealers screen transactions for possible connections with terrorist or narcotics trafficking groups. Now other industries that handle funds must also screen transactions. Suspicious transactions must be reported. The natural result is that some innocent individuals will find their privacy rights have been overcome by competing national security interests. For the foreseeable future, national security interests will nibble at the edges of privacy.

We are very likely to be affected in the US by the privacy regime enacted by the European Union. The EU rules reach far beyond financial and medical institutions and require every industry to limit the sharing of personal information. Specifically, the laws prevent the transmission of personal data into a country whose laws do not offer certain protections for that data. If the complete regime were to be enforced, multinational companies, whether they sell insurance, chemicals, or soft drinks, won't be able to transfer customer or employee data without being concerned about privacy. While it hasn't hit yet, I suspect this is the next step. European companies may be prevented from doing business with US companies unless the US companies can guarantee they provide the same protections the European laws provide.

Currently, this blockade is interfering with some international trade. Many US companies that operate internationally have adopted the European rules. International trade groups and governments are negotiating over this issue, but the result will probably be that US corporations will have to comply or accommodate because, while the European Union may soften its position, it will not give in completely. All US companies, not just financial institutions, that want to sell goods and services in Europe will have to put privacy programs into place.

I expect more privacy protections for employees. Most companies have codes of ethics and conduct that protect the confidentiality of human resources files, but very few laws mandate confidentiality. If legislatures keep privacy on their agendas, then we can expect laws requiring companies to adopt a privacy program that protects the information that employers collect about their workers.

Customer Sensitivity Is Critical

When the privacy provisions of the Gramm-Leach-Bliley Act became effective, the immediate response was to get a program up and running. Soon, another more measured response emerged. Companies could use this as an opportunity to explain their concern for privacy and to offer appealing choices to their customers. Many businesses have been restrained and gracious, as opposed to greedy, in their exercise of the tantalizing data-crunching power of computers. This seems to me to be the correct approach.

As more and more companies fall under some form of privacy regulation, this customer-sensitive approach is most promising. Companies first must develop substantial computer power so they can honor each customer's interest in participating in or being left out of the menu of offerings. Then they may describe their capabilities to the public and offer the benefits. Most important, businesses must then ask each customer to make choices. If we use the power to satisfy consumer demand, rather than to squeeze another nickel onto the bottom line, there may be two results. First, we may forestall an angry public reaction that will lead to more laws. Second, companies that do this job well should increase their pool of happy customers.

Biography

W. Riker Purcell is vice president and regulatory counsel for LandAmerica Financial Group, Inc. He holds degrees from Virginia Military Institute (BA, Honors in English), the University of Virginia (M. Ed.), and Washington and Lee University (JD, managing editor of the Law Review).

After a total of five years of private practice in Savannah, Georgia, and Roanoke, Virginia, Mr. Purcell joined Lawyers Title Insurance Corporation in 1984 and served as associate counsel-Claims for the Pacific states, as underwriting counsel, and as associate regional counsel-Middle Atlantic States. As regulatory counsel, he handles regulatory relations with state insurance departments and federal agencies, works with internal corporate matters, and is also involved with litigation and legislation. Since late 1999, he has been primarily responsible for the development and implementation of LandAmerica's privacy policy. He is a member of the state bars of Georgia and Virginia.

Chapter 20

The Myth of Privacy

William Sterling

The Myth of a "Right" to Privacy

We think of privacy as a pretty straightforward concept. It is easily summarized, but it quickly becomes more complicated as we begin to dig deeper into examples. One of the most widely accepted definitions of privacy comes from Samuel Warren and Louis Brandeis, who described the right to privacy simply as the "right to be let alone." This simple and eloquent description does a great job summarizing what many would argue is their indisputable right as members of a free society. Yet as the debate surrounding privacy shows, this right to privacy is much harder to agree on in the real world. The right to privacy is hard to agree on because privacy is not a right. Everyone values their privacy, but valuing something is very different from saying it is a basic right. The difference between a value and a right is more than just semantics. A right stays with us; no matter what we do, no one can take a right away from us, and we can't do anything to lose our rights. Privacy is different. It's very easy to give up your privacy. In almost every case where we claim a violation of our rights, a deeper look will reveal that we're just doing a poor job protecting something that is valuable to us.

Is it wrong to spy on someone in their own home? What if you do so from a public street? That would imply they have a right to not be seen, even if they're in plain sight from a public street. If someone uses a high-powered telescope to look into someone else's bedroom, most of us would call that a violation of their privacy. If someone is simply walking down the street and happens to see into another person's home from the sidewalk, most of us would not find any fault here. That would suggest the difference between right and wrong is somewhere between glancing in a window from the street and staring into a window using a ...cope. Could the difference that determines whether someone's privacy is ...d be in the telescope? Maybe it's in how long someone looks in your ...w or in the intent of the person looking. The argument might seem clearer if we bring a camera into the picture. Surely we have the right not to have pictures taken of us in our own home. Slight changes can turn a situation from publicly acceptable to an outright violation of privacy.

Satellites have taken detailed pictures of virtually every square inch on the planet, and many of these pictures are now available through inexpensive or freely available services. A cool new Web site at www.earthviewer.com allows you to view satellite pictures of every major city, down to individual homes and buildings. Chances are, if you live in the continental U.S., I can type in your street address and zoom down to see if you have a pool in your backyard. This may seem like a far cry from the example of someone looking into your bedroom window, but the examples actually aren't so different.

The current satellite photos don't have enough resolution to see individual people, but that will change over time. When better pictures are available, someone might see a picture of you in your own backyard. Does that violate your privacy? I wouldn't really mind if someone took a picture of me in my backyard. I personally don't think it would be very interesting, but I might feel differently if I weren't wearing any clothes. I might not like someone having that picture, but where am I drawing the line?

Maybe the satellite companies should be forced to scan through the photos and erase any indecent pictures of people. Someone else may feel strongly about any picture of them in their backyard, even if they're clothed, so maybe the satellite companies should erase all pictures of people. You could even make an argument that you have the right not to have your backyard photographed at all, but would that mean you have some right to every picture taken of your backyard from space? Should the satellite company be forced to get every person's permission before releasing pictures of homes and backyards? Obviously, that would make the service impractical to offer, and it would cease to exist.

In every case, the argument over privacy becomes an argument in degree rather than principle. This is what makes the right to privacy a myth. Taking low-resolution pictures from above in space might be okay, but taking high-resolution pictures into your window from the street is considered a violation of our privacy. Two fundamentally similar practices produce dramatically different responses. Without fundamental definitions of right and wrong when it comes to privacy, we are left in an ambiguous world with a piecemeal set of rules and regulations being patched together as technology enables new practices and creates new public concerns. We can't classify privacy as a fundamental right when it is impossible to create universal definitions of right and wrong when dealing with privacy.

I'm not suggesting privacy is an invalid desire, or even that we shouldn't try to protect our privacy. If we truly desire to keep something private, then we shouldn't give it out to anyone we don't trust. Trust can come in many forms. We give private information to people we trust implicitly without any guarantee they will live up to that trust. If we don't trust someone implicitly, then we can't assume they will keep our information private unless they specifically agree to do so. If I give my phone number to you, and you give it out to a friend or even put it on a Web site, I can blame only myself. Of course, this doesn't mean individuals or companies can say one thing and do another. If someone tells me they will not give out my information, and then they break that agreement by giving out that information, I have a legitimate claim that they violated a contract with me. While we may not have a right to the assumption of privacy, we do have the right to take someone to court if they break an agreement to keep something private. So we can defend our privacy by not giving out anything we value as private. If we need to give out information and want it treated as private in some way, we must either trust the other party implicitly or agree with them on the specific limitations of what they can do with that information. If they violate that agreement, we can take them to court.

Technology as a Red Herring

Technology is a red herring when it comes to privacy. New issues arise as technical advances make practices possible that were never feasible without the efficiencies provided by technology. Cheaper data storage makes it possible for companies and individuals to create and store massive databases of information for relatively low costs. E-commerce makes it possible for retailers to easily track a customer's buying habits over time. The Internet makes the process of accessing this information simple, fast, and very inexpensive. While none of these advances changes the basic way we interact with each other, by making certain practices easier and cheaper, they will end up being more widespread and therefore more widely contested. At first glance, technology seems to be the problem, since it's the only thing changing, but in fact it's enabling people to access information about us that we simply weren't protecting. Technology gets the blame, but technology is not the problem.

Improvements in technology constantly redefine the debate on privacy. As I mentioned, I can see a very detailed picture of your home from space. If I'm willing to pay more for the service, I can get a satellite company to take a recent picture of your home with incredible resolution. I could probably even tell if you had a barbeque that day. I can find out virtually anything I want about you; it's simply a matter of money. Satellite photos are cheap and easy, but I could always just fly over your house in an airplane and take a picture of your backyard; it would just be more expensive. Your credit report, rental history, name, personal stats such as age and height, and what kind of car you drive are all relatively easy facts to obtain online, but private investigators have always been able to obtain that same information for the right price. Technology doesn't change the amount of information available; it only increases the ease and reduces the cost of obtaining it.

We tend to see technology as a sort of anti-privacy tool that's invading our lives and violating our privacy, but maybe this is because technology is harder to understand and less tangible than other forms of communication. Webcams make it easier to record someone or something in a digital format, but small portable video cameras and still cameras have the same basic ability. Digital storage and transfer make every step of the process so much more efficient than paper-based communications. Information can be tracked and stored without us seeing it happen. However, none of these technologies creates fundamental changes in the way we deal with each other; they just make everything easier. In virtually every case, technology isn't creating a completely new practice, but optimizing existing ones.

Just as technology has created some practices we feel are threatening to privacy, it also has the potential to provide us unprecedented protection of our privacy. As technology progresses, online forms of transacting will certainly become infinitely more private than comparable offline transactions. Through anonymous payment mechanisms and anonymous browsing tools, the Internet will provide a more private and secure mechanism for transactions than the offline world could possibly provide.

Encryption technology can allow us to lock any digital e-mail or document so it can't be read without a key. Even if someone can get to our e-mails or files, they won't be able to read them unless they have the digital key. In the real world, if you can intercept a letter, you can simply open it and read its contents. If you intercept an encrypted message in the digital world, it's useless without a key.

Encryption technology will become more seamlessly integrated in tools like e-mail, allowing us to communicate more privately than ever before. Encryption can also allow you to digitally sign messages, so no one can pretend they are you by just by forging your e-mail address. These technologies will provide us a level of privacy and accountability far beyond that which we had in a paper-based world, where physical access to a document was all you needed to read its contents, and forging another's signature just meant you had a copy of their signature. These advances will allow everyone to operate with a heightened level of trust. If I send you a digitally signed e-mail, it can be considered a legally signed document by definition. If you transfer a file to me using strong encryption, you will have a high degree of confidence that no one else will be able to read that file without the key.

As technology continues to advance, we will see new devices that make it easier to protect our privacy, as well as new devices that make it more difficult to protect our privacy. We should accept these opportunities to redefine the way we deal with each other. Technology is only the means of obtaining information. Instead of focusing on technology as the problem, we must focus instead on protecting information in ways that won't be washed away by the next wave of technology.

Online Privacy

Perhaps the best known example of technology forcing the issue of privacy is the evolution of the Internet. The popularity of the Internet makes marketing and customer tracking practices easier. Even though these practices are fundamentally identical to offline practices that have been going on for years, old-fashioned fear of technology has created a privacy outrage.

One of the best examples of the clash between technology and privacy is the outrage that resulted from Double Click's practice of tracking Internet users as they traveled among different Web sites using a technology called Internet cookies. A cookie is an Internet technology that allows a Web site to place information on a user's computer and then subsequently retrieve that information when the user visits that Web site again. Since Double Click was actually serving the ads to users directly through links embedded in other Web sites, users were effectively visiting the Double Click site every time they visited any site that used Double Click's service.

If I go to a Web site that uses Double Click's ad services, my browser gets directed to Double Click's site, where it downloads an ad to display. When my browser is directed to Double Click for the first time, Double Click places a unique identification number inside a cookie on my hard drive. Double Click can then retrieve that cookie each time I visit any Web site that serves Double Click ads. By doing this, Double Click can track us as they visit different Web sites that serve Double Click ads. Double Click is able to demand more money for these ads because their network allows them to deliver the ads more effectively by sending a particular ad to customers who are more likely to respond to that type of ad. The process forms an economic arrangement that is beneficial to all participants. Consumers receive lower-priced (and often free) services because Double Click makes the ad business more profitable for everyone by delivering ads that specific consumers are more likely to respond to.

Companies have been doing this same thing for years, just not quite as efficiently as Double Click. Many top retail companies track everything from personal information to buying habits whenever and wherever possible. Mail-order catalog companies are a perfect example of this. Certain marketers have formed networks of catalog companies. Through these networks, a catalog company can agree to share information about who their customers are and what they purchase. In exchange for that information, those catalog companies receive information about customers who purchased from other catalog companies in that same network. The catalog companies are basically just sharing information about their customers with each other through a marketer. We've all ordered from a catalog and then received new catalogs from other companies the very next week. It wasn't a coincidence.

How are the catalog marketers different from Double Click? They have both created networks to share information between different companies and provide consumers access to products based on our history. But many consumers and privacy advocates were outraged at Double Click. Double Click was even the focus of FTC investigation and a number of class action law suits when they later purchased a catalog marketer to increase their information network. Everyone was upset because they were going to tie our online information with offline information about us. They weren't doing anything new or different. They were doing basically the same thing marketers have always done, only better.

We accept that a department store needs to have security cameras to help prevent theft, but we also expect them to keep our faces and actions while in their store private, and not to use them for any other purposes. Even though they make no guarantee these tapes will be kept private, many of us would be outraged if the department stores began selling these security tapes to other companies to do with as they please.

What if these department stores had face-recognition technology that allowed them to track our movements through their stores? The stores could uniquely identify our face each time we entered their store and track us as we traveled through it. They could then tie our face to other personal information. Now they know who we are, how often we come to their store, what sections we shop in the most, and what we purchased from their store. This could help them arrange their store more efficiently, so items we purchased in a single visit were closer together and easier to find. If they saw that we often looked at furniture in their store but never made any furniture purchases, they might decide to give us a coupon for 10 per cent off any piece of furniture.

These stores would eventually want to share information about their customers with each other so they could find new potential customers who shop at other stores in their area. A marketer might create a network of stores in Manhattan that would share information about other customers who shopped in that area. This would be fundamentally the same as the catalog companies and the Web sites that used Double Click. Face-recognition technology isn't good enough to make this practical, but that will undoubtedly change at some point.

As consumers, we are the ones who actually give up the information to these marketers, either directly or indirectly. Sometimes we don't pay attention to what we give up or to whom, but we do know we're giving out information. For some reason, we just assume no one will track us as we browse the Internet. We tend to have certain expectations of privacy in our daily lives, regardless of where we are or what we're doing. We need to rethink our expectations. Maybe it isn't reasonable to give information to someone with no agreement covering that information, and still have any expectation of what they will or will not do with that information.

Both consumers and companies are finding an acceptable balance. Consumers felt certain practices were inappropriate, and the market reacted swiftly to eliminate, or at least limit, those practices. Companies now weigh the profitability of certain practices with the sentiments of the consumers and their desire for privacy. It's a learning process on both sides, but it seems to be progressing nicely. In the Double Click example, technology enabled consumers to give up information without realizing it. Consumers are now aware that a powerful technology exists with a detailed way of tracking us. Consumers reacted, and companies have become much more explicit about what they would do with that information. Software now gives us more control over how we browse the Internet, forcing companies to develop suitable privacy policies if they want to use cookies to track us.

Company Policies

Your company has the right to monitor everything you do on a computer at work. If an employee uses their company's e-mail, even for personal correspondence, the company is perfectly within their rights to read that e-mail. As an employee, I probably wouldn't want my company to read my e-mail, but I do respect that they own the system and may feel it necessary to monitor any communications over their systems. They may need to check for employees who are harassing coworkers or dealing with customers inappropriately. If a company feels the need to monitor its systems, regardless of the reason, as an employee I have no right to tell them to stop just because I don't like it.

The relationship between an employer and employee is no different from any other relationship. Employment is at will, which means an employee can quit at any time. Employee privacy tends to be a more sensitive topic because people are dependent on their jobs, which puts employers in a strong position when dealing with their employees. Quitting your job is a big deal, much bigger than changing where you buy groceries or furniture. However, that doesn't mean employees have the right to prevent their companies from monitoring their own systems.

Disclosure is key. Employees should find out whether their company has a privacy policy, and if so, what it says. Companies may be able to monitor you, but they should also be willing to disclose their practices. If you ask, they can't lie to you. If they won't tell you what they do, then you should probably assume the worst. As an employee, you should know whether your company monitors or records everything from phone calls to your Internet use. Most employers are very reasonable in their practices and will probably be happy to tell you exactly what they do and why. There's no reason for any company to keep monitoring practices secret.

As an employer, my company has no desire to monitor our employees' use of e-mail or the Internet. Some employers monitor how much time someone spends on certain Web sites, such as eBay or Yahoo, so they can try to judge employee productivity. An employee who spends two hours a day on eBay is probably not doing the best job in the world, but that's a silly way to monitor productivity. If a company's managers can't judge their employee's productivity without playing Big Brother, then the company has much larger problems. It's important, though, to draw a clear distinction between silly and wrong. I may feel that monitoring Web or e-mail activity is a silly way to manage productivity, but that doesn't mean it's wrong.

Employee privacy is still a delicate issue. As an employee, it's scary to think your employer might be monitoring your phone conversations, Web usage, or e-mail correspondence. But you do have other options besides quitting. If you're concerned that your employer is listening to your phone conversations, use a cellular phone. If you really need to send personal e-mail while at work, get a Blackberry or other wireless e-mail device the company doesn't control. If you really need to browse the Internet at work, don't browse inappropriate Web sites. If you really need to spend two hours a day on eBay while at work, you might want to consider getting a new job.

Government Protection

While many people argue that we all have a fundamental right to privacy, the Constitution offers almost no protection in the realm of privacy. The closest thing to privacy law in the Constitution is the Fourth Amendment, which protects us from unreasonable search and seizure. The writers of the Constitution simply did not address privacy between individuals or offer any citizen a broader protection of privacy. Was this an oversight, or did our founding fathers simply not feel privacy was a constitutional right? Since the writing of the Constitution, the government has created hundreds of specific laws affecting our privacy, but nothing has been done to create a broader framework for privacy law. This is probably because there is no good way to create a broad framework for privacy law. By definition, privacy law can be based only on degree, not on principle.

The only appropriate role for government in protecting our privacy is in protecting our information within the government itself. The government is in the unique position of being able to force us to provide information; therefore, it must provide some basic protections to ensure that information is treated appropriately. No other organization can force us to provide information. From local law enforcement to the IRS, the government has a need to obtain and keep information about us to operate effectively. We tell the IRS how much money we made so they know how much we should pay in taxes. The DMV needs to know our height, age, and other personal information to issue driver's licenses. Numerous offices of the government have specific information about us that is necessary for them to perform their functions. I might argue that some of these functions are unnecessary, or that there is too much information in too many places. But the government must force us to give some basic information to be able to operate effectively. The government must therefore protect us from itself by keeping that information as private as possible.

Government does have a responsibility to protect us from itself when it comes to privacy, but what about protecting us from each other? The Video Privacy Protection Act was passed after a newspaper published a list of videos rented by a Supreme Court nominee, but there's still no law addressing magazine subscriptions or book purchases. That means a bookstore can legally tell someone what books I bought, but it would be criminal for Blockbuster to tell someone what movies I have rented. There's nothing unique about video rentals, but public outcry and politics create specific laws to fix specific problems. In this case, public outcry and political power put a law in place to protect consumer information at video stores. The consumer doesn't have any more of a right to privacy than the video store has in this case. What if the video store decided they wanted consumers to keep private their store's name and the movies that store rents to a consumer? I rent a video from a store, and I can tell people what movie I rented and from which store, but the store can't legally tell anyone what I rented or who I am. What gives the consumer more of a "right" to that information than the video store? In this case the stores don't care and the consumers do, but can that be how we determine what is legal and illegal?

What legal protections do we need from each other that common law doesn't already provide? The government protects us from fraud, so if someone claims they will keep our information private and then proceeds to give that information out, then that person (or company) has committed fraud. If we have a contract with someone regarding the use of our information and they violate that contract, you can take them to court, just as you could if they violate any term of a contract. Any other protection we ask the government to provide will force the government to draw arbitrary lines between right and wrong based on the degree. Take the example of the Video Privacy Protection Act, where a video store gave a man's video rental history to a reporter. When the man signed up, did the store pledge to keep that information confidential, or was the issue of privacy not even addressed? If the store committed to keeping that information private, then the man could sue the store for violation of their contract, and his damages would be his loss of privacy. If nothing was mentioned in their agreement, then the store didn't really do anything wrong.

As someone who rents videos, I would rather go to a store that keeps my information private than one that gives out that same information publicly, but that's between the store and me. I do not need the government's help in making that decision. The case where rental information was given out to the press caused public outrage. In that situation, the store would likely lose customers and change their policies as a result of that incident. The store had no real incentive to give out the information to the press in the first place. If a store did have a compelling reason to give out the information, the store may be more resistant to change. Perhaps they'd be willing to compensate the consumer by offering lower prices or an occasional free movie. Maybe they'd do nothing, but consumers could then go to other stores that did agree to keep their information private. Other stores may decide their customers are very privacy sensitive and offer an ironclad privacy policy for their protection. In other words, a natural balance would come as the businesses and the consumers voted with their dollars. In this case, it's likely that most consumers would opt out of having their information shared, if given an option, or rent from a store that keeps rental information private because the customers value their privacy over getting a few free rentals.

This solution to the video rental problem is simply a free market scenario where the market, without any government involvement, solves the problem through changes in policies and practices to react to consumer demands. Since each consumer has the right not to deal with any given business or other individual, we all have the ultimate veto power in any exchange of information — we can simply decide to not deal with that business or person, thereby not giving up any private information. If the cost to your privacy is relatively small and the value you place on a particular service is very high, you may decide the benefit outweighs the cost and use the service despite your privacy concerns. Privacy is just another factor to take into consideration when determining how and with whom you do business.

Some might argue that this free market solution is a dream, and that in reality we need the government to step in and offer more protections. They might argue that companies won't really respond to consumer demand, and we'll be left with too few choices and no privacy. History has consistently proven this view to be incorrect. There are too many choices out there to force us into doing business with any one company. Consumers will continue to value their privacy, and companies will be forced to be sensitive to that value. Many good changes continue to take place that help us protect our privacy, both offline and online. We now have better browsers that offer us more control over how we send information. Companies began releasing privacy policies well before Congress mandated the practice. Many companies that don't have any legal requirement to do so post their privacy policies with a link right on their home page. People are sensitive about privacy, and too many people feel this way for any good company to ignore the issue.

Government involvement in privacy between private individuals and companies is easily the biggest unknown in the future of privacy. Government could continue its attempts to protect our privacy, or it could leave the market to provide the appropriate level of protection. Will the government stick to its job of protecting us from itself, or will it continue to try to protect us from each other?

Real Privacy Protection

Regardless of whether you agree with the view that you have no right to privacy, protecting your privacy through rules and laws can never be as effective as real protection for our information. Real protection exists everywhere, and these protections will continue to be improved as long as there is a market for them.

New technologies will continue to offer increasing protection for our information. You can disable cookies on your browser to prevent marketers from tracking you on the Internet, or you can use anonymous browsing services, such as Anonymizer.com, that allow you to browse the Internet without giving up any information to anyone. At some point you'll have access to anonymous payment services that will allow you to pay through them without disclosing your identity to the person you're paying. It'll be just like cash on the Internet. Encryption technology has already existed for years, but almost nobody encrypts their e-mail. Is that because we don't care about privacy, or because we don't think it's our responsibility to protect our own information? Either way, once e-mail encryption is widely used, you'll be able to trust the security of your e-mail. Other forms of anonymous communication will develop over time. Intermediaries, such as online bill payment services, could become our mask for all online payments and deliveries. They could act as our agent online, and we would only need to trust their privacy to ensure our identities are kept private in online transactions. No one would know who we really are, except the intermediary that acted as our online agent. A retailer simply needs a mailing address and money to transact with us. They may want to know more about us, but they don't need anything more than that. If consumers show an overwhelming demand for privacy and retailers don't provide the appropriate protections, then intermediaries will step in to play that role. Imagine that your online name is "1156454321", and your address is a P.O. Box owned by Paytrust.com (or another bill payment service). You can even change your online name every month, so no one can track your name for more than 30 days. Paytrust pays the retailer for you, and your retailer knows nothing more than your ID number and Paytrust's address.

That is just one example of a solution to a specific privacy concern; there are numerous parallel examples of real solutions for protecting our information. Through a combination of improving technologies, more privacy sensitive businesses, more privacy sensitive consumers, and intermediaries willing to mask our identities when dealing with any "untrusted" parties, we have a strong set of real solutions to protect our privacy without the help of anyone but ourselves and the market.

If we protect our own information through real tools that prevent the information from getting out in the first place, then we don't need any further protection. Protecting our information once it's already in the wrong hands is much harder than protecting it from getting into those wrong hands in the first place.

Biography

William Sterling is the chief technology officer of the Island ECN, an electronic marketplace that enables market professionals to display and match limit orders for stocks and other securities. He is charged with the development and operation of Island's technology, as well as providing strategic direction.

Mr. Sterling started with Island in 1997 as the company's first employee. He began his career in financial services in 1995 at Block Trading in Houston. In 1996, he opened and managed Block Trading's first branch office in Tyler, Texas. He moved to the technical side of the business in 1996, where he was involved in the initial development of CyberTrader. Mr. Sterling resides in New York.

Chapter 21

Starting from Scratch

Richard Brock

Developing a Profitable Customer Relationship

Developing profitable customer relationships is the key to business success. Profitable customers appreciate what you're doing for them and will serve you in return. Great products, great companies and great business leaders are defined by their ability to develop profitable relationships. As a CEO, I find most of my time and energy is devoted to acquiring and maintaining relationships, which will serve this company beyond the life cycle of our current solution. These relationships are truly the lifeblood of our existence.

But, to properly develop profitable customer relationships and achieve the blue ribbon of customer success — customer loyalty — a company must start from scratch. Competitive and product principles need to be evaluated and aligned. Employees must understand that a job well done is only well done if it benefits the customer's business and the customer relationship. This means teaching your employees how to understand the customer, their business processes and their customer acquisition strategy.

The introspection required to acquire and develop loyal customers is arduous, but it is the methodology by which your company differentiates and succeeds in the marketplace. Anyone can have customers, and it's even possible to have customer relationships. But, a company with a long-term market strategy can't simply be a vendor — they need to be a partner, with partner-based relationships that are profitable.

Acquiring New Customers

Introspection — A Look before You Leap

While a majority of efforts and time are spent on marketing and selling to potential customers, the success of those efforts is rooted in a company's customer acquisition philosophy. Congruent to a corporate philosophy, this philosophy is the cornerstone for how a company will compete for customers in the marketplace.

Possibly the most interesting book on the subject, In Search of Excellence by Thomas J. Peters and Robert H. Waterman, Jr., defines three ways you can compete to gain customers: operational excellence, product excellence, or customer intimacy. The book makes the point to choose one and let that lead your company. Another choice may be a secondary goal, but you can't pursue all three. For example, if you're Home Depot, you compete with the lowest price based on operational excellence; if you're Neiman Marcus, you compete with the best service. If you're Intel, you compete with the best technology.

At Firstwave, we focus on customer intimacy (best service). That means that we focus on companies that are searching for a business partner to provide a comprehensive solution to help them solve specific problems and develop customized applications. It means that we have to say we don't just provide out-of-the-box applications; we provide integrated solutions. Not that technology can't be shrink-wrapped, but people who want an out-of-the-box application only don't want to buy from a vendor who is focused on delivering a solution. It affects your pricing, marketing, delivery model, and everything else.

After laying the foundation for your competitive strategy, the most important step to developing a solid customer relationship is to establish credibility as someone who cares about that relationship. Essentially, you are not only a salesperson, but a truly effective partner in solving a business problem. The customer has to know that you have integrity and you will be blatantly honest about your abilities. Based on that honesty, you will seek those opportunities where you fit best. Before you make a proposal for business, you have to earn the right to do so. If you gain the confidence of the customer based on personal integrity, you develop a valuable relationship. If you develop a relationship, it means the customer finds you valuable to their company.

Personal Integrity Requires an Introspective Analysis of Your Company, namely Your Employees

Every employee must focus on customer retention and customer satisfaction — this is priority number one. Furthermore, you must instill a sense of ownership and pride with your employees, so that if they misrepresent anything about the product or fail to gain the customer's confidence, then they know it will reflect upon them personally and professionally. This keeps everyone honest, and customers will be confident that you are a true partner. For your product or company to be successful, there must be people confident in your integrity, whether that is because of your product, your competitors, your price, your service, or a combination of all those things. It's a matter of honestly focusing and aligning goals.

One of the problems in the software industry is that for years the focus was on new account selling. Those companies that focused solely on reaching for the next new deal are experiencing the consequences of their actions. This focus does not add value to any relationship because it compromises both credibility and integrity. If you don't believe in your product or service, if you don't focus on long-term retention, if you just want a quick sale with the cheapest service and cheapest product out there, it is not possible to have a relationship. You have to inspire the sales staff through compensating a job that is not only done, but one that creates a valued relationship that outlasts compensation.

Laying the Foundation for a Long-lasting Partnership
There are three steps to begin a long-lasting relationship with a customer. It starts by identifying their core problem. It is a listening mode. We meet with them to help us understand why they called us, find out their perceived problem and what efforts they've already made to address the problem. The bottom line is people like to open up — and this establishes confidence. Even more important, it establishes a partnership approach to solving the customer's problem.

So, step one is to listen so that you truly understand the requirements. The second step is to repeat the requirements so they are confident that you understand them, and step three is to talk about your solution in light of their requirements. That begins to develop a relationship and starts to separate you from other companies who don't really care who the customer is or where their problem stands, just the available budget. There are too many people out there who do that. But, of course, that's the opportunity for the rest of us.

Here at Firstwave, we prefer to have partnerships with our customers. To do that, we rely on the three steps above to open the lines of communication, honestly set expectations, and communicate our value to the customer's organization. Customers expect Firstwave to solve a problem. We listen to their problem, understand how they feel, and then provide the solution. That's what we do and it is what they expect from us.

Firstwave routinely goes through a process called a gap analysis as a part of each sale. We enumerate the customer's requirements and needs, and have a working session. We get the users involved, because they usually know more of the details than the people on the screening committee. We then can say here is how we understand your requirement, and here's your solution. Determining the gap between what they want and what we offer is a very detailed, step-by-step process. The gap analysis is also a key part of establishing appropriate customer expectations.

All that we expect from the customer is honesty in the relationship. It's important that they give us the proper feedback and fully participate in the partnership. If they're not happy with our service, I would ask them to say so and allow us to address it. A customer is generally unhappy because you didn't set the right expectations going in. Perceived value is truly the heart of the matter—if people are unhappy with your price, maybe you're in the wrong business. But assuming you're not in the wrong business, you have most likely not communicated your value proposition that justifies your price.

Referrals — Testimony to Walking the Walk

One of the best ways Firstwave has been able to sell its vision is through our customers. We've had several sales where a person came to us because they were impressed with our sales support system being used by a company that was trying to sell them their product. Their impression of our solution was so positive that they wanted to buy that system for their own organization. It's being the best example of what you do, walking the walk. We use our CRM solutions internally, which instills internal confidence and experience in your company's product. This is vital to gaining the confidence of your customers.

A referral, such as the example just described, is the best beginning to a new relationship. A customer or partner referral allows you to have initial meetings on a higher-level than you would otherwise because you're not being screened. Instead, you're being perceived as a company of value that can help, and you're being invited in to help discover their requirements and how your product can meet their needs. In essence, without even having made the sale (which will most likely happen), you have become a partner.

At Firstwave, if we acquire a customer correctly, we realize a greater success factor. We expand with their business as they expand, and we expand to other divisions in their company. More importantly, when they go to one of their tradeshows or seminars, they may be talking over a cup of coffee with someone who is looking for a similar system, and they suggest to that person that they should try their vendor-partner. That is the right way to do business.

Customizing Communication and Solutions to Achieve Results

Each person conducts business differently, and we all respond to different stimuli. Some people want an e-mail channel, some want a phone channel, some want to visit you, and others want you to visit them. Therefore, I think the communication channels you use initially depend upon whichever channels are preferred by the customer. You then modify the channel based on whether the initially chosen channel was successful. It's like a restaurant. You offer meat, fish, vegetables and starches, but in the end you serve what people buy. Similarly, when acquiring new customers, you must offer the normal communication channels, and then listen to the customer and find out what he or she wants.

Customization must be addressed on two fronts. As described above, you must tailor your communication channels to reach individual customers. But, you must also offer product or solution customization.

In customer relationship management, if you have the same business processes as your competitors, then you have no competitive advantage. The biggest company will win because of the lowest cost of production. Establishing a competitive position takes strategic tailoring. So we have record keeping systems, if you will, and those can be homogenous. They are contact management systems, and they are part of our basic solutions. You have to have that capability to work "out of the box." But when you get into the business rules and business processes, and the escalation and workflow rules, that's what makes CRM really valuable. Of course, this all varies from company to company, so an effective solution that addresses these rules and issues must be customized.

Building Customer Loyalty

Customer Retention *versus* Customer Loyalty

While customer retention may result from a relationship, customer loyalty should be the desired result. Customer retention equates to someone who is simply using your product. Customer loyalty means that you have earned the customer's trust and confidence. While a loyal customer expects you to be competitive, your business is not always at risk because they view you as a strategic partner, rather than a vendor. Customer loyalty doesn't mean that you serve that customer for the initial life of that particular product, because people may buy things to use for a little while. Customer loyalty means that they buy their subsequent products from you because you are their partner.

Empowering the Customer

Loyal customers are confident partners in your company. As a partner, we feel that it is our duty to empower our customers with more than CRM solutions. We have to also empower them with problem-solving techniques that will allow them to fully understand the benefits of what we bring to the table. It's a win-win situation

— our value is better communicated and customers have confidence in their ability to maximize how well our solution works for them.

A past goal at Firstwave was to reduce the number of support calls we received. Through surveys, we realized that many of our calls were the result of customers failing to use the help documentation and training manuals. So, we developed a new strategy, which has achieved two goals: reducing our support calls, and more important, empowering our customers with the ability to solve their problems.

Our first tactic was to introduce a shift delay in our response to support calls. In other words, when a customer call comes in, their question is logged in to provide tracking and then directed to the most appropriate support manager. That manager then returns the customer's call within five minutes and provides them with the answer.

This process has multiple purposes. First of all, the most appropriate person contacts the customer. It shows our desire and care, and eliminates any room for error. Second, the waiting period has statistically and dramatically reduced the number of calls. In the past, people found that calling the support line would provide an immediate response, as opposed to having to look up the answer in the manual. By introducing the five-minute delay, customers would be more inclined to first find the answer in the manual. But, if they did not find the answer, or they chose not to look in the manual, we were able to get the most knowledgeable person on the phone. This helped us reach our goal and, more importantly, we helped the customers help themselves, resulting in increased confidence in our product.

There is a definite danger in giving too much technical support and therefore not empowering the customer — this is human nature. Human nature states that a person will always want to show off how smart they are. Therefore, a support person or manager might tell a client to type in a lot of highly technical computer code (read: intimidating) to fix the problem, but that shows they didn't have any confidence in the product. It is more important to show the product structure, and work through the product's documentation, which has defined the answer. If the support person gives the client a "geek shortcut", then the client becomes dependent on the support staff. The staff member, on the other hand, thinks he's doing the customer a favor, but really, he's giving them a fish instead of teaching them how to fish. Interestingly, he's also inadvertently setting the client up to believe that the product is not easy to use.

In order to ensure that our support managers were assisting the customers in solving the problem, we added a box on the support call log that required the manager to point out the page number where this item was described or addressed in the manual. This way, if the "cool" support guys aren't properly addressing support complaints, we can confront them. We don't alienate them, but deal with it fairly, inquiring whether they knew that the issue was covered on a particular page. In reality, they didn't know the page number, because they hadn't read the documentation. They were techies, so they didn't need to read the documentation. But they were cheating the customers. So by forcing them to enter the page number on their logs, they had to know the documentation. Then they would give the customer the page number, the customer would look at it, feel good about it, and the call would end positively. Both sides win in this kind of customer relationship.

Customer Support Challenges

One of the greatest customer support challenges is dealing with companies who did not opt to adequately train their workforce on your solution. This results in a high number of customer support calls. We have a system in place to alert us to extraordinarily high calls from one customer. When this happens, we call them and we go not to the person who is calling, but to the person who signed the contract. At this point, we discuss the situation and ask how we can help fix the situation. More often than not, this person hasn't heard anything because he or she bought it and moved on.

We then go on to explain that while you have hundreds of customers using this package, last week you received 22 calls from this particular company, which represented 10 per cent of your calls. You suggest that you haven't done a very good job of training their people, and therefore offer some reduced-fee training, or even free training, to help clear up the problem. You take the stance that your training clearly was not adequate. Instead of suggesting that the customer's employee is not competent to do their job, or the person who understood the system left, you suggest that it might be your fault. You step forward and ask the company to allow you to service this problem.

Basically, we have taken this aberrant problem, which is an untrained person, and turned the relationship around. We initiated the call because we have the system in place to ring a bell that this problem is aberrant. You suggest that the fault is partly yours, and take full responsibility in doing so. We offer a solution, and instead of you being unprofitable because the company is calling too frequently for support, they will realize our fairness and won't take advantage of us. The customer apologizes for the turnover, and subsequent lack of training, and then the profits come back into the relationship and they are probably a better customer and a better reference.

Impact of New Technologies on CRM

Separating the good customer relationship management applications from the not-so-good applications is generally very simple. A product has to be easy to use, intuitive to use, and it has to be available when you need it. No matter how you slice it, if it's not easy to use and not available where it's needed and when it's needed, then it's not going to work. That's the whole secret. New technologies have greatly impacted these basic principles of CRM application success.

I have been in the business for more than 18 years and feel the Internet has made CRM really effective because it is easy to deploy and use. But, while the Internet has improved CRM, I think that it has also screwed up the "local business advantage" because each customer has access to a world of information and options. This translates into a far more efficient market, where people know who has what at what price. Price, geography, and market inefficiencies are no longer issues to deal with. The real focus is on customer satisfaction, which means that you are going to have to serve your customers if you are to compete.

One of the biggest changes in the CRM field right now is the advent of the new tablet PC and the PDA (Personal Digital Assistant). If you're going to be a customer intimate company, you have to have the details on hand. We've seen, however, that in the past, no one would use a standard PC or laptop in front of a customer because it was unnatural; the rep couldn't type fast enough, he was distracted, he wanted to look them in the eyes, and therefore, he usually wanted to take handwritten notes. Information really wasn't captured in the step that it should have been. The new convertible tablet PCs are a tremendous help. You can, in fact, use them in meetings because they allow you to take free-form notes.

There is an 80/20 rule that says 20 per cent of the people will use the handwritten recognition properly, while 80 per cent will just scribble on a pad, but that's what they would be doing anyhow. So, we now have character capture versus character recognition. I believe with the easy-to-use character capture, the people will use it to attach those notes to the customer with whom they're talking. We have improved the salesperson's efficiency, because the notes are in their proper location. Twenty per cent of people will do the handwriting to text translations. But 80 per cent of the time, people will expect them to have captured the notes, which is how we have been doing business. The current generation of these devices is going to replace the pen and paper. And that's pretty powerful.

Major changes are often realized by reaching tipping points. This is where something is good, but when you add it to something else, it gets that much better and it just takes over. Case in point, we can think back to the digital Rolodex. They did not really take off until the Palm Operating System was developed and put to use. Palm gave us a calendar and the personal digital assistant with all of our names and addresses. More importantly, they decided to sync it with our e-mail system. Palm would not have worked without e-mail. E-mail caused people to create databases on their personal computer. Because they had those names and addresses in the personal computer, Palm's secret was to link this information into the little device, and people realized that they could have the calendar, with all of these names and addresses whenever they need them. Furthermore, everybody realized that if you ever had the discipline to put all of that information into the digital Rolodexes, one day the battery crashed or it got rolled over by a chair and you lost everything. Then you realized the same thing could happen with your notebook computer. But, since you can easily synchronize it to your Palm device, the Palm device and my notebook back each other up on key information.

Then PDAs really started getting legs under them when they came out with the phone attached. When you call me, I recognize your phone number because it brings up your name. When I call you, I can look up your name and press "dial" and I don't have to dial the number. Convergent devices are powerful in terms of having information at your fingertips; plus they're always on, which is a main reason why the notebooks are not used. So, you can scribble the handwritten notes of the sales meeting, which is very good, and you don't have to recast them except to attach them. It's no different than what would happen before, but now it's all organized and you take better notes, because the notes are where you need them when you need them.

Another technology tipping point that will change how we work is WiFi, or Wireless Fidelity, which is basically a wireless local area network. You can enter a Starbucks, for example, and pay a couple of dollars and have high-speed Internet access if you have a WiFi card in your PC. Most of the PCs today are shipping with WiFi in the computer as an added benefit. You can pay a few dollars at airports, and have access to it, and you can have WiFi in more and more hotels and other venues.

If your office has WiFi capabilities, I can walk into your office and begin working on a virtual private network from my home office and have total network security while accessing sensitive information such as my e-mail. Furthermore, I can now work flexibly with my customers by being able to perform such activities as checking the status of their account receivables or their inventory, in a manner which is convenient and time-efficient.

The data, which is important in the relationship, is the next step. It's all about the workload and information going back and forth. Information lubricates a good relationship. In the near future, you're going to start to use your notebook, because you're using it in the meeting itself to scribble your notes. You're capturing your notes in real-time; you've also already put this information in your enterprise database because you're using your customer's WiFi connection to do all of this in the background. This is big medicine; it's a big change. Also, if you take the right enabling technology, you can comprehensively view a customer and all the pertinent data that affects both your business and theirs. In this view, you can bring up accounts receivable, which might be in Chicago. Or you might need to access the mainframe in Miami, which has all of the maintenance information. The orders are kept in an Oracle database in Oregon, and your sales are kept in a database in Seattle. Basically, you can bring up a composite screen in front of the customer in real-time view of all these disparate data sources. You can see the back orders, things that just happened, and the current status. A whole bunch of enabling technologies are dramatically changing the way we do business.

To take the success of these technologies further, I think you have to focus on customization capabilities so these technologies can better fit their needs. CRM technologies have to be easy to customize and easy to use. That's the answer. If it is easy to customize and easy to use, everything else will take care of itself.

Success in the CRM Field

You minimize the risk by knowing what you're doing. It's like flying airplanes, motorcycle riding, or scuba diving. You shouldn't be too risky because sooner or later, you will lose. If you take a risk, you should control and manage the risks of that decision to make sure the odds are stacked in your favor. You need to quantify your risk and eliminate risk with low pay-off. If you go into markets where the nature of the product being sold is totally opposite to what you stand for (i.e. "stack them high and sell them cheap"), you're moving away from profitable opportunities.

You must begin by finding your kindred spirits. Find a customer who is dedicated to their customer because you are dedicated to the customer. Birds of a feather flock together. Basically, when you get into a sales situation, if you see that this company is looking for product, but they don't appreciate your unique selling proposition, you're probably not going to change them. So, the best decision for both parties is for you to get out of the relationship. You have to understand what it is you want to get into. I had a friend who parachuted. He was very good at it and then one day, he was parachuting and the wind was dangerously strong. Lo and behold, he parachuted anyway and broke his ankle horribly because he pushed the envelope. He knew he shouldn't parachute when the wind exceeds a certain speed. My advice then is to know your limits; know where your sweet spot is and stay there.

Rule number one: if you don't take care of your customer, someone else will. That's our motto. Rule number two doesn't exist. What I have learned from my experience is that you have to have a perceived value to initially get a sale. But then you have to offer real value to sustain a relationship. That's why you have to market properly, sell properly, and support outrageously to gain customer loyalty and profitable, long-term relationships.

Biography

Named one the 10 Most Influential People in CRM by Sales and Marketing Automation magazine, Richard Brock founded and serves as Chairman and CEO of Firstwave Technologies, Inc. Firstwave, a pioneer in the Sales Force Automation market and a leading provider of web-based Internet Relationship Management applications, was started by Mr. Brock in 1984 to address the needs of companies seeking a complete solution to automate their sales, marketing and customer service. His entrepreneurial spirit has resulted in Firstwave establishing an international presence and serving over 200 companies in 20 countries.

Mr. Brock has also played a significant role in the development and management of several companies. He founded Brock Capital Partners, a capital investment firm, and is a director of Datastream Systems, Inc., a leading provider of maintenance software. Prior to his originating Firstwave, Mr. Brock founded and served as CEO of Management Control Systems, a software provider for CPA firms that is now a division of Research Institute of America. In addition, he has held board positions with three other companies.

Formerly the Chairman of the Technology Association of Georgia, Mr. Brock has assumed numerous industry leadership positions and has received many accolades through his entrepreneurial career. He has served as President and Board Member of the Business & Technology Alliance, President of the Entrepreneur's Division and Board Member of the Information Technology Association of America, President and Board Member of the Southeast Software Association, Chairman of Georgia High Technology Month and Board Member of the Technology Executives Roundtable. He was named Georgia's High Technology Entrepreneur of the Year in 1990.

A Certified Public Accountant, Mr. Brock received his MBA from Louisiana State University and his BS from Spring Hill College.

Chapter 22

Relationship Management

Richard Hochhauser

Overcoming Misconceptions and Customer Relationship Challenges

There is a phrase, relationship management, which is also often called customer relationship management and has the initials CRM associated with it. I prefer to use the first term because an organization could be focusing on GRM (guest relationship management for the travel industry), or DRM (donor relationship management for the non-profit industry), PRM (partner relationship management, for business-to-business marketing), or other client-specific terminology. So relationship management lets you encompass all of them.

During the past five years, we've seen the rise and fall and rise again of relationship management. First, it flourished as a discipline and as a way to organize an enterprise. Then, as an investment, but with no clear-cut vision as to where success would be measured. And now, it has returned, with return on investment (ROI) being the very necessary component, as well as a focus on metrics that seems to have eluded the earlier relationship management tryouts of some businesses.

The biggest misconception about relationship management (RM) is that it is a software buy: buying technology suffices and delivers RM success. However, there is a great deal more to achieving profitable customer relationships than buying technology. Courage is sometimes required to align an organization's objectives and a customer's goals. Profits and customer relationships need to be in sync, and the payback gap is often longer than people may think or plan for, partly because the upfront work — planning, defining objectives, understanding measurements and deliverables — may not get done properly, if at all.

Building enterprise-wide buy-in is one challenge when implementing a relationship management system. The department with which a project is most closely involved is not necessarily the only department in the client company that has an interest in its implementation and success. Other departments may have some level of very real input into the project, such as the sales, marketing, customer service, c-level executives, and the IT [information technology] department.

Sometimes there are political or power struggles between these departments, which seems so silly since the RM is built to help all of them. Regardless, and no matter how much two or more departments don't get along, it makes sense to get the perspective and buy-in of every department that touches the relationship.

To deal with disparate data sources and legacy systems, and to assure data quality in every step of the build and execution, all of these departments must be involved as each owns a different piece of the puzzle. The concept of "garbage in, garbage out" has buried many database and RM systems. In addition, unrealistic measurements of success are also a challenge in dealing with customers, and these measures will vary depending on where in the organization the questions are being asked.

Relationship Management Strategies

As a database marketing and RM partner to many Fortune 1000 consumers and business-to-business organizations, when our customers win, we win. So the first step is to make sure they win. To align our goals with our clients' goals, we make sure we listen, understand, and deliver some innovation in their RM plans and rollouts.

To determine customer needs, we listen twice as hard as we talk. The ability to listen is one of our selling propositions. We are involved in all aspects of direct marketing, and we let the customer know we do all the things they want done. Even if the customer chooses to award us only a portion of its business — a certain aspect of a project — it will know what we do and know how we can take one project and do more with it.

Our strategy is to try to create a unique offering in the marketplace. We have achieved this through a solution set that includes the construction and updating of a database, and then accessing that data and analyzing it in order to translate it into information and then into knowledge. Of course, we then apply that knowledge by creating programs from that application and then physically executing the programs, whether it is building a Web site, or doing a mail or e-mail campaign, or making and taking telephone calls. We do the execution ourselves based on each client's needs and objectives. It is a closed-loop approach, and we do all of the pieces — whether limited or unlimited by each client.

Another strategy is the use of real-time components to monitor transactions that trigger a marketing intervention. Usually, in traditional database applications, some modeling is done and then you must decide whom you will communicate to and then you communicate. Then you must wait for a return and put it back in the database, and then you can measure how well it worked. With our untraditional database applications, it is instantaneous. Somebody behaves, and they automatically receive communication. For example: If it is a bank and a deposit is made that is five times a normal deposit and above a certain dollar amount, there will be an immediate communication from the bank to that client saying, "We'd love for you to keep the money in the bank, and this is how we propose you do that."

Obviously, that's an oversimplification, but that kind of immediate communication (think of it as next day) is very different from traditional database applications. It is based on a predefined trigger mechanism, so in this case, the predefinition might be anything more than four times a traditional deposit, and a minimum traditional deposit of $10,000 makes the trigger work. And that database application, I believe, is a significantly innovative one, which we have found our customers to be excited about and which has resulted in strong ROI for our clients.

Another extension of RM capabilities with growing appeal is the use of the Web to create "marketing portals." A marketing portal is an interactive, Web-based tool used by bank branches, auto dealers, stores, agents and field sales force, etc., to enable the ordering of direct mail program pieces, e-mail and other marketing programs and collateral from enterprise-arranged sources. The portal design and infrastructure is built to meet the needs of specific companies, in specific vertical industries, and is tailored to support lines of business, branch networks and independent agents. Users customize campaigns to their immediate needs, and still do so within the guidelines and regimen of the overall enterprise or brand. Plus, in this day of ROI, just as the branch can see the local payback, the enterprise can size up and evaluate individual participation and see where it has translated into success. This is the ultimate weapon in the strategy of thinking globally and acting locally.

We try to think creatively and give our customers more than they ask for. We strive to understand our customers' customers. We set expectations in a way that helps ensure our success. The worst thing that can happen is to do a great job, but if the expectations were even greater, in effect, there is failure.

Success is what the client says it is. But unlike with many other media, what we do in a direct marketing project is easily measured — we know the cost and the returns. Success usually means we are meeting and exceeding the acquisition goal and achieving the targeted cost per acquisition, and those newly acquired customers end up growing in value and in persistence for the client.

When you look at what dictates success from an internal perspective, for our company it has to do with profit growth, increased earnings per share for our stakeholders and employee shareholders, and creating a work environment for our people that allows them to flourish.

The Role of Technology

Our perspective is highly people-intensive: A good person working on current technology will deliver more value to a client than an average person working on the next generation of technology.

Technology counts, of course, but it doesn't put a project over the top. The person working with technology toward a specific customer solution puts it over the top. And that has to do with understanding the technology and the execution of the technology, understanding the industry that the technology is applied to, and understanding the needs of the customer. And that isn't technology.

Technology is the price of entry; it's not an option. It is the enabler, but it's not the solution. It serves the strategy, not the other way around. Technology without metrics for success is almost always a losing situation.

Technology prowess is surely required, but so is training and timing of early wins, and so are implementation and the demonstration of ROI. And at the end of the day, human capital needs to be in control. Technology is just a tool of the data and marketing professional, not the other way around.

Once someone, whether it is us or someone else, has money inventing a unique, innovative, and wonderful piece of technology, we then can focus on the people side of that, and on the market orientation side of it, and on the technology application side of it, and that's how we make our living.

And that is not to say that we don't develop technology, because we do. It is just that technology spans the spectrum of what we do, and there are literally hundreds of technology elements that ultimately yield applications in which we specialize.

The Human Component in the RM Process

Take data quality, for example, also known as data cleansing or data hygiene. Allow me to discuss briefly our particular offering here, the Trillium Software System®. Trillium Software System is a software solution, and is one of a few enterprise-wide data quality solutions available in the marketplace. In short, it is technology. Through an automated process, it standardizes, enhances and links elements in a marketing organization's database, or in operational transactions for use in an enterprise data warehouse, operational data store or worldwide master file. It is unique, in that it has years of application history, and ROI demonstrations that are often tenfold with clients.

However, Trillium Software System also is based on human intelligence. Its more than 200,000 modifiable business rules understand the context of data. Included are best practices that are learned from human capital, just as there are time-tested business rules identifying and linking customers, there are specific cultural and linguistic rules that enable human-like understanding of data in application specific environments. So, yes, Trillium Software can be thought of as a solution of IT professionals, but in reality, critical business applications such as RM, e-business, and enterprise resource planning suites all benefit from high data quality. Enterprise data quality, done right, is proof positive that "technology" is an enabler for the people who will make it happen.

Related to data quality is data management. Today's smart marketers are everywhere the customer is — using the medium or media of a customer's preference to dialogue, to transact, and to deliver service. Multichannel communication now comes with the territory, demanding data accuracy and customer recognition no matter what channel the customer is happening to use a particular day. Thus, we now have to ensure we have a technology in play to validate customer files so we know that they contain accurate and up-to-date contact information.

We may need to verify and enhance physical addresses so the US Postal Service will deliver. We may need to correct a faulty, outdated or incomplete address, or to verify or add a valid phone number — even if the customer mistakenly provided an error. There may need to be an e-mail address validation. All this is technology at work in a marketing data center, and it is driven in part by a timely, "we need it now" demand that originates with our clients and their customers, most of whom expect immediate, relevant communication in this interactive age with those businesses with which they choose to patronize. So, while data centers deliver this quality and speed, so do the data management account teams — again, human capital — who make sure each channel of communication is optimized and that the marketing organization has a full "360-degree" view for each of its customers.

Another example is analytics. Again, analytics is now touted in many CRM software suites by software vendors — a technology-based solution. That's all well and good, but only if the user understands the discipline, capabilities, pitfalls and reality checks of segmenting customer databases, building predictive models, evaluating those models, and interpreting the results. A common plea from our clients is, "What do the data say?" and "What is the knowledge that is hidden in our data?" Human expertise — experience as a data professional, statistician and industry expert — is vital to answer these questions. It makes productive, optimal use of such software, to help derive substantive action based on accurate data reads. In effect, the software is a tool of the data professional, and not a replacement of the data professional.

Analyzing data is a specialty. Where we engage analytics with customers, for example, we do so using program development teams who interpret data and deliver solutions that make full use of the software and technology toolbox. And these teams have rich vertical industry experience. That means these professionals are adept at recognizing and avoiding "garbage-in, garbage-out" that can fault many segmentation and model-building assignments. Even a trained eye may not spot a model's deficiency until after its first test. These teams understand most diligently the build-test-read-and-refine process. Thus, once again, the most productive analytics engagements, and the unique contributions of a professional's perspective, cannot (yet) be automated fully for any one company. Technology is the enabler, not the deliverer.

Data quality, data management and multiple channel communications are and will be critically important in the foreseeable future. Also real-time monitoring to detect behavior change and the use of predictive modeling that help identify on the fly all the people who need to be communicated with is very young in its implementation. The technology of analytics is not young, but it is not old either. The IT professionals drive things, but technology increasingly will have more normative and "productionized" capabilities over time, which will be exciting to see. The IT department's partnerships with other professionals inside an organization must be strong to capitalize on these capabilities.

Customer Acquisition

Enterprises have to focus on attracting the right customers to try a product or a service. The right customers are the ones with the highest predicted future value and with the necessary propensity to be acquired.

Loyalty is about attitudes, in which we are somewhat interested. We are more interested in loyalty behavior. We view loyalty as an increase in loyal behavior when the share of customer is increased. It is customers coming back to spend more and for more things.

Purchasing behavior defines profitable and unprofitable clients. A company knows what its clients have bought, and it knows the price point at which they bought it. So then the company must dig down below to talk about what kind of profitability the customer has to the company.

A successful business has to identify the most profitable customers, nurture them, and retain them. Those customers allow a business to find look-alikes so it can begin to look for prospects from that customer base. The less-profitable customers are identified and are graduated and retained — and that is an ideal situation. The unprofitable customers are identified and hopefully graduate to profitable status. There are also unprofitable customers that will never be profitable, and an enterprise must allow them to disappear through attrition, which is very hard to do. It is counterintuitive. No one likes to lose business, but it is an important part of this equation.

In order to help our client companies acquire customers, we have to define what specifically is a best customer look-alike. Once that is done, prospects in the marketplace are identified. In our particular company, we have a complete vision of a marketing-focused data strategy: constructing and updating a database, accessing the data, analyzing the data, applying the knowledge and executing the programs. When we share this vision of what we do — this end-to-end approach — our customers don't get stuck on one aspect of a solution. They get a chance to visualize what might happen next because very often they are being exposed to the next steps. They even may learn of needs and opportunities they otherwise did not know they had — or at least better understand where their current thinking may take them. Any enterprise should seek this same complete approach to their data — and have a customer acquisition strategy for RM.

For our own company, the proportion of high-value customers that continue to do business with us defines customer retention for ourselves. As with many organizations, retention for us has to do with order frequency over time and dollar amounts purchased. Targeting high-value customers and growing a base of long-term profitable customers is the goal, as is lowering the cost of acquisition.

Some clients want to establish a vendor relationship — in other words, "Go do this." Other clients adopt a partner relationship and will sit down with us and tell us why they are pursuing the project, allowing us to help them perhaps figure out another way of getting it done less expensively and faster. It pays to know which customers are which, and to treat each customer accordingly.

The Elements of Risk

Taking risks cannot and should not be eliminated in the world of RM. When we take risks for our customers, the fact that we test and retest and test again, almost by definition says there is risk involved, but it also makes improvements on our current state.

In marketing and RM, there is hunch work, which is the risk part. And there is science, which is the reduction-of-risk part. The hallmarks of the direct-marketing strategy are measurability and accountability.

Risk taking is part of doing business. When making decisions on hiring people, a firm hopes a certain percentage will stay. In technology, a business hopes that a high percentage of the technology is optimal. Making decisions on timing and setting expectations for clients is a gamble. One makes decisions on how much risk to take to expand a business — a long-term objective — while still satisfying the short-term objective of trying to optimize earnings per share.

With respect to relationship management, risk can be minimized or managed in part by navigating with someone who has been there before, and knows how to avoid common mistakes, and understands the importance of having defined goals, the right metrics to measure objectives and a solution that is focused. In our particular company, we know that not many companies can say they have three decades of experience building, installing and hosting hundreds of database implementations — and thousands of data-driven primarily marketing solutions. We believe this is more than just a value-add for our clients — it's a means for them to minimize risk in their projects and assignments.

Equally important, in the RM space, is to have internal staff and external partners who are disciplined historically in direct marketing. Direct marketing's emphasis on measurability and accountability go hand in hand with today's database and RM marketing expectations. So where a pure-play software company may appear to be a reliable, stable and attractive partner, it may not understand fully the context, customization and customer demands of a particular client, in a particular industry — and the day-to-day response-driven marketing activity that must enrich the RM solution. Is the supplier going to roll up its sleeves and make it all work?

When a company is not certain if it wishes to in-source or outsource, build versus buy, or simply gain a partner who can help make RM strategies and tactics happen, these aforementioned considerations help to manage risk accordingly.

Golden Rules for Creating Customer Relationships

A sign in my office says it all: The customer is the reason we're here. You should wake up every morning believing that golden rule.

The best advice I ever received was to always do what is best for the customer even if it means we don't maximize our returns. If the client is excited by our willingness to do what it takes to make them win, they are going to be happy long-term, too.

You have to measure customer attitudes and behavior, learn from customer surveys, and understand the value equation: trust times benefits divided by cost.

Some people may say it's all about cost or all about value. Cost is part of value; if you lower the cost, which is the denominator, you are increasing value. But if you increase the benefits, you also increase the value, and trust is there because it is a very important component. It doesn't have as much variability, but without the trust factor being a high index number, the value deteriorates quickly.

Doing what you say you will do is a fundamental step toward establishing trust in a relationship. It's an easy thing to talk about, but it is hard to do. Trust comes from open communication and the ability to convey bad news as well as good news. For instance, instead of declaring, "Here is the problem..." try taking a "this is what we'll do about the problem" approach.

Trust comes from delivering what the customer expects, and over time you have a chance to perform. There is an ethical piece to it and an honesty piece to it, and there's an openness piece to it. In our company, these values are part of our culture, and part of our vision.

Into the Future: Evolving Customer Relationships

John Malone, a cable industry leader, once said that in five years, 80 per cent of his revenue would come from sources that he hasn't even begun to offer yet. That's a provocative point of view about the pace of change and how to stay ahead of it to continue to provide value to customers.

The equation is not quite as dramatic as that for us, although it certainly does apply; we just need to be devoted to our customers and do the right things for them. If we listen hard enough, we'll wind up creating more opportunities for them, such as developing new applications for them because we have listened. We will be able to take them to a new level, and that will fundamentally change the relationship. It will allow us to work with more senior people and in more departments of our client companies.

Growth belongs to those companies that understand how to add value, and that means transforming data into information and applying it to create customer knowledge and to deliver new value based on that. In the end it also means making it happen for your customer.

Biography

Richard Hochhauser is president and chief executive officer of Harte-Hanks, Inc. — a worldwide direct marketing and targeted media company that provides a full range of customer relationship management (CRM) solutions, related direct and interactive marketing services, and regional shopper publications. In addition to his duties as president and CEO of Harte-Hanks, Mr. Hochhauser also serves as a member of the company's Board of Directors. Mr. Hochhauser joined Harte-Hanks in an entrepreneurial capacity 27 years ago. He assumed responsibility for the direct marketing business of Harte-Hanks in 1987, was named president of the parent company in 1999, and was named president and CEO of the company in April 2002.

Mr. Hochhauser has spoken at a wide range of marketing and database conferences, lectured at Northwestern, Carnegie Mellon and Rutgers, and is on the faculty of New York University. He is past Chairman of the Board of Directors of the Direct Marketing Association, served on the Advisory Board of Texas A&M University, Center for Retailing Studies, and is currently a member of the board of directors of Modem Media, Inc., and a board member of the Center for Direct and Interactive Marketing Board of Advisors of NYU's School of Continuing and Professional Studies. Richard Hochhauser graduated from Carnegie Mellon University and received an MBA from Columbia University.

Chapter 23

Finding the Right Fit

Jeffrey Rodek

Developing a Profitable Relationship

Listening to your customer is simply the most important thing you can do to build a profitable customer relationship. The second critical thing is to understand where you can add value and just as importantly, where you cannot — you have to understand the limitations of your domain expertise.

Quick returns on investment and quick wins are needed, especially during the early stages with a new customer. That way, they're winning and your winning and you're building a rapport and building success. You also have to recognize when you can and when you cannot help. For instance, if you listen and they have a pain that they thought you could solve, but you look at it and realize that you cannot help, you have to make the hard decision, the right decision, and refer them elsewhere so that they can get a solution. It may be a loss in the short term, but it is better to win their respect and do right by the customer. If you have the opportunity to say what you can do, maybe they will come back to you later. The alternative is to push something that is not really a fit, which inevitably is unprofitable for you and an unhappy story for the customer. This of course is no way to build a trusting relationship. Ultimately, if you have a solution for their problem, attack it and get some quick wins. On the other hand, if you don't have a fit, you have to pass on the opportunity and recommend the best company for their needs.

For example, our company can often install a new application in two or three months start to finish. With this approach, customers will likely enjoy benefits from their investment very quickly, at a time when many companies are looking to have technology investment paybacks within a year. That's what I would describe as a quick win. The customer is seeing positive returns very quickly.

In listening to the customer, you want to make sure that their requirements are understood and that their expectations are aligned with yours. There should be no communications failures. Taking the time to listen, to build requirements, to build a plan, and work the plan usually leads to success. A second challenge that we face is making sure that the employees of our company are aligned to customer success, as well as some of the more obvious goals in the company, like revenue and profits. When I worked for Federal Express, Jim Barksdale, who you probably remember from his Netscape days, was our COO. I recall being in a meeting with managers from the pickup and delivery operations of Federal Express when Jim was asked what was most important to him: cost numbers, service, or the employees. He told them if he only wanted one of the three, anybody could do it, but because he wanted all three managed, he needed talented managers like them. At Hyperion we like to think of it as the three legs of a stool. Customer satisfaction, profits, and taking care of your people are all equally important — the stool cannot stand on two legs alone.

We take that balanced approach at Hyperion. We have customer satisfaction, profit, and employee satisfaction goals. We have been working hard at this notion, especially in the past year. I have told the story about Jim Barksdale's direction repeatedly, and we've talked about the three-legged stool with our executive committee and to the top hundred leaders in the company. It is a challenge to take this concept and turn it into something that every manager understands. It is also critical that every employee touching the customer understands this idea and a picture is worth a thousand words. So, the picture of a balanced, three-legged stool helps employees keep that in mind in the heat of battle.

Communicating the company's values starts with a culture that is straightforward and honest. Help where you can help; do not help where you don't have domain expertise. You also have to be very clear in your business promise and your mission. We have worked hard, especially over the past six or seven months now, in putting together a very clear vision statement and a mission statement, on articulating our values, and defining a customer promise that can be shared with every employee in our company. Letting our customers know that we promise to deliver world-class enterprise software is imperative.

It's also important to continue to evangelize those values. I talk about our mission and our company's brand promise at every opportunity with employees. You have to evangelize inside and outside of the company all of the time and then back it up. We also talk about why it is important to raise the bar on yourself faster and higher than either the competition or your customers will. For example, think about the high jump or pole vault, two Olympic events that end in a failure. The winner keeps jumping until he or she knocks the bar down. So the winner continues to raise the bar on him or herself, higher and higher and higher. It's up to them to raise it another notch, to try again. In business, if we do a good job of listening to our customers and raising the bar on ourselves, to exceed customer expectations, we will be more successful than if we allow the customers or our competitors to raise the bar.

Hyperion and the Profitable Customer Relationship

It's important to have a clear mission, a clear promise about what your company is all about. You want to have an expectation match. Our customers are increasingly understanding that we are a Business Performance Management software company, and so when they come to us, they are looking for solutions that help them turn strategies into plans, help to monitor execution, and get insight into how they can improve both their financial and operational performance. They want help automating management processes such as analysis, planning, reporting, setting goals, modeling and monitoring results. That's what they expect from Business Performance Management. Just as importantly, you need to make it clear what not to come to us for — we are not in the business of high volume transaction processing. Other software companies do that.

Customers want to use products that work and that are from companies that stand behind them. They want to work with a company that's going to be around a long time. Therefore, they often check out your balance sheet to look at how you are spending your money, to make sure that you are reinvesting in product development. They look at your people, your products and your brand to see if there's a match. They look at all of those things to try and determine who they want to have as a strategic partner. Then they want to talk to other customers; they want references. That is the whole package of what they look for in a software company.

We firmly believe in the adage that you can't manage what you can't measure. So we survey our customers about all aspects of doing business with Hyperion. And to ensure alignment, we make sure rewards match performance vs. goals. For example, customer satisfaction is a key factor in the Hyperion bonus program. If we achieve our customer satisfaction goals, we can add bonus money to the pool. If we don't achieve our goals, we take money away. Everybody is affected and because of the way bonuses work — bonuses generally impact managers more than line employees because a higher percentage of their target compensation is bonus — it impacts our senior management even more than it impacts the front lines. You have to put your money where your mouth is. In aligning the goals, you have to measure them as the customers want them to be measured and you have to impact the reward system.

The keys to profitability in the enterprise software business are different than in many other businesses. You can achieve good margins if your selling cycles are effective, you're not doing a lot of customization, customers are implemented quickly and efficiently, and you're not selling buggy software that requires a lot of support and consulting services. But profitability is more than revenue minus cost — you have to understand the total relationship with the customer. So we look at successful implementations and we measure how much free consulting we have to provide to ensure customer satisfaction. Another set of criteria involves how many commissions are being paid to complete a sale — is the selling process efficient, or are there too many people around and involved in a deal? And we also look at streamlining activities such as license extensions for additional users; we are increasingly turning to the Web to make those transactions both more cost efficient and also simpler for the customer.

Keeping a customer happy is as important as getting a new customer happy. We're doing this in part by putting a lot of energy into improving our support program; such as automating many support initiatives. For instance, we have about 300 customers using new software that with their permission, helps us determine the technical environment, operating system, and hardware they are using. So we short circuit a lot of the questions a support person would normally ask and get a head start on solving the customer's problem. This is easier for the customer and it makes it easier for us to give them an answer. We've learned that using this approach cuts down on customer irritation and helps us resolve a problem in a fraction of the time it used to. That keeps our costs down and the customers much happier.

The purpose of any business is to get and keep a customer. Customer acquisition is about bringing a customer into the fold and selling them software and services, but then also keeping them as a customer and growing with that customer. It is important to recognize that there is a relationship that must be kept with that customer long past the point of selling them software, whether that be further consulting work, more software or perhaps just establishing a great reference.

The software business provides a built-in mechanism to measure continuing satisfaction, since customers pay for ongoing maintenance support. In return, the customer receives updates of the software and gets help resolving any problems. Because of the maintenance contracts, measuring customer retention is pretty easy for a software company; you know how many bought your software and each month you can monitor how many are paying for maintenance to stay with you.

Customer loyalty is the step beyond customer satisfaction. With customer satisfaction, you have sold something to somebody and they are happy. In customer loyalty, they are not only happy, but they often make recommendations to others. It's very much like the old saw about if somebody goes to a restaurant and has a good experience, they might tell 10 people. If they go to a restaurant and have a bad experience, they might tell 110 people. So, customer loyalty goes beyond a satisfied customer toward a customer who is a champion, an advocate, a fanatic about what you're doing, and they're very likely to make unsolicited recommendations for you.

For example, I recently visited Yankee Stadium as a guest of NASDAQ. We were in their box along with quite a few other companies. Within my first five minutes in the box, several different people from different companies saw my nametag and affiliation, and told me how much they love Hyperion. Hearing "you've got great software!" made me feel good but it was also great for everybody else in the room to hear it, since there were probably some potential customers in the group. Another example is when I was in Pennsylvania recently to visit with a customer. The controller, a long time user of our software, said he would only allow Hyperion software to be replaced with another if it was pried from "his cold, dead hands." Fortunately losing the account was not at risk, but this is the kind of relationship that goes beyond satisfaction all the way to loyalty.

Approaching Risk in the Business

Risk — and managing risk — is very important in the software business. There are several things we do in approaching risk while dealing with the customer; such as the way we address quality assurance in product development. Ideally, you want to find any problems in the software while you're testing inside your shop, rather than finding the problems once the customer has installed it. Like many software companies, we restrict Alpha testing, or the very early, unfinished versions of software, to internal review. However we work with customers to test Beta versions, which are not quite ready for prime time but functional. By testing in the customer environment with customers who are willing to give feedback, we improve quality and manage some of the risk involved with introducing highly complex new products.

We also mitigate risk by using our own software — we call it drinking our own champagne. We have a much better sense of how the software works in the real world by virtue of our own experience with it.

Some of the work that we are doing to automate the interaction of customers also helps us manage risk. It's one thing to have a problem with the customer, but it is far worse if the solution to the problem doesn't work. That lesson was reinforced over and over during my career at Federal Express. We did not like being late or losing a package. But if we did, it could be far worse to mishandle the solution. The same thing applies to software companies. A customer calling with a problem is already upset. How that situation is handled is paramount — problems quickly resolved and with honest feedback and communication go a long way toward customer satisfaction and even loyalty. However, problems mismanaged or bungled can get very nasty. From a risk management standpoint, companies have to understand that they're going to have some problems. How those problems are resolved is the difference between world-class customer satisfaction and the also rans.

At Hyperion, the protocol for problem resolution comes through our support organization. Beyond normal call center activities, we work to contain and resolve a problem. But we also go back later and try to make sure that we've addressed the root cause rather than just the symptom.

A new change for us addresses the deployment environment. We have a deployment guide to help our people match our software to the environment and equipment being used at the customer site. In the past, we sometimes weren't aggressive enough in recommending a customer get more horsepower and a bigger machine if in fact the upgrades would have been helpful in supporting our software. But we know that customers would rather understand the requirements up front. And we know from experience in which environments our software performs best, so we should not be shy about communicating this information to customers up front. Logically, if the software works well in an environment, the chances are it will work well in a similar environment with a different customer. Communicating requirements early rather than waiting for problems to surface is a good path to customer satisfaction and part of a proactive approach to risk management.

Technology Now and in the Future

Great technology is scalable in two ways: one way is bigger, better, faster. Another dimension is in terms of making software that scales across a company and allows a great many people to use it and to collaborate with it. The Internet is a great enabler of scalable technology. For instance, our software enables thousands of users in a company to be collaborating and modeling as part of a dynamic planning process. It allows managers and knowledge workers across the company to interact with information. And it supports the notion that everybody is different, everybody has different performance indicators that they are working with. So processing speed and the ability to touch many users in a company and doing that in a way that provides data integrity and a single version of the truth are three important aspects of great technology.

We also think about today and tomorrow. A good solution meets a customer's requirements today. A great solution anticipates the future need. We talked earlier about listening to customers. There are three types of customers that you should listen to very closely. The first ones are those with the squeaky wheel. They have a problem right now; you need to listen to them, contain the problem, and go back and fix the root cause. The second type of customer is one that is interested in a very broad solution. For those, you want to go listen to them to see if you can solve their problem and close the sale. The third type is what I call the design type of customer. Design customers are really thinking beyond how today's features and functions will help them to do today's job. They can help build a vision of where your product should be in the future, which helps us decide what should be happening in our R&D labs and what should come out of the labs in three or five years.

The technology in our business is really at a magical moment. The Internet allows technology to be deployed much more widely and much more effectively, tailored to each user. The Web has simply transformed our business. You'll see companies using Web-based software to support thousands of people — all collaborating on planning, doing real-time reporting off of a single version of the truth for better financial integrity.

The Web has also enabled much broader usage of our software. For instance, for many years our software was chiefly used by finance organizations — the CFO and the controller were our best customers. With the newer Web-based technologies, we have implementations that can span the enterprise. Touching a quarter to a half of all the knowledge workers in a company with our products is a realistic goal.

Technology is a key differentiator too. We're always working for bigger, better, faster, and easier enhancements. And while there is great progress, there is also room for improvement in that area of technology. We are setting new benchmarks every year. We're improving the response times for calculating large amounts of data. And we continually advance ease of use, making the software easier to use for more people. There is no end in sight and that's just on the software side — there are huge advancements on the hardware side of it as well.

It is also important to match the technology with the needs of the customer, with what you do vs. what they need. We offer a suite of products that work together from planning to reporting to goal setting to supporting and monitoring all of these processes that we talk about, but offer customers the option of "starting anywhere." Meaning a customer doesn't have to buy the entire suite to see some immediate benefit. And this comes back to listening to your customers, having a good open dialog with them. We talk about the entire management process and some of them buy solutions to address the entire cycle. Some "get" the big picture but only want to solve an immediate pain. Still others look to enter the suite at one point, to solve an immediate and pressing need, but want to work with us to develop a roadmap to get to the bigger idea. We're ok working with our customers on each of these levels, because ultimately they have to see value and reap a benefit if the relationship is going to succeed over the long haul. Too many companies sell so hard that customers end up with more than they need...which leads to unsatisfied customers. This isn't a long-term strategy but rather a recipe for a bad reputation in the industry. If customers need everything, we're more than happy to sell it and more often than not, our customers want to take it. But one success at a time is also a good selling philosophy.

Customer Relationships in a Nutshell

In a nutshell there are five really key ideas we keep foremost in mind around profitable customer relationships.

First, perception is reality. If the customer thinks there is a problem, there is a problem. Passing the buck, as in, "it's not our problem, it is their problem or another vendor's problem", is not a successful strategy. Rather, the best companies acknowledge problems and work hard to resolve them.

The second idea is based on the reality that companies are going to have problems. Nobody's perfect. Rather, what separates the great companies is how they react and respond to problems. The great companies try to get it right as fast as they can. Then they keep at it until they've determined the root cause. They don't settle for patching over the symptoms but drive to achieve customer satisfaction.

The third idea is organized around people, processes, and systems, which are absolutely integral to customer service. It's about building a culture where those are priorities. It is also about building management systems that are built around commitment and unleashing the discretionary effort of every employee in the interest of both customer satisfaction and also profits. I think that there are things that you tell people, that you try to drill into their heads, but there are also systematic changes to make in the company. It's imperative that we instill a culture of customer service, but we also need to enable people to support that ideal. All of those things have to come together and that's been a constant mantra here.

Fourthly, companies must constantly raise the bar on themselves. The great companies are ahead of customers and ahead of competitors because they never settle, they never rest. They set very high standards and increase those standards every year.

And lastly, you can't manage what you can't measure. Customer satisfaction has to be more than just campaign slogans. It has to be just like profitability or employee satisfaction; you have to find a way to measure it. You have to go back and impact the reward system or it will probably just pay lip service to you. Everything else you need to know flows from these rules.

Biography

Jeff Rodek was named chairman and CEO in October 1999 to provide strategic leadership and direction and drive Hyperion's profitable growth. Prior to joining Hyperion, he served for five years as president and chief operating officer of Ingram Micro, the world's largest wholesale provider of technology solutions, products and services. In January 1998, while at Ingram Micro, Rodek joined the board of directors of Arbor Software, which merged with Hyperion in 1998.

Before joining Ingram Micro, Rodek spent 16 years at Federal Express Corp., a $20-billion global provider of transportation, freight, and e-commerce and supply-chain management services. Rodek's career began in Operations Research, continued in Financial Planning and Analysis, then Operations. His last position at FedEx was Senior Vice President.

Throughout his career as a provider and user of decision support and performance management software, Rodek gained an appreciation for the value of software in measuring performance and driving improved profitability.

Rodek holds a bachelor's degree in mechanical engineering and a master's degree in business administration, with an emphasis in finance, from The Ohio State University. He currently serves on the board of directors of NewRoads, Inc., a leading provider of outsourced business operations solutions to companies engaged in multichannel, one-to-one direct commerce, and EXE Technologies, Inc., a global provider of fulfillment, warehousing and distribution software. In addition, Rodek is a member of the board of Gifts In Kind International and the advisory board to the Fisher College of Business, The Ohio State University.

Chapter 24

How to Make Every Customer a Repeat Customer

Lloyd G. "Buzz" Waterhouse

Profitable Customer Relationships

The science fiction writer Arthur C. Clarke once commented: "Any sufficiently advanced technology is indistinguishable from magic." The problem, of course, is there is no magic. Only technology. Yet, what can be accomplished with technology is magical; it can make every customer a repeat customer and it can create profitable, sustainable customer relationships. But technology alone is not enough. Sustaining successful customer relationships requires a combination of people, process, and technology. And like one of Merlin's magical potions, if any one element is missing, the desired effect will be missing, too. At Reynolds and Reynolds, we have built our business on that principle; the lessons we have learned — and still are learning — can be applied to other businesses in other industries that serve other customers.

The three lessons we continue to learn are focused single-mindedly on making every customer a repeat customer for Reynolds and every customer a repeat customer for our customers. Here's how:[1] Invent the future with your customers;[2] Develop a passion for customer loyalty and move beyond customer satisfaction; and[3] Forget the technology — information is the new magic in profitable customer relationships.

The Market We Serve: Lessons for Other Companies

Reynolds and Reynolds is a billion dollar software and information services company that has served automotive retailing since 1927, when we first developed standardized accounting forms and processes for Chevrolet dealerships across the US Today, the Reynolds brand accounts for the largest installed product base of software and information technology in automobile dealerships and the strongest market position in the industry. Reynolds serves more than 20,000 automotive retailers, every car company in North America, and delivers consulting to automotive retailers in 20 countries worldwide.

Reynolds' leadership is built on deep automotive industry experience, technological knowledge, and the unique ability to bring both together to change how our customers do business, creating value and competitive advantage for them in serving their customers. The value and competitive advantage that make our customers repeat customers is found in connecting, combining, and delivering information in new ways; ways that enable automotive retailers to manage their businesses more profitably and to serve consumers more consistently — whether within the four walls of the dealership or across the expanse of the World Wide Web.

In North America, automotive retailing is a $1.7 trillion market. With more than 25,000 new car franchised retailers, 55,000 used car retailers, 22,000 sport and recreational vehicle shops, and 53,000 collision repair shops, that marketplace generates 22 per cent of all retail activity and pays more than 19 per cent of all sales tax in the US It is a market that encompasses dozens of players, dozens of mega-processes, and billions of transactions — richly complex and poorly connected.

The typical automobile dealer manages on average 2.3 different franchises and several distinct businesses under one roof: new and used vehicles, parts and service, sales and leasing, insurance and financing, rental cars, and increasingly, after market accessories, sports apparel, and upscale café's. Each area is information rich. Yet, automotive retailing, too, often is still characterized by islands of information and separate business operations within dealerships — different information systems and processes, different franchise reporting requirements, and disjointed, scattered touch points with consumers. Although Electronic Data Interchange has been around since the 1960s, less than 5 per cent of the entire automotive value chain is connected. The opportunity to bridge the islands of information — to connect the dots of automotive retailing — is the opportunity to create unprecedented value for businesses and benefit for consumers.

We can serve that market as it exists today — delivering value, certainly — or we can invent the future of automotive retailing with our customers, creating extraordinary value by connecting the dots of automotive retailing. We've chosen to lead the transformation in automotive retailing and invent the future with our customers. For any business, building sustainable, profitable customer relationships — and making every customer a repeat customer — requires inventing the future.

Inventing the Future with Our Customers: The Transformation of Automotive Retailing

Arthur Clarke is also credited with this notion: If a scientist can imagine a future technology, it will happen. What is technologically imaginable in automotive retailing has, in fact, become technologically achievable and has, in fact, begun to resemble magic.

Automotive retailing has undergone more change in the past five years than in the previous one hundred. It began with consumers who, armed with new found knowledge about the vehicle they were seeking, turned the process of buying a car upside down. Today's automotive consumer is increasingly demanding, better informed, and two out of every three consumers starts the car buying process on the Web. In fact, the average consumer now visits more than half a dozen Web sites during the buying process, gathering information and impressions at each stop. They are truly informed consumers.

A decade ago, the process was simple. The consumer walked into a dealership, the dealership held most of the information, the consumer would be told the Manufacturer's Suggested Retail Price, and the consumer would begin negotiating down with the sales person's price. Things have changed. Today, the consumer interacts with the dealership on multiple fronts — the telephone, mail, e-mail, Web Site, kiosk, Telematics devices, and, yes, the new car showroom. The consumer has already done the homework before she (I say she, because almost two-thirds of all car buying decisions are made by women) interacts with the retailer. She knows the wholesale price, vehicle comparisons, option packages, safety record, and national averages for the make and model she is interested in. Now, the tables are turned. The sales person must negotiate up with the consumer, based on their frequently superior knowledge of the product, dealer invoice price, holdbacks, and loads of information recently gleaned from the previously mentioned sources. Simply speaking, it has become much more of a true retailing model, which is why we use the term automobile retailers at Reynolds & Reynolds. While the physical business is a dealership, what now happens in the business is retailing.

As we watched this market change in the last decade, we were reminded of an important lesson in customer relationships: It's not enough to understand your customer; what's required is an understanding of your customer's customer, the forces shaping their behavior, and the forces shaping the world in which both meet. It doesn't matter whether you are selling technology or sheet metal stamping machines. Knowing your customer is important; knowing your customers' customer is more important.

Inventing the future of automotive retailing with our customers is about transforming automotive retailing into a connected model — a seamless consumer experience — bringing together people, processes, and technology that change the business model for automotive retailers and the customer experience for consumers.

A glimpse of the future we are inventing with our customers begins with an electronic service reminder from the automotive retailer — generated automatically and sent anytime 24/7 — to a customer needing a 60,000 mile service. The consumer replies to the e-reminder one evening — at her convenience — using an online service scheduler, selecting the day and time that works best for her and selecting her preferred service technician.

The next morning, the service manager sees the electronic reply and the scheduled service appointment. With one click of the enter key, the service manager can check to verify that parts needed for the service are in inventory and available for this customer's appointment; if the parts were not available and needed to be ordered prior to the customer arriving for service, then the technology would have alerted him of that situation, too, and automatically generated an electronic order for the parts.

With another key stroke, the service manager pulls up a complete record of service and parts for the customer's vehicle and notices that the tires are reaching their maximum mileage life. He makes a note to discuss new tires with the customer when the car is dropped off for service. He even uses the technology to generate a per cent off coupon tied to the specific vehicle and the recommended model of tires.

Next, the service manger checks another screen that displays the entire value history of this customer's relationship with the entire car dealership and sees that she and her family have been long-time customers. This prepares the service manager and his colleagues for the opportunity to treat one of their best customers with something a little extra — in the same way that retailers such as Ritz Carlton and Nordstrom respond to their best customers.

With only a few key strokes, the service manager has gained the knowledge and information that will make the consumer's trip to the service department go more smoothly and hassle free — and go further to meeting the consumer's total automotive needs. But the information doesn't stay in the service department.

Once the consumer has scheduled service, an e-mail alert is sent automatically to the sales manager's Personal Digital Assistant, alerting her that one of her best customers has made a service appointment. The sales manager checks the contacts between the retailer and the consumer — stored in a contact management data base. She reviews this customer's purchase history and vehicle interest, and takes the opportunity to follow-up on a previous desire expressed by the consumer to keep her eyes open for a convertible, if the model and pricing worked.

The sales manager greets the consumer on the morning of the service appointment, they discuss new vehicles, and the consumer takes advantage of viewing the entire new car inventory on the dealership's Web site that evening, constantly updated in real time. The consumer sees a model she likes and asks for a variety of options from lease to purchase. With the click of the mouse, different options are shown and tied directly to the car in which she has an interest.

The next day, the customer picks up the keys to her new convertible, retains her pervious car — with new tires — for her daughter to take to college in the fall, and purchases a "frequent user" card which encourages both of them to return for service.

In this ideal scenario, the unique — the "magical" — combination of technology, processes, and people delivers to the consumer the premium service she deserves, the kind of service and personal attention that can help make her a repeat customer for life. At the same time, the automotive retailer has strengthened its relationship with a repeat customer, created value for the consumer and for the dealership, and all the while has brought the consumer one step closer to being a customer for life.

Far fetched? No. Ideal? Maybe. But the technology is in place to do just that and there are automotive retailers operating in just this manner.

They Have Invented the Future — We Have Simply Helped Them

The market we serve today is not the market we will serve tomorrow. In fact, the product portfolio we take to the market is heavily weighted to what the market will be — not what it is. It's a variation on the comment attributed to hockey great Wayne Gretsky: The secret to his success on the ice is that he skated to where the puck will be — not where it is. We are skating to where the market will be. In this market, the idea of technology, processes, and people creates new ways of selling, buying, and managing a business.

Our objective in inventing the future with our customers — the automotive retailers — is to help them grow their business, capture more revenue, and sustain higher profits. We also are helping our customers create value for their customers. It's the difference between merely providing a product or service that our customers use in the course of business, and creating new tools for the customer to use in changing how they do business and how they create value. In one case, we are meeting the customer's needs today — which is a legitimate, profitable undertaking. In the other case, we are helping that customer invent the future — which creates more value for their business, for their customers, and for Reynolds.

Support a customer's needs today and the customer may be satisfied; help the customer invent the future of his business and you may gain the loyalty that sustains a profitable relationship for years.

Developing a Passion for Customer Loyalty and Moving Beyond Customer Satisfaction

Any successful business will satisfy its customers. The truly successful — the growth companies — also will gain customer loyalty. At Reynolds, we have developed a passion for customer loyalty as a critical business and performance benchmark, which moves us beyond customer satisfaction. Customer satisfaction is still necessary, it's the ante to compete and the antecedent to loyalty, but customer satisfaction alone is no longer sufficient to sustain profitable customer relationships.

Customers can be satisfied with your product and service, yet be willing to switch to another provider who offers the next product iteration, the next feature, the next price reduction. A loyal customer has made a business judgment — a value determination — and concludes: I would choose Reynolds again. That's the key for us. A loyal customer makes a brand decision; a satisfied customer makes a product decision.

Among the customer data we collect is a focus on loyalty and specific measures on a customer's willingness to recommend Reynolds to another company and the customer's intention to continue with Reynolds. We plot "willingness to recommend" and "intention to continue" data points that create a Loyalty Index. The Loyalty Index has several advantages. It is future-oriented and predictive; that is in contrast to most customer satisfaction data, which is backward-looking. "Did the product we delivered six months ago meet your needs?" "Did we respond quickly to the last service call?" Measures that look back are useful but limited. The Loyalty Index suggests what the customer will do in the future — and, therefore, can be combined with sales data around the actual net new business closed with the dealership in order to gauge how well our business is performing.

We map the Loyalty Index score and measure that score against our sales efforts to introduce new technology solutions to this customer. If the customer carries a high Loyalty Index score — meaning they will recommend Reynolds to another company and they intend to continue with Reynolds — then what new business have we created with that customer? We plot where the data suggests we should be on these measures and then plot the actual data. If there is a gap, we ask ourselves, why? Is our incentive compensation not aligned with what we are trying to accomplish in customer loyalty? Are we not identifying the customer's needs correctly and, therefore, not offering solutions that match the true needs? Ultimately, a focus on customer loyalty has caused us to examine our business and organization more critically and to change our economic model.

Our new economic formula (our Hedgehog, to borrow a phrase from Tim Collins's wonderful book From Good to Great) is $E = A + NS$. The E is the economic driver for the company. The A is application penetration, which means the number of applications used by a single customer. For example, if Reynolds offers 200 applications, how many are being used by any particular customer? If the answer is one application, then how do we get 199 more? We'll never get all 200, because some of them are simply different alternatives, but we certainly expect to see the number of applications in our most loyal customers continue to rise. The final variable is NS, which stands for New Start. How do we get new dealerships, new car companies, new heavy equipment dealers, and new sports retailers signed up as customers? This economic model forces a dual focus and balance on increasing penetration with our most loyal customers and creating new starts with new customers. And it provides the framework within which to track the data. Simple, but powerful.

In the ideal life cycle with a customer, to build loyalty we begin with a vision of the way automotive retailing can be done — the future of automobile retailing — and illustrate how our technology and software applications can move the retailer into that future. Our value propositions to these customers are precise and driven by metrics. "Our technology and software solutions will increase your customer retention, your service capture rate, downstream revenue and profit opportunity, and improve your average repair order by x per cent." Those become the business metrics the customer uses to evaluate our solutions and the metrics we use to demonstrate the return on the customer's investment in Reynolds technology. And they're not hollow claims. Each metric is tracked with automated tools and reported to the individual customer and, in aggregate, to other prospects.

In this life cycle with a customer, typically we begin with a series of base applications that demonstrate Return on Investment and the impact on the customer's business. From there, we identify additional applications — additional return opportunities — and continue to move with the customer up the value chain, from automating simple operational processes, such as payroll and accounts payable, through all of the enterprise-wide processing applications and then to more sophisticated applications and services focused on customer loyalty, retention, and Customer Relationship Management.

Finally, the other change a Loyalty Index can drive in an organization is a new look at the allocation of resources. With Reynolds' economic model and loyalty metrics, we are forced to get real clear — real fast — on where to put resources to increase business penetration with a customer, to move a customer up the value chain, to gain a new customer, or to focus on customers who are wavering on using us in the future. At Reynolds, we have realigned our organization, literally, so that the full breath of resources from across the organization — technical, human, and financial — can be brought to bear on any customer at any time to support our economic formula. That means fewer silos. Fewer artificial department lines. Fewer divisions internally. And it's driven by our economic formula. One result is, today, Reynolds has built the largest customer-facing organization in our industry. It is one more investment in long-term, profitable customer relationships, built on customer loyalty.

Forget the Technology — The Magic is in the Information

The technology examples I have described can produce amazing benefits for automotive retailers. But, ironically, the technology we provide might only be a third of the solution. The technology alone is not the magic — the magic comes from the information the technology delivers, the business change the technology creates, and the process reengineering and training within the business that leverages both the technology and the information.

Reynolds provides technologies and strategies that enable automotive retailers to think differently about the information in their business and to manage it differently; transforming information into knowledge and knowledge into insight about their business and their customers, the ones served today and the ones who will be served tomorrow.

Much of the magic in information is best tapped through the alchemy of CRM tools — the new frontier in thinking differently about customers and about information. These are the software and program applications that make it possible to individualize customer relationships, build customer loyalty, and make every customer a repeat customer — one customer at a time. CRM is about information that moves a business closer to individual customers and closer to understanding their individual needs and interests. It's also about tailoring a response, a product, a service. When CRM is done well, it's the difference between simply gathering customer data and actually applying knowledge about the customer in order to change the customer's experience, making it more positive, more personal, more specific to the brand and the retailer. The idea behind Customer Relationship Management is the newest trend based on the oldest concept: know your customers and know your market. Information technology helps automotive retailers apply a bedrock concept of business to business in the 21st Century.

The art of Customer Relationship Management, of course, was first perfected half a century ago by the neighborhood merchant. Then, CRM was face-to-face with each customer, supplemented by dozens of interactions during the week — at school, in the neighborhoods, during worship — and every conversation provided input for the merchant so that the next time an individual was in the store, all of the dimensions of the relationship would come to bear. To do today what the merchant did 50 years ago requires enormously powerful technology and business processes to match. That's what Reynolds delivers to our customers — the technologies that enable customers to tap the information that already is part of their business but that is seldom captured, integrated, synthesized or used to grow the business. With CRM tools, we show them how the magic lies in the information.

And it works. Independent research concludes that automotive retailers implementing CRM in a comprehensive manner can gain double-digit percentage increases in revenue, productivity, and customer satisfaction.

Our customers in automotive retailing — much like customers in countless other industries — are asking how best to reach consumers. With CRM, automotive retailers gain the knowledge and the ability to reach out to individual consumers in unique, personalized ways, to meet their individual needs — whether the first visit to the dealership's Web site or an electronic service reminder after 60,000 miles. The point of CRM is to make the experience for the customer more personal, more positive, and a more specific reflection of the car brand or the dealership brand.

One of the better examples of CRM is automotive telematics, the wireless technology that allows real-time communications and location information between an automobile and an information system. Telematics technologies are capable of collecting and delivering real-time automotive diagnostic and location data across a wireless network that can change the way consumers think about how their car is serviced, maintained, and protected in case of an emergency or theft. It also can change the way automotive retailers think about serving consumers, because it provides a new business model — and new technology — to use in building customer loyalty and in making every customer a repeat customer.

One such telematics technology is provided by Networkcar, which is a Reynolds and Reynolds company. Through Networkcar's small, wireless device that plugs into the standard On Board Diagnostics II port, vehicle performance data and location information are collected continuously, communicated over a wireless network to an information system, and then delivered to the car owner over the Internet on a personalized, secure Web page. The consumer's dealership service department also simultaneously receives information about the vehicle's operation and potential trouble spots.

This device can be installed by an automotive retailer or service center and will plug into 80 million vehicles already on the road and virtually every new vehicle that is manufactured. Instantly, the market for telematics and its application is expanded exponentially from the 2 million (new) vehicles sold with the service factory-installed last year. Just as instantly, there is a new business model for automobile dealerships and service centers that creates a technological link — a tether — to consumers and their cars. Finally, there is an innovation that can ease the chore of maintenance and the worry of safety for millions of vehicle owners. This is technology indistinguishable from magic:

- For consumers there are no added behaviors required: no phone calls, no activation devices, nothing more than driving the way we've always driven.
- Second, the diagnostics can deliver an early warning of mechanical failure: oil pressure that is falling or a water pump that is operating at only 50 per cent capacity. The notification and data are available instantly over the Web. With cell phones now offering web access, real-time information in the car takes on a whole new meaning. The diagnostics can also perform valid emissions testing accepted by state agencies without the time and hassle of waiting at a testing facility.
- Third, if something does go wrong, you'll have GPS-accurate location information (even if your car is stolen) for immediate assistance, as well as engine performance data to understand what led to the failure and required repair. And, it's likely you'll have a higher level of trust and confidence in your vehicle service department, because you will be viewing the same information about the car as the service technician.
- Finally, since the information is delivered through a secure, personal Web site, it changes how you can think about travel by car. A family member taking a long car trip? Visit your secure Web site and view a secure map of the car's progress and location. Your college-aged daughter needs service for the car while on campus? The dealer you trust at your local service department can check and verify the problem and the repair being made hundreds of miles away.

Telematics technology applied this way has the power to change how consumers view the automobile and how automobile retailers view using technology to serve customers. It is an example of a truly connected marketplace, delivered today.

The majority of consumers with a Networkcar device installed in their automobile are twice as likely to return to the dealer for service as those without the device. Good for the automobile retailer, who has an opportunity to build customer loyalty and to improve service department efficiency. Good for the consumer, who receives better, more timely service, and is more informed about the service.

The New Magic of Making Every Customer a Repeat Customer

Information is the new magic, but it is impotent without the right technology. The right technology is indistinguishable from magic, but it, too, is impotent without the process changes that enable technology's power to deliver the magic. And both information and technology are impotent without the right economic and business model. Together all three can lead to sustainable, profitable customer relationships if you invent the future with your customers, if you move beyond customer satisfaction to customer loyalty, and if you recognize how technology turns information into magic.

In our business and in society, the future will see more technology; the technology will be more transparent, yet the impact will be more noticeable. Echoing Arthur Clarke, technology is important when it automates common tasks; technology's impact can be truly magical when it changes how we work and live. Because the point of technology is not to stop at technology, but to take the next step to magic and to ease the work of everyday living. After all, "any sufficiently advanced technology is indistinguishable from magic."

Biography

Lloyd G. "Buzz" Waterhouse has been CEO of The Reynolds and Reynolds Company since November 2002. He joined the company in May 1999 as president and chief operating officer and was elected Chairman in January 2002. He has been instrumental in refocusing the company as an information technology solutions company aimed at driving the transformation of automotive retailing.

Mr. Waterhouse has led an aggressive buildup of technology-based solutions to help automotive retailers and car companies drive productivity, efficiency and revenue growth. The company has developed and introduced solutions like the Reynolds Generations Series™, the company's next generation technology platform and a suite that integrates more than 200 applications and services to meet the needs of the automotive marketplace. Through a combination of acquisitions and internal development, the company has enhanced its strength and market share in emerging growth areas including telematics, Web services, e-

business applications, and markets adjacent to the automotive industry including commercial, heavy truck, marine and power sport dealers.

Before joining Reynolds, Mr. Waterhouse spent 26 years at IBM Corporation. He has extensive experience in international business management, information technology, e-business and organizational change. Mr. Waterhouse was an early participant in the formation of the Internet. Prior to joining Reynolds, he was general manager of e-Business Services, one of IBM's fastest growing business units with annual revenues of over $2.7 billion. From 1996 to 1998 he was general manager of marketing and business development for IBM Global Services, the world's largest IT services company. He served as IBM's director of strategy during 1994-95, and was president of Asia Pacific Services Corporation, an IBM subsidiary headquartered in Tokyo from 1992 to 1994.

As co-chairperson of Dayton's e-Business Task Force, Mr. Waterhouse was instrumental in launching the iZone, which supports the birth and development of information technology-focused companies in the region. The iZone links volunteers from local businesses and development organizations with entrepreneurs so they can get advice about starting a business, obtaining funding, protecting intellectual property, finding a location and developing a business plan.

Mr. Waterhouse serves on the boards of Atlantic Mutual Companies, Pennsylvania State University's Smeal College, Fifth Third Bank, BusinessHere, ChoiceParts, i-Zone, the Downtown Dayton Partnership, Dayton Development Coalition, Dayton Business Committee, Dayton Regional Technology Council, Omega Community Development Corporation, and the Ohio Business Roundtable.

Chapter 25

Best Practices for Offshore Software Development Outsourcing

Eugene Goland

Cost Reduction

The offshore software development industry owes much of its existence to cost reduction. The other side of these savings is the difficulty of risk identification. At the very least, you need a person — be it a full-time staff member, a consultant, or someone you know working for a potential contractor — who is able to see through the physical and cultural barriers presented by countries and organizations. Ten people who know everything there is to know about outsourcing cannot replace one person with hands-on knowledge. The best way to see whether you have found the right person as simple as this: "Can this person ensure friction-free communication flow within the web of stakeholders and team members?" According to DataArt's analysis, more than 80 per cent of process failures were caused by lack of information at decision maker's hands. In most of these cases, however, all the necessary information was present on either client or contractor side.

Focus

While it is widely recognized that choosing outsourcing over in-house development helps to preserve company's business focus, there is one more advantage which is frequently overlooked. The transition to outsourcing means that the CIO is forced to concentrate on managing the processes and information of business, drawing a line between core business and IT services that is visible, tangible and controllable. This is a very healthy transition for those companies which do not consider technology to be the primary driver of their competitive advantage.

Cutting Project Duration

Outsourcing starts with requirements that are supposed to be clear, detailed and verifiable. It is highly desirable that the requirements are complete and non-contradictory, although in reality it is often possible to reach this state only toward the completion of the project. Requirements rarely stay unchanged for the duration of the project — these days business and technical environments change too fast. The faster the first few iterations of a project are completed, the better is a chance of the overall success. Long project cycles affect the team's productivity, accumulate problems and undermine the enthusiasm. How short can this cycle be? Monthly deliverables are common; XP and other agile methods indicate weeks or days, while specially engineered solutions and processes can introduce substantial changes in a matter of hours. The shorter the feedback loop the lower are risks.

Acquiring Unique Resources

Acquiring IT services has a unique component — even when a client pays for services provided by one person, he gains the expertise of a whole company, and often — of an entire industry. Well-organized companies integrate the infrastructure of knowledge dissemination (and access) into their operations. Often, the knowledge base of an average company is not effective enough.

When a corporate infrastructure and company's culture compliment each other and welcome requests for mutual assistance, it's a totally different situation. DataArt provides the following organizational and technical solutions:

DataArt assigns a senior project manager to every 10 to 15 developers. His/her decision making power allows him/her to independently solve upcoming problems, and arrange a comprehensive assistance program when necessary.

DataArt maintains a comprehensive and regularly updated database of human resources, containing information on education, skills, experience, hobbies and access to external sources of information of each employee.

DataArt runs several specializes mailing lists on various IT-related topics, accessible by all employees, who are allowed and encouraged to post their questions and inquires.

DataArt employees can make their own judgments whether they may be helpful in a project they are not directly involved with. In case of resource conflicts the issue is immediately escalated to involve top management of the company. Thus the average time to resolve a problem is two to four hours. This system is by far more effective compared to delegating "from top to bottom" when decision making might take a couple of days.

Pitfalls to Avoid

It is important to be aware what is the primary driver for management decision to outsource. Make sure that decision was not in fact driven by desire to get rid of internal problems and mistakes. Transferring such problems to the vendor might provide temporary relief, but will make relationships complex and ineffective.

We don't recommend outsourcing solely the routine part of the project while keeping the creative part. Crucial aspects are hidden in details, while their implementation always seems routine at first.

We don't recommend letting go of your personnel too fast. After the initial outsourcing success, one of DataArt's clients fired its IT managers along with the developers. It was very soon that he faced the shortage of experts and pricey on-site consultants.

Choosing a Partner
Pricing
While estimating a project, demand two figures: an estimate in dollar value, and an estimate in men/hours or other units. In a bid, it is important to evaluate if efforts involved in the project are adequate. Whereas a price range can fluctuate on a scale from one to 10 and remain meaningful, the reasonable effort estimates should not differ by a factor of more than two, unless there are specific reasons.

Dialogue
Building a relationship with a service provider starts early on, at the selection stage. The crucial aspect of a successful project is a dialogue, when both sides are willing and ready to listen to each other. If a client dominates the communication, while the contractor simply follows, there are certain risks since client might not have a full picture. The goal is to build a constructive dialogue, where both parties pay attention to details, and elaborate on the best possible solution, you have built a solid foundation for a successful project. If the parties enjoy talking to each other early on, chances are high they will have a good communication flow all the way.

The Dowry
In order to lure in a client, contractors often boast of a proprietary software or platform they already developed. This could be both useful and dangerous. The defining measurement is whether they have a similar system or a prototype.

An analogue or a prototype is a piece of software that can be evaluated versus the need. Once there is something tangible, you may be able to progress in smaller steps, improving on the product's functionality and increasing its stability and productivity. This way you can avoid the "dead" time, when there is nothing to test or use.

A platform (or an environment) that can't really be evaluated by the user often disguises potential dangers. As a Trojan Horse, it may contain certain undetectable bugs, limitations and unnecessary complexities which could be fatal for the project.

Think twice before agreeing to use home-made platform if you can't properly evaluate it.

The Journey

It is essential that you visit a subcontractor's office. A personal meeting will allow you to "see and touch" the product, to meet the team, to boost its creativity and build loyalty. A contractor's visits to a client are also highly recommended. It is hard to underestimate the value of these meetings for establishing a constructive and friendly relationship. But don't confuse sporadic meeting with thorough "knowledge transfer" sessions. Either make the visitors part of an ongoing, long-term process, or just take them out to lunch to discuss ongoing issues. Documenting project requirements should be a responsibility of those who understand the actual requirements, not those who just know how to write proper documentation. If a contractor can create the document only as good as that of a client, the task should be left to the client. If the contractor's documents are too complex and overwhelming, it's hard to expect meaningful feedback. The language is the essential part of management, and we don't recommend giving it up to the contractor. If you don't know any specialized languages (such as UML), than use plain English.

Establishing a Relationship

Aligning Contexts

There are only three ways to learn how to understand each other: communicate, communicate, and communicate. One might risk appearing dumb stating the obvious, yet one might be a fool not voicing what is obvious to one party and not to the other.

Teaching masters the art of conveying a thought. It's not the metaphor that matters. It's the repetition, the right questions and exercises that allow conveying a vision.

First Project

The best first project is the one you consider hopeless. It allows you to use the abundant energy of the contractor when he wants to convince you of his capabilities. In case of a successful solution, you are bound to establish a trusting relationship.

If the first project is not critical, it lowers the possibility of risk, yet it doesn't allow to make a sound decision upon its completion. A relatively important project usually turns out rather successfully, and a decision of future projects is made depending on external factors.

Effective Communications

Communication should be direct and uninhibited. Avoid information channeling and especially management ladders. Subscribe as many stakeholders to the mailing list as possible and channel as much communication through this channel as practical. Encourage personal meetings, teleconferencing, and phone calls. Allocate some time for communication process review and enhancement.

Acceptance

The project acceptance should start with a first milestone. A client shouldn't take a position of "first do everything, than we will see." A correct project plan allows for slowing down the deliverables towards the end. For instance, three milestones with an interval of three months each should cover ½ of the project in the first milestone, 5/6 in the second, and completion at the third (not an even division by 1/3).

Developing a Relationship

Mastering the Process

A static balance in a work process is as unstable as in a bicycle standing still. If you don't always develop the relationship, it starts to degrade. We recommend choosing certain metrics and working on their improvements. If the metrics are chosen correctly, they will benefit the relationship. If not — they will at least prevent the process of quality degradation. If the metrics improve, but the quality remains the same — it's time to change the metrics.

Changing Personnel — Good or Bad?

If an IT project manager informs a client that he wants to replace certain developers, it can mean two things: the best are being transferred to a different project, or that a new "star" was assigned to a project. How do you determine the truth? Communicate.

Concluding a Relationship

See Acceptance. Relationships, as all of life, start to end with their beginning. Using outsourcing makes one responsible and vulnerable at the same time. Often you should ask yourself — what will happen if my partner's business collapses? If the project is lucrative enough for a contractor, it can outlast the company. If a client pushes a contractor to the limit by trying to save money, he risks undermining the project as the contractor will be more loyal to better-paying clients.

Biography

Eugene Goland, President of DataArt Inc., is an expert in offshore outsourcing practices by SMB sector. He is a founder of two profitable technology companies with offshore operations. Goland has a strong hands-on knowledge of the outsourcing industry, from both supply and demand sides, and has advised many small and medium businesses on the issues of outsourcing.

Entrepreneurship
Eugene Goland co-founded the first web-based portal for Russian speakers in 1999. Mail.ru became the first company in the segment to ever secure venture capital funding. Until the company became profitable in 2002, Goland managed to raise $7MM in venture funding, acquired dozens of companies (including the second largest rival) and established strategic partnerships with leading industrial companies.

In 1997, Goland founded DataArt, an offshore software outsourcing company. In 2003, DataArt grew to over a hundred employees, with three international offices and world-class clients. The company has been marked by industry researches as an emerging equity play.

Management and strategy
Seven years CEO experience combined with the various c-level roles. As a CEO of Mail.ru, Goland reported to the Board Of Directors, combined of world-recognized leaders in finance and technology. During the three years as the CEO of Mail.ru, Goland structured the company's operation to become the first profitable company in the sector, while preserving the market share (30%) and growing together with the market.

As CEO of DataArt, Goland recognized the potential of offshore software market in 1997 and focused the company's strategy on assembling a world-class technical team to address communication and project management issues. DataArt pioneered NY-based project management personnel and web-based project management tool in early 1998. The company has been profitable every fiscal year and never required venture funding.

Marketing
The Mail.ru brand has achieved an almost 100% recognition in its segment in just under two years. Goland has been actively involved in high-level planning and key executive issues, including subcontracting issues to leading PR and advertising agencies. Since the market was in its infancy, Goland had initiated one of the first market research studies and managed most of it internally.

Technology
Goland participated in the design and development of a web-based portal (Mail.ru), which became one of the most complex projects on the market. By the end of 2003, the portal provided service to 15MM unique visitors per month and half a billion page views spanned over twenty service offerings. The project took three years to complete by a team of fifteen developers and four outsourcing companies.

International
Founded and managed two companies with Russian offices (Moscow and St. Petersburg). Spent four months in DataArt's London office and three years in New York office. In 1998 managed Singapore-based software project with international team.

Appendix 1

Tips and Guidelines

Tips and Guidelines for Upcoming CTO/CIO's

A recent conversation with my mentor, the late Sam Albert, indicated how much he enjoyed watching those whom he had mentored succeed in life and at work.[113] Over his lifetime, Sam's many developers and engineers were promoted to General Manager and President of their companies.

The importance of good mentoring in our profession is often overlooked. However, as CIOs we have a duty and the privilege to share as much of our experiences and life's lessons as we can with the future of our industry. Some of this is done through associations and clubs and some of this is done through direct experiences. More important, we need to leave the future leaders the keys to successful careers as technology executives and visionaries.

Just as a reporter learns the art of opening the doors of confidential sources, our protégés need to learn the art of effective strategies. It's not only important to the development of their career, but it is integral to the successful growth and evolution of our industry.

CIO Magazine's 12-Step Program for Aspiring CIO's

CIO Magazine has clearly outlined a 12-step approach that I would like to share with you in this book. He stressed a couple of major points as part of a CIO Mentoring Program:[90]

- **Customer mentality.** Every person in your company is your customer. And you should treat every customer as if he has the ability to promote you or fire you.
- **Change your dialect.** You must be able to effectively communicate with non-technical people. If you cannot have a short dialogue with other department heads on business issues that are not technical in nature, for example, advertising, finance, merchandising, sales, real estate and so on, the prospect of

you reaching a successful executive level in any organization is slim. You must develop a habit to interact with as many non-IT managers, directors and executives as possible during the week, and intentionally do not discuss technology. You can ask them about current and relevant issues facing their function. Those types of daily exchanges — especially at the senior level — instill the view, if even subconsciously, that you are a managerial peer, not just the "technology guy."

- **Create a service culture.** Demand customer service culture from your direct reports. You must have a zero-tolerance rule for bad customer service and a religious desire to recognize good service. The translation of these values will result in a culture of premium service and will help build your credibility as a good manager.
- **You're only as good as your team.** Remember that your employees are also your customers — so treat them as such. Respect for your subordinates will also help reduce turnover and show senior management that you are a leader
- **Never talk to down to anyone.**
- **Follow up at all cost.** Follow-up is more important than all the technical qualifications in the world. IT people will fix something or complete a project but never let the customer know it's done. Always follow up.
- **Proactive calls.** Make proactive calls to your customers on a regular basis. Ask them how you and your group are doing and if there is anything you can help them with.
- **Skillfully manage expectations.** Never fall victim to the classic IT pitfall of overcommitting and underdelivering.
- **Stay as far away from company politics as you can.** Do not partake in petty infighting in your company. If you are approached or tempted to be drawn in, find a business trip and go on it.
- **Understand financials.** It is important to understand basic financial principles. Finance is the business of business. More specifically, you should know how to read financial statements such as a P&L statement, an income statement, a balance sheet and so on. Identify the relationships and trends between gross margin and sales, how fixed and variable costs impact your company's profitability, the debt position of your company, and so on. Nothing impresses a CEO, COO or CFO more than hearing an IT person intelligently participate in a financial discussion about the business, trends and opportunities.
- **Networking** There's an old saying, "It's not what you know but who you know." Maintain your contacts with former colleagues, bosses and even vendor account representatives. Join and be active in professional associations, which are well worth the dues, and you will build a great circle of contacts in the process.

- **Ethics.** Remember Enron. Never compromise Ethics[90]

Four Ways to Move up a Line

Skarzynski mentions excellent ways to start move up the value chain. Here is how you do it. Let's follow this simple but powerful approach.[81] The formula is similar to Gary Hamel's three-part prescription in *Leading the Revolution* (Harvard Business School Press, 2000):

1. Tighten Alignment with Business Strategy

Ask yourself, "How well do I understand the business?" Chances are, discussing the business side makes you uncomfortable, and your reports even more so. That means it's up to you to demonstrate how IT can help.

2. Increase the IT Group's Business Savvy

Business-conversant CIOs need to be supported by people who can feed them information garnished with the right kind of insights. How well do you understand the benefits your company offers customers?

Here are a couple of ways to raise your staff's business acumen:

- **Do it yourself first.** Take a page out of the playbook of one CEO we know. When was the last time you listened to your company's quarterly call with financial analysts? What might you learn by listening to your CEO's speeches and those of your competitors?
- **Send forth your people.** Assign your canniest people to cross-functional teams working on projects for customers — both external customers and IT's internal customers, such as the market-research folks. Make them available to customers as free resources.
- **Bring in others.** Import business experts to speak about the business of your largest customers — not about their IT concerns, but about their strategy and operations. Establish a matrix structure and joint hiring process, so that each CTO reports to a business-unit head as well as to him.
- **Partner and integrate.** Get close to your CFO. Use the findings and the relationship to build rapport and shared understanding of IT's significance to the business. Show your version of the report card around the company as a way to initiate conversation. Invite the CFO to act as your translator and help you uncover opportunities. Work together on how IT can enact a solution that dovetails with the strategic intent.

3. Isolate the Opportunity to Innovate a Customer Process
Infiltrate the customer. Integrate your people, systems, and goals with those of your customers in pursuit of the common good.

4. Develop an innovation agenda
Learn the three rules of "Strategy 101":

- Strategy has to be different. Copycat strategy is an oxymoron. True strategy is an original.
- The difference has to have value.
- The value has to be competitively advantageous[81]

Tips and Guidelines for Existing CIO/CTO's

I find that it is very useful to follow some practical experts and advice provided by experts and practitioners in this field.

CIO Challenges
Let's begin with listing some common challenges, and talk about how to confront them, and offer an example of one CIO who identified innovative business implications for IT[81]

Typical barriers to change still exist at most IT departments. These include:

- **No time to think.** Business units are continually throwing unplanned, unbudgeted project initiatives over the transom. IT people are so stretched that they unconsciously fall back defensively on old knowledge and behavior patterns. That very human response pulls their standing in the company below the level their talents merit.
- **No way to grasp all the technological possibilities.** In this high-speed, high-tech world, there will always be a better package we haven't seen or a smarter configuration we haven't thought of. Make the best decision you can and move on.
- **IT's menial standing.** Staff is highly trained, yet we're not widely viewed as relevant to the core business. This has always been a problem, and now, with the spotlight on IT's value, it's even more pressing that the company think of us more like engineers and less like plumbers. That's the only way to get the time, budget, and organizational backing to run potentially groundbreaking experiments with the mainstream businesses.
- **The change-resistant organization around us.** From the inside, we look a lot like a government bureaucracy. Specialist silos, turf protection, ingrained attitudes,

incomprehensible jargon, and plain risk aversion preserve the status quo. Even the CEO's efforts are generally thwarted. It's wise to figure that any idea grounded in crash-prone IT will be doubly suspect.[81]

Barriers like these are formidable, but the rewards are even higher.

90-Day Plan

For some of us who need to get things done quickly, I would recommend a 90 day plan improvement. It is time to put together a quick and action oriented plan. Follow this plan for the next 90 days and see if your unit and your company performs better.[52]

First Month: Optimize the present

- **Make sure that you and your savviest IT people understand the business strategy** you're serving and have a vision for its future. Send them into your business community to build understanding, a wider constituency for your perspectives, and a model of the current business.
- **Review the IT portfolio.** Examine whether it directly serves the core value proposition and recent changes in business direction. You will find systems capabilities and IT projects that have lost their way. Identify those that are draining resources, still moving under their own momentum, or propped up by powerful backers.
- **Realign the portfolio.** Kill anything that doesn't pass through the strategy filter. Be direct and forceful, and then be draconian. Free up space in IT to foster innovation and strategic thinking.
- **Define an IT strategy for 2004.** State it in business terms.

Second Month: Develop leaders

- **Assess your organization's skills, capabilities, and assets.** Figure out what combination of these drove past successes. Note who was involved and what values and skills they brought to the table. Review any special circumstances that affected the outcome.
- **Select a core group of current and future leaders.** Your picks should be passionate, curious, and competent. Be sure it's a diverse group; include people of established credibility and new employees with fresh perspectives who can carry innovative ideas and actions outward to the larger organization.
- **Give your action troops an on-the-job MBA.** Hold a boot camp. Let them take aim at the business's core value proposition, value chain, and business model. Offer

apprenticeships in customer service, sales, marketing, and R&D. Let them experience firsthand the pain points of your customers and suppliers.

Third Month: Build innovation into IT strategy
- **Develop a radar on emerging technologies.** Challenge your technologists to periodically propose a set of technologies with potential to help drive your business strategy.
- **Help your team engage the business staff in conversations about the potential of strategic technologies.** Give these conversations a context and structure that help uncover unmet needs and provide solutions.
- **Build an innovation agenda** and a rich set of experimental projects that work on it.
- **Review and revise your strategy** against emergent business needs and technology innovations[15]

Round-the-Year Resolutions for CTOs/CIOs:[15]
- **Spend one day a week with the "one level down" and the "front line."** Identify information that will broaden CIO's perspective and ensure that you apply practical experiences in the real world. "One level down" is a key phrase to influence the opinions of your peers, then influence the opinions of their direct reports. It is important to gain insight in the frontline employees of your organization.
- **Stay alert on service issues.** Delivering the basics and core is priority for your organization's credibility. Other accomplishments will suffer if you are unable to deliver a level of service consistent with what your business delivers to its customers. It is important to analyze underlying root causes and formulate a workable improvement program.
- **Deliver some significant annual efficiency gains.** Every executive is expected to deliver efficiencies. Beyond the one-time benefits of consolidation, the only way to deliver efficiency in a responsible manner is to reduce demand or the cost. Typically IT managers usually know the systems that take the most time to support, the customers who are the most demanding and the services that constantly require exception processing.
- **Facilitate an IT-enabled business strategy.** Strategy is a demand management tactic. Establishing priorities and criteria for future opportunities are two of the most important outcomes of effective strategy-making. It is important to find individuals who can facilitate a process that answers "what should we invest in and why." It is important to get participation at the broadest and highest level.
- **Create a good leadership in CIO.** Build a service organization that shows respect and appreciation for your customers. Ensure that senior IT leaders have good soft

skills, including empathy, network-building, perceptiveness, teaming and persuasion. Design an organization that has the ability to flex capacity by allocating internal headcount on those positions that gate supply such as project managers, business analysts, and senior application and infrastructure design engineers.

- **Project value based results in six months.** Build your credibility and reduce project risk by requiring that all IT-enabled business investments deliver value within six months. Increase the opportunity by understanding what drives value and sequencing these "value dependencies" as early as possible. The company understands improvements in quality, cycle time and efficiency requires many big changes in tandem: consolidated organizations, new order management and fulfillment processes, a single customer image, enterprise visibility on orders and status, and integration with key external vendors. The six-month value rule forced people to a sequence — consolidation of the organization followed by establishment of metrics, an integrated customer database, enterprise order transparency, and so forth.
- **Establish architecture. Focus on standards.** The other focus is the goal of minimizing the technology footprint and operating costs. Set priorities based on application requirements for the next two years or so and invest ahead of need in a disciplined manner.
- **Management of resources.** Run IT like a business by monitoring value, productivity, service and retention trends. Drive value and efficiency using operational metrics — not just financial ones. Monitor project success based on cycle time, use-case analysis and usage.
- **Manage mind share.** Focus on feasibility and importance of tactical plans by summarizing your annual objectives, initiatives, accountabilities and measurements.[15]

Top Tips to Increase Influence

Finally, for the real experts, I would like to suggest some practical tips to increase influence:[52]

- Influence the influencers. Know what your colleagues read and watch, and seek out those they talk to.
- Adopt an executive to focus on and seek a business colleague to be your mentor.
- Keep your message simple and focus on ways to help this executive succeed.
- Position the start of every presentation and report with, "Here's where we were; here's where we are now."
- Provide case studies and examples

- Take road trips to check out technologies — and spend "soak time" with your business colleagues.
- Explain what competitors are doing; show their Web sites.
- Suggest some names as board members or advisers to ensure external — and perhaps IT-savvy — input.
- Equip and coach your executives to be confident IT-linked "road warriors."
- Make your business colleagues savvy IT executives on the road and at home. Suggest a mobile deployment that might spur their imagination concerning mobile deployment.
- And finally, continue to expand your ecosystem and rolodex around the world.

Appendix 2

Technology Brainstormers

1. Where is technology heading? What does the future look like?
2. What are your special skills? What do you do best with respect to technology?
3. If you could successfully create any new technology in the world, what would it do?
4. What areas/industries are poised for or best suited for technology growth?
5. What could become the next "killer application"?
6. How is the way we use technology going to change in the next five years?
7. How will businesses use technology differently in the future?
8. How will consumers use technology differently in the future?
9. What is the best piece of technology advice you have received?
10. What is the piece of technology advice you find yourself most often giving others?
11. How do you use technology as a strategic weapon and to create a sustainable competitive advantage?
12. The technology industry changes everyday (in terms of products/services created, skills needed, etc.). What is your strategy for dealing with change in the industry?
13. How do you use technology to keep your organization technologically nimble?
14. What are some of the biggest opportunities and challenges the wireless industry presents?
15. What are some of the biggest opportunities and challenges other areas of technology face?
16. How should your company use technology(ies) to give your company an edge over your competitors?
17. What are some of the biggest privacy issues from a technology standpoint?
18. What is the difference between cool technologies and technologies that solve problems and can make money?

19. How do you sell yourself, your product, your vision (from a technology standpoint)?
20. How do you do due diligence from a technology standpoint on a company?
21. How important are taking risks/taking the right ones from a technology standpoint? Which are the right ones to take?
22. What do you respect or impresses you most about technology leaders?
23. What technology resources do you have that could give you an edge in the marketplace?
24. What does it take to become a technology leader (as an individual/company)?
25. How do you/your technology go about getting noticed?
26. What are the best skills to have as a technology person?
27. What do you do to stay on top of your technology knowledge and keep your edge?
28. How do you find the right technology people?
29. What resources in the technology industry (not just technical skills) are in the most demand right now? What additional technology skills would be the best to know?
30. What are your short and long term goals with respect to technology/your technology career?
31. What are the golden rules of technology?

What Ifs:

1. What is our worst case scenario from a human resources standpoint? How would I handle it?
2. What is our best case scenario from a human resources standpoint? How would I handle it?
3. What if I am out sick/on vacation? Who would cover for me and are they prepared?
4. Who is my most valuable employee? What happens if I lose this person? Who would replace him/her?
5. What if I am promoted and asked to name my successor? Who would it be?
6. What if my boss quits? How can I prepare to efficiently start helping with some of his/her old responsibilities?
7. What if I have a problem with my boss? How would I handle it?
8. What cross training/job rotating has been done so that each person has a backup if someone is out sick/they leave the company?
9. Who are the key contacts my employees have that we need to make sure we retain good relations with if they leave our company?
10. What if we were hit with a discrimination lawsuit? How would I/we handle it?

11. What if one of my employees is injured on the job?
12. Are my interviewing questions appropriate and thorough? Are there any questions I ask that are inappropriate or illegal to ask?
13. How would I rapidly increase staffing if we landed a big client and needed to hire people very quickly?
14. What if I had to rapidly reduce staff? Who would be the first one(s) to let go?
15. What if I find out one of my employees has been engaging in unethical or illegal business activities?
16. What if one of my employees quits? What is the proper exit procedure?
17. What happens if I lose _____(Insert name here)? Who would replace him/her?
18. Other questions to ask myself.

References

1. Anthes, G.H. (June 19, 2000). The CIO/CTO balancing act. *Computerworld*, 34(25).
2. Aspatore Editors. (2000). *Inside the Minds: Chief Technology Officers*. Bedford, MA: Aspatore Books.
3. Battelle, Business Innovations Technology Forecast, www.battelle.org/forecasts/technology.stm
4. Berinato, S. (December 2002). Calculated Risk. *CSO Magazine*, www.csoonline.com/read/120902/calculate.html
5. Berray, T & Sampath, R. (April, 2002). *The Role of the CTO: Four Models for Success*. Cabot Consultants.
6. Betz, F. (1993). *Strategic Technology Management*. New York: McGraw Hill.
7. Blacktrout Staff, *What is a CTO*, Blacktrout, www.blacktrout.com/whatisacto.html
8. Boloker, D. (January 200). CTO-Emerging Internet Technologies for IBM, *The Role of the CTO at IBM and its clients*. Personal correspondence with the author.
9. Bort, J. (July 23, 2001). CIO: You can beat the discrimination. *Network World*, www.nwfusion.com/you2001/ceiling/ceiling.html
10. Bharadwaj, R. (January, 2002). *The Role of the CTO at Ejasent*. Personal correspondence with the author.
11. Black, J. (MAY 29, 2003) The Women of Tech,. *Business Week*
12. Brunner, G.F. (January, 2001). The Tao of innovation. *Research Technology Management*, 44(1).
13. Business Week, (August 30, 1999). We Are Offering 21 Doors to the Future and Invite You to Explore. *Business Week Online*
14. Burrows, P. (June 23, 2003), Innovation, Lego-Style, *Business Week*
15. Cramm, S. (December 1, 2003). New Year's Resolutions for CIOs .*CIO Magazine* www.cio.com/archive/120103/hs_agenda.html
16. Cardullo, M., PE, Sr. Counselor, US Department of Commerce, CTO Presentation and discussion.
17. CIO Focus: Fundamentals of CIO Role,(2002), *CIO* http://www.theciostore.com/images/CIOFOCUS_FUNDAMENTALS_SUM.pdf
18. CIO Magazine: The Changing Role of the Chief Information Officer 2002-2003, Survey of 500 IT execs. www.theciostore.com/images/CIORESEARCH_STATE_SUM

19. Chen, A. (Sept. 23, 2002). With IT Spending Studies, Estimates Run the Gamut, Eweek, *www.eweek.com/article2/0,3959,547580,00.asp*
20. CNET Staff, *Outsourcing to usurp more US jobs.* CNET News news.com.com/2100-1022_3-5057087.html
21. Cornelius, P. K. et al. 2002. "Introduction." In *The Global Competitiveness Report 2001 — 2002.* New York: Oxford University Press for the World Economic Forum.
22. Cosgroveware, L. (November 04, 2003). Maximizing Value from IT Vendors, *CIO Magazine*
23. Cosgroveware, L. (December 2, 2002). Security and E-business will dominate 2003 IT Spending, *Computerworld, www.computerworld.com / managementtopics / ebusiness / story / 0,10801,76378,00.html*
24. Cosgroveware, L. (Sept. 12, 2002) Security Spending: How much is enough? *CSO Magazine, www.csoonline.com/csoresearch/report6.html*
25. Desmond, P. (October 31, 2002). *META Paints (Relatively) Rosy Security Spending Picture, www.internetnews.com/stats/article.php/1492001*
26. Dixon, P. FutureTechnology. *Global Change, www.globalchange.com / futuretechnology.htm*
27. Dylan, T. (April 10, 2002). Does Your Company Need a CTO? More and more firms are hiring chief technical officers to help them understand and respond to technological change, *Business 2.0*
28. Earl, M. & Feeny, D. (Winter 2000). Opinion: How to be a CEO for the information age. *Sloan Management Review*, 41(2).
29. Earl, M. & Feeny, D. (Spring, 1994). Is your CIO adding value? *Sloan Management Review*, 35(3).
30. Earthweb.com Staff, (February 16, 2001). Becoming a Competitive Weapon in the New Economy, *Earthweb, cin.earthweb.com/reports/article.php/592361*
31. Erickson, T.J., Magee, J.F., Roussel, P.A., & Saad, K.N. (1990). Managing technology as a business strategy. *Sloan Management Review*, 31(3).
32. Farber, D. (October 15, 2002), Ten predictions to shake your world. *ZDNet techupdate.zdnet.com/techupdate/stories/main/0,14179,2885192,00.html*
33. Ferguson, K., TECHNOLOGY GLOBALIZATION, Office of International Technology *Technology Administration, www.technology.gov / International / GlobalTech / p_GlobalTech.htm*
34. Foote, D. (June 3, 2003). Offshoring IT jobs? Consider the risks, not just the rewards. *SearchCIO, searchcio.techtarget.com / originalContent / 0,289142,sid19_gci904410,00.html*
35. Forte, S. (January 2003). CTO-Corzen, *The CTO Role at Corzen and Zagat.* Personal correspondence with the author.
36. Foster, R.N. (January-February, 2000). Managing technological innovation for the next 25 years. *Research Technology Management*, 43(1).
37. Frick, K.A., & Torres, A. (2002). Learning from high-tech deals. *The McKinsey Quarterly*, 2002(1).

38. Gazda, S. From Techie Geek to People Chic:The Transformation of New IT Leaders. *Edizen, http://edizenco.com/insights/textversions/it_study.htm*
39. Geoly ,C. (May 22, 2002). Why the traditional CTO is history, *CNET News, ZDNet.*
40. Gibson, R. (1998). *Rethinking the Future.* London: Nicholas Brealey Publishing.
41. Goldman Sachs, (October 2003), *Dreaming with BRICs: The Path to 2050.* Goldman Sachs global economics paper no. 99
42. Greenspan, R. (April 28, 2002). *EU B2B Expected to Explode. cyberatlas.internet.com/markets/b2b/article/0,,10091_1453831,00.html*
43. Gwynne, P. (March-April, 1996). The CTO as line manager. *Research Technology Management,* 39(2).
44. Halal, W., Kull M, Leffmann A. *The GWU Forecast of Emerging Technologies: A Continuous Assessment of the Technology Revolution,* Department of Management Science, George Washington University
45. Hamm, S., Rosenbush, S., Edwards, C. (June 23, 2003) Tech Comes Out Swinging. *Business Week*
46. Hof, R. (August 2, 2003), Why Tech Will Bloom Again, *Business Week*
47. Hyman, G. (March 19, 2003). Overseas Outsourcing Hurts US Economy, Says Firm. *AtNewYork.com, www.atnewyork.com/news/article.php/2118191*
48. Infoworld,(December 4, 2000). *CTO plays key role in investment strategy.*
49. Infoworld(November 29, 1999). *Web redefines role of CTO.*
50. Inzelstein, S., (February 2002), *The role of the CTO in Value Based Organizations.* Personal correspondence with the author.
51. Kaplan,S. (December,2002) "It's Not Easy Being Breached", *CSO Magazine, www.csoonline.com/read/120902/cost.html*
52. Kitzis, E. & Broadbent, M.(May 2003) *CIOs: Broader Business Roles. Optimize Magazine, (19). www.optimizemagazine.com/issue/019/execreport.htm*
53. Krim,J . (October 10, 2003). Intel Chairman Says US Is Losing Edge.*Washington Post*
54. Kripalani, M., & Engardio, P. (December 8, 2003). The rise of India. *Business Week*
55. Kwak, M. (Spring 2001). Technical skills, people skills, it's not either/or. *Sloan Management Review,* 41(3).
56. Larkin, W. (August 07, 2003). Offshore outsourcing is less of a threat than you think. *Computerworld, www.computerworld.com/printthis/2003/0,4814,83819,00.html*
57. Larson, C.F. (November, 2001). Management for the new millennium-the challenge of change. *Research Technology Management,* 44(6)
58. Lewis, W.W., & Lawrence, H.L. (1990). A new mission for corporate technology. *Sloan Management Review,* 31(4).
59. Lucas, M. (April 4, 2002), CTO: The not-so-popular, misunderstood title. *Computerworld, www.eweek.com*
60. Media Lab. (2001). Overview of the MIT Media Lab. *http://www.media.mit.edu/.*

61. Mark Minevich, Managing Director, Marksoft Holdings, ex CTO IBM Corporation, Author, Chairman of Technology Leadership Council, CIO Collective member
62. Mauzy, J.(August 2003) Should You Be A Chief Creativity Officer? *Optimize Magazine, (22)*. http://www.optimizemag.com/issue/022/briefing.htm
63. McKinsey & Company, (October 2003), *New Horizons:Multinational Company Investment in Developing Economies*, McKinsey Global Institute
64. McKnight, D. (January, 2002). *The Role of the CTO at Titan Corporation*. Personal correspondence with the author.
65. Meinzer, R. & AZupnick, H.(July 2003) Should The CIO Report To The CFO? *Optimize Magazine, (21)*. http://www.optimizemag.com/issue/021/squareoff.htm
66. Millick, S., GLOBAL TECHNICAL WORKFORCE, Office of International Technology — *Technology Administration*, www.technology.gov / International / GlobalTech/Workforce.htm
67. Morgan Stanley, (December 2002), *Morgan Stanley CIO Spending 2003 Report*, Morgan Stanley Research
68. Networld Fusion. (Dec 4, 2002). *The Case Against IM*. www.nwfusion.com/newsletters/gwm/2002/01652867.html
69. Nolan, R. & Bennigson, L. interview (May 4, 2003), The Future of IT Consulting, *CNET News*, news.com.com/2009-1069_3-998618.html?tag=prntfr
70. O'Neill, P.H., & Bridenbaugh, P.R. (November-December, 1992). Credibility between CEO and CTO — A CEO's perspective; Credibility between CEO and CTO — A CTO perspective. *Research Technology Management*, 35(6).
71. Overby, S. (October 15, 2003), The Incredible Shrinking CIO. *CIO Magazine*, www.cio.com/archive/101503/shrinking.html
72. Parker, D.P. (2002). *The Changing Role of the Chief Technology Officer*. www.dpparker.com/article_cto_role.html.
73. Patton, S, (April 1, 2001). CTO/CIO role, *CIO Magazine*, Trendlines / www.cio.com/archive/040101/interview_content.html
74. Phair, M., & Rubin, D.K. (October 26, 1998). Bytes, bucks and big pictures. *Engineering News Review*, 241(16).
75. Prencipe, L. (March 26 2001), Power and influence: CTOs have it. *InfoWorld* www.infoworld.com
76. Robb, W.L. (September-October, 1994). Selling technology to your CEO. *Research Technology Management*, 37(5).
77. Robb, W.L. (May, 2000). Is Your Corporate Lab Taking Enough Risk? *Research Technology Management*, 43(3).
78. Roberts, E. (March-April, 2001). Benchmarking global strategic management of technology. *Research Technology Management*, 44(2).
79. Sanford, W. (November, 2003). Managing Principal, Columbia Strategy. Personal correspondence with the author

80. Santoni, J. (February, 2003). Managing Principal, ITS On Demand, IBM Global Services, *The Role of the CTO at IBM and its clients*. Personal correspondence with the author
81. Skarzynski, P. & Switzer, L.(August 2003) Behold The Conqueror, The CIO! *Optimize Magazine*, (22). http://www.optimizemag.com/issue/022/leadership.htm
82. Spiers, D. (July 5, 2001). CTOs: Technology's easy — It's the people part that's hard to master. *Business 2.0*.
83. Sphorer, J. (March 2003), CTO of IBM Venture Relations and Director of Research-Director, Almaden Services Research, *The Role of the CTO at IBM and its clients*. Personal Correspondence with the author
84. Stephnek, M. (September 15, 2003), Youth at the Gate. *CIO Insight*. www.cioinsight.com/article2/0,3959,1268152,00.asp
85. Thurlings, B. & Debackere, K. (July-August, 1996). Trends in managing industrial innovation — first insights from a field survey. *Research Technology Management*, 39(4).
86. Vaas, L. (February 1, 2003). Offshore Outsourcing: Should You be Worried Yet? *eWeek*. www.eweek.com/print_article/0,3668,a=36491,00.asp
87. Vance Chan, Managing Director, Vance Chan Associates, *Value Added CIO*. www.vancechan.com
88. Waite, W. (January, 2002). *The Role the CTO at Aegis Technologies*. Personal correspondence with the author.
89. Wasserman, E. (October 1, 2003), Labor Pains. *CIO Insight*. www.cioinsight.com / article2/0,3959,1309523,00.asp
90. Williams, S. (April 15, 2003), A 12-Step Program for Aspiring CIOs. *CIO Magazine*, www.cio.com/archive/041503/counsel.html
91. World Economic Forum 2003. *The Global Information Technology Report 2002 — 2003*, ed.by S. Dutta, B. Lanvin, and F. Paua. New York: Oxford University Press for the World Economic Forum.
92. Yates, M., Padmore, L., O'Mahony, R. (October 9, 2003). CIOs Poised to Play Pivotal Role in Creating an 'Innovator's Advantage'. *Accenture, CIO Magazine* www2.cio.com / consultant / report1832.html
93. Zeltzer, D. (January, 2002). *The Role the CTO at the Fraunhofer Institute*. Personal correspondence with author
94. Zuboff, S. & Maxmin, J. (2002). *The Support Economy*. New York:Viking, Penguin Group.
95. Business Week Staff (August 25, 2003). Future of Technology issue, *Business Week* www.businessweek.com/magazine/content/03_34/b3846630.htm
96. Carr, N. (May 1, 2003). *It doesn't matter*. Harvard Business School Press http://www.nicholasgcarr.com / articles / matter.html
97. Morello, D. (July 15, 2003). US *Offshore Outsourcing: Structural Changes*, Big Impact. Gartner Group. www4.gartner.com/DisplayDocument?doc_cd=116284

98. May, N. (Novermber 2003). *Offshore Services: The Impact of Global Sourcing on the US IT Services Market*, IDC. www.idc.com/getdoc.jhtml?containerId=30356
99. DataMonitor (June 19, 2003). Benefiting from Offshore Outsourcing in FS. DataMonitor.www.datamonitor.com/~2f502235690145c69eb3b38aa0d9cf59~/all/reports/product_summary.asp?pid=DMTC0884
100. Deloitte Research (2003). The Cusp of a Revolution: How offshoring will transform the financial services industry. www.deloitte.com/dtt/research/0,2310,sid%253D1013%2526cid%253D15240,00.html
101. US Census Bureau — United States Department of Commerce. www.census.gov
102. Dobbs, R., Jesudason ,R. , Malige, F.(Winter 2002) *Moving up in a downturn*. McKinsey & Company. corporatefinance.mckinsey.com/_downloads/knowledge/mof/2002_no3/3moving_up.pdf
103. Smith, R. (July 2003), The Chief Technology Officer: Strategic Responsibilities and Relationships. *Research Technology Management.* 46(4)
104. Cosgroveware, L. (September 15, 2003). What Do You Think of Your CIO? *CIO Magazine*. /www2.cio.com/research/surveyreport.cfm?id=63
105. Cardullo, M. *Chief Technology Officer: A New Member of the Leadership Team*
106. W. W. Lewis and L. H. Linden, "A New Mission for Corporate Technology", in *Sloan Management Review*, 1990
107. K. S. Colmen, "Benchmarking the Delivery of Technical Support", *IEEE Engineering Management Review*, vol. 22, 1994.
108. J. P. Martino, *Technological Forecasting for Decision Making*, Third Edition ed. New York, NY: McGraw-Hill, Inc., 1993.
109. H. Mintzberg and J. B. Quinn, *The Strategy Process: Concepts, Contexts, Cases*, Second ed. Englewood Cliffs, NJ: Prentice-Hall, Inc., 1991.
110. D. Bannister, "Message from the Chairman: Northern Virginia: Crossroads of the Northern Information Superhighway", in *Perspective: The Voice of Technology Business*, vol. 5, 1996
111. WBJ, "Largest Biotechnology Companies: Ranked by number of employees in the metro area", in *The Book of Lists: 1995-1996*, D. Yochum, Ed., 11 ed. Arlington, VA: Washington Business Journal, Inc., 1996
112. B. Starzynski, "Maryland, Virginia councils push technology together", in *Washington Business Journal.* Arlington, VA, 1996.
113. Sam Albert of Sam Albert Associates. Personal correspondence with the author.